Daily Scripture Companion

Word *of* Life

Celia Sirois

Compiled from the Vatican II
Sunday and Weekday Missals

BOOKS & MEDIA
Boston

Library of Congress Cataloging-in-Publication Data

Sirois, Celia.
  Word of life : daily scripture companion / Celia Sirois.
    p. cm.
  ISBN 0-8198-8318-2 (pbk.)
  1. Church year meditations. I. Title.
  BX2170.C55S525 2008
  242'.3—dc22

                                2008021760

Scripture texts in this work are taken from the *New American Bible with Revised New Testament and Revised Psalms* © 1991, 1986, 1970 Confraternity of Christian Doctrine, Washington, D.C. and are used by permission of the copyright owner. All Rights Reserved. No part of the *New American Bible* may be reproduced in any form without permission in writing from the copyright owner.

Excerpts from the English translation of the *Catechism of the Catholic Church* for use in the United States of America, copyright © 1994, United States Catholic Conference, Inc. — Libreria Editrice Vaticana. Used with permission.

Cover design by Rosana Usselmann

Published by Pauline Books & Media, 50 Saint Paul's Avenue, Boston, MA 02130-3491. www.pauline.org.

Printed in the U.S.A.

Pauline Books & Media is the publishing house of the Daughters of St. Paul, an international congregation of women religious serving the Church with the communications media.

1 2 3 4 5 6 7 8 9   14 13 12 11 10 09 08

For my parents
Cecile B. and Louis F. Sirois,
my first and best teachers

Contents

How to Use This Book

A lamp to my feet is your word, a light to my path.
(Ps 119:105).

Word of Life offers a series of Biblical reflections focused on the liturgical readings for each day. Throughout the year, the Church spreads before us a rich feast drawn from the word of God. When we prayerfully ponder that word, it gradually penetrates our hearts and minds, thus transforming our lives.

The book is arranged by liturgical seasons: Advent, Christmas, Lent, Easter, and Ordinary Time. The Church year begins with the first Sunday of Advent, followed by the Christmas season, Ordinary Time, Lent and the Easter season. Ordinary time then begins again. Because the dates for this vary from year to year, a calendar is included (p. 3).

To get the most out of *Word of Life*, find a time and place that is quiet and conducive to prayer. It is the custom in the Catholic tradition to begin any reflection on Sacred Scripture by invoking the Holy Spirit, either with a formal prayer like the *Veni, Sancte Spiritus* or with a short quote from the Scripture itself, such as the one below from 1 Samuel 3. Read from your Bible the passages for the liturgy of the day, pausing to reflect on any phrase or image that speaks to you. Then turn to the reflection for that day in *Word of Life*. This book is not a commentary but a "conversation starter" facilitating your encounter with the Word of God incarnate in the sacred text.

"Speak, Lord, for your servant is listening" (1 Sm 3:9).

Liturgical Calendar

"Cycle A, B, and C" refers to the Sunday readings. The new cycle begins with the first Sunday of Advent, which is the beginning of a new liturgical year.

"Year I and II" refers to the weekday readings.

Ordinary Time breaks off for Lent on Ash Wednesday and picks up again after Pentecost. Sometimes one or more weeks of Ordinary Time are omitted.

	Page	2008 Cycle A	2009 Cycle B	2010 Cycle C
1st Week of Advent	11	30 Nov–6 Dec	29 Nov–5 Dec	28 Nov–4 Dec
Immaculate Conception	561	8 Dec	8 Dec	8 Dec
2nd Week of Advent	20	7–13 Dec	6–12 Dec	5–11 Dec
3rd Week of Advent	29	14–16 Dec	13–16 Dec	12–16 Dec
December 17–24	40			
4th Sunday of Advent	37	21 Dec	20 Dec	19 Dec
Christmas	51	25 Dec	25 Dec	25 Dec
Octave of Christmas	55	26–31 Dec	26–31 Dec	27–31 Dec
Holy Family	59	28 Dec	27 Dec	26 Dec

		2009 Cycle B Year I	2010 Cycle C Year II	2011 Cycle A Year I
Mary, Mother of God	64	1 Jan	1 Jan	1 Jan
If before Epiphany Jan 2–7	65	2–3 Jan	2 Jan	———
Epiphany of the Lord	72	4 Jan	3 Jan	2 Jan
After Epiphany Mon–Sat (or Jan 7–12)	73	5–10 Jan	4–9 Jan	3–8 Jan
Baptism of the Lord	79	11 Jan	10 Jan	9 Jan
1st Week Ordinary Time	239	12–17 Jan	11–16 Jan	10–15 Jan
2nd in Ordinary Time	245	18–24 Jan	17–23 Jan	16–22 Jan
3rd in Ordinary Time	254	25–31 Jan	24–30 Jan	23–29 Jan
4th in Ordinary Time	263	1–7 Feb	31 Jan–6 Feb	30 Jan–5 Feb

Presentation of the Lord	545	2 Feb	2 Feb	2 Feb
5th in Ordinary Time	272	8–14 Feb	7–13 Feb	6–12 Feb
If before Lent 6th in Ordinary Time	281	15–21 Feb	14–16 Feb	13–19 Feb
7th in Ordinary Time	290	22–24 Feb	——	20–26 Feb
8th in Ordinary Time	299	——	——	27 Feb–5 Mar
9th in Ordinary Time	308	——	——	6–8 Mar
Ash Wednesday	85	25 Feb	17 Feb	9 Mar
1st Week of Lent	89	1–7 Mar	21–27 Feb	13–19 Mar
2nd Week of Lent	98	8–14 Mar	28 Feb–6 Mar	20–26 Mar
3rd Week of Lent	107	15–21 Mar	7–13 Mar	27 Mar–2 Apr
Joseph, Husband of Mary	546	19 Mar	19 Mar	19 Mar
Annunciation	547	25 Mar	25 Mar	25 Mar
4th Week of Lent	117	22–28 Mar	14–20 Mar	3–9 Apr
5th Week of Lent	127	29 Mar–4 Apr	21–27 Mar	10–16 Apr
Holy Week	139	5–8 Apr	28–31 Mar	17–20 Apr
Easter Triduum	145	9–11 Apr	1–3 Apr	21–23 Apr
Easter	151	12 Apr	4 Apr	24 Apr
Octave of Easter	157	13–18 Apr	5–10 Apr	25–30 Apr
2nd Week of Easter	163	19–25 Apr	11–17 Apr	1–7 May
3rd Week of Easter	172	26 Apr–2 May	18–24 Apr	8–14 May
4th Week of Easter	181	3–9 May	25 Apr–1 May	15–21 May
5th Week of Easter	190	10–16 May	2–8 May	22–28 May
6th Week of Easter	199	17–23 May	9–15 May	29 May–4 June
Ascension (If celebrated on Thurs.)	205	21 May	13 May	2 June
7th Week of Easter	211	24–30 May	16–22 May	5–11 June
Pentecost	220	31 May	23 May	12 June
Trinity Sunday	227	7 June	30 May	19 June
Corpus Christi	230	14 June	6 June	26 June
7th Week Ordinary Time	290	——	——	——
8th Week Ordinary Time	299	——	24–29 May	——
9th Week Ordinary Time	308	1–6 June	31 May–5 June	——
10th Week Ordinary Time	317	8–13 June	7–12 June	——

Advent Season

First Sunday of Advent

A

First Reading: Is 2:1–5
Responsorial Psalm: Ps 122:1–2, 3–4, 4–5, 6–7, 8–9
Second Reading: Rom 13:11–14
Gospel: Mt 24:37–44

In today's readings, Advent is imaged as a journey from two directions. From one side, in the vision of Isaiah, we see the pilgrimage of the nations going to Jerusalem, to the mountain of the Lord's house. From the other, we envision the coming of the Son of Man announced by Jesus in the selection from Matthew. Both journeys, the going and the coming, look to a future realization on "that day and hour no one knows" (Mt 24:36). But the future promised in today's readings makes a claim on our present reality as well. Waking to the dawning light of the Lord, we must walk in that light. We must "throw off the works of darkness," says Paul, and "conduct ourselves properly as in the day" (Rom 13:12–13). In Isaiah's words, this means that we must recognize that which beckons the nations to Jerusalem is "instruction" (*torah*) (2:3), the word of the Lord. To walk in the light is to live Torah, God's plan for peace.

Advent sounds a wake-up call. We must heed it lest, like Noah's contemporaries, or like the unsuspecting householder in Matthew, the coming hour finds us unprepared.

B

First Reading: Is 63:16b–17, 19b; 64:2–7
Responsorial Psalm: Ps 80:2–3, 15–16, 18–19
Second Reading: 1 Cor 1:3–9
Gospel: Mk 13:33–37

Advent is about time—not clock and calendar time, but the peculiar experience of time that characterizes the hope of Christians. For those who have put their faith in the revelation of the Lord Jesus Christ, the end time has already come, though it has not yet been fully realized; therefore, Christians live in the time between the now of Jesus' victory over sin and death and the not-yet of his return in glory. And this makes exiles of us all. That is why the prayer of the newly-returned exiles in the reading from Isaiah is our prayer, too. Like them, we also find ourselves stalled between the now of salvation already achieved for us by the Lord, who has "wrought awesome deeds we could not hope for" (Is 64:2), and the not-yet of continued estrangement, our wandering far from God's ways.

The excerpt from 1 Corinthians and the short passage from Mark both tell us how we are to live in this in-between time. We are to use our spiritual gifts as responsible servants, "each with his own work" (Mk 13:34), in the home of our absent Lord, who is coming very soon.

C

First Reading: Jer 33:14–16
Responsorial Psalm: Ps 25:4–5, 8–9, 10, 14
Second Reading: 1 Thes 3:12–4:2
Gospel: Lk 21:25–28, 34–36

∽⟋⊖⟍∼

Today's selections from Jeremiah and the Gospel of Luke are both set amid world-ending events. Jeremiah's words are spoken as Jerusalem falls under siege and the prophet himself is in prison. The defeat of David's house, the destruction of Jerusalem, and the deportation of the people of Judah loom on the horizon. Their world as they know it is coming to an end. The words of Jesus in Luke's Gospel anticipate the end of the world, an event that "will assault everyone who lives on the face of the earth" (21:35). In these dire settings, Jeremiah and Jesus speak with surprising boldness. God "will raise up for David a just shoot ... Judah shall be safe and Jerusalem shall dwell secure," Jeremiah declares (33:15–16). And Jesus counsels in Luke, "When these signs begin to happen, stand erect and raise your heads because your redemption is at hand" (21:28).

Faith and not fear is the response of God's people when collapsing worlds come to an end. In Advent we pray for ourselves, as Paul prayed in 1 Thessalonians, that "blameless in holiness" (3:13), we may with heart's ease greet the world-ending event of Christ's coming.

First Week of Advent

First Reading: Cycles B and C Is 2:1–5; Cycle A Is 4:2–6
Responsorial Psalm: Ps 122:1–2, 3–4b, 4cd–5, 6–7, 8–9
Gospel: Mt 8:5–11

The readings for today look to the future, to the "days to come" when all nations shall make their way to "the house of the God of Jacob" (Is 2:2–3). As the Gospel of Matthew puts it, many will come from east and west to find a place "with Abraham, Isaac, and Jacob at the banquet in the Kingdom of heaven" (8:11). Both Isaiah in the selection for years B and C and Matthew's Jesus proclaim that the God of Israel wills the salvation of all, not just of Jews.

Yet both recognize the privilege of Israel in God's saving plan. So in Isaiah, the house of Jacob must itself "walk in the light" (2:5) before it can light the way for others. This is why Jesus, who expresses amazement at the centurion's faith, is likewise amazed at the lack of faith of so many in Israel.

The selection from Isaiah for year A is also future oriented, but it looks to the more immediate future, when a remnant will be purified and protected by the glory of God, "a smoking cloud by day and a light of flaming fire by night" (4:5). Thus will the house of Jacob come to walk in the light of the Lord and so be light for all nations.

TUESDAY

First Reading: Is 11:1–10
Responsorial Psalm: Ps 72:1–2, 7–8, 12–13, 17
Gospel: Lk 10:21–24

∼⟳∽

In the Hebrew Bible the Spirit of God (*ruach elohim*) denotes Israel's lived experience of God's powerful presence. As "breath" or "wind," God's *ruach* is a driving, divine force, known chiefly by its effects, particularly in Israel's history. The gift of God's Spirit enabled an individual, however insignificant or uncredentialed, to be God's agent. Such was the case of Moses, Joshua, the judges, Saul, David, and the ideal king Isaiah foresees in today's reading. God's Spirit would equip this royal shoot from the stump of Jesse with the qualities needed to do God's work— to "judge the poor with justice, and decide aright for the land's afflicted" (Is 11:4).

The Gospel reading from Luke depicts Jesus, too, as impelled by God's Spirit. Seized by the Spirit, he celebrates God's choice of "the childlike" (Lk 10:21), a preferential option for the powerless and the poor, which he continues in his own ministry. We must situate ourselves among these, for by virtue of the advent of Jesus and the activity of his Holy Spirit, we now enjoy the revelation that prophets and kings wished to see and to hear but never did.

WEDNESDAY

First Reading: Is 25:6–10a
Responsorial Psalm: Ps 23:1–3a, 3b–4, 5, 6
Gospel: Mt 15:29–37

In both of today's readings, the hand of the Lord comes to rest on a mountain. In the passage from Isaiah, the mountain is Zion, the site of the city of Jerusalem. "On this mountain" (Is 25:6), the prophet says, God will rescue a hungry, hurting, humiliated people—by providing a feast of rich food, wiping the tears from their eyes, and removing the stigma of exile. On that day, the prophet assures them, God's people will rejoice in the God who has acted to save them.

In the selection from Matthew, the mountain is symbolic but no less significant. Here again God acts to feed the hungry crowd, having first made the mute speak, the deformed sound, the cripples walk, and the blind see. And "they glorified the God of Israel" (Mt 15:31).

For Isaiah, "that day" (25:9) will be the beginning of the end time. But for Matthew, as for us, "that day" has arrived with the coming of Jesus. With the raising of Jesus, death is destroyed forever, and every Eucharist is a foretaste of the feast God has prepared "on this mountain."

THURSDAY

First Reading: Is 26:1–6
Responsorial Psalm: Ps 118:1 and 8–9, 19–21, 25–27a
Gospel: Mt 7:21, 24–27

In today's Gospel, an excerpt from Matthew's account of the Sermon on the Mount, Jesus tells his disciples that his words must be the firm foundation on which they are to build their lives. As we would expect, these words of Jesus the Jew are undergirded by the words of the Hebrew Bible, such as the words of the prophet Isaiah in today's first reading. Isaiah not only urges his people to build on solid rock, but also insists that a sturdy house, a strong city is one "that is just, one that keeps faith" (26:2). Similarly, Jesus teaches that it is not enough to cry out "Lord, Lord"; one must do the will of the heavenly Father by putting the words of Jesus into practice (Mt 7:21). How do we do that? The responsorial psalm tells us: We make our home secure in the Lord by pushing open "the gates of justice" (118:19).

Jesus comes. But it is not enough for us to give him a home in our hearts. As today's readings both tell us, we must build those homes on "the eternal Rock" (Is 26:4), whose mercy, enduring forever, is the stronghold of our city (Ps 118:1).

This Advent let us open wide the gates of justice to welcome the one "who comes in the name of the LORD" (Ps 118:26).

FRIDAY

First Reading: Is 29:17–24
Responsorial Psalm: Ps 27:1, 4, 13–14
Gospel: Mt 9:27–31

I n literature, blindness is often a metaphor for lack of knowledge, and it seems to function this way in today's two readings.
Clearly, the spiritual eyes of the two blind men in the Gospel
have already been opened by faith. They know Jesus as the Son of
David and trust in his power to save. The miracle that restores
their physical sight is only an outward sign of their spiritual status: "Let it be done for you according to your faith," says Jesus
(Mt 9:29). The passage from Isaiah uses both blindness and deaf-
ness metaphorically to describe the divine reversal that God is
about to work in Judah: "The lowly will ever find joy … For the
tyrant will be no more." Thus will knowledge of God return to
the land. "On that day the deaf shall hear the words of a book …
the eyes of the blind shall see" (Is 29:19–20, 18).

In Advent we wait once again for what God will do in "a very
little while," not the birth of Jesus, an unrepeatable event, but
our own rebirth "out of gloom and darkness" (Is 29:18) into the
light of the knowledge of God. Once again we hope to see the
work of God's hands in our midst so as to sanctify God's holy
name.

Saturday

First Reading: Is 30:19–21, 23–26
Responsorial Psalm: Ps 147:1–2, 3–4, 5–6
Gospel: Mt 9:35—10:1, 5a, 6–8

Both of today's readings attest to God's compassion. In the text from Isaiah, God, who punished Israel for their sin, is moved to pity by their wounds. So the prophet says, "[God] will heal the bruises left by his blows" (Is 30:26). Isaiah depicts the Holy One of Israel as a healer, binding up the people's wounds, blessing them with abundant life, signified by the recurring images of bread and water (cf. vv. 20, 25). And because the Holy One is also their teacher, with abundant life will come brilliant light, "like the light of seven days" (v. 26).

In today's Gospel, Matthew's Jesus, too, is both teacher and healer. "Jesus went around to all the towns and villages, teaching in their synagogues ... and curing every disease and illness." He, too, is moved with pity for the lost, "because they were troubled and abandoned" (Mt 9:35, 36). This motivates him to dispatch his disciples—and all the others whom the Lord of the harvest will send—to prepare people for the coming judgment. This is an Advent mission: sharing the good news of God's reign, giving the gift we have received.

Second Sunday of Advent

A

First Reading: Is 11:1–10
Responsorial Psalm: Ps 72:1–2, 7–8, 12–13, 17
Second Reading: Rom 15:4–9
Gospel: Mt 3:1–12

At first glance, the harsh reality that John the Baptist announced seems far removed from the ideal realm prophesied by Isaiah. But a closer look reveals striking similarities. Both prophets spoke at a time when Israel was experiencing a crisis of authority. The kings of Isaiah's day relied not on the gifts of God's spirit, but on human counselors to govern their people. In John's day, some among the priestly aristocracy colluded with the Romans who ruled Judea. Isaiah and John both delivered a politically charged message. The future king who would "judge the poor with justice" (Is 11:4) would call the present regime to account. The coming wrath would expose the presumption of the privileged who claimed, "We have Abraham as our father" (Mt 3:9). Both Isaiah and John envisioned a new possibility: power at the service of justice and true repentance as social policy.

The prophets' vision reached beyond Israel. The root of Jesse would summon the nations; God would raise up children to Abraham from stones. We Gentile Christians are the living fulfillment of that promise, as Paul tells the Romans. May our faith glorify the God of Israel.

B

First Reading: Is 40:1–5, 9–11
Responsorial Psalm: Ps 85:9–10, 11–12, 13–14
Second Reading: 2 Pet 3:8–14
Gospel: Mk 1:1–8

The opening verse of today's responsorial psalm succinctly summarizes both the reading from Isaiah and the selection from the Gospel of Mark. "I will hear what God proclaims," it declares, "the LORD—for he proclaims peace to his people" (85:9). The passage from Isaiah describes the commissioning of God's messenger, the "herald of glad tidings" (40:9), who is sent to announce good news to the exiles in Babylon. Their service nears its end; God comes to set them free. John the Baptist plays precisely this role as Mark presents him in today's Gospel reading. "One mightier than I is coming after me," he proclaims. "He will baptize you with the Holy Spirit" (Mk 1:7–8).

The first believers in Jesus shared the same expectation as Isaiah and John: an imminent "coming of the day of God" (2 Pet 3:12). This hope had to be revised, however, when the risen Lord did not immediately return in glory. This delay caused some Christians then, as now, to doubt the Lord's promise. The Second Letter of Peter assures them, and us, that the delay of the longed-for day is itself God's gift—the gift of time to repent and receive the Good News.

C

First Reading: Bar 5:1–9
Responsorial Psalm: Ps 126:1–2, 2–3, 4–5, 6
Second Reading: Phil 1:4–6, 8–11
Gospel: Lk 3:1–6

The words of Baruch, today's first reading, are set during the time of the so-called Babylonian Captivity (587–537 B.C.). To the exiles, Baruch offers hope—in the God whose glory will one day lead them home. His message is a song, not a schedule. He has no specific information to impart, only images to keep hope alive. One of the images his song evokes is that of road construction. Like the foreman of a road crew, God orders that mountains be leveled and gorges filled in for the building of a royal road on which "Israel may advance secure in the glory of God" (Bar 5:7). Luke takes up the same image to interpret John the Baptist's message in today's Gospel. John is not speaking to exiles but to a subject people, who are routinely victimized by the collusion of Pilate, Herod, and corrupt high priests. To these oppressed people, John also offers hope: "All flesh shall see the salvation of God" (Lk 3:6).

The salvation promised by Baruch and John is God's work. Our work, Paul says, is to repair the road for God's coming—what Jews call *tikkun olam*—by growing in love, knowledge, and discernment.

Second Week of Advent

MONDAY

First Reading: Is 35:1–10
Responsorial Psalm: Ps 85:9ab and 10, 11–12, 13–14
Gospel: Lk 5:17–26

Today's Gospel, the Lucan version of a familiar story adapted from Mark, introduces an element of conflict in the cure of the paralytic when the scribes and Pharisees ask themselves, "Who but God alone can forgive sins?" (Lk 5:21). For our purposes, the controversy establishes that the authority of Jesus is indeed the authority of the one God. The good news dramatized by the story concerns the incredible things the authority of God effects: forgiveness of sins and fullness of life. This is Isaiah's theme as well.

In today's reading, the prophet announces that God is coming "with vindication" (to judge) and "with divine recompense" (to save) (Is 35:4). This divine visitation will cause barren places to bloom and broken people to burst into song. For God comes to open a highway, a holy way, "for those with a journey to make" (v. 9). On it the redeemed and the ransomed will walk, like the paralytic in the Gospel, returning home with joy. Today's psalm invites us this Advent to hear the Good News that God proclaims through Isaiah and makes present in Jesus: "surely the LORD will-proclaim peace ... to those who trust in him" (85:9).

TUESDAY

First Reading: Is 40:1—11
Responsorial Psalm: Ps 96:1—2, 3 and 10ac, 11—12, 13
Gospel: Mt 18:12—14

The image of God as shepherd informs both of today's readings. The prophet Isaiah depicts the Lord God coming in power, like a shepherd who feeds his flock and gathers the lambs in his arms, "carrying them in his bosom" (40:11). In Matthew, Jesus describes the heavenly Father in the same way as a shepherd who leaves the ninety-nine out on the hills to search for the single sheep that has strayed. But Matthew's version of this favorite parable injects a note of caution, a conditional clause that is missing in Luke's account: "If he finds it" says Matthew (18:13), warning us that the Good Shepherd's search is not always successful, but depends on the lost sheep's readiness to be found. In the readings for Advent, the Church plies us with images of salvation like this one in order to prepare in the wasteland the way of the Lord. We, the lost sheep, hang on every word, straining to hear the herald's cry, the good news of our redemption that "the mouth of the LORD has spoken" (Is 40:5). And as we wait, we are joined by the heavens and the earth in joyful hope "before the LORD, for he comes; / for he comes to rule the earth" (Ps 96:11—13).

WEDNESDAY

First Reading: Is 40:25–31
Responsorial Psalm: Ps 103:1–2, 3–4, 8 and 10
Gospel: Mt 11:28–30

Today's first reading centers on a poignant reproach that God addresses to the exiles in Babylon: "Why, O Jacob, do you say, and declare, O Israel, 'My way is hidden from the LORD, and my right is disregarded by my God?'" (Is 40:27). Discouraged, the exiles doubt the care of their Creator. Isaiah's task is to reassure them: "The LORD is the eternal God ... He does not faint nor grow weary." And more: "They that hope in the LORD will renew their strength, they will soar as with eagles' wings" (vv. 28, 31). In today's Gospel, Jesus also extends a poignant invitation, addressed to "exiles" of another kind—those in Israel who were marginalized for not keeping the law. To them Jesus offers another way: "Take my yoke upon you and learn from me" (Mt 11:29).

The weeks before Christmas can be a time of great weariness. Life can become burdensome beneath the crush of Christmas crowds and Christmas costs. This Advent, let us try to hold on to the words of Isaiah and the wisdom of Jesus, who tell us that the Lord alone is the eternal God. Then the Lord will renew our strength and we may run but not grow weary (see Is 40:31), finding rest for ourselves in him (see Mt 11:29).

THURSDAY

First Reading: Is 41:13–20
Responsorial Psalm: Ps 145:1 and 9, 10–11, 12–13ab
Gospel: Mt 11:11–15

Today's Gospel introduces the great Advent figure John the Baptist. But the text is puzzling. To say, as Jesus does, that "the least in the Kingdom of heaven is greater than he" (Mt 11:11) seems to exclude John from God's kingdom. Scholars like Daniel Harrington take this to mean that, with Jesus, "a wholly new period of salvation history has begun."[1]

The prophet Isaiah suggests that anything "the hand of the LORD" does is always wholly new (41:20). In today's reading, God's intervention on behalf of the exiles in Babylon is described, not just as a new Exodus but as a whole new creation. The most novel feature of this text is the use of the word "redeemer" (*go'el*) as a title for God. The term denotes one's next of kin, who, according to the law of Israel, was obligated to come to one's aid (see Lv 25:25). This, the prophet dares to say, is the relationship God has with Israel! "Your redeemer [*go'el*] is the Holy One of Israel," he says (Is 41:14), a revelation that is underscored by the repetition of the divine "I" in the subsequent verses (15, 17–19). This good news is the basis of Advent hope.

FRIDAY

First Reading: Is 48:17–19
Responsorial Psalm: Ps 1:1–2, 3, 4 and 6
Gospel: Mt 11:16–19

Both of today's readings convey a sense of frustration. Isaiah's oracle depicts God as Israel's teacher, who leads them on the way they should go—morally (by giving them commandments) and materially (by bringing them home from exile). The conditional, "If you would hearken to my commandments," implies that they are chronically reluctant learners (Is 48:18). Similarly, in today's brief excerpt from Matthew, Jesus uses an analogy to describe his contemporaries' refusal to receive the good news of God's kingdom, from either John the Baptist or him. He compares them to capricious children playing games in the marketplace.

Taken together, the two readings present us with a challenge. The Holy One of Israel would teach us, too, what is for our good. But we are as reluctant to hearken to God's way as was ancient Israel or Jesus' generation. We vacillate, as they did, between one religious fad and another, looking for loopholes in God's law. "But wisdom is vindicated by her works" (Mt 11:19). May our good works this Advent prove the wisdom of God's way.

SATURDAY

First Reading: Sir 48:1–4, 9–11
Responsorial Psalm: Ps 80:2ac and 3b, 15–16, 18–19
Gospel: Mt 17:9a, 10–13

❦❧

Today's Gospel presents a distinctly Christian reading of the Hebrew Scriptures. According to the prophet Malachi, Elijah would return to usher in the "great and terrible" Day of the Lord (Mal 3:23–24). Today's reading from Sirach echoes this idea: addressing Elijah, it says, "You are destined, it is written, in time to come to put an end to wrath before the day of the LORD" (48:10a). In the Gospel, Matthew's Jesus identifies John the Baptist as Elijah, and this has become the standard Christian designation of John. In fact, in Luke's Gospel the angel Gabriel in his annunciation to Zechariah describes the role John is to play in God's saving plan. Gabriel alludes to the words of Malachi, saying that God himself "will go before him in the spirit and power of Elijah to turn the hearts of fathers toward children ... to prepare a people fit for the Lord" (Lk 1:17; see Sir 48:10). Elijah's main task then, anticipating the coming Day of the Lord, is to establish peace within the family by reconciling parents and children. This might be a good resolution for the Advent season and a worthy, worthwhile preparation for Christmas when family tensions can run so high.

Third Sunday of Advent

A

First Reading: Is 35:1–6a, 10
Responsorial Psalm: Ps 146:6–7, 8–9, 9–10
Second Reading: Jas 5:7–10
Gospel: Mt 11:2–11

Today's first two readings focus on the coming of God. "Be strong, fear not! / Here is your God," declares Isaiah (35:4). And James echoes, "Make your hearts firm, because the coming of the Lord is at hand" (5:8). Likewise, in both readings the natural world serves as commentary on supernatural events. In Isaiah, the abundant flowers that bloom in the desert announce God's arrival. In James, the coming of the Lord is likened to "the precious fruit of the earth" that the farmer patiently awaits. For both, new growth in nature reflects the newness that God's advent inexplicably brings.

Today's Gospel makes clear just how new the newness is that God's coming inaugurates. John asks Jesus, "Are you the one who is to come?" (Mt 11:3). Jesus' answer, couched in the language of Isaiah, is a qualified yes. The advent John announced as fiery judgment has arrived in Jesus as saving grace; hence, Jesus appeals to John to take no offense at him. Jesus simultaneously praises John and puts him in his place: John's greatness in the old order has been surpassed now by the unpredictably new thing God has done in Jesus. Will we fear it or greet it with joy?

B

First Reading: Is 61:1–2a, 10–11
Responsorial Psalm: Lk 1:46–48, 49–50, 53–54
Second Reading: 1 Thes 5:16–24
Gospel: Jn 1:6–8, 19–28

"Do not quench the Spirit. Do not despise prophetic utter-ances. Test everything" (1 Thes 5:19–21a). With these words Paul exhorts the Thessalonians in today's second reading. Like us, they must practice discernment, actively seeking to know God's will in every circumstance. The reading from the prophet Isaiah suggests a criterion for discerning the will of God and the work of the Spirit. There the Spirit authorizes God's servant "to bring glad tidings to the poor, / to heal the broken-hearted, / to proclaim liberty to the captives / and release to the prisoners" (Is 61:1). Both Paul and Isaiah know that the activity of the Spirit manifests itself in justice and praise.

Discernment is at work in today's Gospel, too. Representatives of the Jewish leaders in Jerusalem, attempting to discern if John's prophetic activity is of God, question him. In answer he tells them, "There is one among you whom you do not recognize" (Jn 1:26). John's words must give us pause, especially in this Advent season. We think we know the Coming One. But do we? Or is he perhaps among us unrecognized? "Test everything."

C

First Reading: Zeph 3:14–18a
Responsorial Psalm: Is 12:2–3, 4, 5–6
Second Reading: Phil 4:4–7
Gospel: Lk 3:10–18

The Third Sunday of Advent was once known in Latin as *Gaudete* ("Let us rejoice") Sunday. And certainly today's first two readings call us, in the words of the responsorial antiphon, to "cry out with joy and gladness." Yet a closer look at these two texts reveals a distinctive feature of Advent joy. The prophecy of Zephaniah, from which the first reading is taken, stands behind another familiar Latin phrase, the title of the ancient hymn *Dies Irae* ("day of wrath"). Zephaniah announces the coming Day of the Lord as a day of unmitigated doom and gloom. That is what makes today's reading so striking. We hear a joyful shout in a situation in which joy seems utterly impossible. Similarly, an emphatic "Rejoice in the Lord always" (Phil 4:4) rises from Paul in prison, where he waits uncertain if he will live or die. Advent joy is the release that comes with finally learning our future is secured by God and not by us.

But the joy of Advent is not passivity. So John the Baptist tells those who receive the Good News: Their joyful hope in the One to come must prove itself in acts of justice. The Lord invites us also to heed that call.

Third Week of Advent

MONDAY

First Reading: Nm 24:2–7, 15–17a
Responsorial Psalm: Ps 25:4–5ab, 6 and 7bc, 8–9
Gospel: Mt 21:23–27

❦❦❦

Both readings today are concerned with legitimizing authority. They establish whether certain individuals or events are "of heavenly or of human origin" (Mt 21:25). The oracle of Balaam recorded in the Book of Numbers legitimizes the rise of David and his conquest of Moab. Foreseen by a prophet, "one who sees what the Almighty sees" (24:4), David's accession is surely of God. Similarly, in today's Gospel, the opponents of Jesus want to know the origin of his authority. But Jesus knows that were he simply to say that his power is from God, they would construe his words as blasphemy. So he avoids answering by asking a question about the authority of John the Baptist.

It is important to note that it was not his opponents' question but their hidden agenda that caused Jesus to demur. In fact their question—"Who gave you this authority?" (Mt 21:23)—is one we must often ask as we seek to discern what in our experience is of God and what is not. Let us ask it seriously this Advent, ready to hear and to heed the answer.

TUESDAY

First Reading: Zeph 3:1–2, 9–13
Responsorial Psalm: Ps 34:2–3, 6–7, 17–18, 19 and 23
Gospel: Mt 21:28–32

Today's Gospel continues the standoff begun in yesterday's reading between Jesus and his opponents, the chief priests and elders. The parable of the Two Sons likens them to the elder son who, when told to go and work in the vineyard, agrees to go but never does. The tax collectors and prostitutes, on the other hand, are like the second son, who at first refuses, but then repents and does what his father wants. Therefore, Jesus says, they are streaming into the kingdom of God ahead of their more reputable religious leaders.

The excerpt from Zephaniah draws a similar distinction. Here "the proud braggarts" who exalt themselves on the temple mount are cast as the elder son (Zeph 3:11), while the remnant of Israel, "a people humble and lowly," plays the part of the repentant second son. They "take refuge in the name of the Lord" (v. 12). The message is obvious. What matters in the end is conversion and concrete action, the obedience of faith. But there is something more. Both Zechariah and Jesus reproach their audiences for being unwilling to hear and accept correction. In Advent we have to ask, are we willing?

WEDNESDAY

First Reading: Is 45:6c–8, 18, 21c–25
Responsorial Psalm: Ps 85:9ab and 10, 11–12, 13–14
Gospel: Lk 7:18b–23

⊷⊶

T he juxtaposition of today's two readings helps us to appreciate the "scandal" Jesus caused. The passage from Isaiah is a magnificent profession of faith in one, and only one, God. This God and no other is the Lord, the Creator and Savior of all, to whom every knee must bend and by whom every tongue must swear. In the Gospel, Jesus responds to the disciples sent by John by summing up his ministry—"The blind regain their sight, the lame walk, lepers are cleansed, the deaf hear, the dead are raised, the poor have the good news proclaimed to them" (Lk 7:22)—thus challenging John to believe that, in him and through him, the Lord and no other is acting to save. Then, as though acknowledging the leap of faith this massive claim requires, Jesus adds, "Blessed is the one who takes no offense [*skandalizo*] at me" (v. 23).

In Advent we prepare ourselves to revisit the jarring juxtaposition of today's readings as it manifests itself in the mystery of the Incarnation. "So great a God, so tiny an infant!" exclaimed St. Francis of Assisi. Blessed is the one who can faithfully hold both humanity and divinity together in one thought.

THURSDAY

First Reading: Is 54:1–10
Responsorial Psalm: Ps 30:2 and 4, 5–6, 11–12a and 13b
Gospel: Lk 7:24–30

Today's readings announce the new future that God creates for exiles and outcasts. The poem from Isaiah is addressed to exiled Israel. Powerful primal images of hopelessness—the barren womb, the broken marriage, the flood in Noah's days—are enlisted to convey the reversal that the "enduring love" of God will bring: "For a brief moment I abandoned you, / but with great tenderness I will take you back ... says the LORD, your redeemer" (Is 54:7–8). The Gospel, too, draws on powerful images to make its point. "What did you go out to the desert to see?" asks Jesus (Lk 7:24). The baptism of John is an oasis in the desert for all the people, even for tax collectors, priming them for the good news of Jesus. The citation from Scripture, combining Exodus 23:20 and Malachi 3:1, reiterates: "I am sending my messenger ahead of you, / he will prepare your way before you" (Lk 7:27).

Like exiled Israel and the eager audience of John, may we this Advent be filled with anticipation at the new future that God continues to create for us in Jesus the Christ. And like Isaiah and Jesus, may we, too, find pertinent and persuasive images to proclaim it.

FRIDAY

First Reading: Is 56:1–3a, 6–8
Responsorial Psalm: Ps 67:2–3, 5, 7–8
Gospel: Jn 5:33–36

Although the brevity of today's Gospel, an excerpt from John, makes it difficult to see, points of contact exist between the two readings. As Isaiah insists that God is the source of his message—"Thus says the LORD" (56:1)—Jesus presents witnesses in defense of his ministry. And both of his witnesses come from God: John the Baptist was sent by God, and the works of Jesus have been given to him by the Father. Isaiah's concern in today's oracle is to say that God welcomes and wills to save not just Jerusalem Jews but all people "who join themselves to the LORD, / ministering to him, / loving the name of the LORD, / and becoming his servants" (56:6). Thus, the religious ritual of God's house is open to others besides the dispersed of Israel. Similarly, the Gospel of John, more boldly than the other three Gospels, attests to the universality of God's saving will revealed in Jesus, and reinterprets the religious feasts of Judaism accordingly.

In its Advent liturgy, the Church also calls John the Baptist and the works of Jesus to testify that the Father has sent Jesus to us and that he is "truly the savior of the world" (Jn 4:42).

Fourth Sunday of Advent

A

First Reading: Is 7:10–14
Responsorial Psalm: Ps 24:1–2, 3–4, 5–6
Second Reading: Rom 1:1–7
Gospel: Mt 1:18–24

Paul begins his letter to the Romans by grounding the Gospel "in the holy [Hebrew] Scriptures." Then, using an early Christian creed, he describes Jesus as "descended from David according to the flesh, but established as Son of God in power according to the spirit of holiness" (1:2–4). This creedal formula holds in tension two dimensions of the mystery of Jesus. What God has done in and through Jesus is both in continuity with previous acts of God in Israel's history and in dramatic discontinuity with all God has done before.

Today's Gospel shows the same dynamic tension. In Matthew, an angel announces Jesus' birth to Joseph. The two things we are told about Joseph—namely, that he is a righteous (Torah-observant) man of David's line—emphasize continuity with Israel's previous experience of God. However, the virginal conception "through the Holy Spirit" (Mt 1:20) is a totally new act of God. Yet even this, as Matthew sees it, is grounded in Scripture. Thus, he applies Isaiah's words—originally spoken of the birth of Ahaz's heir, which would guarantee the future of David's house—to the birth of Jesus. Joseph's righteousness made him ready to receive the new act of God announced by the angel. Are we ready?

B

First Reading: 2 Sm 7:1–5, 8b–12, 14a, 16
Responsorial Psalm: Ps 89:2–3, 4–5, 27, 29
Second Reading: Rom 16:25–27
Gospel: Lk 1:26–38

In today's readings we meet two people who inexplicably found favor with God. The selection from the Second Book of Samuel recounts the story of David's transformation, by the grace of God, from shepherd boy to shepherd king. The occasion is David's intention, confided to Nathan, to build God a house. Rejecting David's proposal, God retells the story of David's rise to power. What is most striking about the story is the repetition of the divine "I" in every sentence. The point is unmistakable: God, not David, is the subject of every verb in David's story.[2] Divine initiative also directs the action of the annunciation scene in Luke. God's grace overshadows Mary and transforms her from Joseph's betrothed to Mother of God.

What God's favor requires of David and Mary is the simple yes that Paul, in today's reading, calls "the obedience of faith" (Rom 16:26). In Advent, may we, who are even now being transformed by the unmerited grace of God in Christ, resolve to say our yes as generously as did David and Mary.

C

First Reading: Mi 5:1–4a
Responsorial Psalm: Ps 80:2–3, 15–16, 18–19
Second Reading: Heb 10:5–10
Gospel: Lk 1:39–45

Today's readings all share the same small scale. In the first reading, the prophet Micah announces God's intention to restore to David's throne a shepherd king who will bring peace to God's people. This ideal king will not come from the city of Jerusalem, however, where corrupt kings hold sway. Rather, he will come from David's humble hometown of Bethlehem, too small to be counted among the clans of Judah (see Mi 5:1). Today's Gospel also shifts the focus from the hub of the Jewish world to the hill country of Judah, a place too small to count by that world's reckoning. There, in the meeting of two pregnant women, the good news of the Lord's coming is joyfully proclaimed. The Letter to the Hebrews also redirects our attention, as Christians, from the sacrifices offered daily in the elaborate Temple liturgy to the offering of the broken body of Jesus on Calvary once for all.

Today's readings teach us that the Lord's coming may be discerned in small beginnings, as imperceptible and as insistent as an infant's stirring in the womb; and yet, who would dare despise it? (see Zec 4:10).

Weekdays of Advent from December 17 to December 24

DECEMBER 17

First Reading: Gn 49:2, 8–10
Responsorial Psalm: Ps 72:1–2, 3–4ab, 7–8, 17
Gospel: Mt 1:1–17

Today's readings serve to both announce and, in some sense, divinely authorize coming events in God's unfolding plan. In the reading from Genesis, taken from the farewell address of the dying Jacob, the patriarch pronounces blessings (or curses) on each of his twelve sons. Today's text is his blessing of Judah, which, with poetic imagery, foreshadows the prominence the tribe of Judah will enjoy when David comes to power. The Gospel is Matthew's version of Jesus' family record. Matthew has imposed a pattern on this genealogy—three sets of fourteen generations. Since fourteen is a multiple of the perfect number seven, this may be his way of telling us that Jesus comes in "the fullness of time." The most striking feature of Matthew's genealogy is the presence of four women whose unconventional marital histories furthered the unfolding plan of God. They prepare us for Mary's role in the birth of Jesus.

In the Bible, farewell addresses and family records serve to demonstrate the continuity of God's saving plan and purpose. So do the readings of Advent.

DECEMBER 18

First Reading: Jer 23:5–8
Responsorial Psalm: Ps 72:1–2, 12–13, 18–19
Gospel: Mt 1:18–25

The prophecy of Jeremiah, in the dark days preceding the fall of Judah, foresees the restoration of the ideal of kingship among God's people. The future king announced in today's reading will be God's agent, governing wisely and doing what is right and just in the land; therefore, he will deserve the title "The LORD our justice" (Jer 23:6). Today's Gospel gives the same title to Joseph. He is a just ("righteous") man, says Matthew (1:19). His justice is demonstrated first of all in his decision not to expose Mary to the law, which would have permitted him some personal satisfaction. Rather, he determines to act in the spirit and not in the letter of the law. His justice is further proven when he becomes the agent of God's justice (God's saving work) by his unquestioning obedience to God's command.

Joseph was a just man whose righteousness made him not rigid but ready at a moment's notice to act on the new word of God that was revealed to him. In Advent the Church gives him to us as an example of how obedience to God's law can open us to the revelation of Emmanuel, "God is with us" (Mt 1:23).

DECEMBER 19

First Reading: Jgs 13:2–7, 24–25a
Responsorial Psalm: Ps 71:3–4a, 5–6ab, 16–17
Gospel: Lk 1:5–25

Today's Gospel, the announcement of the birth of John the Baptist, makes several allusions to the announcement of the birth of Samson in the Book of Judges. In both accounts an angel appears to one member of a barren couple to announce that by the power of God they will be enabled to conceive and bear a son. Therefore, the words of today's responsorial psalm apply to both children: "On you I depend from birth; / from my mother's womb you are my strength" (Ps 71:6). According to the angel, both sons will be Nazirites, never drinking wine or strong drink (see Nm 6:1–21), and both will be consecrated to God from the womb—in John's case, "filled with the Holy Spirit" (Lk 1:15). Finally, both Samson and John will usher in the deliverance of their people.

Luke's infancy narrative is full of allusions like this. It is his way of demonstrating the constancy as well as the consistency of God's activity in every generation. Luke's allusive style is characteristic of Advent, too. In Advent we contemplate God's activity in previous generations, the better to appreciate God's activity in our own.

DECEMBER 20

First Reading: Is 7:10–14
Responsorial Psalm: Ps 24:1–2, 3–4ab, 5–6
Gospel: Lk 1:26–38

The oracle of Isaiah to King Ahaz of Judah during the crisis precipitated by the Syro-Ephraimite coalition against Judah is well known to Christian readers. Confronted with the fear and faithlessness of Ahaz, the prophet announces the birth of a royal son who, unlike Ahaz, will be worthy of the title "Emmanuel." The child will be a visible sign that God has not abandoned David's house, indeed, that "God is with us" (Is 7:14). Today's Gospel announces the birth of another royal son, also of David's line, who "will rule over the house of Jacob forever" and of whose kingdom "there will be no end" (Lk 1:33).

The linking of Isaiah's oracle with the angel's announcement of the birth of Jesus owes more to Matthew than to Luke, however (see Mt 1:22–23). While Luke does want to show the continuity in God's plan, he wants, perhaps, even more to underscore the radical discontinuity; that is, the utterly unpredictable newness of what God has done in Jesus, who is not only son of David, but also Son of God by the power of the Holy Spirit. In Advent we prepare to rediscover this best good news of all, our salvation.

DECEMBER 21

First Reading: Song 2:8–14, or Zeph 3:14–18a
Responsorial Psalm: Ps 33:2–3, 11–12, 20–21
Gospel: Lk 1:39–45

A visitation theme binds today's readings together. In the Song of Songs, a young woman celebrates a springtime visit by her lover. The Gospel is Luke's account of Mary's visit to her cousin Elizabeth. Both visits are joyful occasions: The lover springs gazellelike across the hills, and John leaps for joy in his mother's womb. Here again, Luke's allusive style is evident. The leaping of the baby in Elizabeth's womb recalls the jostling of Esau and Jacob in Rebecca's womb (Gn 25:22) and points to the future roles of John and Jesus. As in the Genesis story, the first-born (John) will in God's plan be surpassed by the One who comes after him (Jesus). The leaping of the baby also recalls David's joyful dance before the ark (2 Sm 6:5, 14). But here, Mary herself is the ark, the new Jerusalem, in whom the presence of God now dwells.

In many ways the alternate first reading from the prophet Zephaniah prepares us for the Magnificat of Mary. As he invites daughter Zion to rejoice and sing joyfully, for "the LORD, your God, is in your midst, / a mighty savior" (Zeph 3:14, 17), so Mary rejoices in God her savior, the Mighty One, who has done great things for her—and for us (see Lk 1:46–55). Praise him.

DECEMBER 22

First Reading: 1 Sm 1:24–28
Responsorial Psalm: 1 Sm 2:1, 4–5, 6–7, 8abcd
Gospel: Lk 1:46–56

In a way, today's first reading simply provides a setting for the responsorial psalm, which is the canticle of Hannah, the mother of Samuel. The reading describes Hannah bringing her young son to the sanctuary in Shiloh to dedicate him to the Lord. She reminds us of another young Jewish mother who will one day present her firstborn son in the Temple in Jerusalem. Today's Gospel records that young woman's canticle, which bears a striking resemblance to Hannah's. Both of these songs, on the lips of women and mothers, anticipate what God will do through the agency of their sons. Both image God's saving activity concretely as toppling unjust structures and disarming oppressive regimes.

"The bows of the mighty are broken," declares Hannah (1 Sm 2:4), and Mary echoes, "He has cast down the mighty from their thrones" (Lk 1:52). "The well-fed hire themselves out for bread," Hannah says (1 Sm 2:5), and Mary answers, "He has filled the hungry with good things" (Lk 1:53). These are songs of the *anawim*, the poor who have no recourse or resource of their own and must wait for God to save them. They capture the true spirit of Advent.

DECEMBER 23

First Reading: Mal 3:1–4, 23–24
Responsorial Psalm: Ps 25:4–5ab, 8–9, 10 and 14
Gospel: Lk 1:57–66

The prophecy of Malachi in today's first reading shaped the Gospel portrait of John the Baptist in many ways. It is given to us today as an aid to interpreting Luke's account of the Baptist's birth. The Gospel scene is homey, even humorous. Elizabeth and Zechariah must insist, over the protests of family and friends, that the child's name is John. With that, Zechariah's "mouth was opened, his tongue freed, and he spoke blessing God" (Lk 1:64). All are astonished and, although the fear that descends on all in the environs is really awe, it is colored to some extent by the words of the first reading. In Christian tradition, John the Baptist is the messenger sent to prepare the way of the Lord. He is the Elijah who will announce that "great and terrible" day.

The Gospel concludes by saying that all who heard of these happenings in the hill country of Judea "took them to heart" (Lk 1:66). Similarly, in Advent we store in our hearts the signs and wonders the Church proclaims, asking ourselves as the friends and neighbors of Elizabeth and Zechariah once did, "What, then, will this child be?" (1:66).

December 24

Mass in the Morning

First Reading: 2 Sm 7:1–5, 8b–12, 14a, 16
Responsorial Psalm: Ps 89:2–3, 4–5, 27 and 29
Gospel: Lk 1:67–79

In today's two readings, the oracle of Nathan and the canticle of Zechariah, God's covenant fidelity comes to the fore. Nathan's dream thwarts David's ambition to build a house for God. Then playing on the word for house (*bayit*), the oracle goes on to say that God will build a house (that is, a dynasty) for David that will stand firm forever. These words signal a dramatic departure from the old covenant theology, which taught that Israel must have no king but God. This divine promise is the essence of God's covenant with David. The canticle of Zechariah picks up this covenant theology and announces a still newer divine initiative. The emphasis falls on God as a covenant maker, who is moved and motivated by mercy (Lk 1:72, 78). This new initiative of God is, of course, the coming of Jesus, whose ways John will prepare (v. 76).

Two of God's covenant partners are named in the canticle of Zechariah, the *Benedictus*. The first is David, whose covenant with God is celebrated in today's psalm, and the other is Abraham. Both were promised salvation from their enemies. John, too, the canticle says, will give people knowledge of salvation, not kingship or conquest but forgiveness of sins.

Christmas Season

Christmas

Vigil Mass

A B C

First Reading: Is 62:1–5
Responsorial Psalm: Ps 89:4–5, 16–17, 27, 29
Second Reading: Acts 13:16–17, 22–25
Gospel: Mt 1:1–25 or 1:18–25

Today's readings call our attention to the function of naming in the biblical tradition, in which a person's name was not just identification but identity. In the prophecy of Isaiah, a decisive change in Jerusalem's fortunes is announced with the words, "You shall be called by a new name / pronounced by the mouth of the LORD." No longer "desolate," the land and the people will now be God's "delight" (Is 62:2, 4).

The genealogy that opens Matthew's Gospel—a long list of names—is his way of showing what Paul tells his fellow Jews in the synagogue in Antioch, namely, God has given Israel a Savior from David's line. Jesus belongs to the family of David through Joseph, himself of David's lineage; at God's command, Joseph names and thereby legally claims Mary's child as his son. The name *Yeshu* (literally, "Yahweh saves") is itself a prophecy of the decisive change that will soon overtake God's people: "he will save his people from their sins." And this, in turn, will lead those people who are touched and transformed by Jesus to name him "Emmanuel," which means "God is with us" (Mt 1:21, 23).

Mass at Midnight

A B C

First Reading: Is 9:1–6
Responsorial Psalm: Ps 96:1–2, 2–3, 11–12, 13
First Reading: Ti 2:11–14
Gospel: Lk 2:1–14

In every age, the birth of a royal son is greeted with joyful hope. Perhaps this will be the king who will bring longed-for peace and prosperity to the realm. Today's oracle from Isaiah may well be a formal announcement of the birth of a new heir to the throne of David. It captures the abundant joy of the people as they anticipate the bounty of the harvest and the breaking, once and for all, of the yoke of oppression. With the words, "In those days a decree went out from Caesar Augustus" (Lk 2:1), Luke also evokes the memory of a ruler whose advent was greeted with joyful hope. The emperor Octavian, who was given the title "August One," ushered in the Pax Romana, a time of unprecedented prosperity and peace. For this, he was acclaimed by the people as "savior of the world."

Against this backdrop, Luke relates the birth of Jesus, which, ironically, goes largely unnoticed. Angels formally announce this royal birth to awestruck shepherds living in the fields. Yet it is in this small child wrapped in swaddling clothes that, as Paul puts it, "the grace of God has appeared, saving all" (Ti 2:11). Come, let us adore him.

Mass at Dawn

A B C

First Reading: Is 62:11–12
Responsorial Psalm: Ps 97:1, 6, 11–12
Second Reading: Ti 3:4–7
Gospel: Lk 2:15–20

The words of Isaiah in today's first reading are addressed to the city of Jerusalem, "daughter Zion," reduced to rubble by the Babylonian conquest. Returning from their years of captivity in Babylon, the exiles are devastated to find their once holy city still so godforsaken. To them the prophet proclaims, "Your savior comes!" (Is 62:11), and where God is, there is renewal and redemption. The coming of the Savior has also been proclaimed to the shepherds in the reading from Luke. They who were once forgotten in the fields have been found and given good news of great joy. And so they hasten to the manger.

Important connections link the shepherds in Luke and Jerusalem in Isaiah. For one thing, the shepherds recall the humble origins of David, and Jerusalem is a monument to David's rise to power. But even more, just as Jerusalem has been defiled by the Babylonians, so are the shepherds ritually unclean. Neither can boast of righteous deeds. That, Paul tells Titus, is what makes the Savior's coming grace—the kind and generous love of God, who saved us, "not because of any righteous deeds we had done / but because of his mercy" (3:4–5). May we share the shepherds' amazement at the wonder of this day.

Mass During the Day

A B C

First Reading: Is 52:7–10
Responsorial Psalm: Ps 98:1, 2–3, 3–4, 5–6
Second Reading: Heb 1:1–6
Gospel: Jn 1:1–18 or 1:1–5, 9–14

Today's two New Testament readings are examples of "Christology from above." In bold, broad strokes, they attempt to situate the mission of Jesus in God's cosmic plan. Both Hebrews and John identify Jesus as the Word through whom all things came to be (Jn 1:3) and through whom, in these last days, God has spoken to us (Heb 1:2). In him, both see "the refulgence of his glory" (Heb 1:3), "the glory as of the Father's only Son" (Jn 1:14). They both trace the Son's earthly sojourn from his pre-existence with God in the beginning to his incarnation and his return—mission accomplished—to take his seat at the Father's side. Clearly, for both Hebrews and John, Christ is the beginning and the end, the author and the heir apparent of cosmic history.

The Christology of Christmas is generally "Christology from below." We reflect on Jesus' birth in humble surroundings. But as Christmas Day comes to an end, we who were summoned to the manger are sent now, like the messenger of Isaiah, to spread the good news, "announcing salvation and saying to Zion, / 'Your God is King!'" (52:7).

DECEMBER 26

Saint Stephen, First Martyr

First Reading: Acts 6:8–10; 7:54–59
Responsorial Psalm: Ps 31:3cd–4, 6 and 8ab, 16bc and 17
Gospel: Mt 10:17–22

In today's Gospel, Jesus warns his disciples that, just as he did, they will suffer persecution at the hands of both religious and civil authorities. But he reassures them that the Holy Spirit will be available to them, telling them how to respond. Jesus' words are dramatized in the account from Acts of Stephen's martyrdom. It is particularly striking how closely Stephen resembles Jesus in this story. Like Luke's Jesus, Stephen is a prophet who works "great wonders and signs among the people" (Acts 6:8). Also like Jesus, he often debates his opponents. And like Jesus, he is executed outside the city of Jerusalem and dies praying, "Receive my spirit" (Acts 7:59; see Lk 23:46).

For both Jesus and Stephen, God was the "rock of refuge" invoked in today's responsorial psalm. Luke places a line from this psalm on Jesus' lips as he breathes his last, having given his all, like Stephen did. "Into your hands I commend my spirit" (Ps 31:6).

On December 25 we remember Jesus' coming to us. On December 26, the feast of St. Stephen, we are reminded of Jesus' coming through us—and of what a costly grace bearing witness to Jesus can be.

December 27

Saint John, Apostle and Evangelist

First Reading: 1 Jn 1:1
Responsorial Psalm: Ps 97:1–2, 5–6, 11–12
Gospel: Jn 20:1a and 2–8

Many modern Catholic scholars question whether the beloved disciple, who figures so prominently in the second half of the fourth Gospel, is in fact John the son of Zebedee, whose feast we celebrate today. Be that as it may, what today's Gospel says of the disciple Jesus loved applies to John and all who, like him, "saw and believed" (20:8). Saw what? Not the cave of Bethlehem but the empty tomb. Not swaddling clothes but burial cloths first spoke of the Word of life, revealed in Jesus the Christ. As today's first reading tells us, the apostles in turn proclaimed this life to us, so that we might share life with them. That is why we profess that our community is indeed "apostolic." It is based on the faithful witness of those who heard, saw, and touched the Word of life.

In poem number 906, Emily Dickinson observes that we see most clearly "through an Open Tomb." So it was for the early Church. In that "Light–enabling Light,"[3] they came at last to understand the true significance of the crib as well as of the cross. In this holy season of light so must we.

DECEMBER 28

The Holy Innocents, Martyrs

First Reading: 1 Jn 1:5—2:2
Responsorial Psalm: Ps 124:2–3, 4–5, 7c–8
Gospel: Mt 2:13–18

Today's Gospel reports the massacre of the holy innocents at the command of Herod, the king of the Jews. Told only by Matthew, the story looks backward to the birth of Moses and forward to the death of Jesus. Moses was born in similar circumstances when Pharaoh, the king of the Egyptians, had ordered the massacre of all Hebrew boys (see Ex 1:16). The Gospel story also announces the death of Jesus when another threatened client of Rome—not Herod this time, but Pilate—will condemn to death the "King of the Jews." In Matthew's scheme, history repeats itself.

Not only in the world of Matthew's Gospel, but also in our own, history seems to repeat itself with depressing regularity. The massacre of innocent children continues, and Rachel weeps inconsolably. "If we say, 'We are without sin,'" the First Letter of John warns us, "we deceive ourselves" (1:8). Therefore, our only hope is to acknowledge our sin and ask forgiveness of the wholly innocent One, who was offered for our sins, "and not for our sins only but for those of the whole world" (1 Jn 2:2). As the psalmist reminds us today, "Had not the LORD been with us" and for us, we would surely have perished (124:2).

DECEMBER 29

Fifth Day in the Octave of Christmas

First Reading: 1 Jn 2:3–11
Responsorial Psalm: Ps 96:1–2a, 2b–3, 5b–6
Gospel: Lk 2:22–35

Today's selection from 1 John could be a commentary on Simeon, the prophet who appears in today's excerpt from the Gospel of Luke. What 1 John says of the man who claims to know God—that he keeps God's commandments—can certainly be said of Simeon. His credentials are, according to Luke, that he is "righteous and devout" (2:25), which means that he keeps the law of God. In the view of the author of 1 John, this would explain Simeon's immediate recognition of Jesus when he is presented in the Temple.

But there is more. With the help of the Holy Spirit, Simeon is given to see, as 1 John puts it, that "darkness is passing away, and the true light is already shining" (2:8). So he greets the arrival of Jesus as "a light to reveal you to the nations, / and glory for your people Israel" (Lk 2:32). Those who pray the Liturgy of the Hours will recognize the words of Simeon's canticle from the night prayer of the Church. May faithfully keeping God's word equip us, as it did Simeon, to continue in the light until that day when the Master dispels all our darkness and dismisses us in peace.

Holy Family

Sunday in the Octave of Christmas

*(Or if Christmas falls on Sunday, this feast is celebrated
on December 30, with only one reading before the Gospel.)*

A

First Reading: Sir 3:2–6, 12–14
Responsorial Psalm: Ps 128:1–2, 3, 4–5
Second Reading: Col 3:12–21 or 3:12–17
Gospel: Mt 2:13–15, 19–23

Through the flight into Egypt, the Gospel reading for today, Jesus relives the family history of his people. As the patriarch Joseph, the son of Jacob, once led his family to safety in Egypt, so here another Joseph—who is also, according to Matthew, a son of Jacob (1:16)—takes his family to Egypt. Then as God once called Israel out of Egypt, even so is Joseph, now in Egypt, told to "take the child and his mother and go to the land of Israel" (Mt 2:20). The same divine providence that protected the comings and goings of Israel now directs the travels of this small family.

God's commitment to family life is evident in the instruction of Sirach, where kindness to parents atones for sins. Similarly, the injunctions in Colossians in today's reading are applied to the Christian family. Parents and children are urged to imitate the compassion, kindness, humility, gentleness, and patience of Christ. Only thus, by doing everything in Jesus' name, can we give thanks to God the Father, whose divine protection we and our families enjoy.

B

First Reading: Gn 15:1–6; 21:1–3
Responsorial Psalm: Ps 105:1–2, 3–4, 6–7, 8–9
Second Reading: Heb 11:8, 11–12, 17–19
Gospel: Lk 2:22–40 or 2:22, 39–40

The first and second readings for today extol the faith of Abraham and Sarah, Israel's first family. In the selection from Genesis, God promises the incredulous Abraham many descendants, as numerous as the stars in the sky. And Abraham, though old and childless, "put his faith in the LORD, who credited it to him as an act of righteousness" (Gn 15:6). The passage from Hebrews is excerpted from a litany praising the faith of Israel's ancestors. It focuses narrowly on Abraham's unconditional trust in God's promise, even when sorely tested.

Today's Gospel reading chronicles the faith of another first family: Mary and Joseph and their newborn son. Their observance of the law of the Lord, which Luke underlines no less than five times in the story (2:22, 23, 24, 27, 39), places them, with Abraham, among the righteous. And like Abraham's faith, theirs, too, will be put to the test. Their child, Simeon tells them, "is destined for the fall and rise of many in Israel, and to be a sign that will be contradicted" (Lk 2:34). With that, Mary and Joseph set out, like Abraham and Sarah, to journey in faith to the place that God would show them (see Gn 12:1). Let us resolve to walk that hard way with them.

C

First Reading: 1 Sm 1:20–22, 24–28
Responsorial Psalm: Ps 84:2–3, 5–6, 9–10
Second Reading: 1 Jn 3:1–2, 21–24
Gospel: Lk 2:41–52

The first and third readings for today were selected in the hope that we would see, as Luke did, points of contact between the family histories of Samuel and of the youthful Jesus. The setting of both stories is the annual family pilgrimage. In the selection from 1 Samuel, Hannah shares with Elkanah her determination to dedicate their son, Samuel, to the Lord. In the Lucan account, Mary and Joseph live through every parent's nightmare. On leaving Jerusalem where they have kept Passover, they discover that their twelve-year-old child is missing. After three frantic days, they find him in the Temple. When his mother asks, "Why have you done this to us? Your father and I have been looking for you with great anxiety," Jesus subtly corrects her. "I must be in my Father's house" (Lk 2:48–49). And in that instance, Mary knows that although he returns with them to Nazareth, he is no longer hers.

The sacrifice required of Hannah and Mary is asked of every parent, that is, to give the children God gives to us back to God. In doing this we trust, as John teaches us in the second reading, in the love the Father has bestowed on us and on them that we may all be called God's children (Jn 3:1).

DECEMBER 30

Sixth Day in the Octave of Christmas

First Reading: 1 Jn 2:12–17
Responsorial Psalm: Ps 96:7–8a, 8b–9, 10
Gospel: Lk 2:36–40

The elderly woman, Anna, who appears in today's Gospel illustrates the teaching of the second part of today's first reading from 1 John. In the words of John's letter, she is a woman who does "not love the world or the things of the world" (2:15). Widowed after seven years of marriage, she spent all her days in the Temple, and "worshiped night and day with fasting and prayer" (Lk 2:37). Coming on the scene of the presentation of Jesus, she is instantly able to see in him what has come from the Father, and "she gave thanks to God" (v. 38).

The first part of the first reading is an awkward literary construction that addresses three age groups—people in three different stages of Christian life—children, youth, and parents or elders. The task of each stage is succinctly suggested. Christian life begins in Baptism with the forgiveness of sin. Next Christian formation requires the strength derived from the power of God's word to conquer evil inside and outside oneself. Then Christian maturity makes one, like Anna, able to see the gift of God "from the beginning" (1 Jn 2:13).

DECEMBER 31

Seventh Day in the Octave of Christmas

First Reading: 1 Jn 2:18–21
Responsorial Psalm: Ps 96:1–2, 11–12, 13
Gospel: Jn 1:1–18

Today's Gospel is the prologue of John's Gospel. It is a Christological hymn summarizing the whole theology of the fourth Gospel. Commenting on the structure of the prologue, Neal Flanagan says it "swings like the arm of a mighty pendulum."[4] It has the literary form of a chain with a suspended pendant. This form, called a chiasm, traces the mission of the Word: His descent from God to this world of ours, where he "became flesh and made his dwelling" (Jn 1:14), and his ascent, mission accomplished, back to the Father's side. The "pendant" that hangs on the chain consists of those verses that tell us why the Word was sent to us: "To those who did accept him he gave power to become children of God" (v. 12).

Having come to believe and be baptized in his name, we count ourselves among God's children. But the reading from 1 John warns us against complacency. He writes about "antichrists" (1 Jn 2:18), defectors from the believing community, and urges true believers to hold fast to the grace and truth that came through Jesus Christ (Jn 1:17).

Mary, Mother of God

January 1—Octave of Christmas

A B C

First Reading: Nm 6:22–27
Responsorial Psalm: Ps 67:2–3, 5, 6, 8
Second Reading: Gal 4:4–7
Gospel: Lk 2:16–21

In today's Gospel, the solemn proclamation of Paul to the Galatians—"When the fullness of time had come, God sent his Son"—is rendered in the vernacular of the infant lying in the manger. As Paul declares, he is "born of a woman," of Mary, who keeps all these things in her heart; and by virtue of his circumcision, he is "born under the law" as well. His birth is good news for Jews first, "those under the law," and then for all who have his Spirit (Gal 4:4).

The first reading for today is the priestly blessing, which Aaron is given to invoke God's name upon the Israelites. Combined as it is with the Gospel for this feast, it serves, like the excerpt from Galatians, to interpret the manger scene. It has been observed that the canticle of the angels announcing peace on earth (see Lk 2:13–14) has a liturgical quality like the song of the seraphim in the theophany of Isaiah 6:2–3. This is Luke's way of shifting the center of worship from Jerusalem to Bethlehem. The priestly blessing has the same effect. From the manger now, the Lord looks kindly upon us and gives us peace.

From January 2 to Epiphany

First Reading: 1 Jn 2:22–28
Responsorial Psalm: Ps 98:1, 2–3ab, 3cd–4
Gospel: Jn 1:19–28

First John was written in the heat of dissension within the Johannine community. Members of the community were denying "Jesus Christ come in the flesh" (4:2). These dissidents are the liars, the antichrists of today's reading. Throughout this passage the author appeals to the indwelling of the Holy Spirit (the Paraclete), whom the Father has sent to guide Christians to all truth (see Jn 16:13). He argues that their anointing with the Holy Spirit at Baptism will enable them to stand firm in the present crisis as well as on the last day, when Christ will reveal himself for all to see. Today's Gospel presents John the Baptist as an example of one who is filled with the Holy Spirit and allows what he heard from the beginning to remain in his heart, even in the heat of conflict and confrontation.

The Gospel suggests that John the Baptist is able to know who Jesus is because he knows so well who he himself is not—not the Messiah, not Elijah, not the Prophet. We must take our cue from him and learn to recognize and revere the humanity of Jesus by reckoning honestly with our own.

JANUARY 3

(if before Epiphany)

First Reading: 1 Jn 2:29—3:6
Responsorial Psalm: Ps 98:1, 3cd—4, 5—6
Gospel: Jn 1:29–34

The prologue of John's Gospel declares of Jesus, "To those who did accept him he gave power to become children of God" (Jn 1:12). Today's reading from the First Letter of John explores what it means to be God's children. Children of God, born of God by water and the Spirit (see Jn 1:13, 3:5), share God's life, which is holy. Therefore, first and foremost, holiness must characterize their lives. Furthermore, although children of God already have eternal life, they await an even greater share of God's life in the future when, says 1 John, "we shall be like him, for we shall see him as he is" (3:2). In today's Gospel, John the Baptist bears double witness to this great good news when he identifies Jesus first as "the Lamb of God, who takes away the sin of the world," and then as the One "who will baptize with the Holy Spirit" (1:29, 33).

In this season of grace, may we come more and more to appreciate "what love the Father has bestowed on us that we may be called the children of God." For this indeed is what we are (1 Jn 3:1). No wonder then that the Church invites us in today's responsorial psalm to "sing to the LORD a new song, / for he has done wondrous deeds" (98:1).

January 4

(if before Epiphany)

First Reading: 1 Jn 3:7–10
Responsorial Psalm: Ps 98:1, 7–8, 9
Gospel: Jn 1:35–42

Both of today's readings reiterate and thus reinforce the message of yesterday's readings. The first, from 1 John, continues yesterday's teaching about the righteousness of God and of those who are begotten by God (2:29). They cannot sin, he boldly declares today, because they are begotten of God (3:9). Furthermore, their righteousness is "made plain" in the love they have for their brothers and sisters (v. 10).

Today's Gospel also echoes the Baptist's declaration in yesterday's Gospel: "Behold, the Lamb of God" (Jn 1:36; see 1:29). The passage is punctuated with John's special vocabulary. Jesus asks, "What are you looking for?" And the disciples reply, "Rabbi ... where are you staying?" (v. 38). In John, a disciple is one who looks for Jesus, seeking him in faith, wanting above all to stay with him. The Greek word for "stay" here is *menein*, sometimes translated "abide" or "remain." In this Gospel, it describes a permanent relationship with Jesus and in him. The Gospel reading ends by expanding on the lesson of the first reading. If righteousness is indeed made plain in love for others, then Andrew shows us that the best way to love our brothers and sisters is to seek them out and bring them to Jesus.

JANUARY 5

(if before Epiphany)

First Reading: 1 Jn 3:11–21
Responsorial Psalm: Ps 100:1b–2, 3, 4, 5
Gospel: Jn 1:43–51

⁓◦◦◦⁓

Today's responsorial psalm calls us to "Know that the LORD is God; / he made us, his we are; / his people, the flock he tends" (100:3). It is instructive to watch Jesus as he gathers his flock in today's Gospel. The call of each is individual, distinctive. First Andrew and an unnamed disciple were led to Jesus by the preaching of the Baptist. Then Andrew brought his brother Simon. In today's reading, Jesus addresses Philip directly, but Nathanael is harder to persuade. They are simple men, conditioned by the biases of their time and place. "Can anything good come from Nazareth?" Nathanael retorts (Jn 1:46), needing to see for himself. Yet these simple men of Israel, having come in time to see the much greater things that Jesus had promised, laid the firm foundation on which the Church is built.

According to today's first reading, the firmness of that foundation would be shown then and now by the love of Jesus' flock for one another. This is how we know "that we have passed from death to life" (1 Jn 3:14). This love to which we are called is an imitation of the love of the Good Shepherd who "laid down his life for us; so we ought to lay down our lives for our brothers" (v. 16).

JANUARY 6

(if before Epiphany)

First Reading: 1 Jn 5:5–13
Responsorial Psalm: Ps 147:12–13, 14–15, 19–20
First option Gospel: Mk 1:7–11
Second option Gospel: Lk 3:23–38 or 3:23, 31–34, 36, 38

All of today's readings are concerned with giving testimony to the humanity of Jesus. Together they span Jesus' entire public life. The first Gospel selection (Mark) begins with the testimony of John the Baptist, who announces the coming of One more powerful than himself, then follows the baptism of Jesus, which signals the start of his ministry. In Mark, Jesus' baptism itself bears witness, assuring the reader that Jesus of Nazareth is indeed the beloved Son of God. In the alternate Gospel selection (Luke), Jesus' family tree attests to his rootedness in the human family. He is indeed a "son of Adam" (Lk 3:38), as well as the only Son of God. As for the first reading, from 1 John, it would seem that dissidents in the Johannine community are denying the role of Jesus' humanity in our salvation; they may well be minimizing the importance of his bloody death on the cross. Therefore, the author of 1 John insists on the testimony of three witnesses: "the Spirit, the water, and the Blood." (5:8). This, he insists, is the testimony of God himself "on behalf of his Son" (v. 9). On the basis of this testimony, we believe in the Son of God and bear witness to him today.

JANUARY 7

(if before Epiphany)

First Reading: 1 Jn 5:14–21
Responsorial Psalm: Ps 149:1–2, 3–4, 5 and 6a and 9b
Gospel: Jn 2:1–11

The ending of 1 John, today's first reading, is a profession of confidence in God: "If we ask anything according to his will, he hears us" (5:14). At first glance, today's Gospel of Jesus' first miracle or "sign" seems to illustrate the point exactly. In this story the mother of Jesus is cast as the persistent petitioner whose prayer is finally answered. But on looking closer, the exchange taking place between Jesus and his mother puzzles us. Jesus' reply to his mother's request—"Woman, how does your concern affect me? My hour has not yet come" (Jn 2:4)—sounds like a refusal. And yet, he proceeds to change the water into wine.

The seeming reluctance of Jesus in this story does two things. First, it shows his mother to be one of those who truly believe in Jesus without having seen miraculous signs (see Jn 20:29). With complete confidence in Jesus, she says to the stewards, "Do whatever he tells you" (2:5). At the same time, by raising the question of Jesus' "hour," this story also makes clear that Jesus acts here, as he will in his "hour," only to do the will of the Father, whose glory he has come to reveal. May we, like Mary, trust in Jesus with complete confidence.

Second Sunday after Christmas

(This mass would be used in countries where the Epiphany is celebrated on January 6.)

A B C

First Reading: Sir 24:1–2, 8–12
Responsorial Psalm: Ps 147:12–13, 14–15, 19–20
Second Reading: Eph 1:3–6, 15–18
Gospel: Jn 1:1–18 or 1:1–5, 9–14

Today's readings celebrate two unique gifts of God to the human family. The reading from Sirach sings the praises of God's wisdom, who comes forth from the mouth of God and makes her dwelling (literally, "pitches her tent") in Israel, the glorious people of God (24:3, 8–12). Later in the same chapter, wisdom is identified as "the book of the Most High's covenant, / the law which Moses commanded us" (24:22). This is the first gift. The second is announced in John's prologue. It is the Word of God, Jesus Christ incarnate, who descends from God to dwell (literally, "to pitch his tent") among us, to show us the Father's glory, and to make us children of God (Jn 1:14, 12). John is saying that the revelation given through Moses is perfected, but not superseded, by the revelation that came through Jesus Christ.

Paul echoes John when he writes that accepting the grace of God revealed in Jesus has given us the power to become adopted sons and daughters of God. Blessed be the God who has blessed us with such a gift!

Epiphany

A B C

First Reading: Is 60:1–6
Responsorial Psalm: Ps 72:1–2, 7–8, 10–11, 12–13
Second Reading: Eph 3:2–3a, 5–6
Gospel: Mt 2:1–12

The word "epiphany" means manifestation, particularly a manifestation of the powerful presence (i.e., the glory) of God. In the Letter to the Ephesians, Paul says that in God's glory manifested in Christ Jesus was revealed "the mystery," that is, God's plan to make Gentiles coheirs with Jews, "members of the same body" (3:6). This is the message of all three readings for today.

The passage from Isaiah invites Jerusalem, brought low by the Babylonians, to "rise up in splendor" (60:1). The long night of exile has ended. A new day dawns, and with it, unbelievably, the welcome sight of sons and daughters coming home. They do not return empty-handed but laden with gifts, "the wealth of nations" (v. 5), signifying not prosperity but praise of the Lord, who has done wonders for all to see, Jews and Gentiles alike. What Isaiah proclaims in song, Matthew relates in story. Instead of Jerusalem, Bethlehem witnesses the pilgrimage of the nations. They are represented by stargazing Magi from the East bearing gifts to honor the newborn King of the Jews. Jews and Gentiles now are partners in glorifying the one God to whom we, too, give honor and praise.

MONDAY AFTER EPIPHANY
OR JANUARY 7

First Reading: 1 Jn 3:22—4:6
Responsorial Psalm: Ps 2:7bc–8, 10–12a
Gospel: Mt 4:12–17, 23–25

Today's first reading from 1 John seems to continue the condemnation of the world begun in John's Gospel. The world is a dangerous place. The spirit of the antichrist "is already in the world," he says (4:3). Therefore, to be popular in the world—as are his opponents, who do not acknowledge "Jesus Christ come in the flesh" (v. 2)—is itself proof that one does not belong to God but to the world that does not accept Jesus. In today's Gospel, however, Jesus himself seems to be enjoying a certain popularity in the world. As he tours all of Galilee, he is followed by "great crowds from Galilee, the Decapolis, Jerusalem, and Judea, and from beyond the Jordan" (Mt 4:25). His reputation reaches even into Syria (v. 24).

Yet Matthew is aware of the world's eventual rejection of Jesus, and begins his account of Jesus' ministry by noting that "John had been arrested" (Mt 4:12). Jesus, as it were, takes up where John left off. His message—"The Kingdom of heaven is at hand" (v. 17)—is John's message. Jesus' fate will be the same as John's—rejection by the world. This sense of foreboding in both readings is relieved by the promise in the responsorial antiphon: "I will give you all the nations for an inheritance." God will have the last word.

TUESDAY AFTER EPIPHANY
OR JANUARY 8

First Reading: 1 Jn 4:7–10
Responsorial Psalm: Ps 72:1–2, 3–4, 7–8
Gospel: Mk 6:34–44

Today's brief selection from 1 John contains one of the central insights of that letter: "In this is love: not that we have loved God, but that he loved us" (1 Jn 4:10). John teaches us that the love of God was revealed by Jesus, who was sent to the world "that we might have life through him" (v. 9). In today's Gospel from Mark, the love of God is revealed in a number of biblical images that are taken up and "translated" into the words and actions of Jesus. In Ezekiel's prophecy, God's love had been depicted as the compassionate care of a shepherd (34:11–16); in Mark, Jesus is moved with pity for the people who are "like sheep without a shepherd" (Mk 6:34). On the desert journey to the Promised Land, God had fed the Israelites with manna (Ex 16:1–4); as Mark describes, in a deserted place Jesus gives the hungry crowd bread and fish. Elisha had once multiplied twenty barley loaves to feed a hundred men (2 Kgs 4:42–44); in Mark, Jesus multiplies five loaves to feed five thousand.

Jesus' revelation of God's love in human words and human gestures informs and enlivens the sacramental life of the Church. No less than the hungry crowd in that deserted place, in the Eucharist we, too, are fed—and so we "have life through him" (1 Jn 4:9).

WEDNESDAY AFTER EPIPHANY
OR JANUARY 9

First Reading: 1 Jn 4:11–18
Responsorial Psalm: Ps 72:1–2, 10, 12–13
Gospel: Mk 6:45–52

Today's two readings are both about seeing God. The Gospel recounts how Jesus' disciples in a boat far out on the lake catch a glimpse of God. They are given a manifestation of God, a "theophany." Several biblical allusions make Mark's intention clear. In the psalms, God's path is "through the mighty waters" (77:20), and in Job, God "treads upon the crests of the sea," passing by the one who does not see (9:8, 11). Finally, Jesus' "It is I" echoes the divine name "I AM" (cf. Ex 3:14). But because the disciples of Jesus are as yet unable to acknowledge "that Jesus is the Son of God" (1 Jn 4:15), the ability to see God eludes them. They are blinded by fear, a fear that only perfect love can banish. And their love has not yet been perfected (v. 18).

The selection from 1 John begins with a statement also found in John's Gospel: "No one has ever seen God" (1 Jn 4:1; see Jn 1:18, 6:46). The point is that only the Son has seen the Father; therefore, only the Son can show us the Father. But today's selection says more: the love of God that Jesus revealed to us is also revealed through us when God's love, dwelling in us, is "brought to perfection" (1 Jn 4:17). The way others will see God in us is "if we love one another" (v. 12).

Thursday after Epiphany
or January 10

First Reading: 1 Jn 4:19—5:4
Responsorial Psalm: Ps 72:1–2, 14 and 15bc, 17
Gospel: Lk 4:14–22

"Whoever is begotten by God conquers the world," declares 1 John in today's first reading. "The victory that conquers the world is our faith" (1 Jn 5:4). Faith gives us a share in Jesus' victory over sin and death, the "world" of 1 John. In the Gospel for today from Luke, Jesus proclaims his victory by quoting Isaiah's words. Anointed by the Spirit, he is sent "to bring glad tidings to the poor ... to proclaim liberty to captives / and recovery of sight to the blind, / to let the oppressed go free, / and to proclaim a year acceptable to the Lord" (Lk 4:18–19; see Is 61:1–2). The Greek word used to describe Jesus liberating captives and releasing prisoners is *aphesis*, the word also used by Luke for forgiveness of sins (see Lk 1:77). Above all, Jesus has overcome the world by freeing us from the power of the evil one.

The Gospel tells us, too, that this victory of Jesus over sin and death is more than a promise; it is a present reality. The words of Isaiah are actualized in the works of Jesus "today." So the victory of Jesus is accessible to us in faith, in the liturgy of the Church, where, as the *Catechism* puts it, we enter into the "today" of the living, liberating God, revealed in Jesus the Christ (see no. 1165).

FRIDAY AFTER EPIPHANY OR JANUARY 11

First Reading: 1 Jn 5:5–13
Responsorial Psalm: Ps 147:12–13, 14–15, 19–20
Gospel: Lk 5:12–16

In today's Gospel, Jesus cures a leper and sends him to the priest as the law of Israel required (see Lv 13–14). Then he adds, "that will be proof [that is, "testimony," *martyrion* in Greek] for them" (Lk 5:14). Scholars are unsure as to whether this testimony is intended for the priest or for Jesus' opponents. What matters for our purposes is that this puzzling remark of Jesus introduces the idea of testimony. Already Jesus is on trial.

Today's first reading, again from 1 John, builds on the thought from yesterday's reading and asks: "Who indeed is the victor over the world ...?" (5:5). Once again the answer depends on who gives testimony. Here the claim is made that it is God who testifies. And the author reasons, "If we accept human testimony, the testimony of God is surely greater" (v. 9). But the testimony of God in this case is not simple, for there are three who testify with one voice, "the Spirit, the water, and the Blood" (vv. 7–8), that is the Spirit-driven ministry of Jesus. "This is the testimony: God gave us eternal life, and this life is in his Son" (v. 11), whose victory over the world has made possible our sharing in eternal life.

SATURDAY AFTER EPIPHANY
OR JANUARY 12

First Reading: 1 Jn 5:14–21
Responsorial Psalm: 149:1–2, 3–4, 5–6a and 9b
Gospel: Jn 3:22–30

Today's readings use two different images to affirm the same reality: The one true God is revealed in Jesus the Christ. The first reading from 1 John takes its lead from the prologue of the fourth Gospel, which says of Jesus, "to those who did accept him he gave power to become children of God," adding, "to those who believe in his name, who were born not by natural genera-tion nor by human choice nor by a man's decision but of God" (Jn 1:12–13). Therefore, 1 John speaks of Christians as being God's children, begotten of God, and adds, "the one begotten by God he protects, and the Evil One cannot touch him" (5:18). Today's Gospel turns instead to the Hebrew Bible, our Old Testament, where Israel is portrayed as God's bride, betrothed to God. In this scheme, Jesus is the bridegroom who comes to claim his bride, and John the Baptist is his best man.

Begotten of God, betrothed to God—however we think of ourselves as believers, baptized in Jesus' name—our joy, like John's, has been made complete by Christ's coming. Therefore, like John, may we, too, seek to decrease—not to lose but to find our true selves in him and in "the one who is true" (1 Jn 5:20).

Baptism of the Lord

SUNDAY AFTER JANUARY 6

A

First Reading: Is 42:1–4, 6–7
Responsorial Psalm: Ps 29:1–2, 3–4, 3, 9–10
Second Reading: Acts 10:34–38
Gospel: Mt 3:13–17

The juxtaposition of today's texts invites the Christian reader to cast Jesus in the role of the anonymous servant of Isaiah's poem. The exchange between Jesus and John the Baptist in Matthew's version of Jesus' baptism highlights the connection. When John tries to prevent Jesus from being baptized, Jesus insists that "it is fitting for us to fulfill all righteousness" (Mt 3:15). In the Bible, righteousness is the victory of justice that the servant of God in Isaiah is called to establish on the earth (42:6). It comes as no surprise, then, when the heavenly voice designates Jesus as the Chosen One "with whom I am well pleased" (Mt 3:17; see Is 42:1).

The selection from Acts further underscores the connection between Jesus and the servant in Isaiah by interpreting Jesus' baptism as an anointing "with the Holy Spirit and power" (10:38). The Spirit of God that comes upon Jesus empowers him, like the servant, to "bring forth justice to the nations" by doing good and healing all who are bruised and broken. Do we count ourselves among them?

B

First Reading: Is 55:1–11
Responsorial Psalm: Is 12:2 3, 4bcd, 5–6
Second Reading: 1 Jn 5:1–9
Gospel: Mk 1:7–11

In the baptism of Jesus we have divine testimony as to who Jesus is. In the words of 1 John, the second reading for today, the Spirit that descends upon Jesus is the one who testifies that Jesus is indeed God's beloved Son, "and the Spirit is truth" (5:6).

Today's first reading is the conclusion of the prophecy of Second Isaiah, the anonymous exilic prophet whose oracles are collected in chapters 40–55 of the Book of Isaiah. In these climactic verses, the prophet, using considerable poetic ability, sums up his good news for the exiles in Babylon. His message takes the form of an invitation to feast on the rich fare of God's grace. This grace, the renewal of the everlasting covenant, is announced with reference to David. The prophet envisions not the revival of David's kingdom but the establishment of the kingdom of God, God's gracious rule over all nations, to which David is called to witness. However Isaiah's intended audience heard his words, for Christian readers they speak of Jesus, who at his baptism is designated David's heir, "a witness to the peoples" (Is 55:4) of the grace and mercy of God. By our Baptism we, too, are called to be such witnesses.

C

First Reading: Is 40:1–5, 9–11
Responsorial Psalm: Ps 104:1b–2, 3–4, 24–25, 27–28, 29–30
Second Reading: Ti 2:11–14; 3:4–7
Gospel: Lk 3:15–16, 21–22

With today's readings we return to Ordinary Time by revisiting an Advent theme. The reading from Isaiah is also the first reading for the Second Sunday of Advent in Year B. It describes the commissioning of heralds of good news sent by God to proclaim a new decree, a new word of God, to the exiles in Babylon: At long last "the glory of the LORD shall be revealed" (Is 40:5). In Advent, the words of Isaiah prepared us for the commemoration of Christ's coming in history. In Ordinary Time they remind us, as Paul reminds Titus, that, although "the grace of God has appeared, saving all," in Jesus we still "await the blessed hope, the appearance of the glory of our great God and savior Jesus Christ" (Ti 2:13).

Luke's account of Jesus' baptism stresses that the grace of God alone works in and through Christ. In Luke, Jesus is clothed with the Holy Spirit as power from on high (see 24:49) only after his baptism and as he prays. This makes it clear that it is not John's ritual but God's response to Jesus' prayer that empowers him— and us—to be heralds of good news.

Lenten Season

ASH WEDNESDAY

First Reading: Jl 2:12–18
Responsorial Psalm: Ps 51:3–4, 5–6ab, 12–13, 14, 17
Second Reading: 2 Cor 5:20—6:2
Gospel: Mt 6:1–6, 16–18 ˙

In many ways today's New Testament readings—from 2 Corinthians and from Matthew—echo the Old Testament reading from the prophet Joel. Joel's words are set in a time of crisis, a defining moment. In that critical moment, he summons the whole people of God to gather in the liturgical assembly to pray and fast. Playing on the Hebrew word *shub*, which means "turn," he tells the people to "return" to the Lord their God in the hope that God may "turn" (relent) and take pity on them. Paul proclaims this message as well. Like Joel, he too addresses people at a defining moment, "the acceptable time" (2 Cor 6:2). As Christ's ambassador, Paul implores the Corinthians to return and be reconciled to the God who has graciously turned to them in Christ.

Joel also warns the people that the public character of their gathering must not detract from the intimately personal nature of true conversion. They must rend their hearts and not their garments. In the same way, Matthew's Jesus warns all of us that our Lenten practices—prayer, fasting, almsgiving—must be for God's eyes only. This is the sentiment of the psalmist who prays for a "clean heart" and a new spirit (Ps 51:12).

THURSDAY AFTER ASH WEDNESDAY

First Reading: Dt 30:15–20
Responsorial Psalm: Ps 1:1–2, 3, 4 and 6
Gospel: Lk 9:22–25

All three of today's Scripture selections convey the same lesson. In Deuteronomy, Moses tells his people that they
choose life by walking in God's ways. Psalm 1:1–2 makes the
same point when it declares blessed the person who does not
walk "in the way of sinners ... but delights in the law of the
LORD." In Luke, Jesus tells his disciples that they choose life by
following in his steps.

Both Moses and the psalmist believe that walking in God's
ways is more than a metaphor; it is a mode of action that requires
keeping God's commandments, statutes, and decrees. Similarly,
Jesus teaches in Luke that following in his steps is more than a
figure of speech; it is a faithful, faith-filled way of life that
demands taking up one's cross each day. Finally, both Moses and
Jesus promise fullness of life—on God's terms.

During this season of Lent, the Church joins its voice with
that of Moses, the psalmist, and Jesus to invite us to walk in
God's way by following in Jesus' steps each day—beginning now.

FRIDAY AFTER ASH WEDNESDAY

First Reading: Is 58:1–9a
Responsorial Psalm: Ps 51:3–4, 5–6ab, 18–19
Gospel: Mt 9:14–15

L ent is a penitential season. Today's readings take up the timely theme of fasting, a common penitential practice among
Jews as well as Christians. The judgment oracle from Isaiah clarifies the purpose of fasting. Fasting—abstaining from food—
allows those who are usually well fed to identify imaginatively
with the hunger of the poor and so to learn compassion. The people to whom the prophet speaks have missed this point. Even as
they fast, they continue to drive their laborers, as did the
Egyptian taskmasters of another time. God says to them and to
us: "This, rather, is the fasting that I wish," says the Lord, "...
sharing your bread with the hungry, / sheltering the oppressed
and the homeless; / clothing the naked when you see them, /
and not turning your back on your own" (Is 58:6–7).

In today's Gospel, Jesus' reply to the objection of John's disciples further situates the practice of fasting. Jesus tells them that
the time for fasting will come when the bridegroom is taken
away. We who live between the Ascension and the Second
Coming of Jesus live in that time. To fast, as we do in Lent,
enables us to recognize Jesus when he manifests himself to us in
the plight of the hungry poor.

SATURDAY AFTER ASH WEDNESDAY

First Reading: Is 58:9b–14
Responsorial Psalm: Ps 86:1–2, 3–4, 5–6
Gospel: Lk 5:27–32

Both of today's readings use striking imagery to announce salvation. The words of Isaiah were apparently written before the walls of Jerusalem were rebuilt after the exile. Salvation, therefore, will not only bring light into the darkness and water to the parched land, but also equip the returning exiles to rebuild the city of God. Thus will the people come to be called "repairer of the breach" and "restorer of ruined homesteads" (Is 58:12). The responsorial psalm for today, Psalm 86, is a prayer for healing, and in the selection from Luke, Jesus presents himself as a doctor. By calling the hated toll collector Levi to join the community of his disciples, Jesus continues his mission of restoring all Israel, including "tax collectors and sinners" (Lk 5:30). To describe his saving work as repairer and restorer, he chooses a medical image, quite common in the ancient world. He is a physician, he says, who comes to restore the sick and repair the human spirit.

The season of Lent gathers us in table fellowship with Jesus and with one another. May his saving work equip us, in turn, to be in our world repairers of the breach and restorers of ruined homesteads.

First Sunday of Lent

A

First Reading: Gn 2:7–9; 3:1–7
Responsorial Psalm: Ps 51:3–4, 5–6, 12–13, 17
Second Reading: Rom 5:12–19 or 5:12, 17–19
Gospel: Mt 4:1–11

In today's selection from the Letter to the Romans, Paul connects the first reading and the Gospel by proposing that we look at Jesus as the new Adam. Just as death entered the world through the old Adam's sin, Paul says, so life has been restored through the new Adam's sacrifice.

In the first reading, we find the story of the fall of the old Adam, which is set in the garden the Lord God planted in Eden. It teems with life, with various trees to satisfy every hunger of soul and body. There Adam is established as God's son and servant. But when tempted, he lets "his trust in his Creator die in his heart," as the *Catechism* puts it (no. 397*). And so it happened that "through one man sin entered the world" (Rom 5:12). The setting of today's Gospel, the testing of the new Adam, is the desert, that place where every hunger goes unsatisfied. There the tempter engages Jesus in conversation, as he did Eve in the garden. But Jesus, trusting absolutely in God's word, withstands the devil's wiles. And so it happened that through one man, God's true Son, sin was overcome. This Lent, how will we allow Jesus to conquer sin in our own lives?

* Cf. Gn 3:1–11; Rom 5:19.

B

First Reading: Gn 9:8–15
Responsorial Psalm: Ps 25:4–5, 6–7, 8–9
Second Reading: 1 Pet 3:18–22
Gospel: Mk 1:12–15

Mark's account of the temptation of Jesus distinguishes itself from that of Matthew's or Luke's by its brevity. It is all of two verses, to which today's reading adds two more. Mark's Jesus comes to establish the rule of God in a world ruled by God's enemy. His entire ministry will be a power struggle in which he will confront and cast out the power of evil by the power of God. This struggle will find him increasingly isolated—from the leaders of his people, from family and friends in his native place, from his own disciples—in a virtual wilderness, surrounded by wild beasts (see Ps 22:13–14, 17, 21–22), where he will die alone and abandoned. Yet, as the reference to ministering angels assures us, this suffering Son of Man is also Son of God, who dwells in the shelter of the Most High (see Ps 91:11–13).

In his trial and triumph in the wilderness of the cross, Jesus suffered for us "the righteous for the sake of the unrighteous" (1 Pet 3:18). According to 1 Peter, it is this that leads us finally to God. For us who were saved by the waters of Baptism, his cross is a bow in the clouds, a sign of the covenant in his blood. This Lent, let us join the psalmist in asking the Lord to make known to us his ways (25:4), even if they lead to the cross.

C

First Reading: Dt 26:4–10
Responsorial Psalm: Ps 91:1–2, 10–11, 12–13, 14–15
Second Reading: Rom 10:8–13
Gospel: Lk 4:1–13

Today's first and third readings share the same background: the people of Israel's wandering in the desert for forty years before they finally enter the Promised Land. God ordained that desert sojourn, Moses says, "to test you by affliction and find out whether or not it was your intention to keep his command-ments" (Dt 8:2). Today's text from Deuteronomy is an ancient liturgical formula that gratefully acknowledges it was God's grace—"his strong hand and outstretched arm" (26:8)—that brought Israel safely through that time of testing to the land flowing with milk and honey. In the Gospel from Luke, Jesus spends forty days in the desert, where he, too, is tested. It is no accident that he answers every onslaught of the devil with a text from Deuteronomy (8:3; 6:13; 6:16). A true Israelite, this Son of God depends absolutely on the grace that has always been Israel's hope and salvation.

In the passage from Romans, Paul also quotes from Deuteronomy (30:14). He wants to say that the grace revealed in Jesus Christ is the same grace revered in the word of Israel's Scripture. On this grace, Jews and Gentiles alike can depend.

First Week of Lent

MONDAY

First Reading: Lv 19:1–2, 11–18
Responsorial Psalm: Ps 19:8, 9, 10, 15
Gospel: Mt 25:31–46

The apparent simplicity of the lesson of today's beloved parable of the Great Judgment from Matthew has become a matter for scholarly debate in recent years. According to some, the phrase *panta ta ethne* is usually translated "all the nations" and should be understood as "all the Gentiles" (that is, non-Jews); the phrase to "the least brothers of mine" (Mt 25:40) refers to Christians of Matthew's church. Be that as it may, placed alongside the reading from Leviticus, the parable has more to say about God than about us, whether we are Gentiles or Jews.

Leviticus instructs all God's holy ones—Jews and Christians alike—to act justly and mercifully in their dealings with one another. But the theological motivation for acting in this way begs for our attention. Leviticus puts it succinctly: "Be holy, for I, the LORD, your God, am holy" (19:2), which is to say that God's holiness is manifest in acts of mercy even as ours must be. In the parable, it is not imitation of God but Jesus' own identification with the least of his/our sisters and brothers that moves us not to "stand by idly" (Lv 19:16) when our neighbor is hungry or thirsty or naked or ill or imprisoned.

TUESDAY

First Reading: Is 55:10–11
Responsorial Psalm: Ps 34:4–5, 6–7, 16–17, 18–19
Gospel: Mt 6:7–15

Today's first reading from the prophet Isaiah affirms the power of God's word. Like rain and snow, it descends to earth from heaven and does not return (ascend) to God until it has achieved the divine purpose for which it was sent.

Today's Gospel, Matthew's version of the Our Father, also affirms the power of words—words offered in prayer to the heavenly Father. Here, too, we discern a pattern as the words Jesus teaches his disciples cut a path covering the distance between earth and heaven. Inspired by his longing for the coming of God's kingdom, the first three petitions ascend into God's presence, while the other four return (descend) to earth, weighted by the human concern for food, forgiveness, and freedom from evil in all its forms. Yet as Jesus teaches his disciples, the power of this prayer does not lie in the multiplication of words, but in the fact that it is the prayer of Jesus, who is himself the Word. So as the Church teaches in the *Catechism*, when we pray the Lord's Prayer we invoke our heavenly Father "by the one Word he always hears" (no. 2769*): Jesus, the Son of the Father.

---

* 1 Pet 1:23; cf. 1 Pet 2:1–10.

WEDNESDAY

First Reading: Jon 3:1–10
Responsorial Psalm: Ps 51:3 4, 12–13, 18–19
Gospel: Lk 11:29–32

The story of Jonah links today's two readings. In the first reading, the original call of Jonah is repeated. This time "Jonah made ready and went to Nineveh, according to the Lord's bidding" (Jon 3:3). Much to Jonah's surprise, when the people of Nineveh heard his warning—the word of the Lord—they responded immediately and all of them repented. In Luke's Gospel, the preaching of Jonah becomes a sign, a standard by which another prophet assesses the response of his hearers. The people of Jesus' day are compared unfavorably to the Ninevites of Jonah's experience, "because at the preaching of Jonah they repented, and there is something greater than Jonah here," Jesus tells them (Lk 11:32).

Another point links the two readings. The message of the Book of Jonah was partly to show that salvation is offered to all, even to Ninevites, the hated Assyrians, whose wickedness was legendary in the ancient world. Similarly, the Gospel proclaims that salvation is offered even to pagans, whose immorality was well known among the Jews. Such is the inscrutable mystery of God's will to save.

THURSDAY

First Reading: Est C 12, 14–16, 23–25
Responsorial Psalm: Ps 138:1–2ab, 2cde–3, 7c–8
Gospel: Mt 7:7–12

Today's Gospel brings us Jesus' teaching on prayer as found in the Sermon on the Mount. Assuming that we are all children of the same heavenly Father, Jesus urges us to ask, seek, and knock, confident that God will answer. The prayer of Esther found in today's first reading is an example of prayer that asks, seeks, and knocks with absolute confidence that God will hear. Interestingly, in the Hebrew Scriptures the story of Esther, which provides the basis for the Jewish feast of Purim, makes no direct reference to God at all. However, our text is taken from the Greek version (indicated by the letter C above), which interjects a religious note. Her prayer makes Esther's religious faith explicit. Clearly in this version, the source of her courage is reliance on God.

Today's readings tell us that courage and confidence in prayer are possible only in the context of a relationship with God. The context of Esther's prayer is her membership in the community of Israel. She relies on the faith of her forefathers. Similarly, Jesus urges his disciples to consider themselves children of the heavenly Father, who gives only "good things to those who ask him" (Mt 7:11).

FRIDAY

First Reading: Ez 18:21–28
Responsorial Psalm: Ps 130:1–2, 3–4, 5–7a, 7bc–8
Gospel: Mt 5:20–26

In today's first reading, the prophet Ezekiel sheds new light on the law of Israel, while in today's Gospel the prophet Jesus does the same. The law Ezekiel is concerned with is found in Deuteronomy and states that each individual is responsible for his or her own actions (see 24:16). Ezekiel expands on this point of law and explores what happens when an individual repents. "If the wicked man turns away from all the sins he committed," he says, "he shall surely live, he shall not die," for, he argues, the Lord derives no pleasure from the death of the wicked (Ez 18:21, 23). The law Jesus is concerned with is, of course, the fifth commandment (see Ex 20:13). Jesus expands the law to include anger, abusive language, and an attitude of contempt, all of which can lead to murder. But Jesus goes even further by making reconciliation the condition and criterion for true worship.

Neither Ezekiel nor Jesus is tampering with the law; rather, each is tempering it with the compassion that each believes is of God. Today's psalmist also makes this point. "If you, O LORD, mark iniquities, / LORD, who can stand?" he asks. Then he answers as both Ezekiel and Jesus would, "But with you is forgiveness, / that you may be revered" (Ps 130:3–4). Lent is the opportune time for repentance and forgiveness.

Saturday

First Reading: Dt 26:16–19
Responsorial Psalm: Ps 119:1–2, 4–5, 7–8
Gospel: Mt 5:43–48

In today's reading from Deuteronomy, Moses solemnly declares the distinguishing mark of Israel's divine election as the cherished chosen people of God: that they wholeheartedly observe God's commandments, statutes, and decrees. In the Sermon on the Mount found in Matthew, Jesus tells his disciples that loving their enemies is what distinguishes them as children of their heavenly Father. In fact, his words echo the Book of Deuteronomy: "You are children of the LORD, your God" (14:1). Both readings tell us that to be chosen by God, to be children of God, brings with it an awesome responsibility. It demands that we act accordingly. The holiness of our lives must show forth the wholeness (the "perfection") of God.

Today's responsorial psalm is from Psalm 119, which is the longest biblical psalm with 167 lines. It is a song in praise of Torah, "the law of the Lord." Its form is an acrostic, using all twenty-two letters of the Hebrew alphabet. Among other things, this illustrates the perfection of God's law. It is a fitting prayer for this Lenten season: "Oh, that I might be firm in the ways / of keeping your statutes!" (Ps 119:5).

Second Sunday of Lent

A

First Reading: Gn 12:1–4a
Responsorial Psalm: Ps 33:4–5, 18–19, 20, 22
Second Reading: 2 Tm 1:8b–10
Gospel: Mt 17:1–9

In the second reading for today, Paul tells Timothy that God's design for our salvation is the grace "now made manifest through the appearance of our savior Christ Jesus, who destroyed death and brought life and immortality to light" (2 Tm 1:10). Paul himself is writing in that light (the resurrection of Jesus). In today's Gospel, however, even before the Son of Man has been raised from the dead, Peter, James, and John are given a glimpse of that grace in the vision of Jesus transfigured.

Matthew's version of the transfiguration sharpens the focus on Peter. In his enthusiasm, Peter offers to build three tents single-handedly—one for Jesus, one for Moses, and one for Elijah. His natural impulse is to want to capture and to cling to the revelation of God's grace manifest in Jesus glorified. But Peter is about to learn what Abraham knew so well: peak experiences are given only to motivate the journey of faith. "Go forth ... to a land that I will show you" (Gn 12:1). Peter must come down from the mount of transfiguration and step onto the road to Jerusalem, the way of the cross. And so must we.

B

First Reading: Gn 22:1–2, 9a, 10–13, 15–18
Responsorial Psalm: Ps 116:10, 15, 16–17, 18–19
Second Reading: Rom 8:31b–34
Gospel: Mk 9:2–10

The story of Abraham and Isaac, today's first reading, captures the imagination of Jews and Christians alike. It stands behind Paul's rhetoric in the Letter to the Romans: "If God is for us, who can be against us? He who would not spare his own Son but handed him over for us all, how will he not also give us everything else along with him?" (8:31–32). Paul seems to suggest that Abraham's offering of his beloved son on Mount Moriah is the model for the sacrifice of God's own beloved Son on Calvary. The *Catechism* interprets the relationship this way: "And so the father of believers is conformed to the likeness of the Father" (no. 2572*).

How are we to read this text in light of the transfiguration of Jesus, today's Gospel? Because of Abraham's willingness to offer his beloved son, the Lord's messenger tells him that his descendants will be abundantly blessed, and in them "all the nations of the earth shall find blessing" (Gn 22:18). The sacrifice of God's beloved Son will mean abundant blessing for all. This is what is revealed to Jesus' disciples in today's reading. But they, like us at times, are uncomprehending. And like us, they will be until their eyes are opened by the risen Lord.

---

* Rom 8:32.

C

First Reading: Gn 15:5–12, 17–18
Responsorial Psalm: Ps 27:1, 7–8, 8–9, 13–14
Second Reading: Phil 3:17—4:1 or 3:20—4:1
Gospel: Lk 9:28b–36

The first and third readings for today describe profound experiences with God in prayer. Abraham's trance and the terrifying darkness that envelops him are like the disciples' sudden sleep and the terrifying cloud that overshadows them. In both of these extraordinary occurrences, God's intention is revealed. To Abraham's descendants God will give the land from the Wadi of Egypt to the Great River. The divine presence, symbolized by the smoking brazier and the flaming torch, guarantees God's gift.

Through the "exodus" that Jesus will accomplish in Jerusalem (Lk 9:31)—his death and resurrection—his disciples will attain the heavenly citizenship of which Paul speaks in his letter to the Philippians. The dazzling glory that shines on the face of Christ is the pledge of that promise. On that day, he will "change our lowly body to conform with his glorified body by the power that enables him also to bring all things into subjection to himself" (Phil 3:21). Meanwhile, we must listen to him in prayer.

Psalm 27 is an apt response to today's readings as it asks the Lord, our light and our salvation, not to hide the brightness of his face from us, that we may see the bounty of his grace.

Second Week of Lent

MONDAY

First Reading: Dn 9:4b–10
Responsorial Psalm: Ps 79:8, 9, 11 and 13
Gospel: Lk 6:36–38

Both of today's readings acknowledge God's compassion. In the prayer from the Book of Daniel, an exiled people cry for mercy. They admit their guilt but boldly remind God: "Yours, O LORD, our God, are compassion and forgiveness!" (Dn 9:9). The Gospel from Luke opens with a call to "Be merciful, just as your Father is merciful" (6:36), that is, not to judge or condemn, but rather to give and to forgive. But because this is Luke's version of this saying of Jesus, it has another meaning, too.

For Luke, sharing material possessions is a hallmark of true discipleship. Today's saying, which occurs in the Sermon on the Plain, carries this economic sense as well. In the verses immediately preceding today's, Luke indicates that loving enemies includes sharing one's goods with them, expecting nothing back (6:35). Similarly, these verses show that pardoning others involves canceling their debts. This concretizes the command of Jesus. Compassion costs, but it will also be richly rewarded; "a good measure, packed together, shaken down, and overflowing, will be poured into your lap," he says (v. 38).

TUESDAY

First Reading: Is 1:10, 16–20
Responsorial Psalm: Ps 50:8 9, 16bc–17, 21 and 23
Gospel: Mt 23:1–12

Today's readings are aimed at rulers responsible for the administration of their respective communities. Isaiah has in mind the princes of Judah whom he urges to act with justice on behalf of the powerless and the poor. In Matthew's Gospel, Jesus seems to be attacking the scribes and Pharisees, but his real targets are Christian leaders who would imitate certain scribes and Pharisees of their day. "You have but one teacher," says Jesus, "you have but one master" (Mt 23:8, 10).

The second part of Isaiah's oracle, on the other hand, is a call to conversion that reaches beyond the ruling class to all God's people, then and now. The prophet says that they stand at a crossroads and must choose the path of salvation or of destruction, to "eat the good things of the land" or to be themselves eaten by the sword (Is 1:19–20). At this critical juncture, God invites them to "set things right" (v. 18). Forgiveness is possible, but the choice is theirs—and ours. It entails making justice our aim (v. 16) because, as the Lord declares in the words of today's psalm, "to him that goes in the right way I will show the salvation of God" (50:23).

Wednesday

First Reading: Jer 18:18–20
Responsorial Psalm: Ps 31:5–6, 14, 15–16
Gospel: Mt 20:17–28

In today's readings, Jeremiah and Jesus face very similar situations. The first reading reveals the plotting of certain citizens of
Jerusalem to kill Jeremiah, while Jesus exposes the threat posed
to him by the chief priests and scribes. This is the context of
Jeremiah's prayer and the content of Jesus' third prediction of his
passion. Both men are tragically misunderstood. Jeremiah's adver-
saries reason that they have nothing to lose by destroying him—
not instruction from the priests, nor counsel from the wise, nor
messages from the prophets. They fail to appreciate how often the
prayer of Jeremiah has averted God's wrath. In the Gospel, even
Jesus' disciples fail to understand the meaning of his words. This
is made embarrassingly clear by the request of Zebedee's sons,
which Matthew has put on the lips of their mother.

Jesus' reply to the request of Zebedee's sons implicates them
in the suffering of Jesus. "Can you drink the chalice that I am
going to drink?" he asks them and us (Mt 20:22). Unlike them,
we know that the cup is a participation in the Blood of Christ (see
1 Cor 10:16). Let us drink it worthily.

THURSDAY

First Reading: Jer 17:5–10
Responsorial Psalm: Ps 1:1–2, 3, 4 and 6
Gospel: Lk 16:19–31

The words of Jeremiah in today's first reading sound a theme that reaches back to Genesis. "More tortuous than all else is the human heart, / beyond remedy," the prophet declares (Jer 17:9). This was God's conclusion, too, in the aftermath of the flood of Noah's time: "The desires of man's heart are evil from the start" (Gn 8:21). Today's Gospel parable probes the mind and tests the heart of a rich man for the instruction of Jesus' hearers. His riches have so deluded this man that even in torment in "the netherworld" he cannot grasp the reality of his situation. Claiming Abraham as his father, he tries to commandeer the services of Lazarus to fetch him water and to warn his brothers. But his efforts are all in vain, for God gives to everyone "according to the merit of his deeds" (Jer 17:10).

Typically, for Luke the perversity of the rich man's heart is revealed in his neglect of the poor man who lay at his door. This may be a clue for us who have not only the words of Moses and the prophets to guide us, but also the witness of Jesus, who rose from the dead.

FRIDAY

First Reading: Gn 37:3–4, 12–13a, 17b–28a
Responsorial Psalm: Ps 105:16–17, 18–19, 20–21
Gospel: Mt 21:33–43, 45–46

J oining the story of the betrayal of Joseph to the parable of the
Tenants sharpens the poignancy of the Gospel portrait of
Jesus. The parable places Jesus in the long line of God's servants
who, sent as messengers to Israel, were sometimes brutally
rejected (see Neh 9:26). To this, the story of Joseph adds the
theme of betrayal by one's own. Both texts, the story from
Genesis and the parable in Matthew, have undergone revision. In
the Genesis account, Reuben vies with Judah to be the hero of
the story, shades of an earlier version. In Matthew's account of
the parable, the punishment of the tenants is meant to evoke the
destruction of Jerusalem by the Romans in A.D. 70. For us, however, the interest lies in how these texts interpret the passion and
death of Jesus.

The parable suggests that the death of Jesus will bring about a
dramatic change in the leadership of Israel, God's vineyard (see Is
5:1–7). No doubt Matthew is anticipating the claim of his community that the vineyard has been given to them. For Christians,
the story of Joseph suggests how the Son of God, betrayed by his
brothers, may in God's plan and purpose be their salvation.

SATURDAY

First Reading: Mi 7:14–15, 18–20
Responsorial Psalm: Ps 103:1–2, 3–4, 9–10, 11–12
Gospel: Lk 15:1–3, 11–32

The prophecy of Micah concludes with a prayer for forgiveness, a prayer made possible by the image that introduces it. The Shepherd of Israel, who performed wonderful signs in "days of old" when they came home from the land of Egypt, is ready to act once more. Therefore, Israel prays with confidence that all their sins will be "cast into the depths of the sea" (Mi 7:14, 19), utterly forgotten. The same image dominates the parable of the Prodigal Son. Here again, true repentance brings about a total reversal of the sinner's lot. The son is fully restored as a son in his father's house, not as a servant.

The second part of the story, however, may address us more directly. As often happens in Luke, the Gospel reveals the thoughts of many hearts (see 2:35). The father's graciousness to the Prodigal Son exposes the smoldering rage and resentment of the dutiful elder son. His fidelity, grudgingly given, has been a kind of slavery. "All these years I served you," he says (15:29). Luke does not tell us what this son does in the end. But for all of us oldest children to the manor born, it is comforting to know that his father came out to him as well.

Third Sunday of Lent

A
*(Readings may also be used
in cycles B and C)*

First Reading: Ex 17:3–7
Responsorial Psalm: Ps 95:1–2, 6–7, 8–9
Second Reading: Rom 5:1–2, 5–8
Gospel: Jn 4:5–42 or 4:5–15, 19b–26, 39a, 40–42

Preparation for Baptism has governed the choice of today's three readings. The controlling image is living water, a biblical symbol for the gift of God. In Exodus, God responds to people's thirst for water. But the water is more than a physical necessity; this is made clear in the last verse, which interprets the action of the story. The people's grumbling about the lack of water is construed as doubt about the gift of God's powerful presence: "Is the LORD in our midst or not?" (Ex 17:7). In Jesus' exchange with the Samaritan woman, the gift of God is again imaged as water, living water that becomes in the one who drinks it "a spring of water welling up to eternal life" (Jn 4:14).

The image of living water appears again in John when on the last day of the feast of Tabernacles Jesus invites all who thirst to come to him and drink. To this John adds the note: "He said this in reference to the Spirit that those who came to believe in him were to receive" (Jn 7:39). This is what Paul means when he declares that "the love of God has been poured out into our hearts through the Holy Spirit" (Rom 5:5). It is not too soon to prepare for Pentecost.

B

First Reading: Ex 20:1–17 or 20:1–3, 7–8, 12–17
Responsorial Psalm: Ps 19:8, 9, 10, 11
Second Reading: 1 Cor 1:22–25
Gospel: Jn 2:13–25

The primary concern of today's three readings is theology; that is to say, all three speak to us of God. The substance of today's first reading concerns the Ten Commandments. The *Catechism* teaches that the "ten words" of God (the Decalogue) are first and foremost words about God. They belong to God's gracious self-communication in the Exodus event (nos. 2059,* 2057**). In that context, they reveal a God who is liberator first and then legislator, a God who wills for us freedom and fullness of life. Psalm 19, in response to the first reading, celebrates the gift of God's law. Not only does it enlighten the eyes, but it also brings joy to the heart.

In Corinthians, Paul argues that the cross of Christ is also a revelatory event. In Christ crucified, God is revealed as powerful and wise, though perhaps not as the world perceives power and wisdom. That slippage between the world's perspective and God's accounts for the challenge posed by Jesus in the fourth Gospel. In John every encounter with Jesus is a summons to see God's glory in and through the signs he does. Some do see his glory, like the disciples after the resurrection. Others never get beyond the signs. In Lent, we pray for the seeing that is believing.

* Dt 5:4.
** Dt 30:16; 5:15.

C

First Reading: Ex 3:1–8a, 13–15
Responsorial Psalm: Ps 103: 1–2, 3–4, 6–7, 8, 11
Second Reading: 1 Cor 10:1–6, 10–12
Gospel: Lk 13:1–9

The memory of the Exodus pervades today's selections from the Book of Exodus and from the First Letter to the Corinthians. In our first reading, we see the great theophany (manifestation of God) at the burning bush that precipitated the drama of Israel's rescue from the hands of the Egyptians by the mighty hand of the living God, I AM. The first four verses of the reading from 1 Corinthians take up this story, recalling the cloud that led them by day and kept them safe from the Egyptians by night (Ex 13:21–22; 14:19–20); their crossing of the Red Sea on dry land (14:22); the manna from heaven (16:4–15); and the water from the rock (17:1–6). But despite all this, Paul continues, the people grumbled and some perished. This he offers as a warning to those who think they stand secure.

Jesus also issues a warning in today's Gospel. As suddenly and swiftly as disaster befell the Galilean pilgrims and the people at the tower of Siloam, he says, so will the Day of Judgment take the unrepentant by surprise. In other words, the Lord may be kind and merciful, as the responsorial antiphon affirms, but even the patience of God runs out.

OPTIONAL MASS
FOR THE THIRD WEEK OF LENT

First Reading: Ex 17:1–7
Responsorial Psalm: Ps 95:1–2, 6–7ab, 7c–9
Gospel: Jn 4:5–42

The climate of Palestine made biblical people appreciate the necessity of water for life. So it is not surprising that in the Bible water became a symbol for life itself. In today's first reading, the people's thirst is the occasion for a revelation of God's saving power, while in the Gospel the revelation of God in Jesus is described as "living water" (4:10). Jeremiah had talked of God as "the fountain of living water" (2:13; 17:13), and the phrase was used as well of the Torah, God's word revealed to Moses. So when Jesus tells the Samaritan woman that he would give her "living water … a spring of water welling up to eternal life" (Jn 4:10, 14), he makes a massive claim. "While the law was given through Moses, grace and truth [the gift of God] came through Jesus Christ" (see Jn 1:17).

"If you knew the gift of God," Jesus says to the woman (4:10). In Lent, we revisit the desert to discover the gift of God once more, as did the wilderness community of the first reading. Meeting Jesus there, we learn, as the *Catechism* puts it, that God thirsts, too, "thirsts that we may thirst for him" (no. 2560*). This is where prayer begins.

---

* Cf. St. Augustine, *De diverris quaestionibus octoginta tribus* 64, 4: PL 40, 56.

MONDAY

First Reading: 2 Kgs 5:1–15ab
Responsorial Psalm: Ps 42:2, 3; 43:3, 4
Gospel: Lk 4:24–30

The two readings for today warn against prejudice and pre-conception. In Luke's Gospel, Jesus is expelled from his hometown of Nazareth because he challenges his people's preconception that God's visitation will be for them only. Alluding to the biblical stories of Elijah, who saved a widow of Zarephath and her son from starvation, and Elisha, who cured the leprosy of Naaman, a Gentile enemy of Israel, Jesus intimates that his own ministry as messianic prophet will extend beyond the boundaries of Israel. For this the people of Nazareth reject him. The first reading is the story of Naaman's cure, and it, too, shatters preconceptions, both Naaman's and the reader's. Who would have thought that a little Israelite slave girl could help the mighty Naaman? Or that he could be healed by doing something so ordinary as washing in the Jordan River? In fact, his preconception of what a prophet should do almost led Naaman to reject the way to health and wholeness.

Naaman discovered, as we must, that the God of Israel acts in unexpected ways that challenge our prejudices and shatter our preconceptions.

TUESDAY

First Reading: Dn 3:25, 34–43
Responsorial Psalm: Ps 25:4–5ab, 6 and 7bc, 8–9
Gospel: Mt 18:21–35

In the first reading, Azariah (his Babylonian name is Abednego) is one of Daniel's Jewish companions in the court of King Nebuchadnezzar. Although he and his friends have attained power in the province of Babylon, they refuse to worship the golden statue that the king had erected; therefore they are consigned to the fiery furnace (see Dn 3:1–23). There Azariah prays not for himself but for his people. He appeals to the "kindness and great mercy" of God, asking for wonders that will bring glory to God's name (v. 42).

In today's Gospel, Jesus teaches his disciples that in their dealings with one another, they must imitate the great mercy of God to which Azariah appeals. The so-called parable of the Unforgiving Servant dramatizes God's mercy by means of the wonderful generosity of the king who writes off the official's large debt. The official fails to understand, however, that having received mercy from the king, he must in turn show mercy to his fellow servants. In fact, as he discovers to his own undoing, the great mercy of the king who delivers him from debt depends on it. Thus, the psalmist says, God "shows sinners [like us] the way" (Ps 25:8).

WEDNESDAY

First Reading: Dt 4:1, 5–9
Responsorial Psalm: Ps 147:12–13, 15–16, 19–20
Gospel: Mt 5:17–19

In the Church's ancient liturgy, this Wednesday was the first "scrutiny" or test of the catechumens preparing for Baptism. The test was on the commandments, so both readings center on that theme. "Whoever obeys and teaches these commandments will be called greatest in the Kingdom of heaven" (Mt 5:19). Jesus tells his disciples that they must practice what they preach (or teach). Specifically, they are to preach and to practice the law of God confided to Israel in the Torah and the teaching of the prophets, that is, the Hebrew Bible. Jesus says that this law will remain in force for Christians as for Jews "until heaven and earth pass away" (Mt 5:18)—until the kingdom of God is fully revealed.

In Deuteronomy, Moses tells the Israelites, who are about to take possession of the Promised Land, that they will preach (or teach) by practicing the statutes and decrees of the Lord, their God. "For thus" he says, "will you give evidence of your wisdom and intelligence to the nations" (Dt 4:6), as will we who have received from Jesus the wisdom of Israel.

Thursday

First Reading: Jer 7:23–28
Responsorial Psalm: Ps 95:1 2, 6–7, 8–9
Gospel: Lk 11:14–23

In today's first reading, the prophet Jeremiah decries the persistent hardness of his people's hearts (7:24) and the stiffness of their necks (v. 26). Both expressions point beyond the symptoms of sin to its source in the very core of the self. As the prophet Jesus casts out demons in today's Gospel, he, too, encounters the obduracy of some of his people. Some accuse him of being Satan's agent; others test him by asking for a sign. In answer, Jesus offers a pithy parable. If Satan is "a strong man fully armed" (Lk 11:21) guarding his possessions, then Jesus is the stronger one (see Lk 3:16), who, "by the finger of God" (11:20), strips Satan of his power and sets free those in his possession. In this way, the works no less than the words of Jesus announce that the reign of God is upon us.

Today's brief parable tells us that there is hope for our hard hearts and stiff necks. Jesus is the stronger one, who by the power of God can take booty from a warrior and rescue captives from a tyrant's grasp (see Is 49:24–25). If you hear his voice today, harden not your hearts.

FRIDAY

First Reading: Hos 14:2–10
Responsorial Psalm: Ps 81:6c–8a, 8bc–9, 10–11ab, 14 and 17
Gospel: Mk 12:28–34

T he epilogue of Hosea, today's first reading, is structured as call and response. Hosea calls the people to return to the Lord, in whom "the orphan finds compassion," he says. In response, God declares, "I will love them freely; / for my wrath is turned away from them" (Hos 14:4–5). Thus is the life-giving love of God—"a verdant cypress tree" (v. 9)—proven once more.

God speaks in today's psalm as well. And again, the longing of God for his sinful people is palpable. "If only my people would hear me," says the unfortunately unfamiliar voice (Ps 81:14, 6).

In the Gospel, a scribe calls on Jesus to tell him which is the first—the greatest—of all the commandments, and Jesus responds with not one but two commandments: "You shall love the Lord your God ... You shall love your neighbor as yourself" (Mk 12:30–31). The scribe repeats Jesus' answer in his own words and, echoing Hosea, adds that such love "is worth more than all burnt offerings and sacrifices" (v. 33; see Hos 6:6). This statement does not negate the need for formal liturgy; it simply affirms the dispositions that must inform true religion as well as true repentance, as in today's first reading. Lent is the time to test if our repentance and our religion are true.

SATURDAY

First Reading: Hos 6:1–6
Responsorial Psalm: Ps 51:3–4, 18–19, 20–21ab
Gospel: Lk 18:9–14c

Like yesterday's reading, today's from Hosea is structured as call and response. Only here the call to "return to the LORD" is insincere, as insubstantial as a morning cloud or "the dew that early passes away" (Hos 6:1, 4). In the parables from Luke, Jesus assesses the piety of the Pharisee in much the same way. Therefore, he did not go home from the Temple justified as the tax collector did.

For Luke, as for many Christians after A.D. 70, the Pharisee had become a stock character, a hypocrite, hard of heart. In reality, the piety of the Pharisees was not any more susceptible to self-righteousness than that of any other religious group then or now. And Jesus knew it. He wanted only to urge on his disciples the true repentance of the tax collector whose sin was before him always (see Ps 51:5). Like Hosea, Jesus did not devalue pious practices like sacrifice and holocaust or fasting and tithing, but he never forgot what the Pharisees themselves believed, that what God desires above all else is love. As we reflect on today's parable, let us embrace the piety of the tax collector without painting all Pharisees with the same brush.

Fourth Sunday of Lent

A

*(Readings may also be used
in cycles B and C)*

First Reading: 1 Sm 16:1b, 6–7, 10–13a
Responsorial Psalm: Ps 23:1–3a, 3b–4, 5, 6
Second Reading: Eph 5:8–14
Gospel: Jn 9:1–41 or 9:1, 6–9, 13–17, 34–38

Today's readings all play on the themes of blindness and sight, darkness and light. Found in the Gospel, the healing of the man born blind is another one of those texts from John that has always figured prominently in the preparation of catechumens for Baptism. Even a cursory reading of the passage makes it easy to see why. Baptismal symbols abound: water, light, and new-found faith in Jesus. However, the conclusion of the story—Jesus' judgment on the religious leaders (represented here by some of the Pharisees)—must cause all believers to wonder, "Surely we are not also blind, are we?" (Jn 9:40).

The passage from Ephesians distinguishes children of light from children of darkness on the basis of their deeds. But this sort of ethical dualism, common enough in the religious writings of the ancient world, can be dangerous. Claiming to be true children of light can too easily lead to crusades exposing the darkness of others. Saying, "We see," our sin remains. This Lent, let us learn to see as God teaches Samuel to see in the first reading, not appearances, but what is in the heart.

B

First Reading: 2 Chr 36:14–16, 19–23
Responsorial Psalm: Ps 137:1–2, 3, 4–5, 6
Second Reading: Eph 2:4–10
Gospel: Jn 3:14–21

⋘◦◯◦⋙

Both of the New Testament readings for today talk in parallel terms about the saving work of God in Christ. "For God so loved the world that he gave his only Son, so that everyone who believes in him might not perish but might have eternal life," says John 3:16. Ephesians repeats, "God, who is rich in mercy, because of the great love he had for us … brought us to life with Christ" (2:2–5). For John, accepting salvation means coming to the light that has come into the world in Christ. For Ephesians, it means being created in Christ as God's handiwork. Both insist that the work of salvation is God's initiative. But Ephesians is more explicit: "By grace you have been saved through faith, and this is not from you; it is the gift of God" (v. 8).

The first reading is also about God's saving work, which, here as well, is motivated by God's compassion (2 Chr 36:15). Although in Chronicles the arena of God's activity is history, not spirituality, the dynamic is the same: the wicked preferred the darkness until God's anger grew beyond human remedy and the people of Judah were carried captive to Babylon. But because God so loved the world, saving light prevailed and Cyrus sent God's people home. This, too, was the gift of God.

C

First Reading: Jos 5:9a, 10–12
Responsorial Psalm: Ps 34:2–3, 4–5, 6–7
Second Reading: 2 Cor 5:17–21
Gospel: Lk 15:1–3, 11–32

In today's reading we see a homecoming—what Paul calls reconciliation in 2 Corinthians. This is what God has done for us in Christ, he says. And as a result, "the old things have passed away; behold, new things have come" (2 Cor 5:17). In the first reading from Joshua, the Israelites stand on the threshold of the Promised Land. The old (their slavery in Egypt, their sojourn in the wilderness) has passed away; new life on the land, their homeland, has come. What they eat signifies this. The manna, desert fare, ceases; in its place are unleavened cakes and parched grain, the yield of the land of Canaan. And all this is from God, who has removed from them the reproach of Egypt.

Similarly, in today's Gospel the old dissolute life of the younger son gives way to new life in his father's house. Instead of the pods on which the swine fed, the son finds a home-cooked family feast. As for the old resentments of the elder son, finally brought to honest speech, they, too, with time, will yield to new ways of relating. All this occurs because of a parent who has learned that we are most like God when we welcome home our children.

OPTIONAL MASS
FOR THE FOURTH WEEK OF LENT

First Reading. Mi 7:7–9
Responsorial Psalm: Ps 27:1, 7–8a, 8b–9abc, 13–14
Gospel: Jn 9:1–41

Today's Gospel was part of baptismal instruction in the early Church. The baptismal elements of the story are easy to see: to St. Augustine, the man's blindness from birth signified original sin; Jesus' smearing the man's eyes with mud could be taken as an "anointing" as in the rite of Baptism; the man is told to wash, an obvious baptismal symbol; the name of the pool is Siloam —"One who has been sent" (Jn 9:7)—which is another name for Jesus; and finally, in the early Church, Baptism was often described as "enlightenment." The story also depicts the "post-baptismal catechesis" of the man whose eyes Jesus opened. Gradually, the man learns to name Jesus more truly as a "prophet," as one who is "from God," and finally as the Lord, whom he worships.

The story is also an object lesson on the need to profess one's faith boldly and bravely before hostile forces. The first reading teaches this as does the psalm. Both authors put their trust in the Lord. Let us make their prayer our own: "The LORD is my light and my salvation; / whom should I fear?" (Ps 27:1).

MONDAY

First Reading: Is 65:17–21
Responsorial Psalm: Ps 30:2 and 4, 5–6, 11–12a and 13b
Gospel: Jn 4:43–54

Today's first reading announces the restoration of Jerusalem as a new creation, using the verb "create" (*bara*) three times. The Bible reserves *bara* for the creative activity of God alone, and what God creates is fullness of life. "No longer shall there be in it / an infant who lives but a few days, / or an old man who does not round out his full lifetime" (Is 65:20). In today's Gospel the new creation asserts itself in the cure of the royal official's son. The emphasis in the story falls on the power of Jesus' word. Coupled with the emphatic repetition of the word *create* in the first reading, it tells us that in and through Jesus, God's word is once again calling new heavens and a new earth into being. In John's Gospel, the miracles of Jesus signify this.

The total transformation announced by Isaiah and anticipated in the ministry of Jesus has not yet been fully realized. Reality for us is not always rejoicing and happiness. But like the royal official in the story, we must put our faith in the word of Jesus. And as Jesus himself did in times of trial, we must find comfort in the words of the psalmist: "At nightfall, weeping enters in, / but with the dawn, rejoicing" (30:6).

TUESDAY

First Reading: Ex 47:1–9, 12
Responsorial Psalm: Ps 46:2–3, 5–6, 8–9
Gospel: Jn 5:1–16

Both of today's readings attest to God's life-giving power. In a vision, the prophet Ezekiel sees from beneath the threshold of the Temple a trickle of water that swells into a river, fresh water that brings life wherever it flows—fish and fruit trees, food and medicine. In the Gospel, Jesus stands by the Sheep Pool in the place called Bethesda and sees a man who needs healing. He has been sick for thirty-eight years. Without waiting for the movement of the water, which was thought to have curative power, Jesus restores the man to fullness of life. Ironically, this life-giving work will in the end cost Jesus his life, for they "began to persecute Jesus" (Jn 5:16).

The healed man is not an attractive character. When Jesus asks if he wants to be healed, he whines self-pityingly. When he is stopped for carrying his mat on the Sabbath, he blames the man who cured him. When he learns who Jesus is, he reports him to the authorities. He never takes hold of the life that Jesus has restored to him. Reborn in the waters of Baptism, have we? Today Jesus says to him and to us, "You are well; do not sin any more" (Jn 5:14).

Wednesday

First Reading: Is 49:8–15
Responsorial Psalm: Ps 145:8–9, 13cd–14, 17–18
Gospel: Jn 5:17–30

The oracle of Isaiah in today's first reading celebrates the works of God the Father, who restores the land, releases prisoners, and returns home an exiled people. In the Gospel, the Father shows the Son these same works, raising the dead and granting life. And so the Son, who does "what he sees the Father doing ..." gives "life to whomever he wishes" (Jn 5:19, 21). But whereas in Isaiah the announcement of salvation is greeted with joyful song in heaven and on earth, in John's Gospel the words and works of Jesus draw an angry response.

The juxtaposition of these two readings also invites us to recognize a mother's love in the works of the Father. "Can a mother forget her infant, / be without tenderness for the child of her womb?" God asks in Isaiah 49:15. The words take on particular force when they are placed alongside the Gospel that affirms that believing in Jesus is the way to eternal life, that is, to becoming children of God. "Even should she forget, / I will never forget you," says the Lord our God (v. 15). And Jesus declares, "The hour is coming ... when the dead will hear the voice of the Son of God ... and live" (Jn 5:25). The hour is coming.

THURSDAY

First Reading: Ex 32:7–14
Responsorial Psalm: Ps 106:19–20, 21–22, 23
Gospel: Jn 5:31–47

In the selection from Exodus, Moses acts as Israel's intercessor, while in the passage from John, he is invoked as their accuser. The episode of the golden calf is the occasion for Moses once again to step into the breach before God in order to save his people. As the psalmist recounts the story, "He [God] spoke of exterminating them, / but Moses, his chosen one, / withstood him in the breach to turn back his destructive wrath" (106:23). Reflecting on this scene, the *Catechism* notes, "The arguments of [Moses'] prayer ... will inspire the boldness of the great intercessors among the Jewish people and in the Church" (no. 2577).

It is often observed that the ministry of Jesus in John's Gospel is cast as a trial; in today's Gospel, court is in session. Arguing in his own defense, Jesus turns the tables on those who accuse him of breaking Mosaic Law by curing the man at the pool of Bethesda on the Sabbath. He tells them that Moses, their intercessor on whom they set their hopes, will accuse them before the Father. In this courtroom drama, even Moses bears witness to Jesus, joining a vast army of witnesses, namely, John the Baptist, Jesus' works, his heavenly Father, and the Sacred Scriptures. Are we also among those who bear witness to Jesus?

Friday

First Reading:Wis 2:1a, 12–22
Responsorial Psalm: Ps 34:17–18, 19–20, 21 and 23
Gospel: Jn 7:1–2, 10, 25–30

Again in a scene from John's Gospel, confusion among the people leads to confrontation with Jesus. Here the people wonder if Jesus might be the Messiah after all. Then they remember that they know where he comes from, and there is a tradition that no one is supposed to know the Messiah's origins. But Jesus tells them that they do not know where he comes from. Only believers, who are themselves "from God," recognize the divine origin of Jesus. Only they know the One whom God has sent.

The first reading from the Book of Wisdom is a meditation on the fourth Servant Song of Isaiah (see Is 52:13—53:12). The anonymous just one of the song is here beset by the wicked because he "styles himself a child of the Lord" and "boasts that God is his Father" (Wis 2:13, 16). As the author of Wisdom reflected on Isaiah, so the author of the fourth Gospel reflected on Wisdom in depicting the mission of Jesus, God's just One, and the motives of his opponents. And no doubt both were influenced by today's psalm: "Many are the troubles of the just man, / but out of them all the Lord delivers him" (34:20). May we also learn to bring God's word to life.

SATURDAY

First Reading: Jer 11:18–20
Responsorial Psalm: Ps 7:2–3, 9bc–10, 11–12
Gospel: Jn 7:40–53

The readings today depict Jeremiah and Jesus as rejected prophets. Controversy swirls around Jeremiah, who is shocked and shaken to discover that his opponents have been "hatching plots" against him while he has been totally unsuspecting, "like a trusting lamb led to slaughter" (11:19). In the Gospel of John, controversy swirls around Jesus, too. The crowd is divided over the question of his origins. The Temple police are taken in by his teaching. Dissent even comes from within the Pharisees' ranks, as Nicodemus objects, "Does our law condemn a person before it first hears him and finds out what he is doing?" (Jn 7:51).

The reappearance of Nicodemus, that "closet Christian" who came to Jesus under cover of night (see Jn 3:2), is an interesting development. His defense of Jesus is weak and ineffective. The sarcasm of his fellows easily dismisses him. He is not a hero, and sometimes defending one's faith in Jesus requires nothing less than heroism. But Nicodemus's heart is in the right place as time will tell (see Jn 19:39). Surely the "searcher of heart and soul" (Ps 7:10) will not find him wanting.

Fifth Sunday of Lent

A

First Reading: Ez 37:12–14
Responsorial Psalm: Ps 130:1–2, 3–4, 5–6, 7–8
Second Reading: Rom 8:8–11
Gospel: Jn 11:1–45 or 11:3–7, 17, 20–27, 33b–45

The raising of Lazarus is the third text from John that traditionally has been used to prepare catechumens for Baptism. In this, the greatest of Jesus' signs, baptismal catechesis comes to a climax. As the dead man Lazarus comes out of the tomb alive, the mission of Jesus is most fully expressed. "I came so that they might have life and have it more abundantly" (Jn 10:10). This is what he tells Martha as well: he is the resurrection and the life. In Romans, Paul develops what this means for us who believe in Jesus and have been baptized in his name. By virtue of the Spirit of Christ that we received at Baptism, we are caught up in his resurrection and can be sure that some day even our mortal bodies will share his life.

Resurrection functions as a sign in the prophecy of Ezekiel, too. Only here it points to the power of God to bring the exiles in Babylon back to the land of Israel. Joined to the other readings for today, it reminds us that resurrection is not a private matter; the new life God gives through the Spirit brings communities, as well as individuals, back to life.

B

The promise of a new covenant announced by Jeremiah is not taken up in John. And yet, an interesting parallel can be drawn between today's two readings. The coming days of Jeremiah seem somehow synchronized with the hour of Jesus. After those days of exile in Babylon, during which Israel will learn obedience from what they suffer, they will be restored and finally come to know the Lord, which in biblical language means to be redeemed. Similarly, in the hour of Jesus that now arrives, he will be lifted up on the cross and, in the language of Hebrews, will learn obedience from what he suffers. Then having been perfected, that is, raised from the dead, he will be the source of ultimate redemption for all who obey him.

Like the author of Hebrews, early Christians believed that the new covenant in Jesus rendered God's covenant with Israel obsolete (see Heb 8:7–13). Since Vatican II, however, the Church has insisted that God's covenant with the Jewish people was not nullified by the saving work of Jesus. In support of this view, the *Catechism* (no. 839) cites the words of Paul in Romans: "For the gifts and the call of God are irrevocable" (11:29).

C

First Reading: Is 43:16–21
Responsorial Psalm: Ps 126:1–2, 2–3, 4–5, 6
Second Reading: Phil 3:8–14
Gospel: Jn 8:1–11

∽⟨⟨◎⟩⟩∾

The poetry of Isaiah in today's first reading celebrates God's infinite capacity to surprise us. The passage captures and conveys this in the implicit summons to remember the Exodus event and in the explicit command not to remember "the events of the past" (Is 43:18). The prophet is saying poetically that this new thing God is poised to accomplish—the return of the exiles from captivity in Babylon—will surpass all of God's previous acts of grace, even the preeminent event of the Exodus. In Philippians, Paul relates his experience of the supreme good of knowing Christ Jesus as Lord. This grace, he says, relativized all those past graces he once considered gain.

The surpassing grace of Christ that took possession of Paul is offered to the woman who is brought to Jesus in today's Gospel. Her sin leaves her without righteousness of her own based on the law. But Jesus, refusing to condemn her, restores her to righteousness. Now she can forget what lies behind and straining forward embrace the new possibility that opens before her by the unmerited grace of God in Christ. That same grace is offered to us in this Lenten season.

OPTIONAL MASS
FOR THE FIFTH WEEK OF LENT

First Reading: 2 Kgs 4:18b–21, 32–37
Responsorial Psalm: Ps 17:1, 6–7, 8b and 15
Gospel: Jn 11:1–45

In John's Gospel, Jesus' miracles are signs (*semeia*) revealing the glory of God in and through the person of Jesus. Jesus, who came so that all who believe in him might have eternal life, in this last sign gives physical life to his beloved Lazarus. The significance of the miracle is stated at both the beginning and the end of the story. To the disciples at the beginning and to Martha at the end, Jesus promises a revelation of God's glory. St. Irenaeus once remarked, "The glory of God is the human person fully alive" (see *CCC* no. 294*). This is the point of John's story, too.

The raising of Lazarus and the raising of the Shunammite woman's child (today's first reading) highlight the response of strong women to the death of those they love. Both Martha and the Shunammite recognize the life-giving power of God in the ministries of Jesus and Elisha, respectively. They have welcomed these men into their homes, and when death strikes, they turn to them expectantly. Miracles will follow. May we who have welcomed Jesus, "the resurrection and the life" (Jn 11:25), into our lives, trust him with our lives and the lives of those we love.

* St. Irenaeus, *Adv. haeres* 4, 20, 7: PG 7/1, 1037.

Monday

First Reading: Dn 13:1–9, 15–17, 19–30, 33–62 or 13:14c–62
Responsorial Ps 23:1–3a, 3b–4, 5, 6
Gospel: Jn 8:1–11 or Jn 8:12–20

In today's first reading, Daniel intervenes on behalf of the chaste Susannah, who has been wrongly condemned for adultery. Similarly in John's Gospel, Jesus intervenes on behalf of a woman "who had been caught in adultery" (Jn 8:3). This Gospel story does not appear in the earliest manuscripts of John. A copyist may have thought it a good illustration of Jesus' words in today's alternate Gospel reading, also from John, "I do not judge anyone" (8:15). If, as John himself tells us, the Jews of Jesus' day were not allowed to put anyone to death (see 18:31), then bringing the unfortunate woman to Jesus may have been an attempt to entrap him. Condemning her to death would violate Roman law; failing to condemn her would be a breach of Jewish law. Jesus avoids the trap by doodling in the sand and challenging her accusers to recognize their own sinfulness.

These stories do not negate the need for judges. Although Jesus did not come to judge the world, even he must pass judgment. And his judgment is true. The scribes and Pharisees in the story, however, are corrupt judges. Like Susannah's attackers, they are using the woman for their own ends. What kind of judgments do we pass on others? Do we defer to the judgment of Jesus?

TUESDAY

First Reading: Nm 21:4–9
Responsorial Psalm: Ps 102:2–3, 16–18, 19–21
Gospel: Jn 8:21–30

In John's Gospel, sin consists of not believing in Jesus, who was sent by God to reveal God the Father, "the one who ... is true" (8:26). So in today's reading, Jesus tells his critics, "You will die in your sins" (v. 24). Similarly in Numbers, the people's sin, the reason for their punishment, is their refusal to believe that God, who led them out of Egypt, can bring them safely through the wilderness. They, too, will die in their sins. In Numbers, salvation lies in looking at the bronze serpent mounted on a pole. In John, it lies in looking at the Son of Man "lifted up" on the cross.

Three times in John's Gospel, Jesus refers to the lifting up of the Son of Man (3:14–15; 8:28; 12:32). The word for "lift up" is *hypsoun*, a word that is used in the New Testament to describe both the crucifixion and the ascension of Jesus. In this way John tells us that the cross is the crown of Jesus' mission—that the glory of God is most fully revealed in the death and raising of Jesus. In Lent, we train our eyes to look on him whom we have pierced (see Jn 19:37; also Zec 12:10), our hope of salvation, and in the words of the psalm, we pray that he will not hide his face from us (102:3).

Wednesday

First Reading: Dn 3:14–20, 91–92, 95
Responsorial Psalm: Dn 3:52, 53, 54, 55, 56
Gospel: Jn 8:31–42

B oth readings today raise the issue of God's power to save. The three young men in Daniel are confident that God can save them. But they refuse to argue the point; instead they act, staking their lives on it. In the end, the truth about God is not proven in theological debate but in the white-hot furnace of daring, decisive action. In the context of John's Gospel, the words of Jesus—"You will know the truth, and the truth will set you free" (8:32)—attest that the saving power of God is made flesh in Jesus. Living according to his teaching, truly being his disciple, is the way to salvation.

Jesus goes on to indict those who claim that Abraham is their father. This passage may have been colored by escalating hostility between John's community and the Jewish leaders. Nevertheless, what Jesus is saying here is that a true son acts like his father. While Jesus acknowledges that his Jewish opponents are "descendants of Abraham," they are not "doing the works of Abraham" (Jn 8:37, 39). They will not believe as Abraham did. So we who also claim God as our Father are warned: we must love the Son and live according to his word.

Thursday

First Reading: Gn 17:3–9
Responsorial Psalm: Ps 105:4–5, 6–7, 8–9
Gospel: Jn 8:51–59

Today's Gospel contains Jesus' boldest claim in all of John: "Before Abraham came to be, I AM" (8:58). Not only is Jesus greater than Abraham, but he also bears God's own name (see Ex 3:14; Is 43:10, 25; 48:12). No wonder Jesus' Jewish listeners "picked up stones to throw at him" (8:59). Stoning was the penalty for blasphemy. Since most scholars agree that the issue of Jesus' divine status was raised only after the resurrection, today's text reflects the faith of John's community. No doubt this is why they were being expelled from the synagogues. Hence, the unremittingly negative portrayal of "the Jews" in John's Gospel.

"Abraham your father rejoiced to see my day," says Jesus. "He saw it and was glad" (Jn 8:56). The context of these words is Genesis 17, from which today's first reading is taken. God makes an everlasting covenant with Abraham and his descendants, "a host of nations" (Gn 17:4). Later, when God promises Abraham a son, Abraham laughs (v. 17). The rabbis interpreted this as rejoicing over the birth of Isaac, the realization of God's promise. John and his community proclaim that God's promise is finally, fully realized in Jesus. Rejoicing, may we proclaim it, too.

Friday

First Reading: Jer 20:10–13
Responsorial Psalm: Ps 18:2–3a, 3bc–4, 5–6, 7
Gospel: Jn 10:31–42

The context of today's reading from John is the Jewish feast of Hanukkah. This winter feast, which John calls the feast of the Dedication (10:22), commemorated the reconsecration of the temple that the Greek King Antiochus IV had desecrated in 167 B.C. In today's Gospel, Jesus, standing in the Temple precincts, refers to himself as "the one whom the Father has consecrated" (Jn 10:36). For John this means that the holiness of the Temple is found now in Jesus, whom the Father has made holy.

If Jesus claims to be God's consecrated one, Jeremiah claims to be God's client. Today's first reading is an excerpt from a prayer of Jeremiah, who finds himself surrounded by trusted friends who have become treacherous enemies. "But the LORD is with me, like a mighty champion," he declares and knows it to be so, "for [God] has rescued the life of the poor from the power of the wicked" (Jer 20:11, 13). The word for "poor" here is *'ebyon,* it describes all those pious, powerless folk whose cause God champions. In the same spirit, Lent invites us to place our cause before God with confidence, for our champion is the consecrated one, whom the Father has "sent into the world" (Jn 10:36).

SATURDAY

First Reading: Ez 37:21–28
Responsorial Psalm: Jer 31:10, 11–12abcd, 13
Gospel: Jn 11:45–56

∽∾⊙∾∾

In today's first reading, the prophet Ezekiel, having joined two sticks into one—representing the kingdoms of Israel and Judah—explains the symbol he has constructed at God's command. He announces the day when God will bring Israel home from exile and "make them one nation upon the land" (Ez 37:22). On that day all twelve tribes of David's kingdom, which had been torn in two by schism after the death of Solomon, will be reunited. "Never again shall there be two nations, and never again shall they be divided into two kingdoms" (v. 22). Today's Gospel extends Ezekiel's vision beyond the boundaries of ancient Israel and Judah. Jesus will die not for Israel only, but also "to gather into one the dispersed children of God" (Jn 11:52).

The scene that follows the raising of Lazarus is found only in John and is carefully crafted to expose the tragic irony of Jesus' death. First, his enemies finally determine to put him to death precisely because he has raised a man to life. Second, the irony is then stated explicitly in the "prophecy" of Caiaphas when he declares that "it is better for you that one man should die instead of the people, so that the whole nation may not perish" (Jn 11:50). As we approach Holy Week, we ponder this bitter irony, the price of our salvation.

Holy Week

Passion Sunday (Palm Sunday)

A

Gospel: Mt 21:1–11
First Reading: Is 50:4–7
Responsorial Psalm: Ps 22:8–9, 17–18, 19–20, 23–24
Second Reading: Phil 2:6–11
Gospel: Mt 26:14—27:66

For Matthew, the passion, death, and resurrection of Jesus is a world-ending event. This is indicated by the use of the verb *eseisthe* ("shook"). It describes the violent shaking of the earth that was expected to announce the arrival of the end time. The verb is used twice in today's readings. The whole city of Jerusalem shook when Jesus entered it (Mt 21:10), and the earth itself shook as he died on the cross (Mt 27:51). For Matthew, the cross of Christ is the axis on which the world turns from the present age ruled by sin and death to the rule of God, the ultimate triumph of life over death. Hence, he reports, "tombs were opened, and the bodies of many saints who had fallen asleep were raised" (v. 52).

With irony, Matthew presents Jesus as the King who enters Jerusalem to announce the turning of the ages. He comes not victorious and triumphant, but "meek and riding on an ass" (Mt 21:5; see Zec 9:9). In this he resembles the obedient servant of the first reading. Because of this, says the hymn in Philippians, God will greatly exalt him, conferring on him "the name which is above every name" (2:9). When life's events shake our personal world, may we look to the cross of Christ in faith and hope.

B

Gospel: Mk 11:1–10
First Reading: Is 50:4–7
Responsorial Psalm: Ps 22:8–9, 17–18, 19–20, 23–24
Second Reading: Phil 2:6–11
Gospel: Mk 14:1—15:47

In Mark, the identity of Jesus as the Messiah, who mediates the power of God, is a well-kept secret until he makes his triumphal entry into Jerusalem. Finally he is greeted as the conquering hero he is. With waving palm branches and shouts of joy, the people hail him as they did Simon the Maccabean when he entered the citadel in Jerusalem (see 1 Macc 13:51). But because Jesus wields the power of God, not the power of Simon, not the kind of power the world understands, the enthusiasm of the crowd quickly wanes. The next time they gather around Jesus, it will be to mock him: "Let the Christ, the King of Israel, come down now from the cross that we may see and believe" (Mk 15:32).

In Mark's Jesus, the features of the suffering servant of Isaiah are most clearly perceived. Abused and abandoned, he does not rebel, does not turn back. "I have set my face like flint," he says, "knowing that I shall not be put to shame" (Is 50:7). And when at last the lone centurion looks into that face, he sees, as we do, that "truly this man was the Son of God" (Mk 15:39).

C

Gospel: Lk 19:28–40
First Reading: Is 50:4–7
Responsorial Psalm: Ps 22:8–9, 17–18, 19–20, 23–24
Second Reading: Phil 2:6–11
Gospel: Lk 22:14—23:56

From the beginning of his Gospel, Luke presents Jesus as King. It is not surprising, therefore, that in the Lucan account of the triumphal entry, Jesus is given a royal welcome. Several details of the story convey royalty; for example, the people spreading their cloaks on the road recalls the way the armies of Israel greeted the news that Jehu had been made king (see 2 Kgs 9:13). It is as though the kingship of Jesus, implied in the announcement of his birth—"the Lord God will give him the throne of David his father" (Lk 1:32)—is made plain and public as he reaches Jerusalem: "Blessed is the king who comes in the name of the Lord" (Lk 19:38; see Ps 118:26). In fact, the proclamation by "the whole multitude" (v. 37) of his disciples, "Peace in heaven and glory in the highest" (v. 38), echoes the proclamation of the "multitude of the heavenly host" at his birth (Lk 2:13).

But this is Jesus, not Jehu. Jesus has no national ambition or agenda, which is why Luke omits the waving of palm branches (see 2 Macc 10:7). This King will rule by humbling himself, "becoming obedient to the point of death, even death on a cross" (Phil 2:8).

Holy Week

MONDAY

First Reading: Is 42:1–7
Responsorial Psalm: Ps 27:1, 2, 3, 13–14
Gospel: Jn 12:1–11

The second part of Isaiah (chapters 40–55) has four passages that scholars designate as the "Servant Songs" (Is 42:1–7; 49:1–7; 50:4–9; 52:13—53:12). These poems depict the call and career of Israel as God's servant. In light of Jesus' death and resurrection, the early Christians reread these poems with reference to Jesus. Hence, the Gospels often identify Jesus with idealized Israel, the true servant of God. Today's first reading is the first Servant Song of Isaiah, which describes the servant's mode of operation. He will serve the "victory of justice" (Is 42:6) not by clamoring in the marketplace nor by crushing his enemies on the battlefield but by his constant, quiet witness before the nations.

Today's Gospel presents us with two contrasting images of servanthood. Both Mary and Judas are disciples of Jesus; both belong to Jesus' inner circle; both have sat at Jesus' feet. So the question arises: What moved one to splendid generosity and the other to betrayal? Though the story does not let us see into their hearts, it does invite us to look into our own hearts as the psalmist does his: "The LORD is my life's refuge; / of whom should I be afraid?" (27:1).

TUESDAY

First Reading: Is 49:1–6
Responsorial Psalm: Ps 71:1–2, 3–4a, 5ab–6ab, 15 and 17
Gospel: Jn 13:21–33, 36–38

The second Servant Song in today's first reading hints at the ups and downs of servant Israel's mission. Armed only with God's word, "a sharp-edged sword," and assured of God's protection "in the shadow of his arm" (Is 49:2), Israel will be the one in whom God will be glorified before all the nations. At times the servant is troubled. "I thought I had toiled in vain," he says, "and for nothing, uselessly, spent my strength" (v. 4). Yet he knows that his reward is with the Lord; he is made glorious in God's sight.

Today's Gospel describes a critical moment in the mission of Jesus. He is troubled at the treachery of Judas, who coolly takes the morsel from his hand and goes out into the night. Once Judas has left, Jesus turns to the others and instructs them one last time. "Now is the Son of Man glorified," he says, "and God is glorified in him" (Jn 13:31). But those words do not rouse them. It is only when he tells them that they cannot follow him that panic sets in. Their servanthood is still self-motivated and self-interested. They have yet to learn, like Jesus and the servant of the song, to yield to the greater glory of God. And what of our servanthood? Is it self-serving or self-giving?

WEDNESDAY

First Reading: Is 50:4–9a
Responsorial Psalm: Ps 69:8–10, 21–22, 31 and 33 34
Gospel: Mt 26:14–25

In the third Servant Song of Isaiah, the servant is described as having the ear and the tongue of a disciple. In Hebrew, the word *disciple* is the passive form of the verb "to teach." A disciple is one who is taught, one whose ear is opened to hear the word of God that must be spoken to the weary. The servant of today's song knows the cost of discipleship, too. "I gave my back to those who beat me," he says. "My face I did not shield / from buffets and spitting" (Is 50:6). His words are echoed by the psalmist who prays, "For your sake I bear insult, / and shame covers my face" (Ps 69:8).

Today's Gospel also brings to the fore the question of discipleship. The early Church never forgot that Jesus was betrayed by one of his own. Although Jesus' death was "according to the Scripture," his words—"Woe to that man by whom the Son of Man is betrayed" (Mt 26:24)—imply that Judas was nonetheless responsible for his action. So Jesus remarks, "It would be better for that man if he had never been born" (v. 24). As the "appointed time" of Jesus again draws near, it is our turn to question ourselves in the presence of Jesus: "Surely it is not I," Lord?

Holy Thursday
Chrism Mass

First Reading: Is 61:1–3a, 6a, 8b–9
Responsorial Psalm: Ps 89:21–22, 25 and 27
Second Reading: Rev 1:5–8
Gospel: Lk 4:16–21

The familiar passage from the prophecy of Isaiah is extended in today's reading to include these words: "You yourselves shall be named priests of the LORD, / ministers of our God shall you be called" (61:6a). They are addressed to the people of God, newly returned from exile, and announce God's intention to reconstitute Israel as "a kingdom of priests, a holy nation" (see Ex 19:6). The reading from Revelation uses the same language concerning the saving work of the risen Jesus. Having "freed us from our sins by his Blood," it says, he "has made us into a Kingdom, priests for his God and Father" (Rev 1:5–6). The context of each reading indicates that both are speaking of the priesthood of the people and not the ordained priesthood. Even today's Gospel, depicting Jesus preaching in the synagogue of Nazareth, must not obscure his status as a layman.

Historically, the struggle that led to the death of Jesus was not between the Jews and the first Christians. It was a struggle between the priests of Jerusalem and a Jewish layman who called them to conversion. On this day, when men renew their commitment to priestly service, that is matter for meditation.

Holy Thursday
Evening Mass of the Lord's Supper

First Reading: Ex 12:1–8, 11–14
Responsorial Psalm: Ps 116:12–13, 15–16bc, 17–18
Second Reading: 1 Cor 11:23–26
Gospel: Jn 13:1–15

Tonight's readings from the Book of Exodus and from the First Letter to the Corinthians are exercises in liturgical remembering (*anamnesis*). The Passover supper is described as "a memorial feast" (Ex 12:14) for all generations, and in the Eucharistic celebration, the bread is broken and the cup drained in remembrance of Jesus. Such remembering, the *Catechism* says, "is not merely the recollection of past events but the proclamation of the mighty works wrought by God.... In the liturgical celebration of these events, they become in a certain way present and real" (no. 1363). Thus in every Jewish Passover in every generation, the liberating act of God is experienced anew. Likewise, as often as we eat the bread and drink the cup of the Lord's Supper, the sacrifice of Jesus on the cross is made present.

Tonight's Gospel also asks us to remember. In John's version of the Last Supper, Jesus interprets his death by washing his disciples' feet. When Peter protests, Jesus tells him, "What I am doing, you do not understand now, but you will understand later" (Jn 13:7). Peter will remember; and so must we. And because we remember, tonight we wash one another's feet.

Good Friday
Celebration of the Lord's Passion

First Reading: Is 52:13—53:12
Responsorial Psalm: Ps 31:2, 6, 12–13, 15–16, 17, 25
Second Reading: Heb 4:14–16, 5:7–9
Gospel: Jn 18:1—19:42

In John's Gospel, the Baptist greets Jesus as "the Lamb of God" (1:29). This title invites the Christian reader to identify Jesus crucified with the suffering servant of Isaiah in today's first reading, who, "like a lamb led to the slaughter / ... was silent and opened not his mouth" (53:7). Isaiah's poem opens with the divine decree: "See my servant shall prosper, / he shall be raised high and greatly exalted" (Is 52:13). That verse sheds light on the ambiguity that characterizes Jesus' predictions of his passion in John's Gospel. Three times he declares that the Son of Man will be "lifted up" (Jn 3:14; 8:28; 12:32). That one verb conveys the double sense of Jesus elevated on the cross and at the same time greatly exalted at the Father's side. So even as he is led like a lamb to the slaughter, he carries in his broken body, pierced for our offenses, the only power that can take away the sin of the world.

The reading from Hebrews suggests another way to look at Jesus crucified, that is, as our high priest. This image of priest also found in John is in Jesus' seamless tunic woven in one piece like the high priest's robe. So our priest and our sacrifice are one; and the cross becomes for us "the throne of grace." Today of all days, let us approach it with confidence (see Heb 4:16).

Easter Season

The Easter Vigil

A B C

First Reading: Gn 1:1—2:2 *or* 1:1, 26–31a
Responsorial Psalm: Ps 104:1–2, 5–6, 10, 12, 13–14, 24, 35 *or*
              Ps 33:4–5, 6–7, 12–13, 20–22
Second Reading: Gn 22:1–18 *or* 22:1–2, 9a, 10–13, 15–18
Responsorial Psalm: 16:5, 8, 9–10, 11

Third Reading: Ex 14:15—15:1
Responsorial Psalm: Ex 15:1–2, 3–4, 5–6, 17–18

Fourth Reading: Is 54:5–14
Responsorial Psalm: Ps 30:2, 4, 5–6, 11–12, 13

Fifth Reading: Is 55:1–11
Responsorial Psalm: Is 12:2–3, 4, 5–6

Sixth Reading: Bar 3:9–15, 32—4:4
Responsorial Psalm: Ps 19:8, 9, 10, 11

Seventh Reading: Ez 36:16–17a, 18–28
Responsorial Psalm: Ps 42:3; 5; 43:3, 4 *or*
              Ps 51:12–13, 14–15, 18–19

Epistle: Rom 6:3–11
Responsorial Psalm: Ps 118:1–2, 16–17, 22–23

In the rites of the Easter Triduum and at the Easter Vigil in particular, we remember the death and resurrection of Jesus. "This is the passover of the Lord," the priest says as the vigil begins. The influence of the Jewish celebration of Passover is evident everywhere in the liturgy of this night. As Anthony Saldarini observes, "The very notion of keeping vigil during the night preceding Easter dawn arises from the biblical regulations for

Passover" (see Ex 12:41–42).[5] The association of the death and resurrection of Jesus with the story and symbols of Passover is natural. This is not only because the events of Jesus' death and rising took place at Passover, but also because in Judaism the event commemorated by Passover, the Exodus, was the paradigm for all the saving acts of God. Saldarini explains that Jewish tradition identified the four crucial nights of God's activity with Passover: the nights of creation, the binding of Isaac, Passover, and the end of the world. The seven Old Testament readings for this night also sound these themes.

The psalms of this night give us words with which to respond to the drama that unfolds in the readings. They invite us to "Sing to the LORD, for he is gloriously triumphant" (Ex 15:1).

A

Gospel: Mt 28:1–10

In his account of the Easter event, Matthew continues to portray the death and resurrection of Jesus as the turning of the ages. He does this most obviously by reintroducing the word *eseisthe* ("shook"), which he used of the city of Jerusalem at Jesus' triumphal entry and of the earth itself when Jesus died on the cross. Here the guards shook with fear at the earthquake (*seismos*) that accompanied the angel of the Lord, who rolled back the stone to reveal the empty tomb. The angel is described in stock apocalyptic language—his appearance like lightning, his clothing white as snow. As the interpreting angel of apocalyptic, he interprets the emptiness of the tomb: "He has been raised just as he said" (Mt 28:6).

Like his death, the resurrection of Jesus is a world-ending event. Yet, as spectacular as this act of God may be, it is not self-explanatory. It must be explained by a divine messenger. The revelation of the angel causes the women to see Jesus the crucified in a new light. Raised from the dead, he is Lord now and commands their homage and their holy fear. The women in Matthew—"fearful yet overjoyed"—acquit themselves better than the women in Mark. They "ran to announce this to his disciples" (Mt 28:8). And so must we.

B

Gospel: Mk 16:1—7

In Mark's Gospel, the good news of Jesus' resurrection is conveyed as a change of location. The young man at the tomb tells the women that Jesus of Nazareth, whom they seek, "has been raised; he is not here" (Mk 16:6). He then instructs them to tell the disciples and Peter, "He is going before you to Galilee; there you will see him, as he told you" (v. 7; see 14:28). Jesus is no longer in the tomb, the realm of death, but in the territory of Galilee that teems with new possibilities.

In today's reading from Romans, Paul describes the impact on believers of Jesus' death and resurrection in much the same way when he says, "You too must think of yourselves as being dead to sin and living for God in Christ Jesus" (6:11). The psalmist's image of the stone rejected by the builders having become the cornerstone (118:22) says much the same thing.

With the silence of the women in Mark—"they said nothing to anyone" (16:8)—the secret of Jesus' identity reasserts itself. It is as though Mark is telling us that the risen Lord will remain a mysterious presence among us until he comes again; only then will we see him. With the stark realism of one who writes under the shadow of the cross, Mark is calling us as well as his contemporaries to walk in faith "in newness of life" (Rom 6:4).

C

Gospel: Lk 24:1–12

A number of Lucan themes converge in today's Gospel. Not surprisingly in what is sometimes called "the Gospel of women," women are the first witnesses of the revelation at the tomb. Finding the tomb empty, they are perplexed; they puzzle over this, as Mary once puzzled over the marvels that surrounded the birth of Jesus (Lk 24:4; also 2:19, 51). Their perplexity is answered by the two men in dazzling garments, who urge them to remember the words of Jesus, whom Luke presents as a prophet whose predictions are invariably fulfilled.

But Luke's account of the resurrection of Jesus is more than a rehearsal of Lucan themes. It is an object lesson in the nature of resurrection faith. What is striking in Luke's story is that the true witness of the women is discredited as "nonsense" (Lk 24:11) by the eleven disciples. More than an example of male superiority, this is Luke's way of warning us that hearing a reliable report—or even, as in Peter's case, seeing the burial cloths—is not believing. Rather, faith in the risen Lord is a matter of remembering his words (see vv. 6, 8) and so seeking—and finding—the Living One among the living. Through faith we know that "By the LORD has this been done" and it is truly "wonderful in our eyes" (Ps 118:23).

Easter Sunday

A B C

First Reading: Acts 10:34a, 37–43
Responsorial Psalm: Ps 118:1–2, 16–17, 22–23
Second Reading: Col 3:1–4 or 1 Cor 5:6b–8
Gospel: Jn 20:1–9

Like its beginning, the end of John's Gospel draws on the themes of Genesis. That the discovery of the empty tomb is made "on the first day of the week … while it was still dark" (Jn 20:1) recalls the first day of the week of creation, when darkness still covered the abyss, just before God spoke the first words, "Let there be light" (Gn 1:3). The passion of Jesus was the hour of darkness (see Jn 13:30). At the death of Jesus, the darkness seemed to have overcome the light—until early in the morning, while it was still dark, when Mary of Madgala discovered the first sign of the new creation.

Because "they did not yet understand the Scripture" (Jn 20:9), neither Mary nor Peter nor even the disciple Jesus loved could, at that moment, comprehend the sign of the empty tomb. This implies that knowing Scripture is a prerequisite for understanding the meaning of the tomb.

Recognizing that the Lord has been raised brings with it the responsibility of sharing that good news with others. As a result, Peter in Acts must go to Cornelius's house. So we, too, are sent to proclaim the resurrection of Jesus by living like people who know they have been raised with Christ (see Col 3:1–4).

Octave of Easter

First Reading: Acts 2:14, 22–33
Responsorial Psalm: Ps 16:1–2a and 5, 7–8, 9–10, 11
Gospel: Mt 28:8–15

The Easter proclamation begins at the empty tomb, which admits several explanations. Today's Gospel presents us with two possibilities. One is the story that was apparently still circulating among the Jews of Matthew's day: the disciples of Jesus stole his body. The other is the burden of Peter's sermon, the first reading for today. Standing with the Eleven, Peter declares that God has freed Jesus from death and "raised him up" (Acts 2:24). Because he is addressing Jews like himself, Peter goes to some length to demonstrate that what God has done for Jesus is according to the Scriptures. He quotes Psalm 16 declaring that God will not allow his "holy one to see corruption" (Acts 2:27).

Peter's lengthy argument from the Scriptures is proclamation, not proof, of the resurrection. He is asking his fellow Jews to believe that Jesus, whom they once rejected, is the Messiah. And he is asking them to take his word for it. In faith, we are the heirs of those Jews who were persuaded by the witness of Peter and the Eleven and their successors. May we, like the women in the Gospel, run to carry the good news to others.

TUESDAY

First Reading: Acts 2:36–41
Responsorial Psalm: Ps 33:4–5, 18–19, 20 and 22
Gospel: Jn 20:11–18

In today's Gospel we see the process whereby Mary Magdalene came to believe in the risen Lord. On finding the tomb empty, she immediately concludes that someone has taken the body of Jesus, and she is devastated. Her tears so blur her vision that she does not recognize the person standing before her. He asks the question that defines discipleship, "Whom are you looking for?" (Jn 20:15). She answers that she seeks the dead Jesus—and hears the living Christ call her by name.

The same process can be discerned in Peter's audience in today's first reading. Empowered by the Spirit, Peter calls them by name. They are Israel, the descendants of Abraham; the promise was made to them and to their children. He declares that the promise has been fulfilled in Jesus, whom they crucified. Deeply shaken, they ask, "What are we to do?" (Acts 2:37). Peter tells them they must repent, that is, turn (like Magdalene) to see in the risen Jesus, their Messiah and Lord. This is the faith that Baptism signifies and celebrates: not devotion to the dead Jesus, but discipleship of the risen Christ. We who are already disciples need to keep on asking ourselves, "What are we to do?"

WEDNESDAY

First Reading: Acts 3:1–10
Responsorial Psalm: Ps 105:1–2, 3–4, 6–7, 8–9
Gospel: Lk 24:13–35

Raymond Brown suggests that today's Gospel may be Luke's answer to those folks in his community—and ours—who look back with nostalgia to the first generation of Jesus' followers. They imagine that their faith would be stronger had they seen the risen Lord with their own eyes. Luke's story aims to show them otherwise. The two disciples walk and talk with Jesus on the road to Emmaus. But reflecting on the Scriptures makes their hearts burn, and they only recognize the risen Jesus in the breaking of the bread. Luke's point is that those same means of knowing the Lord—the Scriptures and the breaking of bread—are available to Christians of every generation in the life and liturgy of the Church.[6]

The reading from Acts makes the same point. In the ministry of the apostles, "in the name of Jesus Christ the Nazorean" (3:6), the powerful words and deeds of Jesus continue to be available to those in need, like the lame beggar in the story. Luke drives the point home by dwelling on the astonishing effect of Peter's words and deeds. Twice the lame man leaps about as Isaiah had promised (35:6) and Jesus had proclaimed (see Lk 7:22). The powerful presence of the risen Jesus is made accessible to us in word and in sacrament. Are we also slow of heart to believe the good news?

Thursday

First Reading: Acts 3:11–26
Responsorial Psalm: Ps 8:2ab and 5, 6–7, 8–9
Gospel: Lk 24:35–48

In today's first reading, Peter and John act on the commission that Jesus gave them in today's Gospel. "Repentance, for the forgiveness of sins, would be preached in his [Christ's] name to all the nations, beginning from Jerusalem" (Lk 24:47). So Peter preaches to his fellow Israelites in Solomon's Portico. His sermon is thoroughly "Jewish." He says that the God who raised Jesus is "the God of Abraham, the God of Isaac, and the God of Jacob, the God of our fathers" (Acts 3:13). He further claims that the suffering of the Messiah was "announced beforehand through the mouth of all the prophets" (v. 18). Jesus is the "prophet like Moses" (v. 22) to whom Moses himself bore witness. But by citing the promise God made to Abraham—"In your offspring all the families of the earth shall be blessed" (v. 25; see Gn 12:3)— Peter hints that the good news is meant for all the nations.

Just as the miracles of Jesus were often misconstrued, the miracle that Peter and John work in Jesus' name is also misinterpreted. So Peter hastens to explain that faith in the name of the risen Jesus has made the lame man whole. Such faith can do the same for us.

FRIDAY

First Reading: Acts 4:1–12
Responsorial Psalm: Ps 118:1–2 and 4, 22–24, 25–27a
Gospel: Jn 21:1–14

All four Gospels tell a story of Jesus calling fishermen to be "fishers of men." In the first three Gospels, these stories take place early in Jesus' public ministry and point to a future still some time away. In John it is an Easter story, inaugurating the mission of the Church in the wake of Jesus' resurrection. The details convey the meaning of the story. In the Gospels, fishing symbolizes the missionary activity of the Church, in which Peter plays a central role. Here that role is dramatized when, in answer to Jesus' request, Peter single-handedly hauls the net ashore. The word for "haul" is the same Greek word that is used to describe the Father's "drawing" disciples to Jesus (see Jn 6:44). The significance of the number 153 has been the subject of much speculation; whatever else, it promises an abundant catch—contained by one unbroken net.

In today's first reading Peter, "filled with the Holy Spirit" (Acts 4:8), casts wide his net among the elders, the leaders of the people, who want to know in whose name he is acting. Peter tells them he acts in the only name "under heaven ... by which we are to be saved" (v. 12). And we, in whose name are we acting?

SATURDAY

First Reading: Acts 4:13–21
Responsorial Psalm: Ps 118:1 and 14–15ab, 16–18, 19–21
Gospel: Mk 16:9–15

In today's first reading, Peter and John continue to share the lived experience of Jesus in Luke's Gospel. When the leaders of the people interrogate them, Peter and John frustrate them by their boldness in defense of the Gospel. They are then dismissed while the council deliberates their fate. Even the Sanhedrin, cannot deny that "a remarkable sign was done" through these companions of Jesus. Even more, "everyone living in Jerusalem" knows it (Acts 4:16). Unable to find a way to punish them, they try to silence the two disciples, ordering them "not to speak or teach at all in the name of Jesus" (v. 18). But Peter and John will have none of it, saying, "It is impossible for us not to speak about what we have seen and heard" (v. 20).

Today's Gospel depicts the disciples of Jesus as being as disbelieving and as stubborn as the leaders of the people in Acts. Only seeing the risen Lord himself brings them to faith. His reprimand of them must strengthen our resolve to put our faith in the witness of those "who saw him after he had been raised" and to proclaim that good news "to every creature" (Mk 16:14–15).

Second Sunday of Easter

A

First Reading: Acts 2:42–47
Responsorial Psalm: Ps 118:2–4, 13–15, 22–24
Second Reading: 1 Pet 1:3–9
Gospel: Jn 20:19–31

Today's Gospel features two appearances of the risen Jesus, taking place a week apart. The first is John's version of the Pentecost event. The gift of the Holy Spirit, which Jesus breathes on the disciples, constitutes them as Church and commissions them to continue his saving work: "As the Father has sent me," declares Jesus, "so I send you" (Jn 20:21). With this, says Jerome Neyrey, "a pattern is established that faith comes from hearing the word preached by the Church."[7] However, that pattern is challenged by Thomas's refusal to accept the witness of the other disciples who tell him, "We have seen the Lord" (v. 25). And so, a week later Jesus must confirm the pattern that was established the week before. This he does with the beatitude "Blessed are those who have not seen and have believed" (v. 25).

In today's second reading, Peter addresses people like us who have not seen the risen Lord, yet believe in him on the strength of the Church's witness—that is, the teaching of the apostles, the communal life, the breaking of bread, and the prayers (see Acts 2:42).

B

First Reading: Acts 4:32—35
Responsorial Psalm: Ps 118:2—4, 13—15, 22—24
Second Reading: 1 Jn 5:1—6
Gospel: Jn 20:19—31

The communal life of the first followers of Jesus, described in today's first reading, is evidence of their self-understanding. The resurrection of the Lord Jesus, with the rush of his Holy Spirit, created a community united in mind and heart—the first-fruits of the new creation. But the new creation had to be lived under the conditions of the old; it must be in the world but not of it. Having everything in common was one very concrete way of declaring "the victory that conquers the world" (1 Jn 5:4).

Of course, there is only one victor over the world and that is Jesus Christ, "the one who came through water and blood" (1 Jn 5:6). In today's Gospel, his victory is announced to the disciples with the words, "Peace be with you," coupled with the gesture by which "he showed them his hands and his side" (Jn 20:19—20). More than a greeting, this peace is the gift the world cannot give (see Jn 14:27). It is theirs now—and ours, too—Jesus tells them, because of his triumph over death. And we, like them, are sent to share it.

C

First Reading: Acts 5:12–16
Responsorial Psalm: Ps 118:2–4, 13–15, 22–24
Second Reading: Rev 1:9–11a, 12–13, 17–19
Gospel: Jn 20:19–31

In today's Gospel, the evangelist take pains to show that all those disciples on whose testimony the faith of the Church rests had an immediate and direct experience of the risen Jesus. According to Lionel Swain, that is the purpose of the story of Thomas.[8] The unique status of the apostles is demonstrated in the reading from Acts. "Many signs and wonders were done among the people at the hands of the apostles," Luke tells us; then he adds, "None of the others dared to join them" (5:12–13). Their direct experience of the risen Lord gives the apostles a numinous quality that causes the people to maintain a respectful distance from them.

Ironically perhaps, it is by "doubting Thomas" that the faith of the apostles is given its fullest expression: "My Lord and my God!" he exclaims (Jn 20:28), bringing the Gospel of John full circle: "The Word was God" (1:1). In the excerpt from Revelation, the risen Lord himself, he who was dead but is now alive forever, makes the same claim. Echoing the word of God in Isaiah, he says, "I am the first and the last" (Rev 1:17; see Is 41:4; 44:6; 48:12). Is the risen Lord first and last in our lives?

Second Week of Easter

MONDAY

First Reading: Acts 4:23–31
Responsorial Psalm: Ps 2:1–3, 4–7a, 7b–9
Gospel: Jn 3:1–8

Today's first reading from the Acts of the Apostles continues the now familiar pattern that characterizes Luke's view of the emerging Church. Having been detained for questioning by the Jewish authorities, Peter and John are released and return to the community, who "raised their voices to God with one accord" (Acts 4:24). As we have come to expect, in their prayer as in their preaching they turn the light of the risen Lord on the Hebrew Scriptures. Their prayer is answered by the gift of the Holy Spirit, as Luke's Jesus had promised (see Lk 11:13). So "filled with the Holy Spirit," they find the courage to continue to speak God's word—"with all boldness" (Acts 4:31).

Such boldness is totally lacking in Nicodemus, who comes to Jesus under cover of night. But then Nicodemus is not yet ready to be "born of water and Spirit" (Jn 3:5). Why not? Is it because he has already formed an opinion of Jesus and cannot move beyond it? Does his concrete thinking—"from below"—make him impervious to the Spirit that, like the wind, blows where it wills? (v. 8).

TUESDAY

First Reading: Acts 4:32–37
Responsorial Psalm: Ps 93:1ab, 1cd–2, 5
Gospel: Jn 3:7b–15

Today's Gospel passage from John repeats Jesus' analogy likening the Holy Spirit to the wind that "blows where it wills" (3:8) and is only "seen" by its effects. Intent on solving the problem of Jesus' words, Nicodemus is impervious to their power. Jesus' analogy urges him to accept the Spirit as he does the wind, as an inscrutable mystery.

The reading from Acts, a Lucan summary of the communal life of the early Church, attests to the power of the Spirit. Like a gust of wind, the gift of God has made this gathering of Christian Jews into an icon of all that is right and good. Because Luke is the author-artist, the image blends the best of all worlds. The Hellenistic (Greco-Roman) appreciation of friendship is evident in the believers being "of one heart and mind" (Acts 4:32). The blessings God promised to Israel are found here as well, in that there is no one needy among them (v. 34; see Dt 15:4). But this is not utopia, a human achievement. This is the effect of the Spirit through the effort of the apostles, who at the heart of the community, "bore witness to the resurrection of the Lord Jesus" (Acts 4:33). Where do we see the effects of God's Spirit in our communities?

WEDNESDAY

First Reading: Acts 5:17–26
Responsorial Psalm: Ps 34:2 3, 4 5, 6 7, 8–9
Gospel: Jn 3:16–21

In today's Gospel, Jesus describes his earthly mission as a struggle between light and darkness. In John, darkness is the world's sinful state, while light is the gift of salvation. Jesus says, "God so loved the world" (Jn 3:16) that he sent his only Son to bring light into the darkness. But the world "preferred darkness to light" (v. 19), passing judgment on itself. The reading from Acts provides a concrete example of the world's refusal of the light. The high priest and all his supporters, the same coalition that acted against Jesus, are assembled again to take action against his followers. The apostles are arrested and thrown into the public jail, only to be released and recommissioned by an angel of the Lord, for the darkness will not overcome the light (see Jn 1:5).

The story in Acts also provides comic relief from the mounting tension between the apostles and the Jewish authorities. The embarrassment to the Sanhedrin caused by the angel releasing their prisoners is truly funny. It is a rare glimpse of divine levity. As Madeleine L'Engle once observed, "It was by gravity that Satan fell."[9] The moral is: lighten up!

THURSDAY

First Reading: Acts 5:27–33
Responsorial Psalm: Ps 34:2 and 9, 17–18, 19–20
Gospel: Jn 3:31–36

Both of today's readings suggest legal proceedings. The Gospel employs courtroom language to summarize the burden of Jesus' message to Nicodemus. Only the one who accepts the testimony of Jesus, who comes from above and "testifies to what he has seen and heard" (Jn 3:32) has eternal life. Anyone who will not accept it must face divine judgment, for "the wrath of God remains upon him" (v. 36). In the first reading, the apostles must endure the wrath of the Sanhedrin for refusing to obey their orders that strictly forbid them to testify to the risen Jesus by teaching about the power of his name. But Peter appeals to a higher law, the heavenly tribunal of the One who "is above all" (Jn 3:31). "We must obey God rather than men," he says (Acts 5:29).

The Son "does not ration his gift of the Spirit," says Jesus in today's Gospel (Jn 3:34). So Peter, testifying to the resurrection of Jesus before the Sanhedrin, boldly calls upon the Holy Spirit, "whom God has given to those who obey him" (Acts 5:32), to bear witness. However unattainable the courage of Jesus and Peter may seem to us, today's psalm tells us that we, too, can bear witness by our steadfast faith while in adversity.

FRIDAY

First Reading: Acts 5:34–42
Responsorial Psalm: Ps 27:1, 4, 13–14
Gospel: Jn 6:1–15

For Christians, the story of Jesus multiplying the loaves has unmistakable eucharistic overtones. While all of the accounts of this miracle of Jesus agree on the basics, John's version departs from them in small but significant ways. First, John is the only one who notes that "the Jewish feast of Passover was near" (Jn 6:4). Second, he is the only one who specifies that barley loaves were used (v. 9), a link to the story of Elisha in 2 Kings 4:42–44. Third, Jesus himself, not the disciples, distributes the loaves (Jn 6:11). Finally, in the scheme of John's Gospel, this miracle functions as a "sign" revealing the glory of God, and the people's misinterpretation of the sign causes Jesus to remove himself from them (vv. 14–15).

Rightly reading the signs of God's glory in our midst demands discernment. In today's first reading, the eminently sane Sanhedrin member, Gamaliel, is a model of discernment. He advises the Sanhedrin to leave the apostles alone, saying that if their activity is human in its origins, it will self-destruct. But if "it comes from God, you will not be able to destroy them; you may even find yourselves fighting against God" (Acts 5:39).

Saturday

First Reading: Acts 6:1–7
Responsorial Psalm: Ps 33:1–2, 4–5, 18–19
Gospel: Jn 6:16–21

John's version of the multiplication of the loaves ends with Jesus fleeing to the mountain alone, while the disciples set out on the lake toward Capernaum. Without Jesus, they soon find themselves in the dark, their boat buffeted by the strong wind and rough seas. Finally, they see him walking on the water. "It is I," he tells them, "do not be afraid" (Jn 6:20). His "It is I" is more than reassurance; it is revelation, a manifestation of the saving power of God, whose name means I AM with you and for you (see Is 43:11). Before they know it, they are safely ashore.

In the reading from Acts, the still small boat, which is the early Church, weathers its first storm. The Greek-speaking Christian Jews complain that their widows are being neglected in the daily distribution of food. This is the first test of the apostles' leadership, and they meet it by sharing the authority Jesus gave them. The imposition of hands signals the transfer of power. As the subsequent stories of Stephen and Philip will show, the seven men will not be administrative assistants but partners with the Twelve in prayer and the ministry of the word.

Third Sunday of Easter

A

First Reading: Acts 2:14, 22–33
Responsorial Psalm: Ps 16:1–2, 5, 7–8, 9–10, 11
Second Reading: 1 Pet 1:17–21
Gospel: Lk 24:13–35

First Peter was written for Christians in Asia Minor whose acceptance of the Gospel alienated them from the society in which they lived. Peter (or a disciple of Peter) wants to bolster their faith and hope in God. He declares to them, for "the time of [their] sojourning" (1 Pet 1:17), what the two disciples in today's Gospel learn on the road to Emmaus: Jesus, whom God raised from the dead, sojourns with them even when discouragement prevents them from seeing him.

Jesus teaches the disciples bound for Emmaus how to reread the Scriptures with reference to himself. And in Acts, Peter interprets Psalm 16—"You will not abandon my soul to the netherworld" (v. 10)—as referring to Jesus' resurrection. Such appeals to the Jewish Scriptures characterized Christian teaching from the start. What is important for the modern reader to note, however, is that Scripture does not prove Jesus' resurrection; rather, reading the Scripture in this way presupposes faith in the risen Lord. Only when they recognized Jesus in the breaking of bread did the disciples recall how their hearts had burned when he, the risen Lord, had opened the Scriptures to them. With hearts burning, let us invite the risen Lord to stay with us in word and sacrament.

B

First Reading: Acts 3:13–15, 17–19
Responsorial Psalm: Ps 4:2, 4, 7–8, 9
Second Reading: 1 Jn 2:1–5a
Gospel: Lk 24:35–48

The harsh words of Peter in today's first reading must not be misconstrued as an indictment of the Jewish people for putting to death "the author of life" (Acts 3:15). Certainly, Peter knew better than most that all sinners are implicated in the death of Jesus. Perhaps that is why he moves so quickly from condemnation to a call to conversion: "Repent, therefore, and be converted, that your sins may be wiped away" (v. 19). He makes the offer confidently because he knows that, as the First Letter of John puts it, by virtue of Jesus' resurrection we now have an Advocate (literally, a Paraclete) with the Father, that is, Jesus Christ the righteous one, who is expiation for our sins.

Repentance for the forgiveness of sins is also the content of the message entrusted to the disciples in Luke's Gospel. Lionel Swain suggests that in this scene, Jesus models the missionary mandate with which he once dispatched the seventy-two.[10] As they were first to say "Peace" in whatever house they entered (Lk 10:5), so does he here; as they were to eat what was set before them (v. 8), he does, too. Here truly the medium is the message, a message that we, too, are sent to proclaim.

C

First Reading: Acts 5:27–32, 40b–41
Responsorial Psalm: Ps 30:2, 4, 5–6, 11–12, 13
Second Reading: Rev 5:11–14
Gospel: Jn 21:1–19 or 21:1–14

A ll three of today's readings attempt to define power. In the selection from Acts, the high priest who presided over the Sanhedrin interrogates Peter and John. Speaking in their defense, Peter appeals to a higher authority than the Sanhedrin's. "We must obey God rather than men," he declares (Acts 5:29). This is exactly the stance that the author of Revelation wants his fellow Christians in the churches of Asia Minor to adopt regarding the Roman Empire. In today's text, he depicts the heavenly host, countless in number, who surround God's throne. Loudly they acclaim the "Lamb that was slain," the crucified and risen Lord, worthy to share the sovereignty of God (Rev 5:12). To proclaim the power of God in this way is to disempower all earthly rulers, those who would be God.

It is interesting to reflect on the commissioning of Peter in today's Gospel against the backdrop of the first two readings. In a sense, Peter is being invited to participate in the sovereignty of the Lamb, who is also the Shepherd. But this is not power as the world knows it. The sovereign power of God is shown in loving service of others, changing their mourning into dancing, as the psalmist would say (Ps 30:12).

Third Week of Easter

MONDAY

First Reading: Acts 6:8–15
Responsorial Psalm: Ps 119:23–24, 26–27, 29–30
Gospel: Jn 6:22–29

To use Johannine language, both readings today tell us that what is "from above" clashes with what is "from below." In Acts, Stephen stands up to his opponents with irrefutable wisdom, his face radiant "like the face of an angel" (6:15). His opponents are no match for such wisdom from above; theirs is the wisdom from below, narrowly focused on preserving their religious institutions, the Temple, and the law. In the Gospel, Jesus is found by a crowd who seek him for all the wrong reasons. Their concerns, like those of Stephen's accusers, are clearly from below. "You are looking for me not because you saw signs," Jesus tells them, "but because you ate the loaves and were filled" (Jn 6:26).

It is all too easy for us as well to look to Jesus to provide our daily bread and preserve our cherished institutions. But the earth-shattering events of Easter shift our focus from our small concerns below to the One sent to us from above. And "this is the work of God, that you believe in the one he sent" (Jn 6:29). In this season of grace, let us make the psalmist's resolution our own and meditate on God's wondrous deeds (Ps 119:27).

TUESDAY

First Reading: Acts 7:51—8:1a
Responsorial Psalm: Ps 31:3cd–4, 6 and 7b and 8a, 17 and 21ab
Gospel: Jn 6:30–35

Today's reading from Acts relies on body language to deliver its message. Stephen looks up "intently to heaven" and proclaims that the risen Jesus stands at God's right hand (Acts 7:55–56). In the vision, Jesus is standing, not sitting, to welcome Stephen into God's presence. Meanwhile, Stephen's accusers grind their teeth in anger and rush at him with their hands over their ears. As Stephen said, they show themselves to be "uncircumcised in heart and ears" (v. 51)—not truly belonging to the people of God, not attentive to God's word. Stephen's cry, "Lord Jesus, receive my spirit" (v. 59), echoes today's psalm as well as the prayer of the dying Jesus (Ps 31:6; Lk 23:46). Then falling to his knees he dies, while Saul concurs in the act, watching the witnesses' cloaks piled at his feet.

The Gospel message, on the other hand, depends on Bible language. Alluding to the Exodus story, the crowd challenges Jesus to match the miracle of Moses, who gave their ancestors manna to eat. Jesus' answer is a rereading of the text. He tells them that God gave the manna, not Moses, and that the same God now gives them the true bread of eternal life—Jesus himself.

WEDNESDAY

First Reading: Acts 8:1b–8
Responsorial Psalm: Ps 66:1–3a, 4–5, 6–7a
Gospel: Jn 6:35–40

In his commentary on Acts, Luke Timothy Johnson suggests the possibility that Saul may have instigated the action against Stephen. He offers three reasons to support his suggestion: First, Saul is from Cilicia, as are some of Stephen's accusers; second, placing clothing at someone's feet, as the witnesses placed their cloaks at Saul's, is to recognize that person's authority; and third, as today's reading records, Saul leads the subsequent persecution.[11] Be that as it may, today's text proves the truth of the old saying "The blood of the martyrs is the seed of the Church." Persecution, not Church policy, accounts for the spread of the Gospel beyond Jerusalem and Judea and even into Samaria.

Philip's conversion of the Samaritans will require the confirmation of the apostles in Jerusalem (see Acts 8:14–17). For the early Church, welcoming the Samaritans into the fellowship of Jesus' followers would give new meaning to the words of Jesus in today's Gospel: "I will not reject anyone who comes to me" (Jn 6:37).

THURSDAY

First Reading: Acts 8:26–40
Responsorial Psalm: Ps 66:8–9, 16–17, 20
Gospel: Jn 6:44–51

In John, disciples are the Father's gift to Jesus. That is the sense of Jesus' words in today's Gospel: "No one can come to me unless the Father who sent me draw him" (Jn 6:44). The Ethiopian eunuch in Acts is a good example of one whom the Father draws to Jesus through the study of the Sacred Scriptures.

That he is returning from a pilgrimage to Jerusalem is important. The law excluded eunuchs from membership in the community of the Lord (see Dt 23:2). But Isaiah had prophesied that someday that would change (see 56:3–5). For the eunuch in the story, that day arrives with Philip.

Not unlike Jesus on the road to Emmaus, Philip meets the eunuch on the road leaving Jerusalem; he interrupts his reading of Isaiah, and converses with him in his carriage. Just as Jesus opened the Scriptures for the two men in the Emmaus story, Philip does so for the eunuch, who asks to be baptized. The eucharistic overtones in the Emmaus story—as well as in today's Gospel—are balanced by the baptismal action in Acts. As Jesus says in today's Gospel: "Everyone who listens to my Father and learns from him comes to me" (Jn 6:45)—through word and sacrament.

Friday

First Reading: Acts 9:1–20
Responsorial Psalm: Ps 117:1bc, 2
Gospel: Jn 6:52–59

Today's first reading recounts the call of Saul, who saw the risen Lord with blinding clarity on the road to Damascus. When Ananias is told to go to Saul, his objection reminds us that this is the man who breathed "murderous threats against the disciples of the Lord" and had authorization from the chief priests to carry them out (Acts 9:1–2). But God has chosen this very man to bring his name "before Gentiles, kings, and children of Israel" (v. 15), and in the words of the psalm, to call all nations to praise and glorify the Lord (see 117:1). So Ananias welcomes Saul now as a brother. Catechizing Saul, Ananias describes the effects of Baptism in two phrases. He tells Saul that he has come to help him "regain [his] sight and be filled with the Holy Spirit" (Acts 9:17), which brings us to today's Gospel.

In his eucharistic discourse, Jesus, the Son who has life from the living Father, shares that life with those who feed on his flesh and drink his blood. This is a hard saying. Only those who through the grace of Baptism have recovered their sight and have been filled with the Spirit can accept it.

SATURDAY

First Reading: Acts 9:31–42
Responsorial Psalm· Ps 116:12–13, 14–15, 16–17
Gospel: Jn 6:60–69

Today's Gospel reports that in the wake of Jesus' eucharistic discourse, "many of his disciples returned to their former way of life and no longer walked with him" (Jn 6:66). In a poignant scene that resembles the confession of Peter at Caesarea Philippi related in the Synoptic Gospels (see Mk 8:27–30; Mt 16:13–20; Lk 9:18–21), Jesus asks the Twelve, "Do you also want to leave?" Always the spokesman, Peter answers for them, "Master, to whom shall we go? You have the words of eternal life" (Jn 6:67–68).

In the selection from Acts, Peter heals Aeneas and raises Tabitha in the name of the risen Jesus. Both miracles are intended to remind us of previous miracles of Jesus in Luke. The healing of Aeneas recalls the cure of the paralytic who, at Jesus' command, "Rise, pick up your stretcher, and go home," stands up at once (Lk 5:17–26). The raising of Tabitha is like the raising of Jairus' daughter: Jesus sends the mourners out of the room, takes the little girl's hand, and says, "Child, arise!" (Lk 8:49–56). Thus, by restoring physical life, Peter, like Jesus, bears witness to the Spirit who gives us eternal life. Peter appears here as an *alter Christus*, another Christ—and each person baptized in the name of Jesus is the same.

Fourth Sunday of Easter

A

First Reading: Acts 2:14a, 36–41
Responsorial Psalm: 23: 1–3a, 3b–4, 5, 6
Second Reading: 1 Pet 2:20b–25
Gospel: Jn 10:1–10

The Jewishness of Jesus and the early Church is evident in all three of today's readings. The conclusion to Peter's Pentecost sermon in Acts is a direct appeal to the whole house of Israel. God has made Jesus, the crucified, Messiah and Lord. Peter announces this as good news for Jews first, for the promise belongs to them and to their children, and then "to all those far off, whomever the Lord our God will call" (Acts 2:39). Although intended for non-Jewish Christians, the passage from 1 Peter is a rereading of the prophecy of Isaiah through the lens of faith in Christ. It appropriates the language of Isaiah's fourth song of the suffering servant (see Is 52:13—53:12) to speak about Jesus, who "bore our sins in his body upon the cross" (1 Pet 2:24; see Is 53:4).

The imagery Jesus uses in today's Gospel is also drawn from the Jewish Bible. Israel's prophets routinely condemned the corrupt leaders of God's people as bad shepherds (see Jer 23:1–8). So does Jesus in today's reading. In their place, he himself will shepherd his people, guiding them in "right paths" (Ps 23:3). As the sheep gate, he himself is the way to salvation, and if we follow him, we have nothing to fear.

B

First Reading: Acts 4:8–12
Responsorial Psalm: Ps 118:1, 8–9, 21–23, 26, 28, 29
Second Reading: 1 Jn 3:1–2
Gospel: Jn 10:11–18

In today's readings, Peter in Acts and Jesus in John use the same strategy to confront the leaders of their people. They expose false leaders with allusions to the Hebrew Scriptures, while reflecting on Jesus' death and resurrection. Following the healing of the man born blind, Jesus uses the parable of the Good Shepherd to continue his argument with some of the Pharisees. In Ezekiel, God dismissed the shepherds of Israel for pasturing themselves and not their sheep, declaring, "I myself will look after and tend my sheep" (Ez 34:1–16). So, unlike the hired hand who works for pay and has no concern for the sheep, Jesus will lay down his life for them—lay it down "in order to take it up again" (Jn 10:17). Peter also exposes the callousness of leaders who would punish him "for a good deed done to a cripple" (Acts 4:9). Then citing Psalm 118, he proclaims that God has raised Jesus, "the stone rejected by the builders," for the salvation of all (v. 11; see Ps 118:22).

Whether we think of ourselves as sheep or as living stones, the message of Easter assures us that because of Jesus' resurrection, we are God's beloved children, even now (see 1 Jn 3:2).

C

First Reading: Acts 13:14, 43–52
Responsorial Psalm: Ps 100:1–2, 3, 5
Second Reading: Rev 7:9, 14b–17
Gospel: Jn 10:27–30

In their guidelines on the presentation of Jews and Judaism in Catholic preaching, the bishops warn that certain selections from Acts that are read in the Easter season must be approached with caution. Today's text in which Paul categorically declares the Jews "unworthy of eternal life" is one example (Acts 13:46). Modern readers must recognize that Acts is Luke's attempt to explain how a Jewish movement became so thoroughly non-Jewish. The reading for today is the first of three passages in which Paul, rejected by his Jewish contemporaries, determines to take the Gospel to the Gentiles.

The only real difference between the excerpt from Revelation and the brief selection from John is their tenses. Both announce the consequence of the death and resurrection of Jesus, the Lamb who shepherds the multitude of people who have washed their robes in his blood. To them he gives eternal life, John says; he will lead them to springs of life-giving water, says Revelation. What one reading announces as a present reality is expected in the other as a future event. The good news of Easter is that the time that is coming is already here. Do we know what time it is?

Fourth Week of Easter

MONDAY

First Reading: Acts 11:1–18
Responsorial Psalm: Ps 42:2–3; 43:3, 4
Gospel: Jn 10:1–10 or Jn 10:11–18

The two Gospel selections for today unpack two separate parables of Jesus, both derived from the biblical image of God as Shepherd of Israel (see Ez 34). The first parable discusses access to the sheepfold, which is only through Jesus, who is himself the sheep gate. The second parable describes the Good Shepherd who "lays down his life for the sheep" who know his voice and follow him (Jn 10:11). In their context in John, the parables are a critique of the Jewish leaders of the previous chapter. Following today's first reading, an example of Peter's leadership, they provide criteria for Church leaders.

In the first reading, Peter acts as gatekeeper and is criticized for it. Through his ministry those "other sheep" are led into the fold, who in this case are the Gentile Cornelius and his household. The boundaries of the sheepfold are being redefined—not at Peter's initiative, but because, as he explains to the Christian Jews in Jerusalem, the gift of God, who is the Holy Spirit, presses irresistibly toward that day when there will be one flock, one shepherd. And who are we to interfere?

TUESDAY

First Reading: Acts 11:19–26
Responsorial Psalm: Ps 87:1b–3, 4–5, 6–7
Gospel: Jn 10:22–30

In today's first reading from Acts, the rush of the Spirit again shakes the church in Jerusalem. The Greek-speaking Christian Jews who have been forced to flee Jerusalem because of "the persecution that arose because of Stephen" spread the Gospel among their fellow Jews "as far as Phoenicia, Cyprus, and Antioch" (Acts 11:19). But soon, by "the hand of the Lord" (v. 21), the message reached non-Jews as well. Many believed and were baptized. When the news reached Jerusalem, that Church dispatched Barnabas to assess the situation in Antioch. There he saw for himself evidence of "the grace of God" (v. 23) and he rejoiced.

In Acts, the growth of the Church is the work of God's hand, while the community's role is to witness and welcome it. This is John's view as well. The Father draws disciples to Jesus (see Jn 6:44). Therefore, says Jesus in today's Gospel, "No one can take them out of my hand." Nor, he adds, can anyone "take them out of the Father's hand" (Jn 10:28–29). In this way the sheepfold, which the psalm describes as the "city of God" (Ps 87:3), is made secure: the one who has established her is the Most High Lord (see v. 5).

Wednesday

First Reading: Acts 12:24—13:5a
Responsorial Psalm: Ps 67:2–3, 5, 6 and 8
Gospel: Jn 12:44–50

T he juxtaposition of today's readings creates an interesting effect. In the Gospel, Jesus concludes his public ministry, while in Acts, Saul begins his. One last time, Jesus proclaims that he has "not come to condemn the world but to save the world" (Jn 12:47). Salvation—eternal life—lies in believing in him, whom the Father has sent. In the reading from Acts, Luke takes great pains to show that Saul and Barnabas are also sent. Once again the Holy Spirit directly intervenes in the life of the community. Saul and Barnabas are to be "set apart" (consecrated). So Paul, "sent forth by the Holy Spirit," embarks on the first of many missionary journeys (Acts 13:2, 4).

Luke's language is important here. He refers to Paul by his Jewish name, Saul. He describes Saul and Barnabas preparing themselves for their commissioning by fasting and prayer, the hallmarks of Jewish piety. He notes what will become Saul's mode of operation on all his missionary journeys: "They proclaimed the word of God in the Jewish synagogues" (Acts 13:5). In this way, Luke reminds us of something we easily forget: like Jesus, Paul was a fervent, faithful Jew.

THURSDAY

First Reading: Acts 13:13–25
Responsorial Psalm: Ps 89:2–3, 21–22, 25 and 27
Gospel: Jn 13:16–20

The concluding verse of today's Gospel is John's version of the saying of Jesus, "Whoever receives you receives me, and whoever receives me receives the one who sent me" (see Mt 10:40). In John the statement is all the more solemn as it leads into Jesus' valedictory, his farewell address to his disciples. It adapts the ancient principle that the one who is sent represents (makes present) the one who sent him, and makes it the foundation of missionary activity. Certainly Luke, like John, understood Christian mission this way, which is why in today's reading from Acts he describes Paul as doing precisely what Jesus did when he undertook his mission: preaching in a synagogue on the Sabbath day (Acts 13:14–15; see Lk 4:16–30).

Paul's "sermon" fast-forwards the tape of Israel's history, only pausing to mention God's testimony on behalf of David from today's responsorial psalm: "I have found David … a man after my own heart; he will carry out my every wish" (Acts 13:22; see Ps 89:21 and 1 Sam 13:14). His point, of course, is the good news that from David's descendants God has now "brought to Israel a savior, Jesus" (Acts 13:23).

FRIDAY

First Reading: Acts 13:26–33
Responsorial Psalm: Ps 2:6–7, 8–9, 10–11ab
Gospel: Jn 14:1–6

In today's Gospel, Jesus declares, "I am the way and the truth and the life" (Jn 14:6). This eminently quotable verse succinctly summarizes the theology of the fourth Gospel. As commentators often note, the words "truth" and "life" qualify the word "way." The Johannine Jesus is here making a massive claim: he is the one and only way to the Father. "No one comes to the Father except through me" (v. 6). He offers those who believe in him this unique access to the Father by sharing with them the truth and the life of the Father. As the Word of God incarnate, Jesus is the fullest expression of the living God available to us, "the fullness of revelation," as we say. But the revelation, accessible through Jesus, is not information about God but intimate communion with God, a share in God's own eternal life.

Paul tells the synagogue in Antioch, "What God promised our fathers he has brought to fulfillment for us, their children, by raising up Jesus, as it is written in the second psalm [today's responsorial], 'You are my Son; this day I have begotten you'" (Acts 13:32–33; see Ps 2:7). Note that Paul is using this psalm to refer to Jesus' resurrection—an early Christological move.

SATURDAY

First Reading: Acts 13:44–52
Responsorial Psalm: Ps 98:1, 2–3ab, 3cd–4
Gospel: Jn 14:7–14

In John's Gospel, Jesus is the one and only way to the Father. But today's reading makes it clear that he is much more than a spiritual guide. When Philip asks him, "Show us the Father," Jesus says, "Whoever has seen me has seen the Father" (Jn 14:8–9). Jesus and the Father are one.

Jesus goes on to declare solemnly, "Amen, amen, I say to you, whoever believes in me will do the works that I do, and will do greater ones than these" (Jn 14:12). Jesus words could be applied to Paul in the first reading today. Like Luke's account of Jesus preaching in the synagogue on the Sabbath (see Lk 4:16–30), Paul's preaching in the synagogue on the Sabbath is greeted first with acceptance and then with rejection. Just as Jesus had indicated in his Sabbath sermon that his mission would reach beyond the boundaries of Israel, so here Paul announces his intention to turn to the Gentiles. He uses the very words of Isaiah that Simeon used in his prophecy of Jesus (see Lk 2:32; Is 49:6). Finally, the same violent abuse that drove Jesus out of Nazareth drives Paul and Barnabas out of Pisidia—rejoicing. Jesus and his disciples are one.

Fifth Sunday of Easter

A

First Reading: Acts 6:1–7
Responsorial Psalm: Ps 33:1–2, 4–5, 18–19
Second Reading: 1 Pet 2:4–9
Gospel: Jn 14:1–12

Recent scholarship recognizes that the Christians addressed in 1 Peter were displaced socially as well as spiritually. Therefore, the author tries to give them a sense of belonging by inviting them to see themselves now as a spiritual house built by God with Jesus as its cornerstone. If the Christian community is a single spiritual household, then the selection from Acts is an example of "home economics." When the Hellenists (Greek-speaking Jews) complain that their widows are being neglected in the daily distribution of food, the whole community, led by the Twelve, decides to enlarge the leadership structure of the young church in order to meet its changing needs. Like everything else in a spiritual house, this is done with the guidance of the Spirit.

The image of the household of God is taken up in today's Gospel, too. Jesus knows that his imminent departure will displace his disciples, so he tells them, "In my Father's house there are many dwelling places" (Jn 14:2). He says he will prepare there a permanent place for them and for us where he is. And we know this is true, for all his words and works are trustworthy (see Ps 33:4).

First Reading: Acts 9:26–31
Responsorial Psalm: Ps 22:26–27, 28, 30, 31–32
Second Reading: 1 Jn 3:18–24
Gospel: Jn 15:1–8

Today's readings are concerned with the vitality of the Christian community. In the selection from John's Gospel, Jesus borrows an image from the Hebrew Scriptures—the vine, often used of Israel (see Ps 80:9–16). He uses it to talk about the network of relationships that constitutes the Christian community: the relationship between the Son and the Father (the vine and the vine grower); between the disciples (the branches) and the Father who prunes them; and between the disciples and Jesus (the branches and the vine). The emphasis in this passage falls on the absolute necessity for disciples to remain in Jesus and Jesus in them. This intimate attachment to Jesus ensures the vitality of the faith community.

But how shall we know we remain in Jesus and he in us? The answer is given in 1 John: "Those who keep his commandments remain in him" (3:24). The commandment John has in mind is the new commandment that we love one another—"not in word or speech but in deed and truth" (v. 18). This is the kind of love that Barnabas extends to Paul in today's reading from Acts.

C

First Reading: Acts 14:21–27
Responsorial Psalm: Ps 145:8–9, 10–11, 12–13
Second Reading: Rev 21:1–5a
Gospel: Jn 13:31–33a, 34–35

The resurrection of Jesus reveals the triumph of God. It is in this sense when Jesus says in today's Gospel: "Now is the Son of Man glorified, and God is glorified in him" (Jn 13:31). In different ways, today's readings all attest to the reality of God's triumph already among us, though always awaited. The excerpt from Acts describes the conclusion of Paul's first missionary journey. Upon returning to Antioch, he and Barnabas call the church together and report on what God has done with them and through them to open the door of faith to the Gentiles. In other words, they bear witness that God has triumphed not only in Israel, but also among the nations. As the psalm puts it, they make known "the glorious splendor of [God's] kingdom" (Ps 145:11).

In the vision of Revelation, today's second reading, the triumph of God is finally, fully realized. God takes up residence with the human race, and all things are made new. But this newness is already accessible to us, says Jesus, if we have love for one another. For in him, God came to dwell with the human race and God remains with us if we love one another as he loved us.

Fifth Week of Easter

MONDAY

First Reading: Acts 14:5–18
Responsorial Psalm: Ps 115:1–2, 3–4, 15–16
Gospel: Jn 14:21–26

In today's Gospel, a disciple's question again interrupts the farewell discourse of Jesus. This time Judas (not Judas Iscariot) asks, "What happened that you will reveal yourself to us and not to the world?" (Jn 14:22). Jesus answers that the world does not love God because it does not keep the commandments of Jesus, which are from the Father, who sent him.

In the account from Acts, however, Paul and Barnabas find the godless Gentile world a little too welcoming of their message. Mistaking the two apostles for the pagan gods Zeus and Hermes, they are not easily dissuaded "from offering sacrifice to them" (Acts 14:18). The words of the responsorial antiphon are apt: "Not to us, O LORD, not to us / but to your name give glory" (Ps 115:1).

Still, the enthusiasm of the people of Lystra bodes well for the Gentile mission. Although they are pagans not yet converted from their follies to the living God, they are not entirely "clueless." As Paul himself observes, they have begun to know God through the benefits bestowed in and through the created order, like the rain and rich harvests God sends down from heaven.

Tuesday

First Reading: Acts 14:19–28
Responsorial Psalm: Ps 145:10–11, 12–13ab, 21
Gospel: Jn 14:27–31a

Both readings today focus on imminent departures. In Acts, Paul is stoned and left for dead outside the city of Lystra. He and Barnabas then conclude their missionary journey by revisiting each of the churches they founded. They admonish the fledgling communities and appoint elders over them to continue the work they have begun, or as they would say, "what God had done with them." They return to their home base at Antioch and report how God opened the door of faith to the Gentiles (Acts 14:27).

In the Gospel, Jesus again tells the still uncomprehending disciples that he is going away for a time. "Peace" (*shalom*) is his farewell gift to them. It is not so much a present as a promise that will be fulfilled on Easter Sunday night when they will receive the Holy Spirit (see Jn 20:19–23). This peace is not what passes for peace in the world. Rather, it is the saving work of Jesus—his death and resurrection—that has made our peace with God. This part of Jesus' valedictory concludes with a profession of love for the Father. It teaches us never to forget that the death of Jesus was, above all, an act of love. How do we respond to his love?

WEDNESDAY

First Reading: Acts 15:1–6
Responsorial Psalm: Ps 122:1–2, 3–4ab, 4cd–5
Gospel: Jn 15:1–8

In today's selection from Acts, early Church leaders confront the burning question of their day: What Jewish practices, if any, should be required of Gentile converts? As one would expect, an array of differing views existed on this issue among early Christians who were predominantly Jewish. These ran the gamut from insistence that Gentile converts be made to observe the whole of Mosaic Law, including circumcision, to the idea that Jewish law had been superseded by the Christian gospel. This debate brought Paul, Barnabas, and others from Antioch to Jerusalem in today's first reading.

The teaching of the fourth Gospel would have placed that community on the more radical side of the spectrum. The image of the vine and branches in today's reading is another way of saying that Jesus (the vine) is the only source of life. "Anyone who does not remain in me will be thrown out like a branch and wither" (Jn 15:6). For these Christians, it was not the practice of Judaism but the person of Jesus who was the only access to God, the sole source of eternal life.

THURSDAY

First Reading: Acts 15:7–21
Responsorial Psalm: Ps 96:1 2a, 2b–3, 10
Gospel: Jn 15:9–11

In Luke's scheme, the original apostle to the Gentiles is Peter, not Paul. Therefore, in today's reading, Peter speaks on behalf of Gentile converts before the Church leaders assembled in Jerusalem. Referring to his experience in the household of Cornelius (see Acts 10:44–49), he argues that Christian Jews should not place the "yoke" of the Jewish law on the shoulders of Gentile converts. "We believe that we are saved through the grace of the Lord Jesus, in the same way as they" (Acts 15:11). The final decision of the assembly comes from James, the leader of the church in Jerusalem. It represents a more moderate view than the one Peter advocated. By requiring that Gentile converts "avoid pollution from idols, unlawful marriage, the meat of strangled animals, and blood" (v. 20), James is asking them to observe the laws that were binding on resident aliens in the land of Israel.

When Peter argues that Gentile converts should not be made to observe the Jewish law, he is referring to requirements like circumcision and the food laws. All God's people must keep the Ten Commandments. As Jesus teaches in today's Gospel, we remain in God's love by keeping the commandments.

FRIDAY

First Reading: Acts 15:22–31
Responsorial Psalm: Ps 57:8–9, 10 and 12
Gospel: Jn 15:12–17

In today's first reading, Silas and Barsabbas carry to Antioch the resolution of the Jerusalem assembly—really "the decision of the Holy Spirit" (Acts 15:28)—concerning the Jewish practices required of Gentile converts. Thus does the early Church seek to act concretely and creatively on the love command that binds all the members of Christ as one.

Jesus' "new commandment" frames today's Gospel. This love command of the Johannine Jesus restates the original love command of the Book of Leviticus (see 19:18) in light of the death and resurrection of Jesus. As the love command in Leviticus was a call to imitate God ("Be holy, for I, the LORD, your God, am holy" [v. 2]), so this one is a call to imitate Jesus, who laid down his life for his friends. As Abraham and Moses were friends of God, so disciples are friends of Jesus. As God's friends dared speak boldly to God in prayer, so may Jesus' followers ask anything of the Father in Jesus' name. As God chose Israel to be a fruitful vine, so Jesus has chosen his disciples to bear lasting fruit. Finally, just as Leviticus 19:18 is the centerpiece of the Jewish Torah, so the love command is the centerpiece of Jesus' moral teaching in John. Is it the center of our lives as well?

SATURDAY

First Reading: Acts 16:1–10
Responsorial Psalm: Ps 100:1b–2, 3, 5
Gospel: Jn 15:18–21

The Holy Spirit, the "Spirit of Jesus," continued to direct the Gentile mission. By the end of today's reading from Acts, Paul is poised to bring the Gospel to Europe on his second missionary journey.

In the words of today's Gospel, "no slave is greater than his master" (Jn 15:20); therefore, Paul will suffer in the service of the Gospel. Already on his first missionary journey with Barnabas, Paul was falsely accused by prominent women of Antioch in Pisidia and expelled from that territory (Acts 13:50). In Iconium "disbelieving Jews stirred up and poisoned the minds of the Gentiles" against them (Acts 14:2). When some of these tried to attack and stone Paul and Barnabas, they fled to Lystra and Derbe (vv. 5–6). At Lystra, Paul was stoned and dragged out of the city (v. 19). In today's first reading, undaunted, Paul returns to Lystra and Derbe, where he meets Timothy.

The words of Jesus in today's Gospel bring Paul to mind. Having been sent into the world as Jesus was, Paul, like Jesus, will come to know the world's hatred. "If they persecuted me, they will also persecute you" (Jn 15:20). So it was that "the churches grew stronger in faith" (Acts 16:5).

Sixth Sunday of Easter

A

First Reading: Acts 8:5–8, 14–17
Responsorial Psalm: Ps 66:1–3, 4–5, 6–7, 16, 20
Second Reading: 1 Pet 3:15–18
Gospel: Jn 14:15–21

In today's Gospel, Jesus reassures his disciples that he will not leave them orphans. "I will come to you," he says (Jn 14:18), through the presence of the Paraclete, the other Advocate the Father will give them in Jesus' name. But the world neither sees nor knows this Advocate, the Spirit of truth. So Peter teaches in the second reading that believers in Jesus must "always be ready to give an explanation to anyone who asks you for a reason for your hope" (1 Pet 3:15). Peter imagines a situation of open hostility to the Gospel in which Christians are being made to suffer for doing good. But however hostility to the Gospel is couched, it must be met with bold witness, inspired by the Spirit of truth.

Philip is an example of such bold witness in today's reading from Acts. Driven out of Jerusalem by severe persecution of the Church, he makes his way to the city of Samaria and proclaims the Messiah to the people there. Preached by Philip in word and deed, the Gospel brings great joy to that city, a joy that is confirmed by the presence of the Paraclete. In this Easter season, may we, too, boldly witness to the tremendous deeds God has done among us.

B

First Reading: Acts 10:25–26, 34–35, 44–48
Responsorial Psalm: Ps 98:1, 2–3, 3–4
Second Reading: 1 Jn 4:7–10
Gospel: Jn 15:9–17

In today's first reading, Peter inaugurates the mission to the Gentiles by baptizing the household of Cornelius, but only after being persuaded that "God shows no partiality" (see Acts 10:9–20). This story gives historical expression to the theology of the Johannine readings for today.

Beginning with the premise that God is love, 1 John makes the sacrifice of Jesus the touchstone of God's love. "In this way the love of God was revealed to us," he says; "God sent his only Son into the world so that we might have life through him" (1 Jn 4:9). Jesus in the Gospel makes the same claim when he says, "No one has greater love than this, to lay down one's life for one's friends" (Jn 15:13). The gift of God's love, revealed in Jesus, is just that: a gift, not a prize and certainly not a possession. To be loved by God, to be chosen as friends by Jesus, makes us not privileged but privy to everything Jesus has heard from the Father. It is to know and to be continually astonished, like Peter's companions, by the range and the reach of the love of God, who shows no partiality. "All the ends of the earth have seen / the salvation by our God" (Ps 98:3).

C

First Reading: Acts 15:1–2, 22–29
Responsorial Psalm: Ps 67:2–3, 5, 6, 8
Second Reading: Rev 21:10–14, 22–23
Gospel: Jn 14:23–29

◦◦◦◦◦◦◦

Today's Gospel addresses two moments in the future of Jesus' disciples: the near future of his departure and the distant future when the Father and Son will come to make their permanent dwelling with them. The seer in Revelation looks to the distant future. He is given a vision of God's permanent dwelling with the human race, "the holy city Jerusalem coming down out of heaven from God" (Rev 21:10). The very construction of this city with its clear crystal walls radiates the glory of the Lord God Almighty and the Lamb, the divine presence.

In the near future when Jesus is no longer with them, the Advocate, the Holy Spirit, whom the Father will send, will teach the disciples everything and remind them of all that Jesus told them. The selection from Acts is a good example of the activity of the Spirit in the life of the early Church. Two things are worthy of note. First, the decision conveyed by James's letter is primarily the Spirit's, although the whole Church affirms it. And second, it aims to restore peace, the hallmark of the Spirit, to the Gentile Christians in Syria and Cilicia. What do you think the Spirit is saying to the Church today?

Sixth Week of Easter

MONDAY

First Reading: Acts 16:11–15
Responsorial Psalm: Ps 149:1b–2, 3–4, 5–6a and 9b
Gospel: Jn 15:26—16:4a

Today's readings introduce two essentials of Christian missionary activity in the person of Lydia in Acts and of the Paraclete in John. On the one hand, like Jesus himself, missionaries depended on the hospitality of women, like Paul depended on Lydia, who in today's reading prevails on Paul and his companions to stay at her house. On the other hand, the world's hatred of Jesus' disciples required the constant help of the Paraclete, "the Spirit of truth who proceeds from the Father" (Jn 15:26), promised in today's Gospel. The courtroom drama that described the ministry of Jesus in John would continue to unfold in the mission of the Church. The Spirit's testimony was as needed then as it still is today.

Lydia and the Paraclete have something else in common. Their respective roles in the life and work of the Church—essential but behind the scenes—are characterized in the *Catechism* as "self-effacement" (no. 687*). But they must never fade from the mind or the memory of the Church. The testimony of the Spirit and the humble service of women and men who have been with Jesus "from the beginning" (Jn 15:27) will always be needed.

* Jn 14:17.

Tuesday

First Reading: Acts 16:22–34
Responsorial Psalm: Ps 138:1–2ab, 2cde–3, 7c–8
Gospel: Jn 16:5–11

The criminal justice system forms the setting for both readings today. The Gospel uses courtroom language, suggested by the name "Paraclete," a term that describes a court official. The Paraclete is sent to "convict the world" (Acts 15:8). In this passage, the attorney for the defense, the Paraclete's usual role, becomes the prosecutor. Thus, the disciples can rest assured that ultimately Jesus will win his suit against the world.

In the story from Acts, Paul and Silas are the victims of anti-Semitism. The two verses that lead into today's story report the charge against them: "These people are Jews" (Acts 16:20). Consequently, they are flogged and jailed "in the innermost cell," their feet chained to a stake (v. 24). There they pray and sing hymns until an act of God releases them, and their jailer becomes their host: "He and all his family were baptized at once" (v. 34). Spreading a table before Paul and Silas, he and his family then joyfully celebrate their newfound faith. Thus was another legal battle won against the hostile world. We can imagine Paul and Silas singing to the Lord, "Your right hand saves me" (Ps 138:7).

WEDNESDAY

First Reading: Acts 17:15, 22—18:1
Responsorial Psalm: Ps 148:1–2, 11–12, 13, 14
Gospel: Jn 16:12–15

Paul writes in 1 Corinthians, "For Jews demand signs and Greeks look for wisdom, but we proclaim Christ crucified, a stumbling block to Jews and foolishness to Gentiles" (1:22–23). This observation may reflect Paul's experience in Athens, reported in today's first reading. In his speech at the Areopagus, he presents a familiar argument, one cited in the new *Catechism*, which concludes as Paul does that the religious beliefs and behaviors of human beings throughout history indicate that they are by nature religious (no. 28*). This is also the psalmist's perspective in today's psalm as he invites all creation to praise the Lord. At the same time, Paul's very modest success among the Athenians shows how difficult it can be to touch and to transform the religious imagination of a people (no. 29**).

Today's Gospel suggests that even people who have been initiated in the following of Christ continue to need the Paraclete's help if they are to grow in their understanding of what Jesus taught. So the Spirit continues to the present day to be "the Church's living memory" and our loving mentor (*CCC* no. 1099†).

---

* Acts 17:26–28.
** *Gaudium et spes* 19 §1, 19–21; Mt 13:22; Gn 3:8–19; Jon 1:3.
† Cf. Jn 14:26.

Ascension

A

First Reading: Acts 1:1–11
Responsorial Psalm: Ps 47:2–3, 6–7, 8–9
Second Reading: Eph 1:17–23
Gospel: Mt 28:16–20

On the feast of the Ascension we remember how Jesus was "taken up, after giving instructions through the Holy Spirit to the apostles whom he had chosen" (Acts 1:2). Although the event of the ascension is depicted only in Luke and Acts, each Gospel in its own way describes the exaltation of the risen Jesus and what it meant for his disciples. In the words of the psalm, "God mounts his throne amid shouts of joy; / the LORD, amid trumpet blasts" (47:6).

Today's Gospel is Matthew's account of Jesus' triumph, which concludes with what is often called the Great Commission. Appearing to the eleven apostles on the mountain, the usual biblical site of divine revelation, Jesus reveals his new status and universal authority as risen Lord. "All power in heaven and on earth has been given to me," he declares (Mt 28:18). He will exercise this power on earth by sharing it with his disciples. So he authorizes them to make disciples of all nations. This is the vision of Ephesians, too. It says that the power God put to work in Christ, raising him from the dead and seating him at his right hand, "far above every principality, authority, power, and dominion" (Eph 1:21) is now at work in the Church, which is his body.

B

First Reading: Acts 1:1–11
Responsorial Psalm: Ps 47:2 3, 6–7, 8–9
Second Reading: Eph 1:17–23 or Eph 4:1–13 or 4:1–7, 11–13
Gospel: Mk 16:15–20

The ascension of the risen Lord is the hinge that holds Luke and Acts together. The scene from Acts, today's first reading, is modeled on the experience of the prophets Moses and Elijah. This is not surprising. Throughout his Gospel, Luke presents Jesus as a prophet after the pattern of Moses and Elijah. Just as Joshua receives a share of Moses' spirit (Dt 34:9) and Elisha receives a double portion of Elijah's (2 Kgs 2:9), the disciples of Jesus are assured that they will receive power to continue his work when the Holy Spirit comes upon them. The influence of the story of Elijah and Elisha is particularly strong. When Elisha asks for a double portion of Elijah's spirit, Elijah tells him his wish will be granted if he sees Elijah "taken up" (2 Kgs 2:9–10). Likewise in today's first reading from Acts, we are told three times that the disciples saw Jesus as he was taken up into heaven (see 1:9–11).

That the spirit of Elijah rested on Elisha was made apparent when he performed signs just as Elijah had done. So in Mark, the work of the disciples is confirmed by signs, and in Ephesians by gifts for building up the body of Christ. What are the signs of the Spirit's activity in our lives as members of Christ's body?

C

First Reading: Acts 1:1–11
Responsorial Psalm: Ps 47:2–3, 6–7, 8–9
Second Reading: Eph 1:17–23 or Heb 9:24–28; 10:19–23
Gospel: Lk 24:46–53

In the structure of Luke's two-volume work, the story of the ascension plays a pivotal role. It concludes volume one (the Gospel of Luke) and begins volume two (the Acts of the Apostles). Both Lucan accounts are given to us in today's readings, a matched set in which the program and the promise of Jesus are the same. The disciples will be his witnesses, beginning in Jerusalem where they are to remain until the promise of the Father, the Holy Spirit, clothes them with power from on high.

The Gospel version of the ascension has a liturgical quality as well, which is no doubt what inspired the choice of today's reading from Hebrews. In this version, Jesus "raised his hands, and blessed" his disciples (Lk 24:50), a gesture reminiscent of the blessing of Simon the high priest as he concluded the Temple liturgy (see Sir 50:19–21). Like Hebrews, Luke presents Jesus as our high priest who enters not a sanctuary made by hands, but heaven itself. For Luke, the Church convened by Jesus' priestly blessing is a worshiping community, as well as a witnessing one, people who praise even as they proclaim.

Thursday

First Reading: Acts 18:1–8
Responsorial Psalm: Ps 98:1, 2–3ab, 3cd–4
Gospel: Jn 16:16–20

In today's Gospel, Jesus puts this riddle to his disciples: "A little while and you will no longer see me, and again a little while later and you will see me" (Jn 16:16). Not for the first time, the disciples are completely baffled by Jesus' words. Even though they have all the pieces of the puzzle—"Because I am going to the Father" (v. 17)—they cannot put them together. It is as though grief at the impending death of Jesus has already overtaken them, and in that breathless "little while" between the departure of one Paraclete and the arrival of the other, they are incapable of understanding. Jesus responds to their perplexity not with a solution but with a solemn promise. "Your grief will become joy," he tells them, because the Spirit of truth will come and will answer all their questions (Jn 16:13, 20, 23).

Impelled by the same Spirit of truth, Paul in the first reading preaches the word to both Jews and Greeks in Corinth. Although, as we have seen, in Acts the mission to the Gentiles emerged as a result of the Jews' refusal of the Gospel, some Jews like Crispus, the synagogue official, and his entire household do come to believe and are baptized.

Friday

First Reading: Acts 18:9–18
Responsorial Psalm: Ps 47:2–3, 4–5, 6–7
Gospel: Jn 16:20–23

Today's reading from Acts is rather strange. In a vision, the risen Lord assures Paul, "No one will attack and harm you" (18:10). Then almost immediately Paul is attacked by his opponents who bring him before the bench of the proconsul Gallio, who has no patience for intra-Jewish disputes. So Paul is released unharmed.

In today's Gospel, Jesus returns to the theme of his departure. He tells his disciples that the throes of death they will soon experience—namely, his suffering and death—will in fact be the pangs of birth. Isaiah used the image of the woman in labor to announce the arrival of a new day, the Day of the Lord (26:16–17; 66:7–10). That day will dawn when Jesus arises. "On that day," he tells his disciples, their hearts will rejoice and all their questions will be answered (Jn 16:23). Still it seems that in some ways, even now after the resurrection, we are still waiting, our questions unanswered, forced like Paul into an uneasy truce with the world around us. So Easter has come once again to tell us that from the tomb, a Man—the risen Jesus—has been born into the world. That joy no one can take from us.

SATURDAY

First Reading: Acts 18:23–28
Responsorial Psalm: Ps 47:2–3, 8–9, 10
Gospel: Jn 16:23b–28

Today's first reading introduces Apollos, the impassioned and eloquent Jew from Alexandria, who was "an authority on the scriptures" and "had been instructed in the Way of the Lord ... although he knew only the baptism of John" (Acts 18:24–25). Where he received his instruction in the new way is a mystery. Alexandria was a cosmopolitan city and a center of learning, but the beginnings of the Church there are not known. Given that the Old Testament had been translated from Hebrew into Greek in Alexandria (ca. 200 B.C.), Apollos's knowledge of the Scriptures is not surprising. In Ephesus and later in Corinth, he distinguished himself by his competence in "establishing from the Scriptures that the Christ is Jesus" (v. 28).

According to John, one role of the Paraclete was to make intelligible what Jesus had said "in figures of speech" (Jn 16:25) and what he had done in his earthly life by referring it back to the Scriptures. In John's view, this activity of the Spirit enabled Christians—like Apollos—to show that Jesus was indeed the fulfillment of all that the Scriptures had promised.

Seventh Sunday of Easter

A

First Reading: Acts 1:12–14
Responsorial Psalm: Ps 27:1, 4, 7–8
Second Reading: 1 Pet 4:13–16
Gospel: Jn 17:1–11a

The Gospel for today excerpts the first part of the prayer of Jesus on the night before he dies. He has just talked at length of his departure, and the air is heavy with dread of the hour that will change everything. So he prays, anticipating the hour that will finally, fully reveal the Father's glory and give eternal life to his disciples. That life, he says (in what most commentators think is a gloss), consists in "knowing" the one true God and the one whom he sent (Jn 17:3)—knowing, not intellectually but intimately, as the Son knows the Father. He does not pray for the world, however, but for the disciples who must remain in the world without him. This is not a rejection of the world, but a realistic assessment of the vulnerability of his disciples. In a hostile world, their hope lies in the fact that they belong to the Father. This same hope moves Peter in the second reading to declare blessed those who suffer in Christ's name.

The selection from Acts finds Jesus' followers also prayerfully anticipating an hour that will change everything. In this time between Ascension and Pentecost, so must we wait and pray.

B

First Reading: Acts 1:15–17, 20a, 20c–26
Responsorial Psalm: Ps 103:1–2, 11–12, 19–20
Second Reading: 1 Jn 4:11–16
Gospel: Jn 17:11b–19

The small part of the prayer of Jesus that is the Gospel for today almost entirely concerns the vulnerability of the disciples. They are vulnerable first of all because their consecration in the truth—the word of God that Jesus gave them—has made them the object of the world's hatred. To be consecrated in the biblical sense is to be set apart, and the world never tolerates those who do not belong to it. But they are also vulnerable to the seductions of the evil one. Jesus' oblique reference to Judas, the one disciple he lost, strikes a poignant note. (The phrase "son of destruction" [Jn 17:12] has the sense of the one under the influence of the power of destruction, that is, Satan, and should be read in this way.) The same poignancy is sounded in Peter's words about Judas in Acts: "He was numbered among us and was allotted a share in our ministry" (1:17).

Jesus also prays that his disciples might share his joy completely. How can this be? The First Letter of John suggests that in our efforts to love one another, God's love—and perhaps Christ's joy—is brought to perfection in us.

C

First Reading: Acts 7:55–60
Responsorial Psalm: Ps 97:1–2, 6–7, 9
Second Reading: Rev 22:12–14, 16–17, 20
Gospel: Jn 17:20–26

All three of today's readings are in the form of prayers. The conclusion of Jesus' priestly prayer pushes back the horizon of his concern even to our own day. He prays for all those who will come to believe in him through the word and witness of his disciples. He asks for us what he earlier asked for his immediate followers: unity with him and with one another. He wants to draw us into the communion he shares with the Father. There is nothing cozy about the unity for which Jesus prays. It has a purpose: that the world may come to know and to believe in the one whom God sent to save it. In the end, it all comes down to this: "God so loved the world that he gave his only Son" (Jn 3:16).

The prayer of Stephen in the reading from Acts gives forceful, faithful witness to the glory of God and to Jesus standing at God's right hand. It seems at first to fall on ears that are deliberately unhearing. But on the sideline stands a young man named Saul, and "the Spirit and the bride say, 'Come'" (Rev 22:17). And he will, compelled like Stephen by "the knowledge of the glory of God on the face of Jesus Christ" (2 Cor 4:6). Will we?

Seventh Week of Easter

MONDAY

First Reading: Acts 19:1–8
Responsorial Psalm: Ps 68:2–3ab, 4–5acd, 6–7ab
Gospel: Jn 16:29–33

Both of today's readings contain examples of incomplete confessions of faith. In Acts, Paul meets disciples who were baptized with the baptism of John, intended only to prepare the way for the stronger One who would baptize with the Holy Spirit (see Lk 3:15–16). Paul lays his hands on these disciples who had never even heard of the Holy Spirit, and they receive the Spirit's gifts.

In the Gospel, thinking they finally understand his words, the disciples of Jesus make a partial confession of faith in him. Like Peter at Caesarea Philippi (see Mk 8:27–30), they say, "Now you are talking plainly ... Because of this we believe that you came from God" (Jn 16:29–30). But they have not yet reckoned with the manner of his return to the Father. So he tells them, "Behold, the hour is coming and has arrived when each of you will be scattered to his own home and you will leave me alone" (v. 32). His hour is still coming, and it will usher in their hour as well. With a view to this—the loneliness of their hour—Jesus assures them and us, "Take courage, I have conquered the world" (v. 33).

TUESDAY

First Reading: Acts 20:17–27
Responsorial Psalm: Ps 68:10–11, 20–21
Gospel: Jn 17:1–11a

Today's readings juxtapose the farewell messages of Jesus and Paul. This prayer of Jesus is his final "report" on his mission, all but accomplished now. It takes us back to John's prologue. There we learned that the Word came from God, and becoming flesh made his dwelling among us that in him and through him we might see God's glory (Jn 1:14). Now the incarnate Word, the Father's only Son, prepares to return to the Father, to the glory that was his "before the world began" (Jn 17:5; see 1:1). He has finished the work he was sent to do and has glorified the Father by entrusting to his disciples the message the Father had entrusted to him. Mindful that he "will no longer be in the world" (v. 11), he prays for these disciples.

Leaving Ephesus, Paul also knows that he is not long for this world. He, too, reports on his mission. He has delivered the message entrusted to him by the Lord Jesus, never shrinking from announcing "the Gospel of God's grace" (Acts 20:24). All he wants now is to finish his race and complete his service. Thus, he commends himself to the elders of the church in Ephesus—and to us.

WEDNESDAY

First Reading: Acts 20:28–38
Responsorial Psalm: Ps 68:29–30, 33–35a, 35bc–36ab
Gospel: Jn 17:11b–19

Commentators often note that Jesus' own prayer resembles the prayer he taught his disciples. Today's excerpt has at least three points of contact with the Lord's Prayer. First, Jesus addresses God as Father, as he taught his disciples to do. Second, he calls upon the Father's holy name, and third, he petitions the Father to deliver his disciples from the evil one.

Paul's prayer in Acts also echoes the prayer of Jesus. As both men prepare to leave those entrusted to their care, they voice their pastoral concerns. They worry that those they so carefully guarded will come to harm and that some may be lost (Jesus' prayer) or go astray (Paul's prayer). They recognize the dangers that threaten their communities, that "the world hated them" (Jesus says in Jn 17:14) and that "savage wolves ... will not spare the flock" (Paul says in Acts 20:29). So they pray. Jesus asks the Father to "consecrate them in the truth. Your word is truth" (Jn 17:17); Paul commends them "to God and to that gracious word of his that can ... give you the inheritance among all who are consecrated" (Acts 20:32). For both men, safety in a hostile world lies in being holy or "consecrated," which simply means knowing not only who, but also whose you are.

Thursday

First Reading: Acts 22:30; 23:6–11
Responsorial Psalm: Ps 16:1–2a and 5, 7–8, 9–10, 11
Gospel: Jn 17:20–26

A t first glance, it may seem that in today's reading, Paul is using a clever ploy to extricate himself from a tight spot. However, a closer look shows Paul speaking the simple truth. He is being tried precisely for his hope in the resurrection of the dead of which the risen Jesus is the firstfruits (see 1 Cor 15:20). However, this time the ensuing debate between the Sadducees, who do not believe in resurrection, and the Pharisees, who do, works to Paul's advantage.

It is entertaining to read Paul's missionary exploits. But it is downright daunting to reflect on what the *Catechism* calls "the prayer of the Hour of Jesus" (no. 2746*), part of which is today's Gospel. In this last section of his prayer, Jesus reaches beyond his immediate circle to include all of us in his oneness with the Father. The reader may find it difficult to appreciate what Jesus is actually saying here, as the Johannine style is somewhat repetitious. To put it simply and succinctly, Jesus is praying for unity among those who believe in him. Jesus stresses this unity has a missionary purpose: "they may be one ... that the world may know that you sent me" (Jn 17:22–23).

* Cf. Jn 17.

FRIDAY

First Reading: Acts 25:13b–21
Responsorial Psalm: Ps 103:1–2, 11–12, 19–20ab
Gospel: Jn 21:15–19

Today's readings foreshadow the deaths of Paul and Peter respectively. In the account from Acts, the Roman procurator Festus refers Paul's case to King Agrippa II and his sister, Bernice—for their entertainment as much as anything else. Jesus had told his disciples that they would be paraded "before kings and governors" because of his name (Lk 21:12), and so it is now with Paul at Caesarea and later before the emperor in Rome.

The appendix of John's Gospel describes Jesus asking a chastened Peter three times to profess his love for him. Much has been made of the fact that in the Greek of John's Gospel Jesus and Peter use different words for love until the third time when Jesus adopts Peter's word, *philia*, rather than *agape*. But more important for our purposes, to each assurance of Peter's love, Jesus answers with the command, "Feed my lambs" (Jn 21:15) . . . "Tend my sheep" (v. 16) . . . "Feed my sheep" (v. 17). So Peter is designated to be shepherd of Jesus' flock. And since, as Jesus taught, "A good shepherd lays down his life for the sheep" (Jn 10:11), there follows a prophecy indicating by "what kind of death [Peter] would glorify God" (Jn 21:19).

SATURDAY

Mass in the Morning

First Reading: Acts 28:16–20, 30–31
Responsorial Psalm: Ps 11:4, 5 and 7
Gospel: Jn 21:20–25

Today's reading from Acts finds Paul under house arrest in Rome. Though he is chained like a common criminal, the word of God is not chained (see 2 Tm 2:9). He spends his days preaching "the kingdom of God" and teaching "about the Lord Jesus Christ" (Acts 28:31).

Behind the fourth Gospel stands the unnamed disciple, "whom Jesus loved," clearly the hero of the Johannine community. He appears in the second half of the Gospel, always in juxtaposition with Peter. So it is not surprising to find him here. When Peter asks, "What about him?" Jesus answers enigmatically, "What concern is it of yours?" (Jn 21:21–22). But does this mean that the beloved disciple is not going to die? Certainly that question has been raised by readers of John in every generation. The final redactor of the Gospel himself confronts it. His answer: "But Jesus had not told him that he would not die, just 'What if I want him to remain until I come?'" (v. 23). The words of Jesus caution us not to worry about the death of the Beloved Disciple, but rather to cling to the truth of his testimony (v. 24).

Pentecost

Vigil Mass

A B C

First Reading: Gn 11:1–9 or Ex 19:3–8a, 16–20b or
Ez 37:1–14 or Jl 3:1–5
Responsorial Psalm: Ps 104:1–2, 24, 35, 27–28, 29, 30
Second Reading: Rom 8:22–27
Gospel: Jn 7:37–39

Today's readings prepare us with a profusion of images for Pentecost. Each of the four suggested readings from the Hebrew Scriptures underscores some aspect of the event. The story of Babel prepares us for the confusion of the devout Jews from every nation as each hears the disciples speaking in his own language (Acts 2:5–6). The theophany on Mount Sinai prepares us for the loud noise and fiery tongues that filled the place where the disciples were gathered (vv. 2–3). The resurrection of the dry bones in Ezekiel's vision prepares us for the Church's creation by the Spirit of the risen Jesus. The outpouring of the spirit upon all humanity announced by Joel prepares us for the conferral of the Spirit on each person in the Upper Room (vv. 3–4).

The New Testament readings speak more directly of our experience of the Holy Spirit. In the Gospel, Jesus promises that the Spirit will be within us as a source of divine vitality. In Romans, Paul tells us that the indwelling Spirit will continue to long within us for the completion of the harvest of which we have only the firstfruits. Let us open ourselves to the power of the Spirit.

Pentecost

Mass During the Day

A

First Reading: Acts 2:1–11
Responsorial Psalm: Ps 104:1, 24, 29–30, 31, 34
Second Reading: 1 Cor 12:3b–7, 12–13
Gospel: Jn 20:19–23

Today's readings present us with two accounts of the Pentecost event. In the first reading, we have Luke's as it appears in Acts, and John's in the Gospel, set not on the Jewish feast of Pentecost but on Easter evening. Both relate the same extraordinary occurrence: the assembled disciples receive the Holy Spirit, who arrives in the form of moved air ("wind" in Acts 2:2, breath in John 20:22), and are sent to proclaim the good news of Jesus' resurrection. They proceed immediately—Peter to the Jews gathered in Jerusalem in Acts and the disciples to Thomas in John.

Luke models his story on the manifestation of God on Sinai when with loud peals of thunder "the LORD came down upon it in fire" (Ex 19:16, 18); the pattern for John's version is the second story of creation in Genesis—reprised in Psalm 104—where God blew the breath of life into the clay figure, who became a living being (Gn 2:7). As the psalmist puts it, "You send forth your spirit, they are created" (Ps 104:30). So it is that today's readings illustrate the unity in diversity that Paul preaches to the Corinthians as the hallmark of the one Spirit. So by the breath of God's Spirit, may we too be constituted as the one body of Christ.

B

First Reading: Acts 2:1–11
Responsorial Psalm: Ps 104·1, 24, 29–30, 31, 34
Second Reading: 1 Cor 12:3b–7, 12–13 or Gal 5:16–25
Gospel: Jn 20:19–23 or Jn 15:26–27; 16:12–15

The readings suggested for today develop and drive home the impact of the Pentecost event on "those who belong to Christ" (Gal 5:24) by describing the function and the fruit of the Spirit in Christian life. In today's reading from John, Jesus discloses in his farewell discourse the work of the Spirit. Two of John's five sayings about the Spirit as Paraclete (Advocate) are found here: first, the Spirit bears witness to Jesus, and second, the Spirit leads the disciples to the truth he takes from Jesus. As the *Catechism* puts it, the Spirit's is a "joint mission" with Jesus (no. 689*).

The truth the Spirit teaches is not a course of study but a way of life that finds concrete expression in "love, joy, peace, patience, kindness, generosity, faithfulness, gentleness, self-control" (Gal 5:22–23). This is the fruit of a life guided by the Spirit. It is interesting to note that this list of virtues does not originate with Paul. Such lists were stock in trade for the moral teachers of the day. But Paul realizes, as we must, that it is not our good deeds but God's grace that bears such fruit, to the glory of Jesus' name.

* Cf. Gal 4:6.

C

First Reading: Acts 2:1–11
Responsorial Psalm: Ps 104:1, 24, 29–30, 31, 34
Second Reading: 1 Cor 12:3b–7, 12–13 or Rom 8:8–17
Gospel: Jn 20:19–23 or Jn 14:15–16, 23b–26

Today's readings explore what it means to live by the Spirit of God. The selection from Romans at first approaches the question negatively. To live by the Spirit is not to "live according to the flesh" (Rom 8:12), which is Paul's way of describing a human life alienated from God by sin. But the passage continues on a positive note: to live by the Spirit is to be no longer alienated from God but adopted as God's children. With the spirit of adoption comes the grace of freely, fearlessly calling on God as "Abba, Father!" (v. 15) and the hope of inheriting with Christ our brother. All this because the Spirit of God dwells in us.

The Gospel text takes up the same theme of divine indwelling. Jesus assures the disciples that the Father will send them another Advocate, the Spirit of truth, to be with them and in them (Jn 14:17). The indwelling Spirit will teach the disciples to love Jesus and to keep his word; then the Son and the Father can make their dwelling with them. So it is that we come home to God by God's making a home with us.

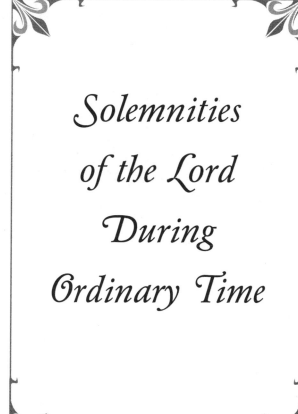

Solemnities
of the Lord
During
Ordinary Time

Trinity Sunday

SUNDAY AFTER PENTECOST

A

First Reading: Ex 34:4b–6, 8–9
Responsorial Psalm: Dn 3:52, 53, 54, 55
Second Reading: 2 Cor 13:11–13
Gospel: Jn 3:16–18

The readings for Trinity Sunday, like the feast itself, invite us to grapple with the inscrutable character of God. The divine revelation given to Moses in the first reading takes place in the aftermath of the debacle of the golden calf. The intercession of Moses, God's intimate friend, prevails upon God not to abandon his sinful people. Then God renews the covenant with Israel by rewriting the commandments on the new stone tablets Moses cut and by solemnly proclaiming the divine name once again. The name of God—"Lord"—does not change. But the character of God as merciful and gracious is more fully revealed in the light of God's willingness to forgive Israel's sin and continue the journey with them. The text teaches us to look for clues to who God is in what God does in history.

In today's Gospel, Jesus calls Nicodemus—and all of us as well—to look even more deeply into the character of God by recognizing in the gift of the Son the love of God the Father, who sent him not to condemn the world but to save it. May we live in the grace of the Lord Jesus Christ and the love of God and the fellowship of the Holy Spirit (2 Cor 13:13).

B

First Reading: Dt 4:32–34, 39–40
Responsorial Psalm: Ps 33:4–5, 6, 9, 18–19, 20, 22
Second Reading: Rom 8:14–17
Gospel: Mt 28:16–20

Paul's letters certainly predate the great Church councils of the fourth and fifth centuries that formulated the doctrine of the Trinity. But an undeniable Trinitarian element exists in the Christian experience that he describes in today's reading from Romans. He says that the Spirit makes us conscious that we are the adopted children of God, making us joint heirs with Christ as well. No doubt this Trinitarian element of the Christian faith experience stands behind the baptismal formula in today's Gospel. "Make disciples of all nations," says Jesus, "baptizing them in the name of the Father, and of the Son, and of the Holy Spirit" (Mt 28:19).

The importance of today's Gospel is underscored by being placed alongside the text from Deuteronomy. In this passage, Moses tells his people that their privileged experience of the one God is manifest in their keeping God's commandments. This is the commission of Jesus as well. He sends his disciples, then and now, to share their faith in him by teaching others to observe "all that I have commanded you" (Mt 28:20).

C

First Reading: Prv 8:22–31
Responsorial Psalm: Ps 8:4–5, 6–7, 8–9
Second Reading: Rom 5:1–5
Gospel: Jn 16:12–15

The doctrine of the Trinity is rooted in the lived experience of God of early Christians like Paul and John. Their discernment of a trinity of persons within the Godhead owes much to the wisdom theology of today's first reading. The speech of personified wisdom in Proverbs prepared these first Christians to recognize the revelation of the incarnate Word. In today's readings we can discern in their experience of God's activity in Christ a certain Trinitarian element. The excerpt from Romans begins with the word "therefore" (5:1). In what follows, Paul enumerates the consequences of God's saving activity in and through Jesus. These are peace with God through Christ; hope of the glory of God; and the love of God poured into our hearts through the Holy Spirit. In Paul's experience, the reconciliation (peace) with God that Christ has won for us—and with it, the hope of future glory—is assured by God's great love, revealed through the gift of the Spirit.

The Gospel focuses on the activity of the Spirit of truth. But here again is an unmistakable Trinitarian element: the Spirit will speak what he hears from the Son, who is the Word of the Father. Are we listening?

Corpus Christi

A

First Reading: Dt 8:2–3, 14b–16a
Responsorial Psalm: Ps 147:12–13, 14–15, 19–20
Second Reading: 1 Cor 10:16–17
Gospel: Jn 6:51–58

Today's reading from Deuteronomy, well known to us from the testing of Jesus in the wilderness (see Mt 4:4; Lk 4:4), provides a key to the eucharistic discourse in John's Gospel. It makes the connection between the word of God and the manna with which God fed the Israelites during their sojourn in the wilderness. Manna, bread from heaven, came to be associated with Torah. By devouring "every word that [came] forth from the mouth of the LORD" (Dt 8:3), the people of Israel were nourished by God as they had been by eating the manna in the wilderness. And the psalm reminds them, "He [the Lord God] has not done thus for any other nation" (147:20). In today's Gospel, Jesus proclaims that the life of God's people will now be nourished and sustained by the Word of God incarnate, his flesh, which is true food, and his blood, which is true drink.

In all three of today's readings, the gift of bread from heaven, be it manna or Torah or the body and blood of Christ, is a test of those who receive it. This is surely the situation of the Christians in Corinth, who apparently must be persuaded that their participation in the body and blood of Christ is the source of their life and unity as one body. And so it is for us today.

B

First Reading: Ex 24:3–8
Responsorial Psalm: Ps 116:12–13, 15–16, 17–18
Second Reading: Heb 9:11–15
Gospel: Mk 14:12–16, 22–26

Today's first reading provides the background necessary for us to understand the words of Jesus in Mark's account of the Last Supper: "This is my blood of the covenant, which will be shed for many" (14:24). Moses spoke similar words when he sprinkled the blood on the people to ratify their covenant with God (see Ex 24:8). Blood was the symbol of life; by virtue of the covenant, they now shared life with God. By speaking these words over the cup of wine, Jesus was inviting his disciples first of all to understand his death within the context of Jewish covenant theology. However, Jesus had come to share God's life not just with Israel but with all. And this is the meaning of the Aramaic phrase "for many."

As the words of Jesus over the cup looked back to Israel's past experience of God, his final words look to the future. On the one hand, they announce his death, but on the other, they assure his disciples of new life in God's kingdom. So he tells them, "I shall not drink again the fruit of the vine until the day when I drink it new in the kingdom of God" (Mk 14:25). So on this feast, let us take up "the cup of salvation" (Ps 116:13) and renew our covenant with our God.

C

First Reading: Gn 14:18–20
Responsorial Psalm: Ps 110:1, 2, 3, 4
Second Reading: 1 Cor 11:23–26
Gospel: Lk 9:11b–17

The story of the multiplication of the loaves, which even includes the eucharistic gestures Paul handed on to the Corinthians—"he took ... he blessed ... he broke ... he gave"—is so familiar to us that it is a challenge to find fresh meaning in it. A close reading of Luke's account, however, does reward the careful reader by highlighting one dimension of the feeding miracle that is often overlooked.

Our first clue to Luke's message in the story of the multiplication of the loaves is that it does not mention Jesus' compassion for the crowd (see Mk 6:34; 8:2). Instead, he receives (welcomes) the people as though he is the host of a long-awaited dinner party. And this is precisely the point. For Luke this miracle, like the Eucharist it signifies, anticipates the end time, which the tradition of Israel and the teaching of Jesus so often portray as a banquet. Not surprisingly then, this end-time feast, which satisfies the hungry crowd, fulfills the beatitude of Jesus, "Blessed are you who are now hungry, / for you will be satisfied" (Lk 6:21), and answers the prayer of Mary, "The hungry he has filled with good things" (Lk 1:53).

Solemnity of the Sacred Heart of Jesus

Friday Following Corpus Christi

A

First Reading: Dt 7:6–11
Responsorial Psalm: Ps 103:1–2, 3–4, 6–7, 8, 10
Second Reading: 1 Jn 4:7–16
Gospel: Mt 11:25–30

Israel's experience of God in history led them to conclude that the spring of all of God's actions in their regard was *hesed*. This word is almost untranslatable in English. Sometimes it is rendered, as in today's psalm, by words like "merciful" and "gracious," or phrases like "slow to anger" and "abounding in kindness" (Ps 103:8). But none of these effectively captures or conveys the active sense of the word. *Hesed* describes God's passion for relationship, God's desire to share life with us. This is what Moses means when he tells his people that God set his heart on them and chose them simply "because the LORD loved you" (Dt 7:7–8).

The revelation of Moses stands behind today's Gospel reading. In Matthew, Jesus continues in the tradition of Moses, who in the Book of Numbers is described as "the meekest man on the face of the earth" (12:3). And like Moses, Jesus, too, is a revealer. Surpassing without superseding the revelation of Moses, he reveals the very heart of the Father, whom he knows so well. First John brings this home when he urges us to "love one another ... for God is love" (4:7–8).

B

First Reading: Hos 11:1, 3—4, 8c—9
Responsorial Psalm: Is 12:2—3, 4, 5—6
Second Reading: Eph 3:8—12, 14—19
Gospel: Jn 19:31—37

Today's readings offer a number of vivid images to describe the love of God that we have come to know in and through the heart of Christ. The parental imagery of the first reading from the prophet Hosea is a poignant depiction of the frustrated love of a parent whose heart is overwhelmed, torn between anger and anguish (11:8). The responsorial psalm is from the prophecy of Isaiah. It discerns the love of God in "his glorious achievement" of salvation for his people and for Zion, their holy city (Hos 12:5—6). The second reading returns to the parental imagery of Hosea when Paul, kneeling "before the Father, from whom every family in heaven and on earth is named," prays for the church in Ephesus, "rooted and grounded in love," that they may "know the love of Christ which surpasses knowledge" (Eph 3:16, 19).

Of all the images presented in today's readings, the most memorable and moving for Christians is that of the dead Jesus' heart exposed by the soldier's lance. "And immediately blood and water flowed out" (Jn 19:34). A number of images interpret the scene. Jesus is cast as the Paschal Lamb whose bones could not be broken (see Ex 12:10) and whose blood saved the people from death, even as the water of Baptism and the blood of the Eucharist save us.

C

First Reading: Ez 34:11–16
Responsorial Psalm: Ps 23:1–3a, 3b–4, 5, 6
Second Reading: Rom 5:5b–11
Gospel: Lk 15:3–7

The words "love" and "heart" appear only in today's second reading from Paul's Letter to the Romans. In the first reading, the responsorial psalm, and the Gospel, the love of God held for us in the heart of Christ is conveyed in the familiar image of the Good Shepherd. The words of Ezekiel in today's first reading were originally addressed to exiles in Babylon, who are likened to lost sheep that "were scattered when it was cloudy and dark" (Ez 34:12). To them the prophet holds out the promise that God, the Good Shepherd, "will gather them from the foreign lands" and "bring them back to their own country" (v. 13). The beloved Psalm 23, an "American icon" as some have called it, turns Ezekiel's prophecy into a prayer. It has also been suggested that it is the prayer of a king, David perhaps, or one of his sons. A king was to be the good shepherd of his people. In this psalm he acknowledges that the Lord alone is his shepherd (v. 1). Finally, Luke's version of the parable of the Lost Sheep stresses the good shepherd's joy at finding the sheep that has strayed. The parable brings us back to Paul, for whom all biblical images are referred to Christ, through whom God proved his love for us once and for all "while we were still sinners" (Rom 5:8).

Ordinary Time

First Week in Ordinary Time

Monday

Year I   *First Reading: Heb 1:1–6*
         Responsorial Psalm: Ps 97:1 and 2b, 6 and 7c, 9
Year II *First Reading: 1 Sm 1:1–8*
         Responsorial Psalm: Ps 116:12–13, 14–17, 18–19
Years I and II *Gospel: Mk 1:14–20*

"The Kingdom of God is at hand!" (Mk 1:15). With these words Jesus begins his public ministry. The phrase he chooses to sum up his message is rooted in the Judaism of his day. In the Hebrew Scriptures, the reign or kingdom of God is a way of speaking about God's powerful rule over all creation. The rule of God is good news, as Psalm 97 proclaims: "The Lord is king; let the earth rejoice" (v. 1). Behind the symbol of God's reign lies the rich, rambling story of God's activity in the world. This story reaches back to creation itself and retells all the words God spoke through the prophets "in times past" (Heb 1:1) and all the wonders God worked on behalf of the poor, of people like Hannah in the first reading. At the time of Jesus, the reign of God was awaited as a dynamic event, God's coming to rule as king. Jesus announces the nearness of that coming.

The message of Jesus demands a reordering of one's whole life. Today's Gospel shows us just how radical this can be as Jesus' first disciples abandon financial security and family ties to follow him. Such literal following may not be asked of us, but our response to Jesus' call must be just as immediate and total.

TUESDAY

❧⟨◦⟩❧

I n his Gospel, Mark presents Jesus as the agent of God's reign, the one who in his words and deeds not only announced but actualized the kingly power of God. So it was that Jesus astonished the crowds, for he both taught and acted with unparalleled authority.

But creation had rebelled, rejecting God's rule, famously celebrated in Psalm 8, and subjecting itself instead to the rule of God's enemy. So the ministry of Jesus was a power struggle, most dramatically enacted in his exorcisms. Invariably the demons recognized the Holy One of God, who had come to destroy them, and Jesus cast them out with one word of command.

Mark notes the amazement of the people, but he does not invite us to share it. He knows that the loud cry, which here signals Jesus' power over the unclean spirit, will one day be torn from Jesus himself as he breathes his last on the cross. This fullest revelation of God's power will be met not with amazement but with abandonment. As the author of Hebrews taught, citing Psalm 8, "We ... see Jesus 'crowned with glory and honor' because he suffered death" (Heb 2:9). As Hannah learned, humiliation precedes exaltation: "The LORD puts to death and gives life" (1 Sm 2:6).

Wednesday

Most of Mark's first chapter describes a day in the ministry of Jesus. Throughout that day Jesus repeatedly acts to "destroy the one who has the power of death, that is, the Devil, and free those who … had been subject to slavery all their life" (Heb 2:14–15). He does this by casting out demons and curing the sick. The next morning finds him rising early and going off to a lonely place to pray.

Mark's Gospel shows Jesus at prayer on three separate occasions (1:35; 6:46; 14:32–42). Each time his ministry is being misunderstood. Clearly, Mark wants us to recognize that Jesus was tempted as we may be at times by the siren song of popular demand. "Everyone is looking for you!" an enthusiastic Peter tells him (Mk 1:37). Jesus prayed at those times. Like Samuel, he turned an attentive ear to God's word, and in communion with God he found his true purpose. The Letter to the Hebrews places Psalm 40 on the lips of Jesus: "Behold, I come to do your will, O God" (Heb 10:7; see Ps 40:9). It should be our prayer, too.

Thursday

The cleansing of a leper that concludes Mark's first chapter is riddled with textual problems, and scholars disagree on how to resolve them. To name a few: some manuscripts say that Jesus was moved with anger rather than with pity (Mk 1:41), and the change of tone in the story is puzzling, because Jesus seems to send the man away with a stern rebuke (v. 43).

The two readings that the Church has attached to this one both shed light on one aspect of this text. The selection from the Book of Samuel demonstrates divine anger: the disastrous defeat of Israel is punishment for the wickedness of Eli's house. As Psalm 44 observes, "You have cast us off and put us in disgrace" (v. 10). The passage from the Letter to the Hebrews sternly warns: "Take care ... that none of you may have an evil and unfaithful heart" (3:12). However, the Gospel is indisputably clear that Jesus has the will and the power to save, whether he is moved by human pity or by divine anger. Because of that, for us it is always "today"—always the day of salvation—if we but hear his voice (Heb 3:7–8; Ps 95:7–8).

Friday

YEAR I   *First Reading: Heb 4:1–5, 11*
         Responsorial Psalm: Ps 78:3 and 4bc, 6c–7, 8
YEAR II   *First Reading: 1 Sm 8:4–7, 10–22a*
         Responsorial Psalm: Ps 89:16–17, 18–19
YEARS I AND II *Gospel: Mk 2:1–12*

The story of Jesus healing the paralytic is sometimes misread, casting Jews and Judaism in a negative light. Parts of the Letter to the Hebrews may be read this way as well, so let the reader beware.

The scribes in Mark's story objected to Jesus' words, "Your sins are forgiven" (2:5), but not because forgiveness of sins was foreign to Judaism. Judaism is a religion of forgiveness. The very words that Jesus spoke were the words the priests in the Temple would say to any sinner who brought a sin offering. What the scribes found blasphemous was Jesus' declaring sins forgiven outside the Temple ritual that God had provided for the forgiveness of sins. Just as in the days of Samuel when the establishment of the kingship had seemed to some like a usurping of God's rule, so it was at the time of Jesus. To some people, the authority Jesus claimed seemed to usurp the role God had given to the priests of the Temple. But God is not bound by roles or rituals. Where there is faith, like that of the friends of the paralytic, miracles happen. These are the "glorious deeds" that we must never tire of declaring to "the generation to come" (Ps 78:4).

SATURDAY

In order to understand why Jesus' table fellowship so often drew the criticism of the Pharisees, it is necessary to know something about both the Pharisees and Jesus. The Pharisees were an association of laymen whose aim was to extend the holiness of the Temple into everyday life. One way they did this was by insisting on a degree of purity in their daily meals that, in fact, was required only for the Temple. For some Pharisees this strict observance worked as a boundary separating them from other Jews whom they judged to be "sinners." Although he agreed with the Pharisees on many points, Jesus' mission was to restore the whole of Israel. So by eating with tax collectors and sinners, he challenged one of the many boundaries that divided his people.

God's grace cannot be measured, managed, or monopolized, but many good people still try to do so, counting themselves among God's chosen. The tragic story of Saul is a case in point. As the passage from Hebrews suggests, the surest way to guard against self-righteousness is to submit oneself regularly to the penetrating judgment of God's word. Do we dare let it penetrate our hearts?

Second Sunday in Ordinary Time

A

First Reading: Is 49:3. 5–6
Responsorial Psalm: Ps 40:2, 4, 7–8, 8–9, 10
Second Reading: 1 Cor 1:1–3
Gospel: Jn 1:29–34

The identity of the unnamed servant of the Lord in the oracles of Second Isaiah remains a mystery. Although Christians understandably tend to read these texts as referring to Jesus, other readings are possible. The servant the prophet had in mind may have been the community of Israel in exile, or a particularly charismatic individual in that community, or perhaps even himself in his capacity as God's spokesman. Paul in some of his letters applies the image to himself as an apostle of Christ Jesus. In today's Gospel, John the Baptist seems to confer the title on Jesus when he testifies that Jesus is "the Son of God" (Jn 1:34) or, in an alternate reading, "God's chosen one." And yet, is not John himself worthy of the name God's "servant ... through whom I show my glory" (Is 49:3)?

However we name the servant, Isaiah's poem makes two important points about all God's servants, whoever they may be. First, the servant is authorized by God's initiative, as Paul is "by the will of God" (1 Cor 1:1) and as Jesus is at his baptism; and second, the servant's mission is to be "light to the nations" that God's "salvation may reach to the ends of the earth."

B

First Reading: 1 Sm 3:3b–10, 19
Responsorial Psalm: Ps 40:2, 4, 7–8, 8–9, 10
Second Reading: 1 Cor 6:13c–15a, 17–20
Gospel: Jn 1:35–42

Like the Gospel, today's first reading is a call narrative. In both texts God is drawing people into his service, while others— Eli and John, respectively—look on. These two are only peripherally involved in today's short stories. They play a necessary interpretive role, however, in the encounter between their disciples and the word of God. Both of today's stories also teach us in what obedience to God's word consists. The psalmist announces the theme when he declares, "ears open to obedience you gave me" (Ps 40:7). Eli instructs the young Samuel to respond to God's call with a prayer, "Speak, LORD, for your servant is listening" (1 Sm 3:9). The two disciples of John the Baptist act immediately on his word, "Behold, the Lamb of God" (Jn 1:36). They not only follow Jesus, but also stay ("remain") with him. These then are the characteristics of obedience: attentive listening in prayer and active seeking that ends in presence.

To these Paul adds another characteristic of obedience. Against those in Corinth whose obedience is purely spiritual, that is, excluding their bodies, Paul affirms that the obedience of faith is the free response of the whole person to God, to whom the body as well as the soul belongs. Let us pray for ears open to obedience.

C

First Reading: Is 62:1–5
Responsorial Psalm: Ps 96:1–2, 2–3, 7–8, 9–10
Second Reading: 1 Cor 12:4–11
Gospel: Jn 2:1–11

The first reading for today is believed to be the work of Third Isaiah (Is 56–66), an anonymous prophet who spoke during the difficult period of rebuilding that followed the exile in Babylon. The high hopes with which the exiles returned to their land were quickly dashed by the enormity of the task before them. Beyond the physical reconstruction of the city of Jerusalem was the need for spiritual renewal. Their return was not the victory that prophets like Second Isaiah (40–55) had promised. In answer, Third Isaiah sets his sights beyond the end of exile to the end time, when Israel will be "a glorious crown in the hand of the LORD" (62:3). Boldly, he announces that day as a wedding, casting God as the bridegroom and Israel as the bride. This is the image that informs today's Gospel. By making the wedding at Cana Jesus' first sign, John tells us that with the ministry of Jesus, God's future arrives.

The end time will reveal the generosity of God, suggested by the extravagant imagery of Isaiah and the abundance of good wine in John. This is the generosity that Paul sees in the manifold gifts of the Spirit now that in Christ the end time has come.

Second Week in Ordinary Time

MONDAY

YEAR I   *First Reading: Heb 5:1–10*
            Responsorial Psalm: Ps 110:1, 2, 3, 4
YEAR II   *First Reading: 1 Sm 15:16–23*
            Responsorial Psalm: Ps 50:8–9, 16bc–17, 21 and 23
YEARS I AND II *Gospel: Mk 2:18–22*

Today's readings mine the Hebrew Scriptures for ways of talking about Jesus. The author of the Letter to the Hebrews depicts Jesus in the language of the Temple as a high priest "according to the order of Melchizedek" (5:1, 6; see Ps 110:4). New Testament writers often quote Psalm 110, which follows the reading; it places Jesus in the royal line of David, whose scepter "the LORD will stretch forth from Zion" (v. 2). The selection from Mark's Gospel identifies Jesus as the bridegroom, a startling designation. In the Hebrew Scriptures and in other Jewish writings, the image of the bridegroom never refers to the Messiah, but only to God.

The presence of the bridegroom in this Gospel is another way of signifying that the reign of God was present in the ministry of Jesus. That startling new thing that God was doing in and through Jesus then as now demanded a brand-new response. The old forms, the old ways would not do. Samuel's censure of Saul suggests what that response might be: "Obedience is better than sacrifice" (1 Sm 15:22). New wine must have new skins.

TUESDAY

YEAR I   *First Reading: Heb 6:10–20*
            Responsorial Psalm: Ps 111:1–2, 4–5, 9 and 10c
YEAR II   *First Reading: 1 Sm 16:1–13*
            Responsorial Psalm: Ps 89:20, 21–22, 27–28
YEARS I AND II *Gospel: Mk 2:23–28*

⟨⟨⟩⟩

The saying of Jesus in today's Gospel—"The sabbath was made for man, not man for the sabbath" (Mk 2:27)—has parallels in the writings of the rabbis. The Pharisees themselves subordinated Sabbath law to human need. In Mark's account, however, the purpose of this story is not to contrast Jesus and the Pharisees, but to compare him to David. Jesus responds to the Pharisees' complaint that his disciples are picking heads of grain on the Sabbath by citing an episode from the story of David in 1 Samuel 21. There David disregarded the sanctity of the tabernacle in order to feed his men. Mark implies that Jesus enjoyed the same freedom that David did.

Walter Brueggemann has suggested that the freedom of David—and Jesus—was rooted in their sense that they were trusted by God. They both believe that God "trusts his men not to bring death but to do what must be done for the sake of his whole community."[12] The same may be said of Abraham, whose call is retold in the reading from Hebrews. For us who are their heirs, the creative fidelity of God on behalf of David, Abraham, and Jesus is, as Hebrews says, a firm anchor, a sure hope (6:18–19).

WEDNESDAY

⤜◯⤏

A t the time of Jesus, Judaism contained a number of religious groups, such as the Pharisees and the Sadducees, who disagreed with one another and among themselves as to how God's law should be lived. Sabbath observance was one issue these groups hotly debated. All Jews, including Jesus, agreed that the Sabbath must be kept holy, as the law of God commanded. But some had differing opinions about what that meant in the practical order. It was understood among the rabbis that when life was at risk, Sabbath observance was superseded. But this was clearly not the case in today's story of the man with the shriveled hand. His life was not at risk. It seems that Jesus was liberal in his view of what could and could not be done on the Sabbath.

But what does this story say to us who are no longer embroiled in such debates? Like all the miracles of Jesus, this one, too, bears witness to the kingly power of God. As all the readings tell us, power is often revealed in the most unlikely places—in the priesthood of Melchizedek, in the victory of David, and in the ministry of Jesus the Jew.

THURSDAY

YEAR I   *First Reading: Heb 7:25—8:6*
          Responsorial Psalm: Ps 40:7–8a, 8b–9, 10, 17
YEAR II   *First Reading: 1 Sm 18:6–9; 19:1–7*
          Responsorial Psalm: Ps 56:2–3, 9–10a, 10b–11, 12–13
YEARS I AND II *Gospel: Mk 3:7–12*

Scholars refer to the verses of today's Gospel as a transitional summary. Mark here recapitulates the ministry of Jesus, mentioning his healing miracles and exorcisms, and noting the vast numbers who followed him. He also refers to Jesus' commanding the unclean spirits "not to make him known" (Mk 3:12). This peculiar feature of Mark's Gospel is sometimes called the "messianic secret."

Throughout the first part of Mark's Gospel, Jesus' miracles are routinely followed by an injunction to silence. As students of Mark have come to understand, this is more than an attempt at crowd control—although for Jesus, as for David, the enthusiasm of the crowds will incite rival powers to jealousy. Rather, the messianic secret is Mark's way of forestalling a premature proclamation of Jesus' messiahship. His messiahship is most fully revealed not in his miracles but, paradoxically, in his suffering and death. So for Mark, there can be no true proclamation of Jesus as Messiah that does not also embrace his cross. To use the language of the psalm, we come to "walk before God in the light of the living" (Ps 56:13) only by way of the cross.

FRIDAY

YEAR I   *First Reading: Heb 8:6–13*
          Responsorial Psalm: Ps 85:8 and 10, 11–12, 13–14
YEAR II   *First Reading: 1 Sm 24:3–21*
          Responsorial Psalm: Ps 57:2, 3–4, 6 and 11
YEARS I AND II *Gospel: Mk 3:13–19*

Mark describes Jesus' choice of the Twelve as a decisive moment in his ministry: "He appointed Twelve" (3:14). The word "appointed" is weak; the Greek says, "he made the Twelve," that is, he created or constituted them. This action of Jesus is a clue to the intent and purpose of his earthly mission. For Jesus and his fellow Jews, the number twelve could refer only to the twelve tribes of Israel. Although in Jesus' time only two and a half tribes remained, since the time of the prophet Ezekiel, the people had hoped that all Israel, all twelve tribes, would be restored in the last days. Against this background, Jesus' creation of the Twelve was a sign that the last days were dawning and the reign of God was at hand.

Like David who refused to seize power on his own terms by killing Saul, Jesus remained firmly and faithfully within the way that God had traced for his people. Only later did Christians and Jews go their separate ways. Hebrews reflects the tension of that time when it speaks of the new covenant negating the old. Our own times, post-Vatican II, however, invite us to rediscover our common heritage with the Jewish people.

SATURDAY

YEAR I   *First Reading: Heb 9:2–3, 11–14*
         Responsorial Psalm: Ps 47:2–3, 6–7, 8–9
YEAR II *First Reading: 2 Sm 1:1–4, 11–12, 19, 23–27*
         Responsorial Psalm: Ps 80:2–3, 5–7
YEARS I AND II *Gospel: Mk 3:20–21*

Two of the three readings for today present us with poignant personal moments. In 2 Samuel, David learns of the defeat of the Israelites and of the death of Saul and Jonathan. In the short passage from Mark, Jesus discovers that members of his own extended family do not understand him or even believe in him. "They set out to seize him, for they said, 'He is out of his mind'" (Mk 3:21). Both David's grief and Jesus' disappointment are emotionally charged moments. Having known bereavement and betrayal in our own lives, we can empathize.

For us, the Letter to the Hebrews holds good news—or perhaps more accurately, hides it in the elaborate comparison it makes between the Temple priesthood and the priesthood of Christ. It says that as high priest, Christ "entered once for all into the sanctuary, not with the blood of goats and calves but with his own Blood, thus obtaining eternal redemption" (Heb 9:12). The good news is that where he has entered, we may follow, bringing our battered, broken hearts into the sanctuary, the one safe place that is the presence of the living God.

Third Sunday in Ordinary Time

A

First Reading: Is 8:23—9:3
Responsorial Psalm: Ps 27:1, 4, 13—14
Second Reading: 1 Cor 1:10—13, 17
Gospel: Mt 4:12—23 or 4:12—17

Today's first reading, excerpted from the prophecy of Isaiah, is adapted and used by Matthew in the Gospel. Like Jews of his day, Matthew understood the prophets were speaking of the distant future. So here he finds the oracle of Isaiah fulfilled in the ministry of Jesus. In effect this enables him to show that Jesus' Galilean ministry is in keeping with God's will and purpose. However, the Isaiah text was originally intended to speak to God's people in the aftermath of the Assyrian conquest. The tribes of Zebulun and Naphtali had been among the first to fall to the Assyrians. But the prophet sees the end of darkness, for God has smashed the yoke, the pole, the rod of oppression.

Paul urges on the Corinthians the abrupt and absolute obedience to the call of Jesus as shown by Simon, Andrew, James, and John. For Paul, following Jesus means belonging to him, not to Apollos or Cephas or even to Paul himself. Just how radically he means this is made clear when he asks, "Is Christ divided?" (1 Cor 1:13). Clearly he is referring to Christ present in the Christian community, which must be united if it is to be the body, the very presence of Christ in the world. The challenge to be "united in the same mind and in the same purpose" (v. 10) remains with us today.

B

First Reading: Jon 3:1–5, 10
Responsorial Psalm: Ps 25:4–5, 6–7, 8–9
Second Reading: 1 Cor 7:29–31
Gospel: Mk 1:14–20

Each of today's readings sounds a wake-up call and suggests a pattern of response. The cry of the prophet Jonah shatters the complacency of the citizens of Nineveh: "Forty days more and Nineveh shall be destroyed" (Jon 3:4). Even before Jonah reaches the halfway mark on his journey through the city, all the people of Nineveh turn from their evil ways. And their repentance causes God to repent as well. The city is saved because the people of Nineveh believed God—they understood that time was running out and reformed their lives accordingly. The psalm response to this reading brings the story home to us for whom time is always running out. "Teach me your paths," we pray (Ps 25:4).

The preaching of Jesus in the Gospel for today disrupts the daily life of four Galilean fishermen. "Come after me," he says (Mk 1:17), and inexplicably they follow. The advent of God's kingdom creates a state of emergency. Here the saying is literally true: "he who hesitates is lost." Similarly, Paul aims to disturb the peace of his Corinthian correspondents when he declares, "The time is running out" (1 Cor 7:29). This realization does not remove them from the world, but it must reorient their lives—and ours—within it "from now on" (v. 29).

C

First Reading: Neh 8:2—4a, 5—6, 8—10
Responsorial Psalm: Ps 19:8, 9, 10, 15
Second Reading: 1 Cor 12:12—30 or 12:12—14, 27
Gospel: Lk 1:1—4; 4:14—21

Today's reading from Nehemiah sets the stage for the scene
from Luke. Both readings depict a liturgical assembly in
which the interpretation of Scripture plays a central role.
Although the actual events that make up the story of Ezra and
Nehemiah are difficult to sort out, there is no question that
today's text depicts a watershed in the history of religion. God
would "speak" now in and through the written word. So, standing on a wooden platform, Ezra opened the scroll and "read
plainly from the book of the law of God, interpreting it so that
all could understand what was read" (Neh 8:8). Years later Jesus
entered the synagogue in Nazareth and, like Ezra, stood up to
read. Unrolling the scroll of Isaiah, he found the passage where it
was written, "The Spirit of the Lord is upon me ..." This, too,
was a watershed, for he added, "Today this Scripture passage is
fulfilled in your hearing" (Lk 4:17—18, 21).

As the word of God encoded in Torah became the constitu-
tion of Israel, so the Word of God made flesh in Jesus became the
foundation of the Church. No wonder, then, that Paul ranks the
ministry of the word so highly on his list of the Spirit's gifts. And
so must we.

Third Week in Ordinary Time

MONDAY

YEAR I   *First Reading: Heb 9:15, 24–28*
          Responsorial Psalm: Ps 98:1, 2–3ab, 3cd–4, 5–6
YEAR II   *First Reading: 2 Sm 5:1–7, 10*
          Responsorial Psalm: Ps 89:20, 21–22, 25–26
YEARS I AND II *Gospel: Mk 3:22–30*

Jesus' exorcisms caused some people to question the source of his power over Satan. In this story, two related charges are brought against him: he is possessed, and he casts out demons with the help of the prince of demons. Jesus answers by drawing two analogies that point out the illogic of the charges. Then he adds: "No one can enter a strong man's house ... unless he first ties up the strong man" (Mk 3:27). In this parable, Satan is the strong man and Jesus is the robber who overpowers Satan and plunders his house. It is typical of Jesus to refer to himself indirectly, for example, as bridegroom or bandit. But massive claims are often implicit in such metaphors. Behind this image is a passage from Isaiah, where God is the robber who takes booty from a warrior and captives from a tyrant (49:24–25). Without using the phrase "reign of God," Jesus proclaims that in his exorcisms God's kingly power is already breaking the power of Satan.

The unstoppable power of God that made David strong against his enemies makes Jesus strong against all the enemies of God's people.

TUESDAY

A ll four Gospels preserve an episode early in Jesus' ministry in which he distances himself from his natural family—mother, brothers, and sisters—and redefines family on the basis of the obedience of faith. "Whoever does the will of God is my brother and sister and mother" (Mk 3:35). And because Mark's Gospel begins with Jesus' baptism, not with his birth, even Mary is counted among those "outside."

The public ministry of Jesus was guided solely by the will of God. In fact, the author of the Letter to the Hebrews sums up Jesus' whole redemptive mission in one verse from Psalm 40: "I come to do your will" (v. 9; see Heb 10:7). To do God's will, as Jesus did, may require us at times to suffer the disapproval of our families.

The sequel of the story of David dancing before the ark is a case in point. The text goes on to say that when David returned to his own family, his wife Michal rebuked him sharply for embarrassing himself and his family by dancing with abandon before all of Israel "as a commoner might do." To which David replied with disarming candor, "I was dancing before the LORD" (Ps 6:20–23).

Wednesday

Year I   *First Reading: Heb 10:11–18*
        Responsorial Psalm: Ps 110:1, 2, 3, 4
Year II   *First Reading: 2 Sm 7:4–17*
        Responsorial Psalm: Ps 89:4–5, 27–28, 29–30
Years I and II *Gospel: Mk 4:1–20*

All three of today's readings attest to the power of God's word. In addition to today's selection, the author of the Letter to the Hebrews explores the mystery of Jesus with constant reference to the inspired word of God, the Hebrew Scriptures. In 2 Samuel the word of God spoken to David through the prophet Nathan will shape the messianic hope of Jews and Christians for ages to come. But of the three, the parable of the Sower is the most compelling.

Scholars often observe that the parable is more concerned with the seed than with the sower. In the Bible, seed is an image for the word of God. Jesus seems to be responding to those among his followers—people like us, perhaps—who are impatient for signs of his mission's success. In the story he tells, the seed undergoes every possible reversal and still yields a rich harvest in the end. Such is the resilience of God's word. When his disciples later question him about parables in general (Mk 4:10), Jesus seems to suggest that this parable is the key to all the others. "Do you not understand this parable? Then how will you understand any of the parables?" (v. 13).

THURSDAY

~∽⊙∽~

Mark chapter 4 explores the purpose of Jesus' parables. Earlier in the chapter, following the parable of the Sower, he seemed to imply that Jesus spoke in parables in order to conceal the mystery of the reign of God from those "outside." In other words, the mystery Jesus revealed was the private property of an in-group. Today's reading corrects that perception. The saying about the lamp is a proverb. It tells us that Jesus did not at all intend concealment when he spoke in parables.

The parables of Jesus were not compact stories with a moral —like Aesop's fables—but puzzles intended "to tease [the mind] into active thought," to use the words of C. H. Dodd.[13] The element of mystery in Jesus' parables was not meant to conceal the good news of God's rule, but to confront his hearers with the unaccountable generosity of God, who always gives immeasurably more (Mk 4:24). Today's story of David preserves his prayer in response to God's gift of kingship. Surely David's story illustrates the truth of the Gospel saying: "To the one who has, more will be given" (v. 25).

Friday

"**Y**ou need endurance to do the will of God and receive what he has promised," declares the Letter to the Hebrews (10:36). This is the point of the first parable in today's Gospel reading. The seed of God's word, the power of God's rule, grows slowly, secretly. Living as we do in the time between sowing and harvesting demands patient endurance.

The second parable contains a comic twist that is easy to miss. In telling the story of the mustard seed, Jesus had in mind two texts from the Hebrew Scriptures. Ezekiel 17 and Daniel 4 both describe Israel in its future glory as a great tree, a noble cedar, in whose ample branches the birds of the air will nest. Jesus announced the dawning of that future glory in words that recalled the grandeur of the prophets' vision only to deflate it. Israel in glory would be a shrub, not a tree. In this way Jesus challenged illusions of grandeur, Israel's and ours. Similarly, David's sin shattered any illusions he may have had about himself as God's anointed. But for us as for David, there is always hope, for God is not taken in by our posturing. With grace and humor, God saves us from ourselves.

SATURDAY

YEAR I   *First Reading: Heb 11:1–2, 8–19*
         Responsorial Psalm: Lk 1:69 70, 71 72, 73 75
YEAR II *First Reading: 2 Sm 12:1–7a, 10–17*
         Responsorial Psalm: Ps 51:12–13, 14–15, 16–17
YEARS I AND II *Gospel: Mk 4:35–41*

In the two first readings given to us today, we meet two men of old whom God approved because of their faith—Abraham in the Letter to the Hebrews and David in 2 Samuel. Set side by side as they are here, they present the light and the dark side of the life of faith. Abraham's faith is proven in his readiness to sacrifice Isaac; not only is his son spared, but also his descendants will be as numerous as the stars (see Gn 22:17). David's faith falters in his sin against Bathsheba and Uriah; not only is he bereft of his son, but "the sword shall not depart from [his] house" (2 Sm 12:10). Although his sin is forgiven, the consequences of that sin remain.

These stories tell us that it is indeed "a fearful thing to fall into the hands of the living God" (Heb 10:31). Yet our only safety lies within those hands. That is the message of today's Gospel. In the Bible, the sea symbolizes chaos. In Psalm 107, for example, God's power is revealed as God quiets the wind and calms the waters of the sea. In this Gospel story, Jesus does what God does—and asks us, "Why are you terrified?" (Mk 4:40).

Fourth Sunday in Ordinary Time

A

First Reading: Zeph 2:3; 3:12–13
Responsorial Psalm: Ps 146:6–7, 8–9, 9–10
Second Reading: 1 Cor 1:26–31
Gospel: Mt 5:1–12a

One theme runs through all three of today's readings, and Paul states it directly: "God chose the lowly and despised of the world, those who count for nothing, to reduce to nothing those who are something, so that no human being might boast before God" (1 Cor 1:28–29). The oracle of Zephaniah, today's first reading, calls upon God's people, already humbled by Assyria, to seek humility (*anawah*) as a claim on God's protection. As Zephaniah sees it, only the powerless and the poor—who, having no resources of their own, must depend wholly upon God—will remain. He thus transforms material want into spiritual wisdom.

God's "preferential option for the poor" is also attested by Jesus in the Beatitudes. Matthew's version of the Beatitudes comes close to the view of Zephaniah. In Matthew, material poverty—Luke's "blessed are you who are poor" (Lk 6:20)—becomes poverty "in spirit" (Mt 5:3), a spiritual posture before God; and hunger and thirst are not for bread or for water but "for righteousness" (v. 6). To us who are neither rich nor poor, these Beatitudes offer a viable spirituality that seeks humility and justice, come feast or famine.

B

First Reading: Dt 18:15–20
Responsorial Psalm: Ps 95:1–2, 6–7, 7–9
Second Reading: 1 Cor 7:32–35
Gospel: Mk 1:21–28

The verses from Deuteronomy in today's first reading describe the divine authorization of a prophet like Moses. This future prophet in Israel will teach with the authority of Moses; he will command the people's attention and demand their obedience. Thus says the Lord, "I . . . will put my words into his mouth; he shall tell them all that I command him. Whoever will not listen to my words which he speaks in my name, I myself will make him answer for it" (Dt 18:18–19). The identity of this prophet is unspecified in the text of Deuteronomy. But early Christians discerned the authority of Moses in the teaching of Jesus, as Mark does in today's Gospel. It was Jesus' authority that set him apart from other teachers of his day. The authority of his new teaching was manifest in his miracles. To the amazement of the people, even the unclean spirits obeyed his word.

The passage from Deuteronomy concludes with a warning to those who presume to speak without divine authorization. This caution governs Paul's advice on marriage. It is advice, he is careful to note, not authoritative teaching; what Paul says, not the Lord (see 1 Cor 7:12). The instruction of the psalmist is the flip side of Paul's: If today you hear God's voice, harden not your hearts (see 95:7–8).

C

First Reading: Jer 1:4–5, 17–19
Responsorial Psalm: Ps 71:1–2, 3–4, 5–6, 15, 17
Second Reading: 1 Cor 12:31—13:13 or 13:4–13
Gospel: Lk 4:21–30

All three of today's readings are contextualized by conflict. Set in the promising days of King Josiah, the call of the prophet Jeremiah anticipates other days when the prophet will meet with violent opposition from "Judah's kings and princes ... priests and people" (Jer 1:18). In the same way, Jesus' first visit to his hometown of Nazareth after the start of his public ministry anticipates the violent opposition that will continue to characterize his relationship with his native place. The enthusiasm with which they greet him gives way to fury when the meaning of his words becomes clear. "They rose up, [and] drove him out" (Lk 4:29).

Because 1 Corinthians 13, the so-called "hymn to love," is generally read apart from its context in Paul's letter, most readers do not realize that it is, in fact, part of Paul's response to the conflict in Corinth. It is not so much a hymn as an instruction for those who boast of their spiritual gifts. The one gift that matters, Paul says, is love—love that is practical and permanent. And such love is only possible because the God who knew Jeremiah and Jesus from the womb knows us fully, too. Let us praise him as the psalmist does, saying, "On you I depend from birth; / from my mother's womb you are my strength" (Ps 71:17).

Fourth Week in Ordinary Time

MONDAY

YEAR I   *First Reading: Heb 11:32–40*
         Responsorial Psalm: Ps 31:20, 21, 22, 23, 24
YEAR II *First Reading: 2 Sm 15:13–14, 30; 16:5–13*
         Responsorial Psalm: Ps 3:2–3, 4–5, 6–7
YEARS I AND II *Gospel: Mk 5:1–20*

Today's Gospel is the story of an exorcism that betrays the raw humor of a folktale, the episode of the pigs stampeding to their deaths. The description of the demoniac is horrifying and repulsive. Only in the light of the other two readings does the message of this one come into focus.

The rebellion of Absalom reduced David to a shadow of his former self. He made his way weeping up the Mount of Olives, head covered and feet bare, while Shimei cursed him and threw stones at him. David was not so different from the Gerasene demoniac. David, too, was tragically alienated—from his son, his subjects, and his royal self. The plight of God's people as described in Hebrews—"they went about . . . needy, afflicted, tormented," wandering in deserts, dwelling in caves (11:37–38)—is also reminiscent of the Gerasene's. The psalmist weighs in as well: "Many are saying of me, / 'There is no salvation for him in God' " (Ps 3:3). Each of these desperate human situations cries out for God to see and to save.

The Gospel tells us that in Jesus, God does just that.

TUESDAY

The two miracle stories in today's reading from Mark present us with "a cloud of witnesses," as Hebrews would say (12:1): Jairus, the synagogue official whose daughter is near death; the desperate woman afflicted with a hemorrhage for a dozen years; and, of course, Peter, James, and John, the privileged witnesses to Jesus' saving work. The first story begins, is interrupted by the second story, and then finally the first story is completed, creating what scholars describe as a "sandwiching" effect. Mark intends that we read one story in light of the other. Doing so, we discover that the salvation from death that Jairus sought for his daughter is accessible only to those who have faith, like the woman with the hemorrhage.

If there is a point of contact between this Gospel and the selection from 2 Samuel, it lies in the anguish of the two fathers, Jairus and David. More often than not, our lived experience is like David's rather than that of Jairus. At these times, above all, we must keep "our eyes fixed on Jesus, the leader and perfecter of faith" (Heb 12:2).

WEDNESDAY

YEAR I   *First Reading: Heb 12:4–7, 11–15*
          Responsorial Psalm: Ps 103:1–2, 13–14, 17–18a
YEAR II   *First Reading: 2 Sm 24:2, 9–17*
          Responsorial Psalm: Ps 32:1–2, 5, 6, 7
YEARS I AND II *Gospel: Mk 6:1–6*

In a way, the story of David in 2 Samuel inverts today's Gospel story from Mark. By ordering a census of all the tribes of Israel, David was in effect setting himself over and against his people. As Walter Brueggemann explains, "A royal census is not a neutral tool of policy." Rather, it served one of two purposes, both oppressive: taxation or military draft.[14] In the Gospel story, his people set themselves over and against Jesus. Sadly, because of their lack of faith, he could work no miracle there.

The whole dynamic of Mark's Gospel is summed up in this one brief episode. The wisdom and miraculous deeds of Jesus are greeted with amazement, which soon gives way to suspicion and scandal. "They took offense at him" (Mk 6:3). At times, all of us find Jesus and his Gospel too much for us too. That is when Hebrews is most persuasive: "Strengthen your drooping hands and your weak knees. Make straight paths for your feet, that what is lame may not be dislocated but healed" (12:12–13).

THURSDAY

YEAR I   *First Reading: Heb 12:18–19, 21–24*
            Responsorial Psalm: Ps 48:2–3ab, 3cd–4, 9, 10–11
YEAR II   *First Reading: 1 Kgs 2:1–4, 10–12*
            Responsorial Psalm: 1 Chr 29:10, 11ab, 11d–12a, 12bcd
YEARS I AND II *Gospel: Mk 6:7–13*

As David counseled Solomon, so Jesus counsels the Twelve. They are to continue his ministry in word and deed. Mark makes this clear by the words he chooses to describe their commission. Like Jesus, they are to preach "repentance," expel demons, and heal the sick. The instructions Jesus gives are the rules of the road for traveling missionaries. As an itinerant teacher, Jesus depended on the hospitality of those to whom he ministered, and so would his disciples. Their dependence on the generosity of others would be absolute and practical; they were to take "no food, no sack, no money in their belts" (Mk 6:8). They were to receive graciously whatever hospitality was offered. The instruction to stay in one house "until you leave from there" (v. 10) was meant to keep missionaries from shopping for better accommodations.

If we have "approached … the city of the living God," as Hebrews says (12:22), it is only because God has drawn near to us, through the mission of Jesus continued by his Church. Let us pray with the psalmist that God may make it firm forever (Ps 48:9).

FRIDAY

YEAR I   *First Reading: Heb 13:1—8*
          Responsorial Psalm: Ps 27:1, 3, 5, 8b—9abc
YEAR II   *First Reading: Sir 47:2—11*
          Responsorial Psalm: Ps 18:31, 47 and 50, 51
YEARS I AND II   *Gospel: Mk 6:14—29*

The selection from Hebrews urges us: "Remember your leaders who spoke the word of God to you" (13:7). The reading from the Old Testament Book of Sirach and the passage from Mark's Gospel present us with two great men whose lives speak to us of God—one a messiah, the other a martyr. In the life and death of each, the early Church found resonance with the life and death of Jesus. Sirach's praise of David is poetic and prayerful. He was the Lord's "anointed" (messiah)—to whom, according to Psalm 18, God "gave great victories" (v. 51)—and his whole life rose like a sacred offering before God. On the other hand, Mark's account of the martyrdom of John the Baptist is pointedly prosaic. He was the Lord's prophet, and his life was sacrificed to ensure the political survival of a corrupt client-king. Both converge in the experience of Jesus.

And in ours? The martyrdom of John is "sandwiched" between Jesus' sending out his disciples and their returning to him. This is Mark's way of telling us that disciples of Jesus may expect to share John's fate, as Jesus himself did. "Consider the outcome of their way of life and imitate their faith" (Heb 13:7).

Saturday

The three readings for today invite us to reflect on pastoral leadership. The author of the Letter to the Hebrews exhorts his readers to obey their leaders and to submit to them, mindful of the responsibility they bear. The excerpt from 1 Kings contains the prayer of a young king who, wanting to be a good leader, asks only for "an understanding heart" (3:9). The brief episode from Mark vividly describes the tireless service that will be required of the apostles of Jesus. Solomon's question seems to lie just under the surface of all three readings: "Who is able to govern this vast people of yours?" (1 Kings 3:9).

Each reading suggests the same answer. Mark shows the apostles simply participating in Jesus' pastoral ministry to the vast crowd, who are "like sheep without a shepherd" (6:34). In the reading from Kings, it is clearly by God's favor that Solomon rules with a wise and understanding heart. But the prayer in Hebrews says it best: it asks that through Jesus, "the great shepherd of the sheep," God may "carry out in you what is pleasing to him" (13:20—21). In short, the answer to Solomon's question is: not you, but God in you.

Fifth Sunday in Ordinary Time

A

First Reading: Is 58:7–10
Responsorial Psalm: Ps 112:4–5, 6–7, 8–9
Second Reading: 1 Cor 2:1–5
Gospel: Mt 5:13–16

The context of today's selection from the prophecy of Isaiah is a critique of fasting as an act of piety. True piety, the prophet declares, does not consist in such ritual acts but in responding to the practical demands of justice: feeding the hungry, sheltering the homeless, clothing the naked. Ironically, these acts of piety do as much to restore the community that practices them as they do to rescue the poor. The effect of removing oppression and relieving affliction from their midst is to make them a vital, visible faith community. In Corinthians, Paul critiques preaching that is nothing more than an empty exercise in rhetoric. The art of persuasion was held in high regard in Paul's day, and he was as able as the next man to turn a phrase. But because true faith rests "not on human wisdom but on the power of God" revealed in Jesus, Paul made "Jesus Christ, and him crucified," the sole object of his preaching (1 Cor 2:5, 2).

Combined with these readings, the words of Jesus warn us: "Your light must shine before others, that they may see your good deeds and glorify your heavenly Father" (Mt 5:16). But when our piety becomes ritual and our preaching rhetoric, the salt loses its taste and the light no longer shines.

B

First Reading: Jb 7:1–4, 6–7
Responsorial Psalm: Ps 147:1–2, 3–4, 5–6
Second Reading: 1 Cor 9:16–19, 22–23
Gospel: Mk 1:29–39

The New Testament readings for today present us with two men with a mission, both in a sense driven to accomplish the work they have been given to do. The brief selection from Mark sums up a busy day in the life of Jesus; then in his curt exchange with Simon Peter, it conveys the urgency of Jesus' mission. There is no time to bask in the admiration of the crowds, as Peter suggests. Rather, Jesus says, "Let us go on to the nearby villages that I may preach there also." And he adds, "For this purpose have I come" (Mk 1:38). Jesus, no less than Paul in the second reading, is under the compulsion of the Gospel. Paul explains the urgency of this compulsion with a striking analogy: paradoxically, the freedom of the Gospel in which he is so deeply invested has made him a slave to all.

In a very different sense, Job, too, speaks of himself as a slave. Lacking purpose, his days are an unremitting drudgery, like those of a day laborer who waits for his wages. Perhaps his misery is given to us today as a foil for the mission of Jesus and Paul. When time weighs heavy upon us, we might do well to assess our share in the Gospel. Are we waiting for the adulation of the crowd— "Everyone is looking for you" (Mk 1:37)—or are we motivated solely by God's purpose?

C

Every one of today's readings describes a privileged experience of God. The call of Isaiah takes place within a theophany (a manifestation of God) in the Temple. In the presence of God, Isaiah immediately becomes aware that he is "a man of unclean lips" (Is 6:5). God, however, comes not to condemn but to call. So cleansed, Isaiah is sent to speak God's word. In the second reading, Paul refers to a number of appearances by the risen Jesus to those who would become the foundation of the Church. He counts himself among this originating group. Recalling his experience of the risen Lord makes him, even in retrospect, mindful of how unfit he is to be called an apostle. Yet the grace of God has made him an effective minister of the Gospel. Finally, Simon Peter, recognizing the word of God in the work of Jesus, falls to his knees and prays, "Depart from me, Lord, for I am a sinful man" (Lk 5:8). And in answer, Jesus makes him a fisher of men.

Such privileged experiences are not ours. We come to God through the word of Isaiah and the witness of Peter and Paul, who hand on to us what they themselves received. Mindful of our own unworthiness, we can only pray as the psalmist does, "Forsake not the work of your hands, O Lord" (Ps 138:8).

Fifth Week in Ordinary Time

MONDAY

YEAR I   *First Reading: Gn 1:1–19*
          Responsorial Psalm: Ps 104:1–2a, 5–6, 10 and 12, 24 and 35c
YEAR II *First Reading: 1 Kgs 8:1–7, 9–13*
          Responsorial Psalm: Ps 132:6–7, 8–10
YEARS I AND II *Gospel: Mk 6:53–56*

Today's three readings deal with the theme of homemaking. Describing the first three days of creation, the Book of Genesis shows God overcoming the deep and the dark in order to make the earth a habitable, hospitable place for human beings —a home. In the First Book of Kings, the priests of Israel carry the ark of the covenant into the holy of holies. The dark cloud symbolizes the presence of God, who takes up residence in the princely house—the home—that Solomon has built. Finally, the Gospel of Mark suggests that the powerful presence of God has found a new home in the ministry of Jesus. Mark says that the crowds "began to bring in the sick on mats to wherever they heard he was," and all who touched the "tassel on his cloak ... were healed" (Mk 6:55–56).

Mark's meaning is only fully disclosed in the Greek verb translated here as "were healed." That word (*esozonto*) connotes more than mere physical healing. In the vocabulary of the early Church, it described the total experience of salvation: not just wellness, but wholeness—in other words, coming home.

TUESDAY

YEAR I   *First Reading: Gn 1:20—2:4a*
         Responsorial Psalm: Ps 8:4–5, 6–7, 8–9
YEAR II   *First Reading: 1 Kgs 8:22–23, 27–30*
         Responsorial Psalm: Ps 84:3, 4, 5 and 10, 11
YEARS I AND II *Gospel: Mk 7:1–13*

❧∽◅◦▻∾❧

Mark is not entirely accurate in his presentation of the issue under discussion in this Gospel story. In Jesus' time, there were many different types of Pharisees. Not all of them, and certainly not all Jews, practiced the ritual hand washing described in this passage. This was one way that group sought to live God's law by bringing the ritual holiness of the Temple into their daily lives. Jesus' concern was that too much attention to such human customs could lead to the neglect of God's commandments. One example was the practice of *korban*, which involved declaring something "sacred" and thereby removing it from the claims of others.

In his prayer found in 1 Kings, Solomon asks: "Can it indeed be that God dwells on earth?" (8:27). Genesis answers with a resounding yes! Having created men and women "in the divine image" (Gn 1:27; see Ps 8:6), God dwells with us, within us. Sacred places like the Temple of Solomon and sacred practices like the hand washing of some Pharisees all pale in comparison to the sacred dignity of the human person, which the law of God— the commandments—proclaims and protects.

Wednesday

In Mark's version, Jesus' debate with some Pharisees on the issue of ritual purity leads him to make a striking public statement, which Mark sums up in an editorial comment: "Thus he declared all foods clean" (7:19). Many scholars doubt that Jesus, the observant Jew, did in fact abolish the Jewish food laws. If he did, why then did the earliest Christians continue to keep them, as Acts says they did? Rather, the words of Jesus make an important distinction between ritual purity and moral purity.

In the Gospel, Jesus offers a catalog of the wickedness that may come from within people, from their hearts (see Mk 7:21–22), to render a person impure. Psalm 37 takes a more positive approach. It says that wisdom comes out of the just man, because "the law of God is in his heart" (vv. 30–31). Such was the case of Solomon as long as his heart was with his God. And Genesis tells us that such was the condition of all humanity—in the beginning. Let us ask God to send forth his Spirit that we may be recreated and the face of the earth be renewed (see Ps 104:30).

THURSDAY

Women are prominent in all three of today's readings. In the passage from Genesis, God determines to make "a suitable partner" (2:18) for the man. Interestingly, the Hebrew word *ezer*, rendered here as "partner," is routinely used in the psalms to refer to God, who is Israel's covenant partner. This choice of words is one way in which the author of this story points to the dignity of woman. The author of 1 Kings, however, blames the wives of Solomon for turning his heart away from the Lord, thus making these foreign women ultimately responsible for the schism soon to follow. In the selection from Mark, Jesus himself is confronted by a foreign woman.

In this story Jesus seems strangely out of character. He answers the pleading woman with an awkward rebuff, dismissing her as a "dog," an epithet that Jews sometimes used for Gentiles. He seems reluctant to heal. On the other hand, she is every woman who loves her child. She will not be put off. At that moment, she is a "suitable partner" for Jesus: they match wits and Jesus yields, turning his face to the Gentile world.

FRIDAY

YEAR I   *First Reading: Gn 3:1–8*
           Responsorial Psalm: Ps 32:1–2, 5, 6, 7
YEAR II   *First Reading: 1 Kgs 11:29–32; 12:19*
           Responsorial Psalm: Ps 81:10–11ab, 12–13, 14–15
YEARS I AND II *Gospel: Mk 7:31–37*

Commenting on the Genesis account of the fall, the *Catechism of the Catholic Church* attributes the first sin to the fact that the man and the woman let their trust in their Creator die in their hearts (no. 397*). As a result, they hide in shame from God as well as from each other. In the First Book of Kings, Solomon is deprived of his kingdom, having turned his heart away from the Lord, the God of Israel. The prophet Ahijah therefore gives ten tribes to Jeroboam. Alienation and division are the consequences of sin.

If the two first readings underscore the tragic effects of sin, the reading from Mark declares the joyous event of the dawn of salvation among the nations. The last verse is an allusion to Isaiah 35. It is Mark's way of indicating that God's glorious future, which the prophet had announced as a time when the ears of the deaf would be open and the tongue of the dumb would sing (Is 35:5–6), had arrived. It was already present and palpable in the ministry of Jesus. Therefore, all of us who have been baptized in his name must listen to his word with open ears, and proclaim it with clear voices.

* Cf. Gn 3:1–11; Rom 5:19.

SATURDAY

YEAR I   *First Reading: Gn 3:9–24*
         Responsorial Psalm: Ps 90:2, 3–4abc, 5–6, 12–13
YEAR II *First Reading: 1 Kgs 12:26–32; 13:33–34*
         Responsorial Psalm: Ps 106:6–7ab, 19–20, 21–22
YEARS I AND II *Gospel: Mk 8:1–10*

Adam's overreaching will be punished: he will eke out a mea-
ger living from the hard ground to which he will finally
return (Gn 3:17–19; see Ps 90:3). Similarly, Jeroboam's overreaching will also be punished: his house will be "cut off and
destroyed from the earth" (1 Kgs 13:34). Such is the lot of those
who grasp at God's gifts.

In contrast, the Gospel story of the multiplication of the
loaves signifies and celebrates the bounty of God's kingdom. The
miracle points in three directions: past, present, and future. The
setting in a "deserted place" recalls God's goodness in the past,
the gift of manna in the wilderness. That the people in the story
"ate and were satisfied" (Mk 8:8), and that seven baskets were
leftover looks to the future to the abundance of the messianic
age. As Isaiah foretold, God will then set before all peoples a feast
"of rich food and choice wines" (25:6). Finally, the verbs used to
describe the actions of Jesus—he took, he gave thanks, he broke,
he gave—bring us back to the present, to the Eucharist where,
already though not yet, we "learn to savor how good the LORD is"
(Ps 34:9).

Sixth Sunday in Ordinary Time

A

First Reading: Sir 15:15–20
Responsorial Psalm: Ps 119:1–2, 4–5, 17–18, 33–34
Second Reading: 1 Cor 2:6–10
Gospel: Mt 5:17–37 or 5:20–22a, 27–28, 33–34a, 37

The Book of Sirach, from which today's first reading is taken, is an example of wisdom literature. Israelite wisdom, like that of other ancient cultures, was primarily concerned with living a good life. Therefore, it addressed the human issues that confronted individuals and communities in daily living, such as marriage and family, loyalty in friendship, honesty in business, and so on. In time, wisdom in Israel came to be identified with Torah (see Sir 24:22) and assumed the weight of moral authority, as today's psalm makes clear. In today's reading, Sirach teaches that the immense wisdom of God wills good—keeping the commandments—and not evil, which is the abuse of human freedom.

In the Sermon on the Mount, Matthew depicts Jesus authoritatively interpreting the Torah. He takes up the old questions—about anger and divorce and oaths—in the light of the new reality, the rule of God he has come to proclaim. Thus both wisdom and Torah are fulfilled in him. Paul says that this Jesus is the only wisdom he preaches, the mysterious wisdom of God prepared before the ages and revealed to us now through the Spirit. Can we say the same?

B

First Reading: Lv 13:1–2, 44–46
Responsorial Psalm: Ps 32:1–2, 5, 11
Second Reading: 1 Cor 10:31—11:1
Gospel: Mk 1:40–45

◦◦◦◦◦◦

Today's first reading from the Book of Leviticus provides background for Mark's account of Jesus cleansing a leper as told in the Gospel. The word "leprosy" in ancient Israel covered a number of diseases of the skin. The law in Leviticus prescribed that the priest diagnose the disease and declare the person unclean. Isolation was imposed in all cases until it could be determined if the case was infectious. It was also the priest who decided that a leper was "clean" or healed. Therefore, when Jesus sends the leper in today's reading to show himself to the priest and to make the offering prescribed by Moses, he is acting as a Torah-observant Jew.

The leper who is cleansed by Jesus, on the other hand, acts like a Christian missionary: he "went away and began to publicize [*keryssein*] the whole matter. He spread the report [*logos*] abroad" (Mk 1:45). *Keryssein* means "to proclaim" and *logos* means "word." So, he "proclaimed the word" and thus gave glory to God, as that other missionary Paul urges the Christians in Corinth to do in today's reading when he says, "So whether you eat or drink, or whatever you do, do everything for the glory of God" (1 Cor 10:31). We who have had the guilt of our sin taken away (Ps 32:5) should also give glory to God.

C

First Reading: Jer 17:5–8
Responsorial Psalm: Ps 1:1–2, 3, 4 and 6
Second Reading: 1 Cor 15:12, 16–20
Gospel: Lk 6:17, 20–26

The sequence of woe and blessing in Jeremiah's oracle is inverted in the blessings and woes of Jesus' sermon. In Jeremiah, trust forms the basis for blessing and woe—"Cursed is the one who trusts in human beings.... Blessed is the one who trusts in the LORD" (Jer 17:5, 7). This is the sentiment of today's psalm as well: "The LORD watches over the way of the just, / but the way of the wicked vanishes" (Ps 1:6). The Sermon on the Plain in Luke is addressed to the disciples of Jesus, the poor who have placed their trust in him. The Beatitudes are the direct consequences of discipleship, while the woes warn away would-be disciples who are rich. The danger is not in riches, but in the false sense of security they inspire.

Luke's version of the Beatitudes differs from Matthew's not only in number, but also in their reference to material, rather than spiritual, conditions; for example, Luke's "Blessed are you who are poor" (Lk 6:20) versus Matthew's "Blessed are the poor in spirit" (Mt 5:3). These bold proclamations are made from the perspective of God's future, which in Jesus is somehow already present. It is also the perspective of Paul, who recognizes in the risen Lord the "firstfruits of those who have fallen asleep" (1 Cor 15:20) and the hope of those who mourn for them.

Sixth Week in Ordinary Time

MONDAY

YEAR I   *First Reading: Gn 4:1–15, 25*
          Responsorial Psalm: Ps 50:1 and 8, 16bc–17, 20–21
YEAR II   *First Reading: Jas 1:1–11*
          Responsorial Psalm: Ps 119:67, 68, 71, 72, 75, 76
YEARS I AND II *Gospel: Mk 8:11–13*

The mysterious story of Cain and Abel offers no explanation as to why God accepted Abel's sacrifice and rejected Cain's, although popular wisdom has certainly sought one. Psalm 50 may be construed as a partial answer: "Not for your sacrifices do I rebuke you," it says, but for attacking "your brother … your mother's son" (vv. 8, 20). Still it seems best to defer to the freedom of God. This seeming inequality originating in the free will of God gives rise to Cain's resentment. Yet God makes it clear to Cain that his resentment, understandable though it may be, need not control him. He can master it and live in dignity with the tension of divine freedom. A similar tension underlies the Gospel story. Jesus' opponents want to solve the mystery of his claims with a sign from heaven. They would force God's hand, as it were. But Jesus is adamant: no such sign will be given.

The Letter of James calls us to full maturity in the Christian life and says that this requires endurance, among other things. Endurance is not passivity but patience. It is the ability to live in dignity with the tension of God's freedom.

Tuesday

Year I   First Reading: Gn 6:5–8; 7:1–5, 10
         Responsorial Psalm: Ps 29:1a and 2, 3ac–4, 3b and 9c–10
Year II First Reading: Jas 1:12–18
         Responsorial Psalm: Ps 94:12–13a, 14–15, 18–19
Years I and II Gospel: Mk 8:14–21

In the Gospel story, Jesus experiences the same frustration that God expresses in the reading from Genesis. Leading into the story of Noah, the author of Genesis writes that God—who, according to Psalm 29, "is enthroned above the flood" (v. 10)—"regretted that he had made man on the earth, and his heart was grieved," seeing how evil were the desires of the human heart (Gn 6:5–6). Jesus, too, is grieved to discover that his disciples have closed their minds and still do not understand, even after the miracle of the loaves. "Are your hearts hardened?" he asks, incredulous (Mk 8:17).

Closer to home, the Letter of James may cause us to wonder how often we ourselves must grieve the heart of God. James suggests, for example, that when the tug of our passions tempts us, we say, "I am being tempted by God" (Jas 1:13). Or when we blame God for the blindness of our minds and the bankruptcy of our hearts, must not God be grieved—the God who wills only to bless us with every worthwhile gift and to bestow on us the crown of life? (vv. 12, 16).

WEDNESDAY

YEAR I   *First Reading: Gn 8:6–13, 20–22*
        Responsorial Psalm: Ps 116:12–13, 14–15, 18–19
YEAR II *First Reading: Jas 1:19–27*
        Responsorial Psalm: Ps 15:2–3a, 3bc–4ab, 5
YEARS I AND II *Gospel: Mk 8:22–26*

Throughout his Gospel, Mark describes Jesus' ministry as one in which demons are cast out immediately and the sick are cured instantly. The miracle recounted in today's Gospel does not fit that pattern. Perhaps in this story Mark is more interested in describing the progress of recovery than the pattern of Jesus' power. In the early Church, Jesus' healing of the blind was a symbol of Baptism. In the life of faith there are no quick studies. Sight comes gradually for us, as it did for the man in the story. To change the metaphor, that is why James tells us to "welcome the word that has been planted in you and is able to save your souls." We are not just to listen to it, but also to "be doers of the word," which is the only way that faith can grow (Jas 1:21–22).

The story of Noah was also a symbol of Baptism in the early Church. Saved by water in the ark, Noah could not immediately walk out onto the surface of the earth. Saved by the waters of Baptism, it, too, takes time for us to walk with confidence into the dawning light of the new day God has made. As we reflect on the gift of our Baptism, we ask ourselves, "How shall I make a return to the LORD?" (Ps 116:12).

Thursday

Year I   *First Reading: Gn 9:1–13*
            Responsorial Psalm: Ps 102:16–18, 19–21, 29 and 22–23
Year II   *First Reading: Jas 2:1–9*
            Responsorial Psalm: Ps 34:2–3, 4–5, 6–7
Years I and II   *Gospel: Mk 8:27–33*

Today's reading from Genesis describes the covenant God made with Noah and his descendants under the sign of the rainbow. In the view of Judaism, the covenant with Noah reveals God's will for the salvation of all human beings without distinction. The author of the Letter of James also underscores God's impartiality. After all, he asks, "Did not God choose those who are poor in the world to be rich in faith and heirs of the Kingdom?" So he warns us, "show no partiality as you adhere to the faith in our glorious Lord Jesus Christ" (Jas 2:5, 1).

In today's Gospel, Jesus also shows himself impartial. Peter's profession of faith in Jesus as the Messiah is incomplete, for Peter has not yet recognized or reckoned with the true nature of Jesus' messiahship. This is made dramatically clear when he adamantly refuses to accept Jesus' prediction of the passion. Jesus responds with his eyes on his disciples—those present and those still to come, like us. "Get behind me, Satan!" he says (Mk 8:33). His point is inescapable: any disciple, even Peter, who denies the cross, stands on the side of Satan and not of God.

FRIDAY

YEAR I   *First Reading: Gn 11:1–9*
          Responsorial Psalm: Ps 33:10–11, 12–13, 14–15
YEAR II   *First Reading: Jas 2:14–24, 26*
          Responsorial Psalm: Ps 112:1–2, 3–4, 5–6
YEARS I AND II *Gospel: Mk 8:34—9:1*

In Genesis, the central problem of the story of Babel is answered in the story of Abraham. In the story of Babel, the people of the land of Shinar decide to secure their own existence. "Come, let us build ourselves a city and a tower with its top in the sky," they say, "and so make a name for ourselves" (Gn 11:4). But their efforts end in disaster, and they are scattered all over the earth, just as they feared. In the language of today's Gospel, they sought to save their lives but lost them. Abraham, on the other hand, surrendered his life in faith and saved it. And because he did not succumb to the temptation of Babel, of trying to make a name for himself, God made his name great (see Gn 12:3).

The Letter of James goes on to show that Abraham's faith was proven in his works, specifically in his readiness to sacrifice Isaac. In offering his only son, Abraham was surrendering his own future as well. James says that for such faith in action, "he was called 'the friend of God'" (2:23). What God asked of Abraham, Jesus asks of all his disciples. Faithful following of Jesus entails self-denial and self-sacrifice. There is no other way.

Saturday

Year I   *First Reading: Heb 11:1–7*
         Responsorial Psalm: Ps 145:2–3, 4–5, 10–11
Year II *First Reading: Jas 3:1–10*
         Responsorial Psalm: Ps 12:2–3, 4–5, 7–8
Years I and II *Gospel: Mk 9:2–13*

The Letter to the Hebrews defines faith as "the realization of what is hoped for and evidence of things not seen" (11:1). In the transfiguration, Peter, James, and John are given a glimpse of what all Christians hope for and long to see: Christ in glory. The vision overwhelms Peter, who exclaims, "It is good that we are here!" (Mk 9:5). Then as he tries to capture the moment by suggesting that they build tents on the site, the heavenly voice speaks: "This is my beloved Son" (v. 7). These words, confided to Jesus at his baptism, are addressed now to his disciples. With this, the vision ends.

The selection from James is addressed to Christian teachers. The author, himself a teacher, realizes that teaching is an awesome ministry. The conclusion of the transfiguration story depicts Peter, James, and John, future Christian teachers, struggling to reconcile what they have just seen and heard with what they have previously learned from scribes and from Scripture about resurrection. As they do so, the voice from heaven insists: "Listen to him" (Mk 9:7). Do we?

Seventh Sunday in Ordinary Time

A

First Reading: Lv 19:1–2, 17–18
Responsorial Psalm: Ps 103:1–2, 3–4, 8, 10, 12–13
Second Reading: 1 Cor 3:16–23
Gospel: Mt 5:38–48

At times Christians, anxious to show the moral superiority of Jesus, oppose his teaching to that of the Jews. Today's readings offer a corrective for this tendency to set Jesus over and against his people. In the verses from the Sermon on the Mount from today's Gospel, Jesus looks beyond legal redress for alternative ways to respond to insult and injustice. In this he acts in the spirit of Leviticus, which in today's reading teaches: "Take no revenge and cherish no grudge against any of your people" (19:18). Jesus adheres to Torah, too, when he teaches love of enemies. The statement "and hate your enemy" is neither in the text of the Hebrew Bible nor in the teaching of the rabbis, although it does appear in some sectarian writings like the Dead Sea Scrolls. Jesus, like Leviticus, makes love the center of the moral life in imitation of God. Jesus' "Be perfect, just as your heavenly Father is perfect" (Mk 5:48) echoes "Be holy, for I, the Lord, your God, am holy" of Leviticus 19:2. And it is such holiness that, in Paul's words, makes the community of faith God's temple.

The Hebrew Scriptures and the Christian New Testament both see love at the core of God's character. How do our lives reflect this love?

B

First Reading: Is 43:18–19, 21–22, 24b–25
Responsorial Psalm: Ps 41:2–3, 4–5, 13–14
Second Reading: 2 Cor 1:18–22
Gospel: Mk 2:1–12

I n today's first reading, the prophet Isaiah prepares the exiles in Babylon for the new thing God is about to do for them. This act of God on their behalf is so new that it will make all God's past favors forgettable, he says. And this is all because of God's own willingness to forget their past failures and forgetfulness. In the second reading, Paul seems to affirm the promise of Isaiah when he says, "God is faithful" (2 Cor 1:18). But for Paul, God's promise of newness is most fully realized in Christ Jesus. He tells the Corinthians, "For however many are the promises of God, their Yes is in him," that is, in Christ (v. 20).

In today's Gospel, Mark gives us the same message. The physical cure of the paralytic is but the outward sign that his sins are forgiven. This is the newness of life Jesus offers those who in faith can perceive it. In today's story, perceiving the possibility of new life for their friend, four men cut a hole in the roof in order to bring the paralytic to Jesus. To the astonishment of all the people, their resourcefulness is rewarded with newness never seen before. "He rose, picked up his mat at once, and went away in the sight of everyone" (Mk 2:12). The story must give us pause: are we as imaginative in bringing our friends to Jesus?

C

First Reading: 1 Sm 26:2, 7–9, 12–13, 22–23
Responsorial Psalm: Ps 103:1–2, 3–4, 8, 10, 12–13
Second Reading: 1 Cor 15:45–49
Gospel: Lk 6:27–38

J esus' teaching on love of enemies is put with inescapable clarity in the Gospel for today, the continuation of the Sermon on the Plain in Luke. The love command is cast in active verbs, showing that this is a practical demand made on those who hear what Jesus says (his disciples). "Do good to those who hate you, bless those who curse you, pray for those who mistreat you" (Lk 6:27–28). It is also apparent in the concrete examples that follow.

Love of enemies flies in the face of our every natural impulse. But the other two readings for today shed light on this seemingly impossible teaching. When David refuses to harm Saul, he acts not on abstract principle but on practical faith. He will not usurp God's role as judge, even to avenge himself on his sworn enemy. In the reading from 1 Corinthians, Paul makes a distinction between the first Adam and the last Adam (Christ), between the natural and the spiritual. What is impossible in the order of nature is made possible by the grace of God in Christ. The point is that faith and grace make love of enemies possible if not easy. For only with the eyes of faith can we recognize that "not according to our sins does he deal with us" (Ps 103:10). Just so we should not deal with others according to theirs.

Seventh Week in Ordinary Time

MONDAY

YEAR I   First Reading: Sir 1:1–10
         Responsorial Psalm: Ps 93:1ab, 1cd–2, 5
YEAR II   First Reading: Jas 3:13–18
         Responsorial Psalm: Ps 19:8, 9, 10, 15
YEARS I AND II Gospel: Mk 9:14–29

Today's Gospel story is a preview. Here we see the disciples attempting in Jesus' absence to carry on his work—driving out demons and debating with scribes. It is a glimpse into the future of the Church. Although Jesus gave them authority over unclean spirits, the disciples cannot expel the demon that torments the boy. No doubt the scribes have outclassed them in discussion as well. The answer to their predicament lies in the miracle story sandwiched between two references to the disciples' powerlessness. They must admit their lack of faith in Jesus and make the prayer of the desperate father their own: "Help my unbelief!" (Mk 9:24).

Called to share his wisdom and power, the followers of Jesus can do so only through faith. "Everything is possible to one who has faith" (Mk 9:23). This is not to say that faith can do anything, but that faith does not put limits on what God can do. James calls such faith "wisdom from above" (3:17); as Sirach says, it is a gift lavished on God's friends (1:8). When later the disciples ask Jesus, "Why could we not drive the spirit out?" he recommends the power of prayer (Mk 9:28–29).

TUESDAY

YEAR I   *First Reading: Sir 2:1–11*
         Responsorial Psalm: Ps 37:3–4, 18–19, 27–28, 39–40
YEAR II *First Reading: Jas 4:1–10*
         Responsorial Psalm: Ps 55:7–8, 9–10a, 10b–11a, 23
YEARS I AND II *Gospel: Mk 9:30–37*

T he two first readings highlight different aspects of today's
     Gospel story. Predicting his passion, Jesus shows himself to
be well schooled in the way of wisdom. He knows that God's servants are often tried by adversity and crushed by misfortune, as
Sirach teaches in today's reading. Having studied "the generations
long past," he knows, too, that God "saves in time of trouble" (Sir
2:10, 11). The argument that preoccupies Jesus' disciples in the
same Gospel story—namely, "Who was the greatest?" (Mk 9:34)
—deserves the stern warning of James: "Where do the conflicts
among you come from?" he asks; then admonishes, "Humble
yourselves before the Lord and he will exalt you" (Jas 4:1, 10).
More gently, Jesus tells them the same thing. In Jesus' day, the
child that he set before the Twelve was not a symbol of innocence
but of poverty and powerlessness. Children in that world were
vulnerable and voiceless, as they are in ours. Jesus was telling the
Twelve—and us—that true greatness consists in extending a
warm welcome to the least of his brothers and sisters.

Wednesday

In today's reading, James warns against "boasting in your arrogance" (4:16). John's words to Jesus in the Gospel story show more than a little arrogance and pretension: "We saw someone driving out demons in your name, and we tried to prevent him because he does not follow us" (Mk 9:38)—that is, he is not one of us. In answer, Jesus the teacher takes his cue from Moses, that other great teacher. The Book of Numbers recounts how Joshua wanted to stop Eldad and Medad from prophesying because they had not gone as commanded to the tent of meeting. But Moses answered him, "Are you jealous for my sake? Would that all the people of the Lord were prophets!" (Nm 11:29). In a similar situation, Jesus also counsels tolerance: "Whoever is not against us is for us" (Mk 9:40).

As Christians, we have been baptized in Jesus' name, but that name does not belong to us. We do not have exclusive rights to the wisdom and power of God revealed in Jesus. Being wise men, Moses and Jesus both recognized that wisdom, the power of God, often walks with us "as a stranger" (Sir 4:17). Let us learn to welcome the stranger.

THURSDAY

All the readings for today sound an alarm. "Delay not your conversion to the LORD," Sirach insists (5:8). "The way of the wicked vanishes," the psalmist warns (Ps 1:6). "Weep and wail over your impending miseries," cries James (5:1). The foolish will be "herded into the nether world," adds Psalm 49:15. "If your hand causes you to sin, cut it off!" commands Jesus (Mk 9:43). These hard sayings relentlessly force us to acknowledge that one day God will judge all of us. In these verses, Mark again shows Jesus' concern for those "little ones" so easily led astray. But Jesus knows, too, that we are often our own worst enemies. Occasions of sin arise from within ourselves, as well as from outside. Borrowing the vivid imagery of Isaiah, he says in no uncertain terms: whatever in you causes sin must be rooted out at all cost, so that you may enter life and avoid the fires of hell, "where 'their worm does not die, and the fire is not quenched'" (Mk 9:48; Is 66:24).

Such hard sayings are rarely heard in our day. But the truth they convey is as essential as salt: "Salt is good," says Jesus, "but if salt becomes insipid, with what will you restore its flavor?" (Mk 9:50).

FRIDAY

YEAR I First Reading: Sir 6:5–17
Responsorial Psalm: Ps 119:12, 16, 18, 27, 34, 35
YEAR II First Reading: Jas 5:9–12
Responsorial Psalm: Ps 103:1–2, 3–4, 8–9, 11–12
YEARS I AND II Gospel: Mk 10:1–12

D ivorce was as live an issue in Jesus' day as it is in ours. Mark's account preserves the earliest memory of Jesus' teaching on this painful human dilemma. The question is put to him as a test: Is divorce legal? Jesus answers with a question of his own: "What did Moses command you?" (Mk 10:3). It is important to note how vague Moses' teaching is on this point. No law in the written Torah—the first five books of the Hebrew Scriptures—clearly states the grounds for divorce. Deuteronomy 24:1–4, however, does assume the practice of divorce, and on that basis the opponents of Jesus respond that Moses permitted it. Jesus' teaching is also based on Torah. Turning to Genesis, he declares that God intended "from the beginning of creation" (Mk 10:6) that marriage be indissoluble.

The teaching of Jesus is as important for what it says about marriage as for what it says about divorce. Clearly, he honors the union of two people whose "Yes" means "Yes," as James might put it (Jas 5:12). And surely all that Sirach says of the "faithful friend" is true of the faithful spouse as well—he or she is "a sturdy shelter ... a treasure ... beyond price ... a life-saving remedy," another self (6:14–17).

Saturday

Today's three readings have a sacramental quality. The Council of Trent found scriptural evidence in this passage from James for the practice of anointing the sick (see 5:13—15). According to Tertullian, some early Christians used this selection from Mark as scriptural justification for infant baptism (see 10:13—16). In both cases, the Church discovered in the human words and gestures of Jesus—his healing the sick and welcoming the children—a precedent and a pattern for its own sacramental ministry. The reading from Sirach uncovers the anthropology—the understanding of the human person—on which sacramental theology is built. Made in the image of God, human beings are uniquely equipped, Sirach says, to discover and "glory in the wonder of his deeds and praise his holy name" (17:8).

The human warmth of Jesus is evident in today's Gospel as well. Of the three Gospel writers who relate this incident, Mark is the only one who says specifically that Jesus "embraced the children" (10:16; see Mt 19:15; Lk 18:17). Psalm 103 picks up this nuance when it sees and celebrates the love of God—embodied in Jesus—as the compassion of a father for his children (see v. 13).

Eighth Sunday in Ordinary Time

A

First Reading: Is 49:14–15
Responsorial Psalm: Ps 62:2–3, 6–7, 8–9
Second Reading: 1 Cor 4:1–5
Gospel: Mt 6:24–34

Today's readings are all about trust. The two short verses that make up the first reading are the reassuring words of Isaiah to the exiles in Babylon. Their doubt—"the LORD has forsaken me; my Lord has forgotten me"—is answered with a mother's firm promise: "I will never forget you" (Is 49:14–15). In today's response, the psalmist puts his trust in God alone, saying, "He only is my rock and my salvation." In the Gospel excerpt from the Sermon on the Mount, Jesus confronts his disciples with a choice and a challenge. They must choose between the service of God and the service of mammon; that is to say, they must decide to secure their future by trusting in God rather than in their portfolios. To do so is to acknowledge that even the most basic necessities of life are the gift of the heavenly Father.

In the First Letter to the Corinthians, the stewardship of God—the God who provides like a father and a mother who never forget—is imitated by the apostles Paul and Apollos. They are "stewards of the mysteries of God," writes Paul (1 Cor 4:1). Yet trustworthy as their stewardship may be, it is exercised within the stewardship of God's providence, and therefore God alone can be trusted to judge them. In whom do we place our trust?

B

First Reading: Hos 2:16b, 17b, 21—22
Responsorial Psalm: Ps 103:1—2, 3—4, 8, 10, 12—13
Second Reading: 2 Cor 3:1b—6
Gospel: Mk 2:18—22

Covenant love, God's *hesed*, is depicted in daring speech in today's readings. The oracle of Hosea declares God's intention to renew the covenant with wayward Israel by returning with them to the desert, the place where, coming up from the land of Egypt, they first came to know God. God's hope is that a fresh encounter will lead again to espousal, "in right and in justice, in love and in mercy" (Hos 2:21). The same imagery controls the presentation of Jesus in today's Gospel. Defending his disciples for not fasting, Jesus casts himself as the bridegroom, a role reserved for God in the writings of the prophets. In him and through him, he seems to say, God's people are being wooed and won. As wedding guests, his disciples witness and celebrate the arrival of the new covenant.

In 2 Corinthians, Paul describes himself and his fellow apostles as ministers of this new covenant. And like Hosea and Jesus, Paul, too, understands the new covenant in spousal terms. Later in the same letter, he will tell the Corinthians, "I betrothed you to one husband to present you as a chaste virgin to Christ" (2 Cor 11:2). So in today's reading, like a proud father, he tells his recalcitrant children that their names are written on his heart, "not in ink but by the Spirit of the living God" (2 Cor 3:3).

C

First Reading: Sir 27:4–7
Responsorial Psalm: 92:2–3, 13–14, 15–16
Second Reading: 1 Cor 15:54–58
Gospel: Lk 6:39–45

The Book of Sirach and the Sermon on the Plain are both forms of wisdom literature: they aim at building character on the assumption that character determines action. The instruction of Sirach makes speech the test of a person's character. "In his conversation is the test of a man," it says, then uses an agricultural analogy to reinforce the point: "The fruit of a tree shows the care it has had; / so too does a one's speech disclose the bent of one's mind" (Sir 27:5–6).

The teaching of Jesus in today's Gospel has a similar structure. But his parable, in the form of a rhetorical question, seems to make sight the touchstone of character. "Can a blind person guide a blind person?" he asks. This is also followed by an agricultural image: "Every tree is known by its own fruit," which goes on to reaffirm that speech is key to character after all, as the mouth reveals what is in the heart (Lk 6:44–45). Today's psalm also consists of an agricultural allusion comparing the just to fruitful trees (see Ps 92:13–15).

The last line of 1 Corinthians 15 is an exhortation. Like Sirach and Jesus, Paul is concerned with action that is firm, steadfast, fully devoted, and not in vain (1 Cor 15:58). Such "good fruit" is possible, he says, because of the victory of our risen Lord Jesus Christ.

Eighth Week in Ordinary Time

MONDAY

YEAR I *First Reading: Sir 17:20–24*
       Responsorial Psalm: Ps 32:1–2, 5, 6, 7
YEAR II *First Reading: 1 Pet 1:3–9*
       Responsorial Psalm: Ps 111:1–2, 5–6, 9 and 10c
YEARS I AND II *Gospel: Mk 10:17–27*

Today's Gospel is a story of missed opportunity. A man approaches Jesus with the question: "What must I do to inherit eternal life?" Jesus' answer is thoroughly Jewish: "You know the commandments." To which the man replies, "All of these I have observed from my youth," (Mk 10:17, 19, 20). Moved, Jesus invites him to do one thing more: "Sell what you have, and give to the poor" (v. 21). In Judaism, the word *zekhut* describes the hundred-fold to which Jesus is calling the rich man. As Jacob Neusner explains, "it is gained . . . by an act of renunciation . . . which heaven cannot compel but highly prizes."[15] For the man in the Gospel story to give all he had to the poor and to throw in his lot with Jesus would have been such an act. But he "had many possessions" (v. 22).

Christians have usually depicted the man in this story as young, as though such opportunities are offered only to the young. But Jesus repeats his invitation throughout our lives. To accept it is to gain the "inheritance that is imperishable" (1 Pet 1:4). To refuse it is to go away sad, like "those who have never lived" (Sir 17:23).

TUESDAY

YEAR I   *First Reading: Sir 35:1–12*
    Responsorial Psalm: Ps 50:5–6, 7–8, 14 and 23
YEAR II   *First Reading: 1 Pet 1:10–16*
    Responsorial Psalm: Ps 98:1, 2–3ab, 3cd–4
YEARS I AND II *Gospel: Mk 10:28–31*

I n today's Gospel, Jesus promises the hundredfold to all who have left everything to follow him. Such total renunciation and reliance on God goes beyond the rules and rituals of religious observance. This is the sense of Sirach's words when he says that the worship most pleasing to God consists in justice and generosity (35:6–7). This sentiment is echoed by the psalmist when he exhorts, "Offer to God praise as your sacrifice" (Ps 50:14).

Jesus assures Peter that God's response to such total self-giving, as he required of the rich man who went away sad, is made "in this present age" as well as "in the age to come" (Mk 10:30). In the present, the disciples are given back everything they thought they had left—with one exception. Jesus says they will receive "a hundred times more now in this present age: houses and brothers and sisters and mothers and children and lands"— but not fathers (Mk 10:30). This is not to exclude male parents from the community of Jesus. It is rather to ensure that that community remains free of male domination. In the community of Jesus' disciples there is one Father, only one—and that is the Holy One, who, as Peter writes, calls us to be holy (1 Pet 1:15).

WEDNESDAY

In Mark's Gospel, each prediction of the passion is followed by a dramatic example of the disciples' failure to grasp what Jesus is telling them. Today's selection is a case in point. Following the third prediction of his passion, the sons of Zebedee ask Jesus to give them places of honor when he comes into his glory. Jesus couches his answer in biblical imagery—the cup and the bath of pain. Both symbolize suffering and death, but James and John do not understand that. Neither do the other ten, who are indignant at the two brothers for trying to gain an edge on the rest of them. One more time Jesus must explain: "It shall not be so among you" (Mk 10:43).

In the failure of the disciples, Mark holds up a mirror and invites us to see ourselves. Like James and John, how often do we make requests of Jesus without knowing what we are asking? "Give new signs and work new wonders," we pray, unmindful of the cup and the bath of pain (Sir 36:5). When will we realize that we were ransomed not with perishable things "but with the precious Blood of Christ as of a spotless unblemished Lamb" (1 Pet 1:19)?

THURSDAY

YEAR I   *First Reading: Sir 42:15–25*
         Responsorial Psalm: Ps 33:2–3, 4–5, 6–7, 8–9
YEAR II *First Reading: 1 Pet 2:2–5, 9–12*
         Responsorial Psalm: Ps 100:2, 3, 4, 5
YEARS I AND II *Gospel: Mk 10:46–52*

"**I** want to see," says blind Bartimaeus (Mk 10:51). In the Gospels, to believe is to have one's eyes opened to the revelation of God in nature and in history. "How beautiful are all his works!" exclaims Sirach, awestruck at the glory of God that fills all creation (42:23). Peter's letter is crowded with colorful images as he invites the newly baptized to see themselves now as God's own people—"newborn infants ... living stones ... 'a chosen race, a royal priesthood, a holy nation'" (1 Pet 2:2, 5, 9).

The story of Bartimaeus is the story of a call as well as a cure. The careful reader will see that it has been shaped by Jesus' call of his first disciples in Mark 1:16–20. When Jesus summons, the blind beggar throws off his cloak and comes. This gesture recalls the response of the first disciples who immediately left their nets when Jesus called them (see vv. 18, 20). The beggar's cloak is the "tool of his trade," the net in which he catches the alms on which he lives. He abandons all this for the chance to see, and seeing, he "followed him on the way" (Mk 10:52). "I want to see," we cry, too. And to us Mark says, "Get up! Jesus is calling you!" (v. 49).

FRIDAY

YEAR I   *First Reading: Sir 44:1, 9–13*
        Responsorial Psalm: Ps 149:1b–2, 3–4, 5–6a and 9b
YEAR II   *First Reading: 1 Pet 4:7–13*
        Responsorial Psalm: Ps 96:10, 11–12, 13
YEARS I AND II *Gospel: Mk 11:11–26*

In today's Gospel, Mark has combined two symbolic actions of Jesus—cursing the fig tree and cleansing the Temple—with a group of Jesus' sayings on prayer. The two symbolic acts must be understood against the background of Jesus' conviction that, in the words of Peter, "The end of all things is at hand" (1 Pet 4:7). With the end always in view, when God would come to rule the world with justice (Ps 96:13), Jesus dramatically demanded that the Temple be purified and prepared to be the focal point of the new thing God would do in the last days, when all the nations would come to Jerusalem to pray, as Isaiah had promised (see Is 2:2–3). By sandwiching this action of Jesus within the strange story of the cursing of the fig tree, Mark underlines the critical nature of Jesus' action. Like those other "godly men" (Sir 44:1), the prophets before him, Jesus, too, condemned the corruption that had stripped Temple worship of its good fruit.

The First Letter of Peter urges us to take Jesus at his word— "all that you ask for in prayer, believe that you will receive it and it shall be yours" (Mk 11:24)—by remaining calm and always able to pray.

SATURDAY

The Old Testament Book of Sirach concludes with a canticle on wisdom. Clearly the wisdom Sirach celebrates is not esoteric knowledge but ethical instruction. He says that from his youth it has kept his feet on the level path (Sir 51:15). Such wisdom is practical; it issues in praise of God, its author.

In today's Gospel, Jesus also demonstrates practical wisdom. His enemies want to trap him into making a public claim that he acts with God's authority. This would set him up for the charge of blasphemy. So Jesus evades their question with a question of his own.

The Letter of Jude contains practical wisdom as well. Jude offers a program for Christian life, counseling prayer "in the Holy Spirit" and perseverance "in the love of God" (vv. 20–21). He also gives sound advice on how to deal with those who have gone astray. "On those who waver, have mercy" (v. 22), he says, but be realistic in rescuing the others. He urges his readers to recognize their limitations and not to associate with those who have succumbed to false teaching, confiding them instead to the mercy of the one, the only God who can save.

Ninth Sunday in Ordinary Time

A

First Reading: Dt 11:18, 26–28, 32
Responsorial Psalm: Ps 31:2–3, 3–4, 17, 25
Second Reading: Rom 3:21–25, 28
Gospel: Mt 7:21–27

It is generally acknowledged that the setting and structure of the Sermon on the Mount are patterned on Moses' giving of the Law (Torah) to Israel on Mount Sinai (see Ex 19:20—23:33; Dt 4:44—26:19). The choice of an excerpt from Deuteronomy to accompany today's Gospel, the conclusion of the Sermon on the Mount, calls attention to this relationship between the texts. Just as Moses sets two possibilities before his people—a blessing for keeping the commandments of the Lord, or a curse for not keeping them—so does Jesus confront his disciples with two possibilities. They can build their lives on the secure foundation of his teaching—the word of God, who alone is our "rock of refuge" (Ps 31:3)—or failing to do that, they can build their lives on shifting sand and be utterly ruined.

In the teachings of both Moses and Jesus, blessing and curse, security and ruin all depend on doing the will of God. Paul insists in Romans that we are not saved by the law; but neither are we lawless. Crying, "Lord, Lord" is not enough (Mt 7:21). Only by doing the will of the heavenly Father can we, Jews and non-Jews alike, enter the kingdom of heaven.

B

First Reading: Dt 5:12–15
Responsorial Psalm: Ps 81:3–4, 5–6, 6–8, 10–11
Second Reading: 2 Cor 4:6–11
Gospel: Mk 2:23——3:6 or 2:23–28

Just how important Sabbath observance was and still is in Judaism is made clear in today's first reading. In light of this, it is also important to understand that, in the Gospels, Jesus does not deny the necessity of keeping holy the Sabbath day. The controversy, rather, revolves around the question: What exactly is involved in keeping the Sabbath? How to define the work that was prohibited by the commandment was an ongoing debate in the Judaism of Jesus' day, and it continues to be in our own. In today's Gospel, Jesus weighs in on the liberal side of the issue with a statement echoed in rabbinic literature: "The sabbath was made for man, not man for the sabbath" (Mk 2:27). Even the cure of the man with a withered hand is not a break with Sabbath law but a rereading of it in light of the authority Jesus claims.

A number of biblical traditions explain the significance of keeping the Sabbath. In Deuteronomy it is presented as a way for Israel to embody the saving act of God, who, as the psalm puts it, "led you forth from the land of Egypt" (Ps 81:11), that makes them who they are as God's people. Even so must we, Paul says, carry in our body the sacrifice of Jesus that makes us who we are as his Church.

C

First Reading: 1 Kgs 8:41–43
Responsorial Psalm: Ps 117:1, 2
Second Reading: Gal 1:1–2, 6–10
Gospel: Lk 7:1–10

At first glance it may seem that the elders of the Jews who appeal to Jesus on behalf of the centurion, a God-fearing foreigner, are taking their cue from the words of today's first reading. This is the prayer of Solomon, who at the dedication of the Temple intercedes with God for all the peoples of the earth who may come to the Temple to pray. But on closer inspection, the motive of the elders may not be so pure. "He loves our nation and built the synagogue for us," they say. "He deserves to have you do this for him" (Lk 7:4). In short, one good turn deserves another. To his credit, the centurion himself recognizes that he is not worthy, that he does not deserve to have Jesus enter his house. The authority that has allowed him to act as a benefactor to the Jews in Capernaum is not symmetrical to the divine authority of Jesus. Even Jesus is amazed at such faith.

The Galatians whom Paul addresses are also foreigners, non-Jews who have come to believe in Jesus. But it is their little faith that amazes Paul. Unlike the centurion, they cannot distinguish the authority of the Gospel of Christ from cheap imitations. Can we?

Ninth Week in Ordinary Time

MONDAY

YEAR I   *First Reading: Tb 1:3; 2:1a–8*
         Responsorial Psalm: Ps 112:1b–2, 3b–4, 5–6
YEAR II   *First Reading: 2 Pet 1:2–7*
         Responsorial Psalm: Ps 91:1–2, 14–15b, 15c–16
YEARS I AND II *Gospel: Mk 12:1–12*

The parables of Jesus that the Gospel writers recount natural-ly reflect their respective concerns. Here Mark has expanded Jesus' parable of the Vineyard and appended to it two verses from Psalm 118 in order to drive his point home: the rejection of Jesus by some of the leaders of Israel was a tragic mistake. To discover the original meaning of the parable as Jesus told it is more difficult. Pheme Perkins suggests that we consider the owner of the vineyard and the manner in which he deals with the tenants.[16] In a way he is like Tobit, a good man who does not conform to the logic of the world but conducts himself by another law. So he appeals repeatedly to the tenants and even sends his son, while his neighbors and perhaps even we wonder, "Will this man never learn!"

Jesus seems to say: such is the power of God. Peter adds that this is the divine power that has "bestowed on us everything that makes for life and devotion" (2 Pet 1:3). This is the divine nature we are called to share.

Tuesday

Year I   First Reading: Tb 2:9–14
         Responsorial Psalm: Ps 112:1–2, 7–8, 9
Year II First Reading: 2 Pet 3:12–15a, 17–18
         Responsorial Psalm: Ps 90:2, 3–4, 10, 14 and 16
Years I and II Gospel: Mk 12:13–17

The tax this Gospel story mentions was a poll tax the Romans levied on all the people of Judea. It caused controversy among the Jews because of its political and religious implications. Paying the tax would seem to support the political claim of Rome. Because it had to be paid in Roman currency, the tax also carried the implication of idolatry, for the coin was inscribed with the words "Tiberius Caesar, august son of the divine Augustus." Jesus' answer spoke to both levels of the debate. His "Repay to Caesar what belongs to Caesar" (Mk 12:17) allowed for limited cooperation with Rome, which was the position of the Pharisees as well. His reference to "what belongs to God" (v. 17) (in Greek, "the things of God") made a subtle but significant religious distinction. Since all things belong to God, all things are owed God.

This story is often used to define Christian duty to God and nation—as if the two were on a par. This is not the meaning of Jesus' answer. Because as Peter says we "await new heavens and a new earth" (2 Pet 3:13), we must, with the conscientiousness of Tobit, continually assess where our allegiance to the state must yield to the absolute claim of God.

WEDNESDAY

YEAR I   *First Reading: Tb 3:1–11a, 16–17a*
        Responsorial Psalm: Ps 25:2–3, 4–5ab, 6 and 7bc, 8–9
YEAR II   *First Reading: 2 Tm 1:1–3, 6–12*
        Responsorial Psalm: Ps 123:1b–2ab, 2cdef
YEARS I AND II *Gospel: Mk 12:18–27*

Today's selection from Tobit presents us with parallel lives. Tobit and Sarah both suffer, and in their suffering are verbally abused by those closest to them—Tobit by his wife, Sarah by her maid—and both contemplate death as release from suffering. But God heard their prayer. And God is "not God of the dead but of the living," as Jesus will demonstrate in the Gospel (Mk 12:27). The Sadducees accepted as authoritative only the first five books of the Bible; therefore, they rejected the Pharisees' and Jesus' teaching on resurrection. The hypothetical case they put to Jesus in today's Gospel was an attempt to reduce that teaching to absurdity. In answer, Jesus showed that they did not understand either the true nature of resurrected life or their own Scriptures.

Our hope in resurrection rests on the power of the living God revealed in Christ Jesus. As 2 Timothy declares, "Christ Jesus ... destroyed death and brought life and immortality to light through the Gospel" (1:10). A highly scientific age may not easily accept this good news, but we must proclaim it boldly, knowing in whom we have trusted.

THURSDAY

Since the written Torah has 613 commandments, Jewish teach-ers were routinely asked, "Which is the first?" Jesus' answer combines two commandments: the first concerns loving God (from Deuteronomy 6), and the second concerns loving others (from Leviticus 19). This exchange with a scribe provides a pleas-ant interlude in a phase of Jesus' ministry that is riddled with controversy. Since his arrival in Jerusalem, Jesus has been chal-lenged by the chief priests and leading men of the city, by a coali-tion of Pharisees and Herodians, and by some Sadducees. In con-trast, this conversation is open and honest. The scribe's study of Torah has made him ready to receive the reign of God.

The same may be said of Tobiah and Paul. Like his father, Tobiah has taken to heart the words of Torah. His prayer makes that clear. So, accompanied by an angel, he, too, is not far from God's reign. Finally Paul, the zealous Jew, formed in the way of Torah and never far from God's reign, preaches even while in chains. He is absolutely convinced that God is ever faithful, "for he cannot deny himself" (2 Tm 2:13). Are we also convinced of this?

FRIDAY

YEAR I   *First Reading: Tb 11:5–17*
        Responsorial Psalm: Ps 146:1b–2, 6c–7, 8–9a, 9bc–10
YEAR II *First Reading: 2 Tm 3:10–17*
        Responsorial Psalm: Ps 119:157, 160, 161, 165, 166, 168
YEARS I AND II *Gospel: Mk 12:35–37*

The two first readings for today deal with sight. Tobit is enabled to see his son Tobiah, the light of his eyes, and Paul encourages Timothy, his "son," to see him—his "way of life, purpose, faith, patience, love, endurance" (2 Tm 3:10). Both Tobit's and Paul's stories are for us Sacred Scripture. They are part of that library of inspired books that speak to the Christian community with the authority of God's own word. Jesus' Bible was the Jewish Scriptures—the Law (the written Torah), the Prophets, and the Writings. The creative fidelity with which he approached them, evident in today's Gospel, should be the model for our own biblical study. In this passage, for example, Jesus interprets Psalm 110 to expose the narrowness of the messianic expectations of some scribes.

Sacred Scripture was part of Jesus' "equipment" as a teacher in Israel, and the Second Letter to Timothy says it should be ours, too (see 2 Tm 3:16–17). Although our methods of biblical interpretation will be different from those of Jesus' or Paul's day, they must always recognize and respect the word of God as a living word that demands a lived response. How are we "equipped for every good work" (v. 17) by the word of God?

Saturday

Year I   *First Reading: Tb 12:1, 5–15, 20*
         Responsorial Psalm: Tb 13:2, 6efgh, 7, 8
Year II   *First Reading: 2 Tm 4:1–8*
         Responsorial Psalm: Ps 71:8–9, 14–15ab, 16–17, 22
Years I and II *Gospel: Mk 12:38–44*

A s Raphael exhorted Tobit and Tobias before his departure, so Paul exhorts Timothy before his death. Both Raphael and Paul, angel and apostle, counsel good works and promise "a full life" (Tb 12:9) and "a crown of righteousness" (2 Tm 4:8) to those who endure. The Gospel story also contains exhortation. Observing the people putting money into the collection box opposite the Temple treasury, Jesus seizes the opportunity to teach his disciples a lesson. He directs their attention to a poor widow and her two small copper coins. He tells them that hers is the greater gift, for "she, from her poverty, has contributed all she had, her whole livelihood" (Mk 12:44).

Scholars often note that the widow is presented as a foil for those scribes whose piety is showy and self-serving. But she prepares us as well for the self-giving of Jesus. As she gave her livelihood, so he will give his life. Perhaps Mark is suggesting that almsgiving—so highly valued in the Book of Tobit as better than either prayer and fasting, able to save one from death and expiate every sin (12:8–9)—is one practical way for us to follow Christ.

Tenth Sunday in Ordinary Time

A

First Reading: Hos 6:3–6
Responsorial Psalm: Ps 50:1, 8, 12–13, 14–15
Second Reading: Rom 4:18–25
Gospel: Mt 9:9–13

The point Paul is trying to make in today's selection from Romans can be more easily grasped if the verse immediately preceding is included. In Romans 4:17b, Paul says of Abraham, "He is our father in the sight of God, in whom he believed, who gives life to the dead and calls into being what does not exist." Like many Jewish writers of his day, Paul mines the story of Abraham in order to find support for his theology: in this instance, for his teaching that we are saved by faith in Christ. The connection between Abraham and the Christian believer, as Paul sees it and says here, is that both put their faith in God, who has the power to bring life from the dead womb of Sarah as from the tomb of the dead Jesus.

The power of God to bring the dead to life is also attested by both the prophecy of Hosea and the pronouncement of Jesus in today's readings. The God who slew Ephraim with the prophet's words will raise them up "on the third day" (Hos 6:2). And the divine physician looks for the spiritually sick, the sinners, and restores them to life because, says Jesus citing Hosea, "I desire mercy, not sacrifice" (Mt 9:13; see Hos 6:6). Let us then "go and learn the meaning of the[se] words" (Mt 9:13).

B

First Reading: Gn 3:9–15
Responsorial Psalm: Ps 130:1–2, 3–4, 5–6, 7–8
Second Reading: 2 Cor 4:13—5:1
Gospel: Mk 3:20–35

In today's selection from Mark, Jesus makes a massive claim, a claim that is magnified when placed alongside the first reading. In answer to the scribes who accuse him of casting out demons by the prince of demons, Jesus offers a short parable. "No one can enter a strong man's house to plunder his property unless he first ties up the strong man" (Mk 3:27). Jesus is claiming the power of God to bind up the forces of evil on the last day (see Is 24:22). And because he wields the power of God—the Holy Spirit—those who reject him reject God and put themselves beyond forgiveness. Christian tradition has sometimes applied God's words to the serpent in Genesis, today's first reading— "He will strike at your head, / while you strike at his heel" (3:15)—to the power of Jesus over the enemy of God and of God's people.

Today's Gospel begins and ends with references to Jesus' family. In the concluding verses, Jesus redefines membership in his family on the basis of active faith—"whoever does the will of God is my brother and sister and mother" (Mk 3:35). This is the community Paul also envisions, the family of those who believe and therefore speak tirelessly to the glory of God. Is this our family?

C

First Reading: 1 Kgs 17:17—24
Responsorial Psalm: Ps 30:2, 4, 5—6, 11, 12, 13
Second Reading: Gal 1:11—19
Gospel: Lk 7:11—17

All three readings for this Sunday are stories of God interven-ing in people's lives to comfort the afflicted in the stories from the First Book of Kings and the Gospel of Luke, and to afflict the comfortable in the case of Paul. Several points of con-tact can be seen between the raising of the widow of Zarephath's son by Elijah, and the raising of the widow of Nain's son by Jesus. This is to be expected, since Luke modeled his story on the one from Kings, even to the phrase, "[Jesus] gave him to his mother" (Lk 7:15; see 1 Kgs 17:23). Yet, prescinding from these formal similarities, it is striking to see in both stories God's intervention on behalf of women who, bereft of husbands and sons, find them-selves largely unprotected in a male-dominated world.

The intervention of God in Paul's life works in the opposite direction. God's grace calls Paul from his former way of life in Judaism and deprives him of the privileged status he once enjoyed as a zealot for his ancestral traditions. Yet in all three sto-ries, the result of divine intervention is the same: God is glorified—by the widow of Zarephath, by the audience of Jesus, and by the church in Jerusalem finally persuaded of Paul's con-version. "So they glorified God because of me," he says (Gal 1:24). Has the intervention of God in our lives worked to the glory of his name?

Tenth Week in Ordinary Time

MONDAY

YEAR I   *First Reading: 2 Cor 1:1–7*
         Responsorial Psalm: Ps 34:2–3, 4–5, 6–7, 8–9
YEAR II *First Reading: 1 Kgs 17:1–6*
         Responsorial Psalm: Ps 121:1bc–2, 3–4, 5–6, 7–8
YEARS I AND II *Gospel: Mt 5:1–12*

❦❦❦

Matthew's version of the Beatitudes of Jesus emphasizes their thoroughly Jewish character. In form and in content, each one echoes the Hebrew Scriptures, with the difference that Jesus' Beatitudes are eschatological. They announce happiness in the future, when the reign of God inaugurated by Jesus will be fully realized. As Daniel Harrington explains, "the Beatitudes function not as 'entrance requirements' but rather as ... an appropriate eschatological reward" for the meek and the merciful, the pure of heart, and the makers of peace.[17] Jesus says that the reign of God belongs to such as these.

Consolation is the theme of all three of today's readings. Paul assures the Corinthians that "the God of all encouragement" (2 Cor 1:3) will comfort them who share in the sufferings of Christ. God comforts Elijah, one of the few faithful servants of God left in Israel during the reign of Ahab and Jezebel. The Beatitudes of Jesus console the poor and the persecuted by promising them abundant life in God's kingdom. May the God of all consolation touch and transform our lives so that we, in turn, may touch the lives of others.

Tuesday

Year I   *First Reading: 2 Cor 1:18–22*
       Responsorial Psalm: Ps 119:129, 130, 131, 132, 133, 135
Year II   *First Reading: 1 Kgs 17:7–16*
       Responsorial Psalm: Ps 4:2–3, 4–5, 7b–8
Years I and II *Gospel: Mt 5:13–16*

The sayings of Jesus that Matthew records in today's Gospel are biblically based. In the Hebrew Bible, salt as a preservative is used as a metaphor in a number of different senses. But combining light with the city on a hill clearly points to the prophecy of Isaiah. There the prophet speaks of the days to come, when all the nations shall stream to the mountain of the Lord's house that towers above the hills to be instructed in God's ways. Therefore, he calls the house of Jacob to "walk in the light of the Lord!" (Is 2:5). The image of light dominates today's psalms as well. Psalm 119 associates light with the revelation of God's word (v. 130), while in Psalm 4 it describes God's face (v. 7).

Jesus' message is clear. Just as the miracle Elijah worked invited a Sidonian widow to recognize the power of Israel's God, and just as God intended faithful Israel to be a beckoning light to the nations, so must we who follow Jesus incite others to praise God our heavenly Father by our good works. As Paul would say, it is for this that God has anointed us, sealed us, and deposited the Spirit in our hearts (see 2 Cor 1:21–22).

WEDNESDAY

YEAR I   First Reading: 2 Cor 3:4–11
            Responsorial Psalm: Ps 99:5, 6, 7, 8, 9
YEAR II   First Reading: 1 Kgs 18:20–39
            Responsorial Psalm: Ps 16:1b–2ab, 4, 5ab and 8, 11
YEARS I AND II Gospel: Mt 5:17–19

The somewhat complicated distinction that Paul makes in 2 Corinthians 3 between the surpassing glory of the new covenant and the fading glory of the former one may be misleading. He seems to be saying that the new covenant has rendered the Mosaic Law obsolete. But scholars are not so sure he meant that. For our purposes, it is enough to note the force of Jesus' own words, reported by Matthew in today's Gospel: "Until heaven and earth pass away, not the smallest letter … will pass from the law, until all things have taken place" (5:18).

Paul's main concern in 2 Corinthians 3 is to defend his ministry as an apostle. His credentials have been challenged, and he responds by affirming that his qualifications come from God alone. In the contest on Mount Carmel, Elijah challenges the prophets of Baal to give proof of their credentials, and his success shows him to be the true prophet of the Lord, who alone is God. As for us, Jesus tells us that whatever credibility we have as followers of Christ lies in our obeying God's commandments and teaching others to do so, too.

THURSDAY

J esus does not claim that his teaching is superior to Jewish tradition in the Law and the Prophets; rather, he calls his followers to a superior observance of that tradition. Their holiness must surpass that of the scribes and Pharisees. He explains what he means in a series of "antitheses," or contrasts, all structured in the same way: "You have heard … But I say to you. . . ." In each case, Jesus' interpretation of a given law cuts to its core, the better to expose its meaning and to express it in practical terms. In today's reading, for example, he recognizes that anger and abuse often lie at the root of murder, and so he prohibits these behaviors. But Jesus' teaching is more than prohibition; he also underscores the overriding importance of reconciliation.

Reconciliation characterizes the ministry of Elijah and Paul as well. Elijah's whole life is spent calling Israel and its royal house to return to the Lord their God, as expressed in today's selection. Never preaching himself but only Jesus Christ, Paul works to remove the veil that keeps his people and all peoples from knowing "the glory of God on the face of Jesus Christ" (2 Cor 4:5–6).

Friday

In today's Gospel, Jesus continues to interpret the law and the prophets. He says that as anger lies at the root of murder, so lust lies at the root of adultery. He adds a stern warning: "If your right hand causes you to sin, cut it off and throw it away" (Mt 5:30). The urgency and the intimacy of his language betray his personal knowledge of our frail and fallen humanity. After all, he is our brother. Paul, too, knows all about human frailty. "We are afflicted in every way," he writes to the Corinthians (2 Cor 4:8). And in 1 Kings the prophet Elijah, having been "constantly … given up to death," as Paul might say (2 Cor 4:11), finally gains the safety of Mount Horeb (Sinai) only to have God send him back into the fray.

Elijah, Paul, and the human Jesus were all "earthen vessels" like us (2 Cor 4:7). Through them and through us the power of God is revealed. Like them, we must often seek out the mountain, that place of prayer, where God speaks in "a tiny whispering sound" (1 Kgs 19:12) and then sends us back into the fray.

SATURDAY

YEAR I   *First Reading: 2 Cor 5:14–21*
          Responsorial Psalm: Ps 103:1–2, 3–4, 9–10, 11–12
YEAR II   *First Reading: 1 Kgs 19:19–21*
          Responsorial Psalm: Ps 16:1b–2a and 5, 7–8, 9–10
YEARS I AND II *Gospel: Mt 5:33–37*

In this Gospel, Jesus may seem to be abolishing the commandment against swearing, but in fact, he is challenging his hearers to live it radically and rigorously. This is what it means to "fulfill" the law, that is, to bring it to its fullest expression. Some have argued that Jesus is presenting an ideal beyond the reach of all but the most heroic. But that misses the point. According to Joachim Jeremias, the Sermon on the Mount in Matthew was a catechism for newly baptized Christians. Therefore, he says, "it was preceded by conversion, by a being overpowered by the Good News."[18] The rigorous, radical way of life that Jesus outlined is intended for those who are already, in Paul's words, "in Christ ... a new creation" (2 Cor 5:17). Thus reconciled with God, they are able to live a new life.

The brief episode from 1 Kings describes the call of Elisha, who is "overpowered" by Elijah and compelled to leave everything and follow him. So the love of Christ impels us to live for him.

Eleventh Sunday in Ordinary Time

A

First Reading: Ex 19:2–6a
Responsorial Psalm: Ps 100:1–2, 3, 5
Second Reading: Rom 5:6–11
Gospel: Mt 9:36—10:8

Today's readings sound the theme of divine election, that is, God's choice of Israel and us. The familiar passage from Exodus is the preamble to the great covenant-making event on Mount Sinai. In these verses God makes an overture. The people of Israel have already experienced God's initiative on their behalf in their divinely-driven Exodus from Egypt. But if they are to be God's cherished possession, they must freely ratify God's choice of them. God does not want puppets but partners in a relationship of mutual respect. In the Gospel, too, a group is selected and set apart to be partners in Jesus' ministry. However, the text is carefully structured to make clear that God has chosen them. Moved by the enormity of the work to be done, Jesus does not immediately recruit the twelve disciples. Rather, he tells them to ask God to send laborers. So when he later summons them, it is as though God has answered their prayer.

The text from Romans is a meditation on the death of Jesus, the cost of God's choice of us. Like Israel, we, too, have been ransomed, but at what price! To acknowledge this is really to "know that the LORD is God; / he made us, his we are" (Ps 100:3).

B

First Reading: Ez 17:22–24
Responsorial Psalm: Ps 92:2–3, 13–14, 15–16
Second Reading: 2 Cor 5:6–10
Gospel: Mk 4:26–34

Today's excerpt from the prophecy of Ezekiel enables us to understand and appreciate the humor of Jesus' parable of the Mustard Seed. The imagery of Ezekiel speaks to Israel's hope of future glory among the nations of the earth. God will take a tender shoot and plant it on a high mountain where it will become a majestic cedar, like the one mentioned in today's psalm (see Ps 92:13). That this image inspired the parable of Jesus is apparent in his observation "that the birds of the sky can dwell in its shade" (Mk 4:32; see Ez 17:23). But Jesus has comically reduced the scale of the image from lofty tree to large plant. As Pheme Perkins explains, this is Jesus' way of recasting "people's images of themselves and of what it means for God to rule in the world."[19]

Points of contact are present between today's second reading from 2 Corinthians and Jesus' parable of the seed that grows in secret. Both describe a time of waiting before the harvest, when we must walk and work "by faith, not by sight" (2 Cor 5:7). And for this time, both counsel courage and creative fidelity. Only thus shall we "bear fruit even in old age" (Ps 92:15).

C

First Reading: 2 Sm 12:7–10, 13
Responsorial Psalm: 32:1 2, 5, 7, 11
Second Reading: Gal 2:16, 19–21
Gospel: Lk 7:36——8:3 or 7:36–50

Reflecting on this Sunday's readings leads to the conclusion that only those who recognize the grace of God are moved to act hospitably toward others. The story from Luke makes the point most clearly. The once sinful woman loved much, says Jesus, because she was grateful that God had forgiven her many sins. On the other hand, Simon's inattentiveness to Jesus, a guest at his table, revealed his failure to recognize and respond to the offer of God's grace. The same logic applies in God's rebuke of David for the murder of Uriah. Because he failed to acknowledge the countless ways in which God had graced him—and having counted a few, God says, "I could count up for you still more" (2 Sm 12:8)—David acted with murderous inhospitality toward the Hittite and his wife.

The brief excerpt from Galatians continues Paul's account of how he confronted Peter on the issue of hospitality to Gentiles. Paul says that if indeed we recognize that we have been saved by the grace of God in Christ, if we truly believe that by God's grace we live now, not our old lives as Gentiles or Jews, but the new life of the risen Lord, then we must not allow the divisions of the old order to keep us from the same table.

Eleventh Week in Ordinary Time

Monday

Year I   *First Reading: 2 Cor 6:1–10*
         Responsorial Psalm: Ps 98:1, 2b, 3ab, 3cd–4
Year II *First Reading: 1 Kgs 21:1–16*
         Responsorial Psalm: Ps 5:2–3ab, 4b–6a, 6b–7
Years I and II *Gospel: Mt 5:38–42*

A t first glance, Naboth's refusal of King Ahab's offer seems to contradict the spirit that Jesus urges upon his hearers in today's Gospel. But it is only a seeming contradiction. The teaching of Jesus did not oppose the law of Israel but sought only to fulfill it. The "law of retaliation," which he cites in today's reading, can be found in Exodus 21, Leviticus 24, and Deuteronomy 19. The purpose of the law was to prevent the escalation of violence. Far from abolishing the law, Jesus proposes another way of accomplishing the same goal. Ahab's offer to purchase Naboth's vineyard, however, was a violation of Israel's law. Leviticus 25:23 prohibited the sale of ancestral lands, "for the land is mine," says God, "and you are but aliens who have become my tenants."

On the other hand, Paul exemplifies Jesus' teaching by always acting with patient endurance in the face of violence. Armed with only the "weapons of righteousness" (2 Cor 6:7), he not only endures but enriches many.

Tuesday

Year I   *First Reading: 2 Cor 8:1–9*
        Responsorial Psalm: Ps 146:2, 5–6ab, 6c–7, 8–9a
Year II   *First Reading: 1 Kgs 21:17–29*
         Responsorial Psalm: Ps 51:3–4, 5–6ab, 11 and 16
Years I and II *Gospel: Mt 5:43–48*

The "law of retaliation" fully operates in today's reading from 1 Kings. God sends Elijah to confront and condemn Ahab for the murder of Naboth. Ahab will suffer the same fate as Naboth, even to the goriest detail. Yet sincere repentance wins Ahab a reprieve. The destruction of his house is postponed to the next generation. Thus do we see that the God of Israel is indeed the God of Jesus, the heavenly Father who makes the sun to rise and the rain to fall on "the bad and the good . . . the just and the unjust (Mt 5:45). This is the "wealth of generosity" (2 Cor 8:2) that Paul wants to inspire in the Corinthian community as well. To that end, he holds up the example of the churches of Macedonia, whose generous donation to the collection spills over from their total self-donation to God.

Totality is the key to the last verse of the Gospel reading, which tells us to be perfect "as your heavenly Father is perfect." The Hebrew Bible never describes God as "perfect" (Mt 5:48). The word here points rather to God's wholeness revealed in his surpassing and sometimes surprising generosity. It is this we are called to imitate.

WEDNESDAY

YEAR I *First Reading: 2 Cor 9:6–11*
        Responsorial Psalm: Ps 112:1bc–2, 3–4, 9
YEAR II *First Reading: 2 Kgs 2:1, 6–14*
        Responsorial Psalm: Ps 31:20, 21, 24
YEARS I AND II *Gospel: Mt 6:1–6, 16–18*

In today's Gospel taken from the Sermon on the Mount, Jesus comments on three acts of traditional Jewish piety—almsgiving, prayer, and fasting. The fact that Matthew has preserved these sayings of Jesus indicates that Christians also practiced these religious acts. As he touches on each one in turn, Jesus cautions against making any one of these private acts of piety into a self-serving public display. To do so is to forfeit any reward from the heavenly Father. In 2 Corinthians, Paul is especially concerned with the practice of almsgiving. He writes to encourage everyone to give "without sadness or compulsion" (2 Cor 9:7), confident that the Father who sees in secret will repay. The psalmist proclaims this message as well when he declares blessed the God-fearing man who gives lavishly to the poor (Ps 112:1, 9).

The reading from 2 Kings may help us to appreciate how private prayer may be richly repaid. It describes the powerful and empowering religious experience of Elisha. Leaving the fifty guild prophets on the other side of the Jordan, Elisha learns the secret of Elijah's power and returns with the prophet's mantle and a double portion of his spirit.

THURSDAY

YEAR I   First Reading: 2 Cor 11:1–11
         Responsorial Psalm: Ps 111:1b–2, 3–4, 7–8
YEAR II   First Reading: Sir 48:1–14
         Responsorial Psalm: Ps 97:1–2, 3–4, 5–6, 7
YEARS I AND II Gospel: Mt 6:7–15

The relationship between Elijah and Elisha, celebrated by Sirach in today's reading, was Luke's model for the relationship between Jesus and his followers. As Elisha stood watching Elijah being taken up to heaven, the disciples watched the ascension of Jesus. And as Elisha received a double portion of Elijah's spirit, the disciples on Pentecost received the Spirit of their risen Lord. Thus it was that they came to share his passion and his power. Although he was not there on the day of Pentecost, Paul was filled with the same fiery zeal and made the Gospel of God revealed in Christ Jesus his unceasing boast. The new *Catechism* tells us that when we pray the first three petitions of the Our Father—the Gospel for today—we, too, are seized by "the burning desire ... of the beloved Son for his Father's glory" (no. 2804*).

The first three petitions of the Our Father are summed up in the central one: "Thy Kingdom come" (Mt 6:10). All three long for the reign of God to come in its fullness. To pray for this is to ask the Father to bring to completion the saving work begun in Christ.

"This is how you are to pray," Jesus teaches us today (Mt 6:9).

---

* Cf. Lk 22:14; 12:50.

FRIDAY

YEAR I   *First Reading: 2 Cor 11:18, 21–30*
          Responsorial Psalm: Ps 34:2–3, 4–5, 6–7
YEAR II   *First Reading: 2 Kgs 11:1–4, 9–18, 20*
          Responsorial Psalm: Ps 132:11, 12, 13–14, 17–18
YEARS I AND II *Gospel: Mt 6:19–23*

In today's selection, the author of 2 Kings concludes the story of Ahab. The promised destruction of Ahab's house, punishment for the murder of Naboth, was deferred until his children succeeded him. Athalia, Ahab's daughter, ruled the land of Judah for six years. Then in the seventh year, Jehoiada the priest made a clean sweep of the royal house. For the people of Judah, his action was a defining moment. Not only did he return Ahaziah's son to power, but he renewed the people's covenant with God as well. Thus, having recovered their heavenly treasure, they were able to reorder their hearts. "All the people … rejoiced and the city was quiet" (2 Kgs 11:20).

In the Gospel for today, Jesus, like the priest Jehoiada, calls his disciples to clarify their vision and values, too. He reminds them that what they cherish will determine what they choose. Second Corinthians shows Paul as living proof of that. This catalog of Paul's sufferings in the service of the Gospel is truly remarkable. Only a man whose "eye is sound" (Mt 6:22), who sees everything in the light of Christ, could bear such hardships and more.

SATURDAY

YEAR I   *First Reading: 2 Cor 12:1–10*
         Responsorial Psalm: Ps 34:8–9, 10–11, 12–13
YEAR II   *First Reading: 2 Chr 24:17–25*
         Responsorial Psalm: Ps 89:4–5, 29–30, 31–32, 33–34
YEARS I AND II *Gospel: Mt 6:24–34*

"No one can serve two masters," Jesus declares in today's Gospel. "He will either hate one and love the other, or be devoted to one and despise the other" (Mt 6:24). The short story from 2 Chronicles is a case in point. Torn between their priest and the princes of Judah, Joash and his people forsook the God of their fathers, ignored God's prophets, and slew Jehoiada's son, Zechariah, in the Temple court.

The word "mammon," sometimes rendered as "money," may be the key to Jesus' meaning in today's Gospel. It is derived from the Hebrew *'mn'* which means "trust." Jesus' words raise precisely that issue: in whom or in what will we put our trust? There is no doubt as to where the psalmist stands: "Those who seek the LORD want for no good thing" (Ps 34:11), he declares. There is no doubt of Paul's answer either. Trusting absolutely in the power of God, whose grace is always enough, he boasts only of his weaknesses. He says, "I am content with weaknesses, insults, hardships, persecutions, and constraints, for the sake of Christ," then adds paradoxically, "for when I am weak, then I am strong" (2 Cor 12:10). Why are you anxious?

Twelfth Sunday in Ordinary Time

A

First Reading: Jer 20:10–13
Responsorial Psalm: Ps 69:8–10, 14, 17, 33–35
Second Reading: Rom 5:12–15
Gospel: Mt 10:26–33

The themes of mission and suffering converge in today's readings from Jeremiah's prophecy and from Matthew's Gospel. The confession of Jeremiah exposes the depth of his suffering in the service of God's word, but also the depth of his trust that God is with him. This trust is based on his knowledge of God as the mighty champion of the powerless and poor. As the psalmist proclaims, "The LORD hears the poor, / and his own who are in bonds he spurns not" (Ps 69:34). The so-called "mission discourse" in Matthew 10 assumes that some suffering is inevitable for those who share the mission of Jesus. In these few verses, Jesus repeats the phrase "do not be afraid" no less than three times (Mt 10:26, 28, 31), and he encourages the disciples to place their trust in God on the basis of their knowledge of God's care for all creation, even for the smallest sparrow.

Such trust in God can only be bolstered by reflection on Paul's instruction to the Christians in Rome. For "the gift is not like the transgression" (Rom 5:15), which is to say that in and through the gift of Christ comes the overflow of God's grace that sweeps away transgression. For us who place our trust in God, eternal life, not death, prevails. Do not be afraid.

B

First Reading: Jb 38:1, 8–11
Responsorial Psalm: Ps 107:23–24, 25–26, 28–29, 30–31
Second Reading: 2 Cor 5:14–17
Gospel: Mk 4:35–41

The significance of the authority Jesus demonstrates in Mark's account of the calming of the sea is elucidated by the few verses from Job in the first reading and anticipated in the words of Psalm 107. God spoke to Job "out of the storm" (Jb 38:1) and "hushed the storm to a gentle breeze" (Ps 107:29). Jesus displays this power, and none other, when he calms the storm at sea. And it answers the disciples' question: "Who then is this whom even wind and sea obey?" (Mk 4:41).

Such cosmic display of Jesus' power enables us to better appreciate what Paul tells the Corinthians in today's second reading. He writes to explain the consequence of the death of Jesus. Recalling a familiar creedal formula, "one died for all," he says that "therefore, all have died" (2 Cor 5:14). Having died with Christ on the cross means that the life we live now is in every way "a new creation" (v. 17). We no longer see things as we did before. Furthermore, our new perspective is cosmic in scope. Now we know that the old order has passed away and that the new heavens and the new earth have been established by the death and rising of Jesus, in which we share.

C

First Reading: Zec 12:10–11; 13:1
Responsorial Psalm: Ps 63:2, 3–4, 5–6, 8–9
Second Reading: Gal 3:26–29
Gospel: Lk 9:18–24

The mysterious oracle of Zechariah may seem to resonate with the two New Testament readings for today. But the reader must be warned that the meaning of these verses is far from certain. The prophet announces an outpouring of the spirit that will move the people to true repentance in which the whole society will take part (see Zec 12:12–13). Their new inner attitude will be the result of God's initiative, for it is God who will pour out the spirit. This is akin to what Paul says of Christian baptism. To be baptized into Christ is to live a new life, to have a new inner attitude, which is Christ's. This new life in Christ has ramifications for the whole social order. The divisions of the old order—on the basis of ethnic identity, socioeconomic status, and gender—cease to exist (see Gal 3:27–28).

In a very difficult verse to decipher, the oracle of Zechariah also alludes to one "whom they have pierced" and for whom they shall mourn as "for an only son" (12:10). Whoever Zechariah had in mind, Christians can only think of Jesus (see Jn 19:37), who, in today's Gospel, predicts his passion and calls us to follow him. In this setting, it is interesting to hear the words of today's Psalm 63 as coming from the lips of Jesus, the suffering Son of Man, as well as our own.

Twelfth Week in Ordinary Time

MONDAY

YEAR I   *First Reading: Gn 12:1–9*
         Responsorial Psalm: Ps 33:12–13, 18–19, 20 and 22
YEAR II   *First Reading: 2 Kgs 17:5–8, 13–15a, 18*
          Responsorial Psalm: Ps 60:3, 4–5, 12–13
YEARS I AND II *Gospel: Mt 7:1–5*

The gift promised to Abram in the reading from Genesis is for-feited by Israel in the selection from 2 Kings. Unlike Abram, who "went as the LORD directed him" (Gn 12:4), the Israelites went their own way, rejecting "the covenant which [God] had made with their fathers" (2 Kgs 17:15). So God condemned them to the cruel tyranny of Assyria. God's anger here, as elsewhere in the Bible, gives God's judgment an emotional force, which is difficult for us to bear. But as Abraham Heschel explains, in the Bible, "Anger, too, is a form of [God's] presence in history. Anger, too, is an expression of [God's] concern."[20] That is why biblical people, though fully aware of the terrifying reality of God's anger, came not only to tolerate it, but to trust it as well.

The biblical image of God as judge underlies Jesus' warning against passing judgment in today's Gospel. Jesus tells us that God alone is judge, and this God will pass on us the verdict we so glibly pass on others.

TUESDAY

YEAR I   *First Reading: Gn 13:2, 5—18*
          Responsorial Psalm: Ps 15:2—3a, 3bc—4ab, 5
YEAR II   *First Reading: 2 Kgs 19:9b—11, 14—21, 31—35a, 36*
          Responsorial Psalm: Ps 48:2—3ab, 3cd—4, 10—11
YEARS I AND II *Gospel: Mt 7:6, 12—14*

The sayings of Jesus in today's passage from Matthew seem to comment on the two first readings. Jesus' summary of "the Law and the Prophets" (Mt 7:12) is reminiscent of a well-known story about Hillel, a rabbi who died when Jesus was about ten years old. A scoffer once asked Hillel if he could teach him the whole Torah while he stood on one foot. Hillel replied, "What is hateful to you do not do to your neighbor; that is the whole Torah; go and study it" (Babylonian Talmud, *Shabbat* 31a,b). In the view of both Hillel and Jesus, Abraham's treatment of Lot in today's reading from Genesis anticipates the Golden Rule and so fulfills the Torah.

Jesus goes on, calling his hearers to "enter through the narrow gate ... that leads to life" (Mt 7:13—14). The notion of the two ways, or two gates as Jesus puts it, is also found in the Hebrew Scriptures. In Deuteronomy 30, for example, Moses sets before his people life and death, blessing and curse, and urges them to "choose life" (v. 19). Hezekiah faces this choice in the reading from 2 Kings: to take the path of least resistance by submitting to Assyria's demands, or to take the less-traveled road of trust in the living God. And his trust is rewarded, his kingdom spared. And we, where do we place our trust?

WEDNESDAY

YEAR I   *First Reading: Gn 15:1–12, 17–18*
          Responsorial Psalm: Ps 105:1–2, 3–4, 6–7, 8–9
YEAR II   *First Reading: 2 Kgs 22:8–13; 23:1–3*
          Responsorial Psalm: Ps 119:33, 34, 35, 36, 37, 40
YEARS I AND II *Gospel: Mt 7:15–20*

Today's two first readings take up the theme of covenant. In Genesis, God "cuts" a covenant with Abraham in a ritual that seems strange to us but is attested to in Jeremiah 34. In 2 Kings the people of Judah, having recovered "the book of the law" (22:8) that was lost when the Temple was desecrated during the reign of a previous king, renew their covenant with God. These stories convey two aspects of covenant. God's covenant with Abraham underscores the graciousness of God, who here goes so far as to assume the obligations of the covenant by passing like a flaming torch between the animals. The account from 2 Kings, on the other hand, focuses on the covenant obligations that fall upon the people. These are contained in the book of the law, which scholars believe to be a version of Deuteronomy. The sayings of Jesus in today's Gospel stress this point, too.

Jesus declares that false prophets are known not by their words but by their deeds. For prophets, as for all God's people then and now, covenant fidelity consists in keeping God's statutes and decrees with their whole hearts and souls.

Thursday

In today's two first readings, Sarai and Jehoiachin are both trag-ically conditioned by the world in which they find themselves. Sarai's abuse of Hagar is deplorable, but Sarai is the product of a patriarchal society in which a woman's worth was determined by her ability to bear male heirs for her husband. She is caught in what Megan McKenna describes as "an interlocking set of oppressions" that pit one woman against the other.[21] The young king Jehoiachin "did evil in the sight of the LORD," but Jehoiachin is the end of a long line of unscrupulous kings and queens who routinely ignored the warnings of God's prophets (see 2 Kgs 24:9). He is heir to a royal house that was built "on sandy ground" (see Mt 7:26). So it will collapse, completely ruined. This is not to excuse either Sarai or Jehoiachin, but only to note that they were products of the culture in which they lived.

We are no different. Born and raised in a Christian culture, we easily cry out, "Lord, Lord" (Mt 7:21). But Jesus demands more. It is not enough to hear his words, but we must put them into practice with raised consciousness and renewed heart.

FRIDAY

YEAR I   *First Reading: Gn 17:1, 9—10, 15—22*
         Responsorial Psalm: Ps 128:1—2, 3, 4—5
YEAR II   *First Reading: 2 Kgs 25:1—12*
         Responsorial Psalm: Ps 137:1—2, 3, 4—5, 6
YEARS I AND II *Gospel: Mt 8:1—4*

In today's Gospel, a leper approaches Jesus and asks to be
cured. Having just concluded the Sermon on the Mount, Jesus
responds in a way that shows him as powerful in deed as he has
been in word. Just as he insisted in the Sermon that he had not
come to abolish the law and the prophets, so here he sends the
leper to the priest to fulfill the requirement of the law as set forth
in Leviticus 14. Clearly, Matthew wants us to see Jesus as a true
son of Abraham, a faithful Jew who walks blamelessly in God's
presence.

Sadly, the same cannot be said of Zedekiah in the reading from
2 Kings. Zedekiah was Jehoiachin's uncle, whom the Babylonians
installed as king after Jehoiachin and his entourage were led into
captivity. But Zedekiah would not heed the word of the Lord
spoken through the prophet Jeremiah. Had the king done so, he
would have died in peace. Once again divine judgment is accomplished in the history of God's people. Only this time, the agent
of God is not Assyria but Babylon. The Temple is burned, the city
walls torn down, and fifty years of exile begin "by the streams of
Babylon" (Ps 137:1).

Saturday

Year I   *First Reading: Gn 18:1–15*
        Responsorial Psalm: Lk 1:46–47, 48–49, 50 and 53, 54–55
Year II *First Reading: Lam 2:2, 10–14, 18–19*
        Responsorial Psalm. Ps 74:1b–2, 3–5, 6–7, 20–21
Years I and II *Gospel: Mt 8:5–17*

All three of today's readings are child-centered. In the passage from Genesis, Abraham's three visitors announce that Sarah will bear a child. In the poem from Lamentations, the laughter of Sarah is answered by the tears of the mothers of Jerusalem, whose children faint from hunger and breathe their last in their arms. And in the Gospel, a centurion asks Jesus to cure his servant boy. Although the passages are not at all alike, an air of expectancy pervades all three and finds explicit expression in the Canticle of Mary that serves today as a responsorial psalm. Sarah, the desperate women of Jerusalem, and the centurion all wait on the power of God that has done great things for Mary. They hope it will do for them, too, what they cannot do for themselves— bring new life to the barren womb, the ravaged city, the sick child.

Jesus commends the centurion's words: "I too am a man subject to authority" (Mt 8:9), which is to say, "I know power when I see it." So must we, for recognition of God's power revealed in Jesus admits us from east and west to the table with Abraham, Isaac, and Jacob, in the kingdom of heaven (Mt 8:11).

Thirteenth Sunday in Ordinary Time

A

First Reading: 2 Kgs 4:8–11, 14–16a
Responsorial Psalm: Ps 89:2–3, 16–17, 18–19
Second Reading: Rom 6:3–4, 8–11
Gospel: Mt 10:37–42

Jesus' saying in today's Gospel—"Whoever receives a prophet because he is a prophet will receive a prophet's reward" (Mt 10:41)—is illustrated in the short story from the Second Book of Kings. For receiving Elisha because he is a prophet and "a holy man of God," the Shunammite woman receives as reward the biblical equivalent of eternal life. She will have a son. In a sense, this is the principle operative in the excerpt from Paul's Letter to the Romans. By receiving Jesus Christ "raised from the dead" because we know him to be the Christ, we receive a share in his "reward," that is, in his life for God "by the glory of the Father" (Rom 6:4). This is no cheap grace, however, for receiving Jesus worthily means dying to sin, to self, and finding newness of life in him.

The death to self required of those who would follow Jesus has social, as well as spiritual, ramifications. It may even disrupt family life. Although Matthew has softened the saying of Jesus considerably by rendering the verb "hate" (see Lk 14:26) as "loving more than," his words warn us that the Gospel may require everything we cherish, including family life. But as the psalm says, the promises of the Lord are sure; his faithfulness—and our reward—are confirmed in heaven.

B

First Reading: Wis 1:13–15; 2:23–24
Responsorial Psalm: Ps 30:2, 4, 5–6, 11, 12, 13
Second Reading: 2 Cor 8:7, 9, 13–15
Gospel: Mk 5:21–43 or 5:21–24, 35b–43

In today's Gospel, Mark interweaves two stories of Jesus in order to make the point that the author of the Book of Wisdom makes in the Old Testament reading: God wills life, not death; and the death that entered the world by the envy of the devil is undone by faith in Jesus.

The interweaving of the two stories by Mark depends on their similarities, most obviously on the desperation of each one and the daring faith required of them both in the face of contrary "professional" opinions—the many doctors, in the woman's case, and the mourners at Jairus's house. Both Jairus and the ailing woman seem to be people of means. His position as synagogue official suggests as much; and although she has exhausted her resources, it has apparently taken her twelve long years to do it. Yet, as they both must acknowledge, all the money in the world cannot save or secure life. Thus the categories of poverty and riches are redefined by "the gracious act of our Lord Jesus Christ," whose poverty makes us rich (2 Cor 8:9), or in the words of the psalmist, whose "good will" changes mourning into dancing (Ps 30:6, 12).

C

First Reading: 1 Kgs 19:16b, 19–21
Responsorial Psalm: Ps 16:1–2, 5, 7–8, 9–10, 11
Second Reading: Gal 5:1, 13–18
Gospel: Lk 9:51–62

⋘⊙⋙

"**F**or freedom Christ set us free" (Gal 5:1). Paul's words are a clarion call, urging us to live in the freedom of the children of God. As Paul himself goes on to say, however, that freedom is not license but a call to serve. It is exemplified in today's Gospel by Jesus' resolute determination to journey to Jerusalem where he will be "taken up" on the cross (Lk 9:51), then in the cloud into heaven (see Acts 1:9–11).

The divine necessity that impels Jesus must move his followers as well; this is made clear by his response to the three would-be disciples. If Luke's Jesus is Elijah-like, then Jesus' disciples resemble Elisha, Elijah's successor, who was endowed with a double portion of Elijah's spirit (see 2 Kgs 2:9). In today's readings the juxtaposition of the call of Elisha with the Gospel text makes the point. As the cloak of Elijah falls upon Elisha, so will the disciples of Jesus be clothed with power from on high, that is, the Holy Spirit. Also the request to bid farewell to kith and kin, missing from Matthew's version of this story, again points to Luke's intention that the call of Jesus' disciples be likened to that of Elijah's successor. The point is that the Spirit of God both calls us to freedom and compels us to follow the prophet Jesus, who sets his face to Jerusalem and never looks back.

Thirteenth Week in Ordinary Time

MONDAY

YEAR I   *First Reading: Gn 18:16–33*
         Responsorial Psalm: Ps 103:1b–2, 3–4, 8–9, 10–11
YEAR II *First Reading: Am 2:6–10, 13–16*
         Responsorial Psalm: Ps 50:16bc–17, 18–19, 20–21, 22–23
YEARS I AND II *Gospel: Mt 8:18–22*

D ivine judgment appears in both of today's first readings. In Genesis, the Lord visits the cities of Sodom and Gomorrah to determine if their actions correspond to the outcry against them, while the prophecy of Amos announces a day of judgment for "three crimes of Israel, and for four" (Am 2:6). In both, the Lord God is understood to be "the judge of all the world" (Gn 18:25). Abraham's conversation with God probes and proves the justice of the divine judge. As judge, God is as anxious as Abraham to distinguish between the innocent and the guilty, so the bargaining is pressed to its natural limit. Abraham, who has been called to father a people who keep the way of the Lord by doing what is just, learns that the judge of all the world does indeed act justly.

The excerpt from Matthew's Gospel includes a hard saying about discipleship. Scholars agree that the words of Jesus—"Let the dead bury their dead" (Mt 8:22)—are a "hyperbole," a deliberate exaggeration intended to shock. Jesus means that even the solemn obligation of burying the dead must yield to the demands of true discipleship.

TUESDAY

YEAR I   *First Reading: Gn 19:15–29*
        Responsorial Psalm: Ps 26:2–3, 9–10, 11–12
YEAR II *First Reading: Am 3:1–8; 4:11–12*
        Responsorial Psalm: Ps 5:4b–6a, 6b–7, 8
YEARS I AND II *Gospel: Mt 8:23–27*

The two first readings present two sides of divine election. God's choice of Abraham meant blessing not only for himself, but also for everyone associated with him. Lot is a good example. As we hear in today's reading, God spared Lot and his family because of Abraham. But with God's choice of Abraham and his descendants came the responsibility of keeping God's commandments. When they failed to do so, as at the time of Amos the prophet, the people of Israel were not spared the fury of God's wrath, despite their being God's chosen people. "You alone have I favored, / more than all the families of the earth," says the Lord, "therefore I will punish you / for all your crimes" (Am 3:2). Clearly, divine favor was not divine favoritism.

Today's Gospel depicts the familiar scene of Jesus calming the storm, a story found in Mark and Luke as well. One distinctive feature of Matthew's version is Jesus' addressing his disciples as *oligopistoi*, "little-faiths" (8:26). They have some faith, but not always enough. They are like us. So like them we pray to the one "whom even the winds and the sea obey": "Lord, save us!" (vv. 27, 25).

Wednesday

Year I   First Readings: Gn 21:5, 8–20a
          Responsorial Psalm: Ps 34:7–8, 10–11, 12–13
Year II   First Reading: Am 5:14–15, 21–24
          Responsorial Psalm: Ps 50:7, 8–9, 10–11, 12–13, 16bc–17
Years I and II Gospel: Mt 8:28–34

The story from Genesis and the words of Amos stand in a jar-ring juxtaposition. Sarah's jealousy and Hagar's banishment strangely seem to be condoned by God, the same God who condemns the sacrifices of Israel, asking only that "justice surge like water, / and goodness like an unfailing stream" (Am 5:24). The key may be to borrow Matthew's strategy in today's Gospel. As Matthew retells the story of the Gerasene demoniac (actually, Gadarene demoniacs, plural, since there are two in Matthew), which he took from Mark, he makes several changes. For example, he sums up in a few words Mark's detailed description of the demoniac's behavior before the exorcism, and omits altogether his request to follow Jesus after it. These changes keep the story focused on Jesus.

In the same way we must keep our eyes on God when we read the story of Hagar. God's command, not Sarah's contempt, controls the action of the story. "Do not be distressed about the boy or about your slave woman," God tells Abraham (Gn 21:12). Then God acts to vindicate both women—Sarah, through whose child Abraham's line will continue, and Hagar, whose son will also be made a great nation.

THURSDAY

YEAR I   *First Reading: Gn 22:1b–19*
         Responsorial Psalm: Ps 115:1–2, 3–4, 5–6, 8–9
YEAR II *First Reading: Am 7:10–17*
         Responsorial Psalm: Ps 19:8, 9, 10, 11
YEARS I AND II *Gospel: Mt 9:1–8*

Controversy swirls around Amos and Jesus in today's readings. The words of Amos threaten the priest of Bethel, who tells Jeroboam, "The country cannot endure all [the prophet's] words" (7:10). Similarly, Jesus' words trouble some scribes. "This man is blaspheming," they think (Mt 9:3). Amos responds by recounting the story of how God took him from his flocks and his sycamore trees to be a prophet. Jesus answers by healing the paralytic. "Which is easier to say?" he asks (v. 5). By dramatizing his power over sickness, he raises the possibility at least that he also has power over sin. Even his critics are awed.

In the Bible, testing proves the faith of God's people. As he reads the story of the testing of Abraham, Sean McEvenue finds that it tests the reader as well. The author's narrative technique, he says, aims "directly at making readers participants in the story."[22] The dialogue, sparse as it is, and the painfully detailed description of the action of the story keep the reader enthralled until the angel's call breaks the tension. With Abraham, we are challenged to trust God absolutely and to learn again that God will provide.

Friday

Year I   First Reading: Gn 23:1–4, 19; 24:1–8, 62–67
         Responsorial Psalm: Ps 106:1b–2, 3–4a, 4b–5
Year II First Reading: Am 8:4–6, 9–12
         Responsorial Psalm: Ps 119:2, 10, 20, 30, 40, 131
Years I and II Gospel: Mt 9:9–13

Today's Gospel finds Jesus once again at odds with the Pharisees who object to his eating with sinners. When reading such conflict stories, we must remind ourselves of Jesus' close association with the Pharisees. Some scholars believe that the Pharisees so strongly criticized Jesus' table fellowship because he sometimes also ate with them. Even the quote from Hosea that Matthew has added to the punch line of this story, "'I desire mercy, not sacrifice'" (Mt 9:13; see Hos 6:6) is not intended to depict Jesus against the Jews. As Matthew certainly knew, after the Temple was destroyed in A.D. 70, the rabbis themselves read this passage to mean that works of mercy could replace Temple sacrifice as a way of attaining forgiveness of sins. In today's reading, Abraham's last task is to insure that Isaac will continue his father's journey without ever turning back. Jesus and the Pharisees wanted this for all Israel; they simply disagreed on how to achieve it.

Amos also proclaimed that God wants mercy, not sacrifice, and that he would turn their feasts into famine because they exploited the poor. As mercy defined the mission of Jesus, who came to call sinners, so must it describe our lives as his disciples.

SATURDAY

YEAR I   *First Reading: Gn 27:1–5, 15–29*
          Responsorial Psalm: Ps 135:1b–2, 3–4, 5–6
YEAR II   *First Reading: Am 9:11–15*
          Responsorial Psalm: Ps 85:9ab and 10, 11–12, 13–14
YEARS I AND II *Gospel: Mt 9:14–17*

In the Bible, blessing means fullness of life. This theme holds together today's three readings. In the passage from Genesis, "the fertility of the earth" shows forth God's blessing as it yields an "abundance of grain and wine" (27:28). The prophecy of Amos also expresses that same abundant life in agricultural terms: "The plowman shall overtake the reaper, / and the vintager, him who sows the seed" (9:13). In the Gospel, however, Jesus prefers wedding imagery to talk about the blessings that accompany the arrival of God's reign in him and his ministry.

These passages also show that God's blessing often comes in unexpected ways. Rebekah orchestrates Jacob's deception of Isaac to secure the all-important birthright for her second son. Yet, far from passing a moral judgment on mother or son, the inspired author simply acknowledges that God is not bound by the conventional arrangement that gave preference to the first-born son. The point is that, in the words of the psalm, "The LORD has chosen Jacob for himself" (135:4). Similarly in the Gospel, Jesus, speaking in parables, declares that in him God is again blessing Israel in a new way that shakes up and shatters old categories and conventions.

Fourteenth Sunday in Ordinary Time

A

First Reading: Zec 9:9–10
Responsorial Psalm: Ps 145:1–2, 8–9, 10–11, 13–14
Second Reading: Rom 8:9, 11–13
Gospel: Mt 11:25–30

Because we have the Spirit of Christ, Paul tells us in the reading from Romans, we are debtors of God. This means that we are under obligation to God alone; we belong to God. Today's Gospel tells us further that our belonging to God is by God's choice, and the prayer of Jesus expands on the biblical theme of God's preference for the "childlike," the powerless, and the poor who "labor and are burdened" (Mt 11:28).

This divine preference for the poor may be because, unlike the privileged, the poor are debtors by definition. They can more readily understand what it means to be under obligation, dependent on God, as they so often must depend on others. Perhaps, too, God knows that because they are powerless, the poor must be able to imagine other ways of having than by owning, other ways of ruling than by conquering. This makes them more apt to recognize in the one who comes riding on an ass a King who brings the hope of peace to the nations. To submit to the yoke of Christ is to slip out of the yoke of convention. It is a quantum leap of the imagination that sees indebtedness to God as the only true freedom.

B

First Reading: Ez 2:2–5
Responsorial Psalm: Ps 123·1–2, 2, 3–4
Second Reading: 2 Cor 12:7–10
Gospel: Mk 6:1–6

"**A** prophet is not without honor except in his native place and among his own kin and in his own house" (Mk 6:4). These words of Jesus from Mark's Gospel apply to all three of the readings for this Sunday. Ezekiel is warned in a vision that he will meet with resistance from the rebellious house of Israel, his own people to whom he is sent. Paul's words to the Corinthians are excerpted from a section often referred to as his "letter in tears" (2 Cor 10–13). It is Paul's appeal to his beloved Corinthians; they have betrayed him by transferring their allegiance to the high-powered "super apostles" who have seduced them with their eloquent, ecstatic speech. In the Gospel, Jesus is rejected by the people of Nazareth, his native place.

The experience of all three—familiarity breeding contempt —invites us to ask ourselves: Do we, obstinate of heart, refuse to hear the prophet's word? Are we, like the Corinthians, impressed by showy rhetoric but impervious to the grace that comes in weakness? Or are we, like the people of Nazareth, so lacking in faith that Jesus cannot act powerfully among us? The psalmist's prayer is interesting in this light: "Have pity on us, O LORD ... / for we are more than sated with contempt" (123:3). Are we?

C

First Reading: Is 66:10–14c
Responsorial Psalm: Ps 66:1–3, 4–5, 6–7, 16, 20
Second Reading: Gal 6:14–18
Gospel: Lk 10:1–12, 17–20 or 10:1–9

Paul concludes his letter to the Galatians by returning to a theme that appears in virtually all of his uncontested letters. He writes, "May I never boast except in the cross of our Lord Jesus Christ" (Gal 6:14). "Boasting" is a favorite Pauline expression. More than bragging rights are intended. For Paul, boasting is an expression of absolute confidence not in oneself as Jew or Gentile, "circumcision or uncircumcision" (see Gal 6:15) but in God, whose grace is revealed in Christ. Far from glory seeking, it gives glory to the God who seeks to make us in Christ a new creation. Likewise, Jesus in the Gospel tells the seventy-two disciples, newly returned from their first foray as missionaries, not to glory in their success, however sensational, but "because your names are written in heaven" (Lk 10:20), that is, because they belong to God, to whom all glory is ultimately due.

In today's first reading, the prophet, who is also a poet, looks to the eventual restoration of Jerusalem not by human achievement but by God's grace. He invites Israel to boast in the Lord whose power "shall be known to his servants" (Is 66:14). This invitation is extended to all the earth, even by the psalmist when he calls upon all to see and to sing praise to the glory of God's name (Ps 66:2).

Fourteenth Week in Ordinary Time

MONDAY

YEAR I   *First Reading: Gn 28:10–22a*
         Responsorial Psalm: Ps 91:1–2, 3–4, 14–15ab
YEAR II *First Reading: Hos 2:16, 17c–18, 21–22*
         Responsorial Psalm: Ps 145:2–3, 4–5, 6–7, 8–9
YEARS I AND II *Gospel: Mt 9:18–26*

Today's two first readings speak of a sacred place where human beings come close to the living God. Genesis speaks of Jacob's so-called "ladder" with the messengers of God "going up and down on it" (28:12). The ladder connects earth and heaven, suggesting "open lines" of communication between the two. In Hosea, the desert to which God draws Israel is the place of espousal, where God speaks and Israel responds "as in the days of her youth" (2:17). More striking still is the content of God's speech in both selections. To Jacob, God says, "Know that I am with you; I will protect you wherever you go" (Gn 28:15). And to the people of Israel, God's words are a pledge of everlasting love.

In today's Gospel, the person of Jesus is the sacred place where two individuals come into contact with the living God. Here as well is movement in two directions. The synagogue leader wants Jesus to touch his daughter; the ailing woman wants to touch Jesus. As the new *Catechism* says, this is the dynamic of prayer, where God's desire and ours intersect (no. 2560*).

---

* Cf. St. Augustine, *De diversis quaestionibus octoginta tribus* 64, 4: *Patrologia Latina* 40, 56.

TUESDAY

YEAR I   *First Reading: Gn 32:23–33*
       Responsorial Psalm: Ps 17:1b, 2–3, 6–7ab, 8b and 15
YEAR II *First Reading: Hos 8:4–7, 11–13*
       Responsorial Psalm: Ps 115:3–4, 5–6, 7ab–8, 9–10
YEARS I AND II *Gospel: Mt 9:32–38*

The story of Jacob's struggle with God, one of today's first readings, is variously interpreted. The *Catechism of the Catholic Church* secs it as "the symbol of prayer as a battle of faith" (no. 2573*). All the readings for today deal with this battle. An irony underlies the idolatry of Israel, which Hosea so strenuously condemns: when they "made many altars to expiate sin," he says, their "altars became occasions of sin" (8:11). Hosea did not condemn the altars but the lack of discernment of the people who used them. Similarly in the Gospel, the mixed reaction to Jesus' healing of the demoniac who was also mute suggests the necessary struggle that Jesus' ministry precipitated among his people.

The spiritual life is a mysterious battle, demanding a daily, disciplined discernment, lest our altars become occasions of sin. Struggling with God is a costly grace. It may mean many dark nights of wrestling with beings divine and human. But from this battle we emerge as "wounded healers," like Jacob, who goes limping to meet his long lost brother.

---

* Cf. Gn 32:24–30; Lk 18:1–8.

WEDNESDAY

YEAR I   *First Reading: Gn 41:55–57; 42:5–7a, 17–24a*
          Responsorial Psalm: Ps 33:2–3, 10–11, 18–19
YEAR II   *First Reading: Hos 10:1–3, 7–8, 12*
          Responsorial Psalm: Ps 105:2–3, 4–5, 6–7
YEARS I AND II *Gospel: Mt 10:1–7*

⌘

Agricultural motifs figure in all three of today's readings. The Genesis text is a much abridged version of the story of Joseph and his brothers. A famine brings Jacob's sons to Egypt and leads to their eventual reconciliation with Joseph. Hosea uses agricultural imagery to reinforce his claim that God, not the Baals, controls fertility. In the Gospel, Jesus directs his newly named apostles not into pagan territory but to "the lost sheep of the house of Israel" (Mt 10:6). In all three passages, God is at work, however imperceptibly, to create new opportunities.

In Genesis the poignant self-recriminations that his brothers make in his hearing move Joseph, a God-fearing man, not to revenge but to a reconciliation that will mean prosperity for his brothers. The words Hosea addresses to Israel are as much a summons as a sentence. They are motivated by God's hope that Israel might once again sow justice and reap piety. And from our vantage point, we know that Jesus' instructions to the Twelve that the good news of God's reign be proclaimed first to the house of Israel will one day expand to include the ends of the earth.

THURSDAY

YEAR I   *First Reading: Gn 44:18–21, 23b–29; 45:1–5*
              Responsorial Psalm: Ps 105:16–17, 18–19, 20–21
YEAR II   *First Reading: Hos 11:1–4, 8e–9*
              Responsorial Psalm: Ps 80:2ac and 3b, 15–16
YEARS I AND II *Gospel: Mt 10:7–15*

The two first readings for today paint powerful pictures of parental love. The climax of the story of Joseph and his brothers—Joseph's self-disclosure—is preceded by Judah's moving speech. Dramatically, he pleads with Joseph to spare Benjamin for the sake of Jacob, their father, who dotes on his youngest child. It is a plea for Jacob's life, for he has warned Judah that the loss of Benjamin would send his "white head down to the nether world in grief" (Gn 44:29). In the passage from Hosea, God is the doting parent whose heart is overwhelmed at the thought of his child's destruction. So God determines not to vent his anger against them. Even a cursory reading of the Old Testament shows that this is a recurring theme in Israel's experience with God. What makes this passage uniquely powerful, however, is that it exposes the very core of God's being as totally other than ourselves. "I will not destroy ... For I am God and not man, / the Holy One present among you" (Hos 11:9).

Against this background, today's Gospel exhorts all of us who are sent to do what Jesus did. We must work as he did to make present and palpable in the world the holiness of God, who has no will to destroy.

FRIDAY

YEAR I   *First Reading: Gn 46:1–7, 28–30*
          Responsorial Psalm: Ps 37:3–4, 18–19, 27–28, 39–40
YEAR II   *First Reading: Hos 14:2–10*
          Responsorial Psalm: Ps 51:3–4, 8–9, 12–13, 14 and 17
YEARS I AND II *Gospel: Mt 10:16–23*

A ll three of today's readings sound the theme of divine reassurance. On his way to Egypt, Jacob (aka Israel) stops at Beersheba, where God speaks to him in a vision: "Do not be afraid to go down to Egypt, for there I will make you a great nation" (Gn 46:3). The prophecy of Hosea concludes with divine reassurance that, though he has collapsed through his guilt, Ephraim (Israel, the people this time) will prosper once more, for God's wrath will turn away from them. In the Gospel, Jesus sends his disciples out "like sheep in the midst of wolves" (Mt 10:16). They will be tried by rulers and kings, but they must not worry about their defense. For just as the God of his father will go down to Egypt with Jacob, so will the Spirit of their Father speak for the disciples of Jesus.

In Matthew's arrangement of Jesus' words in today's Gospel, signs of God's future—such as the gift of the Spirit and the division of families—appear as present realities. Already the Gospel divides family members, and the Spirit must defend disciples persecuted for their faith. For Matthew, God's future has already arrived.

Saturday

All of today's readings call our attention to God's holiness. In the Bible, holiness is not static perfection but the total and dynamic otherness of God. It is dramatically displayed in today's account of Isaiah's call. Here God's holiness is acclaimed by seraphim and accompanied by earthquake and smoke, elements that usually attend the manifestation of God. Isaiah knows that in the presence of such holiness, a sinful human being is doomed. In the Gospel, Jesus urges his disciples not to fear human beings but God, who alone is Lord of life. In the Bible, such fear of God consists in recognizing that only God is God.

The story of Joseph offers a practical example of the biblical fear of God, experienced by Isaiah and expressed in Jesus' teaching. After the death of their father, Joseph's brothers fear that he may now want to kill them, so somewhat disingenuously, they beg his forgiveness. Joseph's answer acknowledges that there is one God, only one. "Can I take the place of God?" he asks (Gn 50:19). Thus he shows himself to be a God-fearing man. In the language of the psalmist, he is "a descendant of Abraham" and a true "son of Jacob" (Ps 105:6).

Fifteenth Sunday in Ordinary Time

A

First Reading: Is 55:10–11
Responsorial Psalm: Ps 65:10, 11, 12–13, 14
Second Reading: Rom 8:18–23
Gospel: Mt 13:1–23 or 13:1–9

In Romans 8, Paul boldly declares his faith in the future: "I consider that the sufferings of this present time are as nothing compared with the glory to be revealed for us," he says (v. 18). How can he be so confident? Because he trusts absolutely in the firstfruits that the Spirit, that seed of fire, has already produced, namely, the resurrection of Jesus in which we and all creation can hope to share. Jesus' parable is also a confident assertion about the future of the Gospel, which, borrowing the language of Isaiah, he likens to seed. As the word of God in Isaiah will surely achieve the end for which it was sent, so will the good news of Jesus, against all odds, produce an abundant harvest.

A subtle shift takes place in the focus and the intended audience of the explanation of Jesus' parable. The focus moves from the seed to the soil that receives it, and the hearers are no longer the crowd but the disciples of Jesus. What this does is draw us who consider ourselves disciples into the line of fire. Jesus asks us now as he asked his inner circle then to test the quality of the soil we bring to the hearing of the Gospel.

B

First Reading: Am 7:12–15
Responsorial Psalm: Ps 85:9–10, 11–12, 13–14
Second Reading: Eph 1:3–14 or 1:3–10
Gospel: Mk 6:7–13

Today's readings juxtapose blessing and curse. Ephesians opens with an extravagant prayer in which God is blessed —thanked and praised—for every spiritual blessing (gift). According to Ephesians, of all these gifts the greatest by far is God's choice of us in Christ. Every spiritual blessing is summed up in this one: holiness, adoption as God's children, redemption, forgiveness of sins, wisdom, and knowledge of the mystery of God's plan and purpose. As a result of this incomparable gift, we exist for the praise of God's glory; that is to say, our whole lives must be a prayer of praise and thanksgiving. Today's psalm strikes the same note: it celebrates God's gifts ("benefits"), above all, his salvation as "glory dwelling in our land" (Ps 85:13, 10).

If praise is to be the first response to the gift of God in Christ, then proclamation must follow immediately. So Jesus sends the Twelve to preach repentance to the villages around Nazareth. They are authorized to proclaim in word and deed the gift of God revealed in Jesus. But Jesus warns them from his own experience, like that of Amos before him, that they must be prepared to meet rejection by "shaking the dust from their feet" (see Mk 6:11), symbolically rejecting those who, to their peril, reject God's blessing.

C

First Reading: Dt 30:10–14
Responsorial Psalm: Ps 69.14, 17, 30–31, 33–34, 36, 37; Ps 19:8, 9, 10, 11
Second Reading: Col 1:15–20
Gospel: Lk 10:25–37

An element of deflation appears in each of today's three read-ings. In the passage from Deuteronomy, Moses assures the people that the word of God, Torah, is not so exalted or exotic as to be beyond their reach. Rather, it is very near, already in their hearts; they have only to do it. The hymn in Colossians depicts an exalted cosmic Christ. Yet the author of Colossians, with one small addition to the text, brings Christ very near, within reach of everyone, by locating him not only in the cosmos, but also in the Church, which is his body.

Jesus' injunction, "Do this and you will live," deflates the ego of the lawyer who is commended for correctly quoting the law of love from the Jewish Scripture. It is as though the greatest commandment loses luster when it becomes a practical demand. But Jesus, like Moses, will not relent. He tells the man the para-ble we know perhaps too well and repeats: "Go and do likewise." In the Torah of Israel and the teaching of Jesus, it all comes down to being a good neighbor to all in need (Lk 10:28, 37).

Fifteenth Week in Ordinary Time

MONDAY

YEAR I   *First Reading: Ex 1:8–14, 22*
       Responsorial Psalm: Ps 124:1b–3, 4–6, 7–8
YEAR II   *First Reading: Is 1:10–17*
        Responsorial Psalm: Ps 50:8–9, 16bc–17, 21 and 23
YEARS I AND II *Gospel: Mt 10:34–11:1*

"The one sent by a man is as the man himself."* This Jewish legal principle stands behind Jesus' words in today's Gospel: "Whoever receives you receives me, and whoever receives me receives the one who sent me" (Mt 10:40). This saying uncovers the deepest meaning of Christian mission. The Christian missionary is to make Christ present as Christ makes God present in the world.

The identity of the one sent to represent Christ gives a key to the other two readings. He or she is "one of these little ones" (Mt 10:42). In other words, acceptance or rejection of Christ is signified by one's treatment of the lowly. They are his representatives. This is the sense of the passage from Isaiah as well. God tells the people that true worship lies in hearing the orphan's plea and defending the widow, the lowly who are God's agents among us. Finally, the words of Isaiah and Jesus both reflect the touchstone of Jewish law recalled in the reading from Exodus: for you were once despised strangers yourselves in the land of Egypt (see Ex 22:20).

* m. *Bereshit* 5:5.

TUESDAY

❧⟐❧

Fear is a moving force in the two first readings. Fear of Pharaoh makes a fugitive of Moses, and fear of the Syro-Ephraimite alliance causes the hearts of King Ahaz and his people to tremble "as the trees of the forest tremble in the wind" (Is 7:2). In both situations, faith in God is lacking. Moses has not yet met the God of his father, and Ahaz lacks the courage that Isaiah urges upon him.

The last line of the reading from Isaiah—"Unless your faith is firm, / you shall not be firm!" (7:9)—serves as a bridge to the Gospel reading. This verse is a play on words, using two forms of the same verb, *aman*, which means "to be firm," and is the root of our word "amen." This verb is used often of the house of David, whose throne, God has promised, shall stand firm forever. But this promise, Isaiah tells Ahaz, requires faith to be effective. Jesus says much the same thing to Capernaum and the neighboring towns. They have been privileged to see his miracles, "mighty deeds" that would have moved the people of Sodom to repent (Mt 11:23), but they have failed to respond with firm faith. So they, like the house of David, will be liable to judgment—as will we unless we repent.

WEDNESDAY

YEAR I   *First Reading: Ex 3:1–6, 9–12*
         Responsorial Psalm: Ps 103:1b–2, 3–4, 6–7
YEAR II *First Reading: Is 10:5–7, 13b–16*
         Responsorial Psalm: Ps 94:5–6, 7–8, 9–10, 14–15
YEARS I AND II *Gospel: Mt 11:25–27*

Taken together, the two first readings are a study in contrasts. Both Moses in the passage from Exodus and Assyria in the prophecy of Isaiah are chosen to be God's instruments. God sends both against "an impious nation" (Is 10:6). But what a difference in their response! The overweening pride of Assyria as it boasts, "By my own power I have done it" (v. 13), contrasts sharply with the meekness of Moses, who protests, "Who am I that I should go to Pharaoh and lead the children of Israel out of Egypt?" (Ex 3:11). As Jesus proclaims in the Gospel, God is revealed "to the childlike"—the meek like Moses (see Nm 12:3) —and not to "the wise and the learned" (Mt 11:25).

The conclusion of today's Gospel selection is sometimes called the "Johannine logion" because it resembles the rhetoric of the fourth Gospel. It depicts Jesus as the Son who knows the Father and who alone can make the Father known. In a sense, Jesus, too, is God's instrument, God's servant, as well as God's Son, sent to reveal the Father, who is "Lord of heaven and earth" (Mt 11:25). Like Moses, Jesus recognizes with thankful praise "All things have been handed over to me by my Father" (v. 27).

THURSDAY

YEAR I   *First Reading: Ex 3:13–20*
           Responsorial Psalm: Ps 105:1 and 5, 8–9, 24–25, 26–27
YEAR II   *First Reading: Is 26:7–9, 12, 16–19*
           Responsorial Psalm: Ps 102:13–14ab and 15, 16–18, 19–21
YEARS I AND II *Gospel: Mt 11:28–30*

Both the reading from Exodus and the selection from Matthew offer rest to the weary. Indeed, the invitation Jesus extends to his disciples is very much like the invitation God extends to the Israelites through Moses. It is a promise of rest—release from oppression and fruitless toil. Jesus describes this rest as a "yoke," and this word, often used to refer to the Law of Moses, links the two invitations. What is promised here is not cheap grace. The people of God will find rest in the land "flowing with milk and honey" (Ex 3:17) by keeping God's commandments, just as the disciples of Jesus find refreshment by conforming to the likeness of Christ, who is "meek and humble of heart" (Mt 11:29). As Matthew says, this is the lighter, more liberating yoke.

The passage from Isaiah is a psalm of lament. It is the prayer of the man or woman who looks back contritely on days of fruitless labor—"We conceived and writhed in pain, / giving birth to wind" (Is 26:18)—and longs now, with joyful hope, for the salvation that only God can give.

FRIDAY

YEAR I   *First Reading: Ex 11:10—12:14*
          Responsorial Psalm: Ps 116:12–13, 15 and 16bc, 17–18
YEAR II   *First Reading: Is 38:1–6, 21–22, 7–8*
          Responsorial Psalm: Is 38:10, 11, 12abcd, 16
YEARS I AND II *Gospel: Mt 12:1–8*

Today's two Old Testament readings depict the saving work of God. The selection from Exodus recounts "the Passover of the Lord," when God devastated the Egyptians and delivered the Israelites from their oppression. The story from Isaiah retells Hezekiah's recovery from a mortal illness by the grace of God, who heard his prayer and saw his tears. The prayer of Hezekiah is reprised in the responsorial psalm. "Those live whom the LORD protects," he declares (Is 38:16).

Today's Gospel attests to Jesus' liberal view of Sabbath law. By recalling the example of David and the exception made for the priests, Jesus seems to say that, although the Pharisees sharply criticize his view, it has a precedent in Jewish Scripture. However marginal, he remains a Jew. But even more important, by referring to the text of Hosea—"I desire mercy, not sacrifice" (6:6)—Jesus, Lord of the Sabbath, seems to suggest that Sabbath is best kept by practicing compassion and so imitating the saving work of God. Surely, "something greater than the temple is here" (Mt 12:6).

SATURDAY

YEAR I   *First Reading: Ex 12:37–42*
          Responsorial Psalm: Ps 136:1 and 23–24, 10–12, 13–15
YEAR II   *First Reading: Mi 2:1–5*
          Responsorial Psalm: Ps 10:1–2, 3–4, 7–8, 14
YEARS I AND II *Gospel: Mt 12:14–21*

The two first readings present two contrasting images—one of imminent triumph, the other of impending tragedy. The Exodus reading describes the triumphal march of the Israelites when the Lord "led them out of the land of Egypt" (12:42). Micah's prophecy, however, proclaims punishment for these people who are now oppressing one another after having escaped oppression in Egypt. The prophet knows that rampant injustice has already led to the downfall of Samaria; he announces the same tragic end for Judah. On that day, he warns, they will not "walk with head high, / for it will be a time of evil" (Mi 2:3).

In today's Gospel, Matthew uses the words of another prophet to shed light on the activity of Jesus. Scholars tell us that these words were originally addressed to the people of Judah in exile in Babylon, and the servant is a symbol of the chosen people. Isaiah promises that they will again triumph not by war but by a way of life that "will proclaim justice to the Gentiles" (Mt 12:18; see Is 42:1–4). Many years later, Matthew saw in the ministry of Jesus the fullest realization of the vocation of God's people.

Sixteenth Sunday in Ordinary Time

A

First Reading: Wis 12:13, 16–19
Responsorial Psalm: Ps 86:5–6, 9–10, 15–16
Second Reading: Rom 8:26–27
Gospel: Mt 13:24–43 or 13:24–30

In today's Gospel, the lesson of the parable of the Weeds and the Wheat is succinctly stated in the lines from Wisdom, which speak of God as just but kind. What is particularly striking in these verses is the balance the author achieves between God's might and God's mercy. In his view, God's leniency proves God's power. As he puts it, "Your mastery over all things makes you lenient to all" (Wis 12:16). The same sense is conveyed in Jesus' parable. It presents an interesting contrast between the calm restraint of the householder and the high anxiety of his slaves. As soon as the weeds appear, the slaves look for someone to blame. They even suggest that the householder has not sown good seed, and they are ready to act immediately to rid the crop of noxious weeds. He, on the other hand, acts with practical wisdom, confident that his wheat can tolerate the presence of the weeds. He knows his patience will be rewarded at the harvest.

The power and patience of God is also demonstrated in Romans in the intercession of the Spirit, who takes our muddled and mixed messages and turns them into prayer.

B

First Reading: Jer 23:1–6
Responsorial Psalm: Ps 23·1–3, 3–4, 5, 6
Second Reading: Eph 2:13–18
Gospel: Mk 6:30–34

The first and second readings for today seem to play on a number of contrasting images. The oracle of Jeremiah contrasts false leaders with that righteous shoot who shall govern wisely; bad shepherds with the Good Shepherd, who is God; the present time of dispersion and distress with the coming days of salvation. His message is a word of hope for exiled Israel. The excerpt from Ephesians invites Gentile Christians to contrast their prior status with their present life in Christ. They who were once far off have been brought very near. The dividing wall that separated Jew and Gentile has given way; there is now, in place of the two, one new humanity with one route of access to the Father. The message is a word of hope for Jews and Gentiles estranged from God and from one another. Both readings proclaim God's intention to gather the sheep so that there will be one flock and one shepherd (see Jn 10:16).

That is the mission of Jesus in today's Gospel. The sight of "the vast crowd ... like sheep without a shepherd," fills him with compassion. "And he began to teach them" (Mk 6:34). What he will teach them and us is another contrast: bread in the wilderness, a table spread before us in the sight of our foes (Ps 23:5).

C

First Reading: Gn 18:1–10a
Responsorial Psalm: Ps 15:2–3, 3–4, 5
Second Reading: Col 1:24–28
Gospel: Lk 10:38–42

The theme of hospitality links today's reading from Genesis with the Gospel from Luke. In the first reading Abraham hastens to extend the hospitality of his camp to three strangers. Unbeknownst to him, they are welcoming angels (see Heb 13:2). He has food prepared and waits on them while they eat. In the Gospel, Martha and Mary welcome Jesus. Martha is clearly head of that household, and it is she, like Abraham, who waits on their guests. Martha is ennobled by association with Abraham. She is no longer the distracted and disgruntled housekeeper of Christian preaching, an image never intended by Luke. Rather, the key to Luke's meaning lies in the word "serving" (*diakonian, diakonein*), which appears twice in the story. His point is that the Church, the household of God, must never become so caught up in service that it neglects the word of God (see Acts 6:2).

Today's reading from Colossians places Paul in the company of both Martha and Mary by describing him as a minister (*diakonia*) of the Church, whose stewardship is to bring to completion the word of God.

Sixteenth Week in Ordinary Time

MONDAY

YEAR I   *First Reading: Ex 14:5–18*
         Responsorial Psalm: Ex 15:1bc–2, 3–4, 5–6
YEAR II *First Reading: Mi 6:1–4, 6–8*
         Responsorial Psalm: Ps 50:5–6, 8–9, 16bc–17, 21 and 23
YEARS I AND II *Gospel: Mt 12:38–42*

Today's readings deal with the identity of God as Lord. God declares that in the crossing of the sea, "the Egyptians shall know that I am the LORD" (Ex 14:18). The Israelites will also find in this event an authenticating sign that indeed the Lord God is fighting for them. The passage from Micah indicts the people for their failure to remember this sign (see 6:4).

In the Gospel, Matthew depicts scribes and Pharisees asking for a similar authenticating sign from Jesus. But Jesus says that God will not give them a sign except the sign of Jonah, which for Matthew has a double meaning. On the one hand, it points to the death and resurrection of Jesus, the confirming sign par excellence that he is Lord. On the other hand, it likens Jesus to Jonah, just as the concluding verses liken him to Solomon. But the comparison is ironic: people responded positively to the preaching of Jonah and to the wisdom of Solomon, but negatively to the ministry of Jesus, who is greater than both Solomon and Jonah. And for this they will be indicted by the people of Nineveh and the queen of the south. And we, how do we respond to the sign of Jonah, the death and resurrection of Jesus?

Tuesday

Year I   First Reading: Ex 14:21—15:1
         Responsorial Psalm: Ex 15:8–9, 10 and 12, 17
Year II First Reading: Mi 7:14–15, 18–20
         Responsorial Psalm: Ps 85:2–4, 5–6, 7–8
Years I and II Gospel: Mt 12:46–50

If the theme of yesterday's Gospel was the identity of Jesus, authenticated by the sign of Jonah, the theme of today's reading is the identity of Jesus' family. The two first readings provide the link. The passage from Exodus recounts the awesome demonstration of God's power at the crossing of the sea, the authenticating sign that the God of Israel is Lord of all. The responsory that follows this reading is the so-called "Song of Moses"—a dramatic elaboration of the older "Song of Miriam" also in Exodus 15. The Song of Moses retells the story of that fateful night when God saved his people by casting "horse and chariot ... into the sea" (Ex 15:1). The prayer of the prophet Micah invokes this memory, asking God to act powerfully once again: "As in the days when you came from the land of Egypt, / show us wonderful signs" (Mi 7:15). Psalm 85 hints at the rest of that story. It celebrates the end of exile, many years after Micah's prayer. The need for authenticating signs goes on.

In the Gospel, however, Jesus asks us as his followers for a sign. Pointing to his disciples—then and now—he says that doing the will of his heavenly Father is the authenticating sign of membership in his family. The Gospel challenges us to ask ourselves how authentic is our membership in Jesus' family.

WEDNESDAY

YEAR I   *First Reading: Ex 16:1–5, 9–15*
          Responsorial Psalm: Ps 78:18–19, 23–24, 25–26, 27–28
YEAR II   *First Reading: Jer 1:1, 4–10*
          Responsorial Psalm: Ps 71:1–2, 3–4a, 5–6ab, 15 and 17
YEARS I AND II *Gospel: Mt 13:1–9*

Today's Gospel parable primarily concerns the seed, not the sower. The action of the story, which would have been so familiar to Galilean farmers, traces the "mission" of the seed. It meets with resistance and reversal of all kinds, yet still yields a rich harvest. Since the seed in the story is the word of God, the parable is a profession of faith in the power of God's word to overcome every obstacle.

The parable sheds light on the two first readings. Jeremiah is called and commissioned to speak the word of God, "to root up and to tear down, to destroy and to demolish, to build and to plant" (1:10). In his career as a prophet, he will come to know all too well the resistance and reversals that so often greet the seed of God's word. In the reading from Exodus, the grumbling of the Israelites—"Would that we had died ... in the land of Egypt" (16:3)—reminds us again of the unpromising condition of the soil in the parable—the human condition, which only the grace of God can make ready to receive God's word. Let us open our hearts to the action of God's grace in our lives.

Thursday

YEAR I   *First Reading: Ex 19:1–2, 9–11, 16–20b*
         Responsorial Psalm: Dn 3:52, 53, 54, 55, 56
YEAR II   *First Reading: Jer 2:1–3, 7–8, 12–13*
         Responsorial Psalm: Ps 36:6–7ab, 8–9, 10–11
YEARS I AND II *Gospel: Mt 13:10–17*

Their covenant with God on Sinai that is described in the account from Exodus fashioned Israel into the people of God. Thus, in the words of Jeremiah, they became "the first fruits of [God's] harvest" (2:3). Throughout their subsequent history, the people often debated the question: What constitutes membership in the community of God's people? This is the context of Matthew's Gospel.

The Christians for whom Matthew wrote were convinced that belonging to the people of God meant believing in Jesus as Messiah and Lord. They agonized over the question of why so many of their fellow Jews rejected the Gospel. In today's reading, Jesus tells his disciples that God has given them a privileged insight into the mysteries of God's reign. So they are more blessed than the prophets and saints before them. As for those who do not hear or understand, their refusal is part of God's plan, too. For us living in other times, today's Gospel may invite us to recognize and to reflect upon the inscrutable mystery of God's choice of Israel and of us.

FRIDAY

YEAR I   *First Reading: Ex 20:1–17*
         Responsorial Psalm: Ps 19:8, 9, 10, 11
YEAR II   *First Reading: Jer 3:14–17*
         Responsorial Psalm: Jer 31:10, 11–12abcd, 13
YEARS I AND II *Gospel: Mt 13:18–23*

Most scholars agree that the interpretation of the parable of the Sower found in today's Gospel is, in all likelihood, the work of the early Church. Note how the focus has shifted from the seed to the soil. In a message for the first Christians as well as us, the passage warns against all those things that may threaten the life of faith: the wiles of "the Evil One."

All the readings for today serve as examples of how the teaching of the Scriptures developed. The passage from Exodus is the earliest version of the Decalogue, the Ten Commandments. These words of God not only undergird the whole law of Israel, but they also undergo development as they are handed down to a generation in changed circumstances (see Dt 5:6–21).

The text from Jeremiah announces a development in which the Jerusalem Temple will replace the Ark of the Covenant as the Lord's throne (see 3:16). And the response to that reading, also from Jeremiah, foresees a further development, when the people now scattered among the nations are finally gathered and brought home (31:10).

The Gospel then shows how even the parables of Jesus were developed in new directions to speak to the needs of the emerging Church.

Saturday

Year I   *First Reading: Ex 24:3–8*
            Responsorial Psalm: Ps 50:1b–2, 5–6, 14–15
Year II   *First Reading: Jer 7:1–11*
            Responsorial Psalm: Ps 84:3, 4, 5–6a and 8a, 11
Years I and II *Gospel: Mt 13:24–30*

All three readings for today challenge God's people to faithful living. In the passage from Exodus, all twelve tribes of Israel formally ratify their covenant with God, committing themselves to observing all the words and ordinances of the Lord contained in the book of the covenant (Ex 24:3). But even as their covenant is sealed by blood, the readers know that they will struggle to live it faithfully in the midst of the uncovenanted nations who worship alien gods. In the selection from Jeremiah, the prophet reminds God's people of their covenant obligations by paraphrasing the Ten Commandments: "Are you to steal and murder, commit adultery and perjury, / burn incense to Baal, / go after strange gods...?" he asks them (7:9). His words are addressed to Temple-goers who in their everyday lives are continually being seduced by the wiles of the evil one.

With the realism characteristic of Jesus' parables, the Gospel story recognizes that those who live faithfully in this world often do so surrounded by those who do not. But the sower of the good seed, who is also the Lord of the harvest, is confident that the wheat can withstand the weeds and grow the stronger for it.

Seventeenth Sunday in Ordinary Time

A

First Reading: 1 Kgs 3:5, 7–12
Responsorial Psalm: Ps 119:57, 72, 76–77, 127–128, 129–130
Second Reading: Rom 8:28–30
Gospel: Mt 13:44–52 or 13:44–46

❧❧❧

"Do you understand all these things?" (Mt 13:51) Jesus asks in today's Gospel. Then he goes on to explain that understanding brings the old in contact with the new. Today's parables convey his meaning. Like the fisherman whose net collects fish of every kind, the person who is wise in God's ways must learn to discern the bad from the good. That goes without saying in view of the final judgment. But wisdom in the kingdom of heaven requires taking risks, too, like that of the merchant who sells all he has to buy the pearl of great price. Above all, Jesus seems to say, the wise must expect the unexpected. In the poet Wordsworth's phrase, borrowed by C. S. Lewis to speak of his conversion, they must be ever ready to be "surprised by joy." Such joy radically transforms by turning one's world on its head. All that was once so important is reassessed from this new perspective. This is the wisdom that Solomon seeks and that Jesus urges on his disciples.

Paul also invites us to see all things from the new perspective of God, who wills only what is good. "Do you understand all these things?" (Mt 13:51).

B

First Reading: 2 Kgs 4:42–44
Responsorial Psalm: Ps 145:10–11, 15–16, 17–18
Second Reading: Eph 4:1–6
Gospel: Jn 6:1–15

John's version of the multiplication of the loaves has points of contact with Elisha's miracle, today's first reading. Among them are the skepticism of the disciples, who object like Elisha's servant; the presence of the boy (not unlike Elisha's servant); and the mention of barley loaves. But this episode, set on a mountain at Passover time, is also reminiscent of Moses, who gave his people bread from heaven. Jesus' question, "Where can we buy enough food for them to eat?" (Jn 6:5) echoes the question of Moses, "Where can I get meat to give to all this people?" (Nm 11:13). As manna was given by God to test the people (see Ex 16:4), so does Jesus test Philip; and when all have had their fill, Jesus instructs the disciples to gather the fragments as Moses taught Israel to gather the manna each day (Ex 16:17).

The Greek of Jesus' command to gather the fragments— *klasmata*—is associated with Eucharist in the *Didache*, an early Christian manual. It likens the gathering of the Church for Eucharist to the gathering of eucharistic fragments into one. This is Paul's vision of unity as well—"one body and one Spirit" (Eph 4:4) because of the one loaf we share (see 1 Cor 10:17).

C

First Reading: Gn 18:20–32
Responsorial Psalm: Ps 138:1–2, 2–3, 6–7, 7–8
Second Reading: Col 2:12–14
Gospel: Lk 11:1–13

"**S**hould not the judge of all the world act with justice?" (Gn 18:25). Abraham's question lies, spoken or unspoken, on the tongue of every petitioner. Will God hear a just suit? Does God answer every prayer? Does God care? In today's New Testament readings, Jesus and Paul both join with the psalmist in responding to these questions with a resounding yes. Psalm 138 declares, "When I called you answered me; / you built up strength within me" (v. 3). "For everyone who asks, receives; and the one who seeks, finds; and to the one who knocks, the door will be opened," Jesus says emphatically (Lk 11:10). And Paul reiterates: "Even when you were dead in transgressions," incapable of hope or of prayer, God brought you to life with Christ, "having forgiven us all our transgressions" (Col 2:13).

But prayer requires persistence. Jesus is emphatic about that, too. The one who asks must ask repeatedly, like Abraham; the one who seeks must seek untiringly, like the grateful psalmist; the one who knocks must knock loudly, like the persistent Paul. And God, like a good father, will answer every prayer, if not with what we want, surely with all we need: the Holy Spirit.

Seventeenth Week in Ordinary Time

MONDAY

YEAR I   *First Reading: Ex 32:15–24, 30–34*
          Responsorial Psalm: Ps 106:19–20, 21–22, 23
YEAR II   *First Reading: Jer 13:1–11*
          Responsorial Psalm: Dt 32:18–19, 20, 21
YEARS I AND II *Gospel: Mt 13:31–35*

In the two first readings, Moses and Jeremiah are given similar roles to play: both are moved to identify sympathetically with God and with God's people. According to the *Catechism*, Moses' sympathy with God, as well as with his people, makes him "the most striking example of intercessory prayer ... [who] 'stands in the breach' before God in order to save the people" (nos. 2574,* 2577**). Today's reading from Exodus is one example of Moses' role as intercessor. In the passage from Jeremiah, the rotted loincloth is more than an image of destruction. By being made to wear the loincloth, Jeremiah comes symbolically to share God's own intimate attachment to "the whole house of Israel and the whole house of Judah" (Jer 13:11).

To grasp the message of the parables in today's Gospel also requires imaginative identification. Both a humble agent (the seed) and a hidden activity (the yeast) yield impressive results. Jesus invites us to take on the humble, hidden work of providing sheltering presence and nourishing bread in and for the world.

* 1 Tm 2:5.
** Ps 106:23; cf. Ex 32:1–34:9.

TUESDAY

YEAR I *First Reading: Ex 33:7–11; 34:5b–9, 28*
        Responsorial Psalm: Ps 103:6–7, 8–9, 10–11, 12–13
YEAR II *First Reading: Jer 14:17–22*
        Responsorial Psalm: Ps 79:8, 9, 11 and 13
YEARS I AND II *Gospel: Mt 13:36–43*

Again in today's Gospel we hear the early Church's interpretation of a parable of Jesus, the parable of the Wheat and Weeds. Note the shift in emphasis: the parable urges patience; the interpretation stresses punishment.

Without denying punishment, patience dominates the two first readings. In the text from Exodus, which the *Catechism* considers pivotal, "God hears Moses' prayer of intercession and agrees to walk in the midst of an unfaithful people" (no. 210*). Thus does God's name express God's patience: "The LORD, the LORD, a merciful and gracious God, slow to anger and rich in kindness and fidelity, continuing his kindness for a thousand generations, and forgiving wickedness and crime and sin" (Ex 34:6–7; CCC no. 211**). These qualities of God, elaborations of the divine name, are reprised in Psalm 103. Jeremiah's lament in the midst of the double calamity of drought and war also appeals to the divine patience promised by the name God revealed to Moses: "For your name's sake spurn us not" (Jer 14:21). Psalm 79, following upon the prayer of Jeremiah, also calls upon God to "deliver us and pardon our sins / for your name's sake" (v. 9).

* Cf. Ex 32; 33:12–17.
** Eph 2:4.

WEDNESDAY

YEAR I   *First Reading: Ex 34:29–35*
         Responsorial Psalm: Ps 99:5, 6, 7, 9
YEAR II   *First Reading: Jer 15:10, 16–21*
          Responsorial Psalm: Ps 59:2–3, 4, 10–11, 17, 18
YEARS I AND II *Gospel: Mt 13:44–46*

Today's three readings recall a phrase in which Paul assesses the cost of discipleship: "For this momentary light affliction is producing for us an eternal weight of glory beyond all comparison" (2 Cor 4:17). The phrase "an eternal weight of glory" is interesting because it is so etymologically precise. The Greek *doxa* translates the Hebrew *kavod*, which literally means "weight," hence "the weight of glory." The radiance of Moses' face signals his share as God's friend in God's unfading glory. The autobiographical passage from Jeremiah reveals his struggle under the weight of God's hand. Yet a glorious future awaits him, too: "If you bring forth the precious without the vile, you shall be my mouthpiece," God says (Jer 15:19).

The two short parables in today's Gospel cast Paul's statement in story form. When the treasure and the pearl are discovered, they relativize the value (the weight) of everything else. Both men eagerly sell all that they have in order to secure them. With these stories Jesus invites us into the company of Moses, Jeremiah, and Paul, the company of those who have glimpsed God's glory and have gladly given all to attain it.

THURSDAY

YEAR I   *First Reading: Ex 40:16–21, 34–38*
         Responsorial Psalm: Ps 84:3, 4, 5–6a and 8a, 11
YEAR II *First Reading: Jer 18:1–6*
         Responsorial Psalm: Ps 146:1b–2, 3–4, 5–6ab
YEARS I AND II *Gospel: Mt 13:47–53*

Each of today's readings discloses a different facet of God's dealings with people. Through the symbols of the dwelling (the tabernacle), the cloud by day and the fire by night, the Exodus text describes God's constant presence with the house of Israel "in all the stages of their journey" (40:38). The episode retold by Jeremiah depicts God as a potter, patient and painstaking in fashioning and refashioning the house of Israel, the work of his hands. The parable of the Net returns to the theme of God as judge at the end of the world, when "angels will go out and separate the wicked from the righteous" (Mt 13:49).

Taken together, these readings provide the outline for the life of every person in relationship with God. Each life is a journey, a pilgrimage with many stages. As Psalm 84 suggests, the goal is finally to attain the true dwelling of the living God. All along the way, the pilgrim is being shaped and reshaped like clay in the potter's hands. At the end comes the judgment, the sorting out described in Jesus' parable and ascribed by Matthew to the discerning scribe who brings from his stores "both the new and the old" (13:52).

Friday

Year I   *First Reading: Lv 23:1, 4–11, 15–16, 27, 34b–37*
         Responsorial Psalm: Ps 81:3–4, 5–6, 10–11ab
Year II *First Reading: Jer 26:1–9*
         Responsorial Psalm Ps 69:5, 8–10, 14
Years I and II *Gospel: Mt 13:54–58*

Today's readings show us Jeremiah and Jesus as two prophets found to be too much for those to whom they are sent. The people of Judah react angrily to the words of Jeremiah, refusing to heed his warning of impending doom. The amazement of the people of Nazareth gives way to incredulity as they reflect on Jesus' roots in their village. "Is he not the carpenter's son? Is not his mother named Mary...?" (Mt 13:55). Consequently, having rejected the prophet's words, the house of Judah will fall. The Temple will be destroyed and the city devastated. Similarly, the lack of faith among the people in his native place will mean that Jesus cannot work many miracles there. These stories may cause us to wonder if we also fail to hear the words of God-sent prophets, either because they are too fearsome or too familiar.

Participation in liturgy is one way of remaining attuned to God's word. The text from Leviticus is a schedule of feasts, Israel's liturgical calendar. In these festivals, God commands the attention of the people and calls them to acknowledge that the Lord alone is God. There is no other.

SATURDAY

Today's reading from Leviticus established in Israel the observance of Jubilee. This fiftieth year, announced on the Day of
Atonement (Yom Kippur), was to be a sacred time, "proclaiming
liberty in the land for all its inhabitants" (Lv 25:10). The text outlines the goals of the Jubilee year as human liberation (releasing
captives and so curbing the institution of slavery), economic liberation (restoring land to its original owner and so controlling
the distribution of wealth), and ecological liberation (respecting
the earth and the animals on it by allowing them to rest and
replenish themselves). Scholars do not know if the Jubilee was
ever actually implemented in Israel. But in time it came to symbolize that day when God's reign would be finally, fully revealed.

Throughout the ages prophets have announced this "year of
favor from the LORD, / and a day of vindication by our God" (Is
61:2; see Lk 4:19). Confronting powerful, political regimes, they
have risked all by speaking "in the name of the LORD, our God"
(Jer 26:16). This is the witness of Jeremiah and of John the
Baptizer in today's readings.

Eighteenth Sunday in Ordinary Time

A

First Reading: Is 55:1–3
Responsorial Psalm: Ps 145:8–9, 15–16, 17–18
Second Reading: Rom 8:35, 37–39
Gospel: Mt 14:13–21

For some time now, scholars have recognized Matthew's tendency to associate Jesus with the biblical metaphor of Lady Wisdom. The juxtaposition of today's Gospel with a text from Isaiah cast in the style of wisdom invites us to make the same connection. Lady Wisdom personifies God's outreach in the world by inviting people to feast at her table in words that are very like those of Isaiah in today's reading: "All who are thirsty, / come to the water! ... / Come, without paying and without cost, / drink wine and milk!" (Is 55:1). Often Wisdom's invitation must compete with Folly's, who is also personified. What Lady Folly offers is sweet stolen water that fails to satisfy (see Prv 9:17). Matthew's editing of the story of the multiplication of the loaves also presents us with two banquets: Herod's birthday banquet, to which the opening verse refers, and the banquet that Jesus sets before the crowd. The one deals death; the other leads to life.

In Romans, Paul joins his voice to Isaiah's, to Lady Wisdom's, and to Jesus' to affirm beyond all doubt that God is for us and nothing can separate us from God's love.

B

First Reading: Ex 16:2–4, 12–15
Responsorial Psalm: Ps 78:3–4, 23–24, 25, 54
Second Reading: Eph 4:17, 20–24
Gospel: Jn 6:24–35

Jesus' exchange with the crowd in John's Gospel is meant to remind the reader of Moses' frequent exchanges with the Israelites, as in today's passage from Exodus, which is recapitulated in Psalm 78, "He rained manna upon them for food / and gave them heavenly bread" (v. 24). The crowd's dialogue with Jesus moves along typically Johannine lines. Three times they question him and each time fail to grasp the deeper meaning of his words, which they persist in taking literally. They seem unable to let go of the intriguing possibility that there might in fact be such a thing as a free lunch. This, as John intends, requires Jesus to speak bluntly: "I am the bread of life," he finally tells them, "whoever comes to me will never hunger, and whoever believes in me will never thirst" (Jn 6:35).

When the crowd, hoping to gain access to an inexhaustible food supply, asks Jesus, "What can we do to accomplish the works of God?" (Jn 6:28), he answers in language that sounds more like Paul than like John. Not works but faith in the one God sent is what God wants, he says. The thought is further developed in Ephesians. By faith, believers are renewed in the spirit of their minds and become a new creation (see Eph 4:23).

C

First Reading: Eccl 1:2; 2:21–23
Responsorial Psalm: Ps 90:3–4, 5–6, 12–13, 14, 17
Second Reading: Col 3:1–5, 9–11
Gospel: Lk 12:13–21

The readings for this Sunday warn us against investing too heavily in material possessions. In the words of Jesus, "Take care to guard against all greed, for though one may be rich, one's life does not consist of possessions" (Lk 12:15). It is important to note what Jesus does not say. He does not condemn the rich, nor does he promote poverty. What he counsels is perspective. The parable makes the point. The man in the parable comes under judgment not because he is rich but because he is a fool for thinking that a bumper crop can secure his life for many years to come. He trusts inordinately in his possessions and gives no thought to God, who alone secures and sustains life. This is why Colossians refers to greed as idolatry (see 3:5).

The question that indicts the rich fool in the parable echoes the sentiments of Qoheleth in the first reading. If "you can't take it with you," he argues, what is the point? But this is the perspective of a man who does not believe in life after death. Paul and Luke, on the other hand, urge us to grow rich in what matters to God, that is, to seek what is above. The psalmist puts it this way: "Teach us to number our days aright, that we may gain wisdom of heart" (Ps 90:12).

Eighteenth Week in Ordinary Time

MONDAY

YEAR I   *First Reading: Nm 11:4b–15*
         Responsorial Psalm: Ps 81:12–13, 14–15, 16–17
YEAR II *First Reading: Jer 28:1–17*
         Responsorial Psalm: Ps 119:29, 43, 79, 80, 95, 102
YEARS I AND II *Gospel: Mt 14:13–21*

It is easy to see a connection between the passage from Numbers and Matthew's account of the multiplication of the loaves. The setting of Jesus' miracle is "a deserted place" (Mt 14:15), recalling another desert where God provided manna for the Israelites to eat. In today's reading from Numbers, the people demand meat as well. Some scholars interpret the fish mentioned in the story of the multiplication of the loaves as a reference to the quail with which God will answer the people's request. The quail, after all, came from the sea (see Nm 11:31).

Each servant of God in today's readings experiences in his own way the burden of caring for God's needy people. Moses is most direct: "I cannot carry all this people by myself," he complains, "they are too heavy for me" (Nm 11:14). Jeremiah is forced to compete with the false prophet Hananiah, whose empty promise of peace better suits God's people who are in denial. Even the disciples of Jesus want to dismiss the hungry crowds. When our own resources are depleted, each one must trust the unbounded resourcefulness of God.

TUESDAY

Today's Gospel makes a profound Christological statement. In the story of Jesus walking on water, Matthew depicts Jesus doing what only God can do: "He alone stretches out the heavens / and treads upon the crests of the sea" (see Jb 9:8). When his terrified disciples cry out, Jesus' answer echoes the divine name: "It is I" (Mt 14:27). Finally, the power of Jesus is revealed in his fully restoring sick people to wholeness. This is the same divine power announced by Jeremiah. Note the repetition of "I" as the prophet declares God's intention to restore the tents of Jacob.

In the Gospel, Peter is a little like Aaron and Miriam in the text from Numbers. They fail to appreciate Moses' status as God's servant, and Peter fails to appreciate Jesus' status as God's Son. They want to do what Moses does; he wants to do what Jesus does. All are brought up short.

Critics have rightly noted the unequal treatment of Miriam in the text from Numbers. This reflects the historical conditioning of human writers and not inequity on the part of the divine Author.

WEDNESDAY

YEAR I   *First Reading: Nm 13:1–2, 25—14:1, 26a–29a, 34–35*
         Responsorial Psalm. Ps 106:6–7ab, 13–14, 21–22, 23
YEAR II   *First Reading: Jer 31:1–7*
         Responsorial Psalm: Jer 31:10, 11–12ab, 13
YEARS I AND II *Gospel: Mt 15: 21–28*

In today's Gospel we find Matthew taking a story from Mark and making it his own. In his commentary on Matthew, Daniel Harrington explains how Matthew has heightened the theme of prayer in his version of this story. Where Mark simply relates that the desperate woman begged Jesus to cast the demon out of her daughter, Matthew reports her words. She speaks three times. The first two times her words are prayers: "Have pity on me, Lord, Son of David!" and "Lord, help me" (Mt 15:22, 25). In the end, Jesus himself remarks on her great faith. In this way, Harrington says, Matthew portrays this woman as a "model of praying faith."[23] In today's episode from Numbers, the Israelite community lacks precisely this—praying faith.

The poem from Jeremiah makes an important point about the power of prayer. It is not praying faith that causes miracles to happen—like the cure of the woman's daughter or the restoration of the tribes of Israel. Rather, it is the mercy of God who loves us, all of us, "with age-old love" (Jer 31:3).

THURSDAY

YEAR I   *First Reading: Nm 20:1–13*
           Responsorial Psalm: Ps 95:1–2, 6–7, 8–9
YEAR II   *First Reading: Jer 31:31–34*
           Responsorial Psalm: Ps 51:12–13, 14–15, 18–19
YEARS I AND II *Gospel: Mt 16:13–23*

The image of the rock links the reading from Numbers to today's Gospel. In both texts the rock ensures the community's survival. From the rock God gives the people water to drink; on the rock, who is Peter, Jesus will build his Church. But in both texts the rock also becomes a stumbling block. For Moses and Aaron it is an occasion of sin; and Peter, the rock, becomes for Jesus the instrument of Satan. He is literally "a stumbling block," *skandalizo* in Greek. Although the exact nature of their sin is unclear, Moses and Aaron's angry outburst obscures the holiness of God, who is acting to save. Similarly, Peter's own inadequate interpretation of messiahship obscures God's saving plan and tempts Jesus to trip and fall.

Like all of us at times, Moses, Aaron, and Peter are "little-faiths," to use Matthew's favorite phrase. Jeremiah offers hope both to them and to us. The newness of the new covenant lies in a new capacity on the part of God's people, from least to greatest, to know the Lord who will remember their sin no more. At the psalmist's urging, let us today bring our contrite hearts before the One who will not spurn them.

Friday

At first glance, the good news of Deuteronomy and that of today's Gospel seem to be diametrically opposed. The one speaks of salvation as prosperity and long life; the other talks of saving one's life by losing it. But the message of the two texts is not so different. Deuteronomy tells the Israelites that their unique vocation as the people of God flows from the revelation of God's own uniqueness in the Exodus event. God asks: Has any other god ever acted like this? In the Gospel, Jesus teaches his followers that their vocation as crucified disciples flows from the revelation of his vocation as crucified Messiah in the events of his death and resurrection. Thus, Jews and Christians alike are called to witness to the one, the only God, who acts in unexpected ways to save all people.

The prophet Nahum's name means "consolation," but as is often observed, there is little consolation for the Ninevites in his message as he foresees that city's bloody end. The words of Jesus are no less ominous: "The Son of Man," he says, "will come with his angels in his Father's glory ... then he will repay each according to his conduct" (Mt 16:27). Be warned.

SATURDAY

YEAR I   *First Reading: Dt 6:4–13*
         Responsorial Psalm: Ps 18:2–3a, 3bc–4, 47 and 51
YEAR II *First Reading: Hb 1:12—2:4*
         Responsorial Psalm: Ps 9:8–9, 10–11, 12–13
YEARS I AND II *Gospel: Mt 17:14–20*

Each of today's three readings is a statement about faith. The text from Deuteronomy contains the principal profession of faith of the Jewish people, the *Shema*. It begins with the words, "Hear, O Israel! The LORD is our God, the LORD alone!" (Dt 6:4). The verses that follow describe how totally their faith in the one God must pervade the life of this people.

When in a time of national crisis the word of the Lord finally comes to the prophet Habakkuk after a long delay, it tells him, "The just man, because of his faith, shall live" (2:4). In a fitting response, the psalm declares, "They trust in you who cherish your name" (9:11). In such times, faith must be resilient.

Today's Gospel is also a statement about faith. Here again Matthew adapts a story from Mark. Mark's story focuses on the faith of the boy's father; in Matthew it focuses on the little faith of Jesus' disciples. When they wonder why they could not expel the demon, Jesus answers, "Because of your little faith." Then he goes on solemnly to declare to them—and to us—that even a little faith can move mountains, even if it is only "the size of a mustard seed" (Mt 17:20).

Nineteenth Sunday in Ordinary Time

A

First Reading: 1 Kgs 19:9a, 11–13a
Responsorial Psalm: Ps 85:9, 10, 11–12, 13–14
Second Reading: Rom 9:1–5
Gospel: Mt 14:22–33

In all of today's readings, we meet faithful servants of God who, when they find themselves momentarily overwhelmed by circumstances, are steadied by the felt presence of God in their lives. The context of the excerpt from the first reading is the threat of retaliation by Jezebel for the slaughter of the prophets of Baal on Mount Carmel. Fearing for his life, Elijah flees into the desert and prays for death. But God acts to revive him by bringing him to Horeb, the mountain of God, where God speaks in "a tiny whispering sound" (1 Kgs 19:12). The appearance of Jesus walking on the water has all the elements of a theophany, a manifestation of God, such as Elijah experienced in the cave at Horeb. He calms his terrified disciples with the revelatory formula, "It is I [literally, I AM, the divine name]; do not be afraid" (see Is 41:10), and they respond by calling him Lord. So when the wind is too much for Peter, it is the Lord who stretches out his hand to catch him.

In Romans 9 Paul is overwhelmed with sorrow that his fellow Jews have not accepted the Gospel of Christ. But his faith is steadied by recalling all the irrevocable gifts of God to Israel.

B

First Reading: 1 Kgs 19:4–8
Responsorial Psalm: Ps 34:2–3, 4–5, 6–7, 8–9
Second Reading: Eph 4:30——5:2
Gospel: Jn 6:41–51

Today's readings examine the mysterious gift of faith. On the one hand, faith is the free human response to divine revelation; on the other hand, that response is possible only by the God-given gift of faith. In today's selection from John, Jesus says, "No one can come to me unless the Father who sent me draw him" (6:44). This suggests that every disciple is the Father's gift to Jesus. The same paradox is at work in Elijah the prophet's crisis of faith. His prayer under the broom tree is an admission of failure that would be better translated "I am not as good as my fathers in faith [specifically, Moses and Joshua]." But because he allows God to draw him, he is given the strength to retrace the steps of Moses to Horeb—another name for Sinai—and is rewarded there with a manifestation of God.

The paradox of the life of faith shapes Paul's grammar in Ephesians. The passage is an exhortation, but typical of Paul, he matches every imperative with an indicative. Thus, every human activity required by faith is made possible by the prior activity of God in Christ; for example, we can be forgiving because God has forgiven us in Christ. In other words, it is all God's gift.

C

First Reading: Wis 18:6—9
Responsorial Psalm: Ps 33:1, 12, 18—19, 20—22
Second Reading: Heb 11:1—2, 8—19 or 11:1—2, 8—12
Gospel: Lk 12:32—48 or 12:35—40

A ll three of this Sunday's readings assume an eschatological perspective. Eschatology is from the Greek *eschaton*, which means "last things," "end time," "world-ending event." The concern of eschatology, however, is not primarily with the end of a world (prophetic eschatology) or even with the end of the world (apocalyptic eschatology), but with the triumph of God in the world God created. The reading from Wisdom recalls the death of the firstborn of the Egyptians, which took place as Israel was keeping "the divine institution" (18:9) of Passover. That feast would ever after commemorate God's triumph over the enemies of Israel, a world-ending event if ever there was one. In Hebrews, Abraham's journey to the unknown land that was to be his inheritance takes on an eschatological significance, becoming a search for a heavenly homeland, a city whose architect and maker is God.

The Gospel from Luke continues to discuss the responsible use of material things from an eschatological perspective. The message of the parables is that all is to be assessed in the light of the triumphant return of the Son of Man "at an hour you do not expect" (Lk 12:40). Are we ready?

Nineteenth Week in Ordinary Time

MONDAY

YEAR I *First Reading:* Dt 10:12–22
       Responsorial Psalm: Ps 147:12–13, 14–15, 19–20
YEAR II *First Reading:* Ez 1:2–5, 24–28c
        Responsorial Psalm: Ps 148:1–2, 11–12, 13, 14
YEARS I AND II *Gospel:* Mt 17:22–27

⁕⁕⁕

The selections from Deuteronomy and Ezekiel bear witness to "the God of gods, the Lord of lords, the great God, mighty and awesome," who is the glory of Israel. In Deuteronomy that glory is revealed in the "great and terrible things" (10:17, 21) God did in order to secure the freedom and the future of Israel. In Ezekiel the glory of God appears in human likeness resplendent with fire and electrum, an alloy of silver and gold (1:27).

By comparison, the Gospel story seems very prosaic. It begins with the second prediction of Jesus' passion that leaves the disciples grief-stricken. Then it continues with a somewhat mundane exchange about paying taxes. Still we catch a glimpse of God's glory even here. When Jesus asks Peter whether the kings of the world take tribute from their sons (*huion* in Greek) or from strangers, he makes a profound claim. The tax in question was levied on Jews for the upkeep of the Temple. Jesus' question and the expected answer from Peter imply that Jesus is exempt from paying this tax for the maintenance of God's house because he is the very Son of God.

Tuesday

Year I   *First Reading: Dt 31:1–8*
          Responsorial Psalm: Dt 32:3–4ab, 7, 8, 9 and 12
Year II   *First Reading: Ez 2:8–3:4*
          Responsorial Psalm: Ps 119:14, 24, 72, 103, 111, 131
Years I and II *Gospel: Mt 18:1–5, 10, 12–14*

In all three of today's readings, servants of God and of God's people are being commissioned. In every case, they are urged to internalize the saving will of God. As Moses' successor, Joshua will lead Israel on the last stage of their journey, bringing them into the Promised Land. As he prepares to commission Joshua, Moses tells the people what he will soon repeat to his successor: he will accomplish the task only if he trusts that God, who "will never fail you or forsake you," marches before him (Dt 31:6). Ezekiel is called to speak God's word to the rebellious house of Israel and is required literally to ingest that word, taking it in and making it his own word of "lamentation and wailing and woe" (2:10).

Today's Gospel is from Matthew 18, sometimes called the "ecclesiastical discourse," which contains Jesus' instructions to those who will one day lead his Church. Clearly, concern for the "little ones," the most vulnerable members of the community, is of paramount importance. Why? The parable gives the answer: because the heavenly Father, the Good Shepherd, wills that not "one of these little ones be lost" (Mt 18:14).

WEDNESDAY

YEAR I   *First Reading: Dt 34:1–12*
        Responsorial Psalm: Ps 66:1–3a, 5 and 8, 16–17
YEAR II   *First Reading: Ez 9:1–7; 10:18–22*
        Responsorial Psalm: Ps 113:1–2, 3–4, 5–6
YEARS I AND II   *Gospel: Mt 18:15–20*

The powerful presence of God links all three readings today. In each one, the same divine presence is symbolized in a different way. In the passage from Deuteronomy, the powerful presence of God descends on Joshua as he is filled with the spirit of wisdom. In the vision of Ezekiel, the powerful presence of God is glory, and it departs from the Jerusalem Temple because of "all the abominations that are practiced within it" (9:4). In the Gospel selection, Jesus' name conveys the reality of God's powerful presence.

Today's Gospel is also of interest for what it tells us about life in the church of Matthew. Clearly, that community of Christians found it necessary at times to deal firmly and forcefully with its sinful members. The three-step process outlined in these verses counsels confrontation, intervention, and, as a last resort, excommunication. Strangely enough, this step is described as treating the offender "as you would a Gentile" (Mt 18:17). But the most important aspect for us to note is that the community must take this action only while united in prayer, assuring them of God's powerful presence.

THURSDAY

YEAR I   First Reading: Jos 3:7–10a, 11, 13–17
             Responsorial Psalm: Ps 114:1–2, 3–4, 5–6
YEAR II   First Reading: Ez 12:1–12
             Responsorial Psalm: Ps 78:56–57, 58–59, 61–62
YEARS I AND II   Gospel: Mt 18:21–19:1

E ach of the three readings for today presents a sign and urges us to heed it. The Israelites' long journey from Egypt to the Promised Land began with the crossing of the Red Sea and ended, as reported in today's excerpt from Joshua, with the crossing of the Jordan River. Joshua tells the people, "This is how you will know that there is a living God in your midst" (Jos 3:10). It is a sign that God is with them. The prophet Ezekiel lives among a rebellious people who "have eyes to see but do not see, and ears to hear but do not hear" (Ez 12:2). Ezekiel's charade is a sign for these people about the exile that will soon befall them.

In the Gospel, Jesus answers Peter's question—How often must I forgive? As many as seven times?—with a numerical sign. "Not seven times," he says, but "seventy-seven times," an unlimited number (Mt 18:21–22). The parable drives the point home: if God places no limit on forgiveness, neither can we. Unless we learn to forgive wholeheartedly, as the heavenly Father forgives us, we cannot presume on God's forgiveness. This is not a quid pro quo; this is the logic of grace. Let the one who has ears hear.

FRIDAY

YEAR I   *First Reading: Jos 24:1–13*
        Responsorial Psalm: Ps 136:1–3, 16–18, 21–22 and 24
YEAR II   *First Reading: Ez 16:1–15, 60, 63 or Ez 16:59–63*
        Responsorial Psalm: Is 12:2–3, 4bcd, 5–6
YEARS I AND II   *Gospel: Mt 19:3–12*

In each of today's readings, three different sacred writers employ the same basic strategy in order to proclaim God's will and purpose. That strategy is to recount God's gracious deeds of the past in order to call God's people in the present to grateful, graceful living. In the two first readings, the recital of God's past favors is the historical prologue that culminates in a renewal of the covenant. Joshua presides at such a covenant renewal ceremony at Shechem, where he prepares the tribes of Israel to take possession of the Promised Land. Ezekiel uses an allegory to relate God's graciousness to Israel from the beginning and to announce an everlasting covenant. In the Gospel, Jesus appeals to God's past activity as Creator in order to support his prohibition of divorce.

The disciples' astonished response to Jesus' teaching on divorce leads him to make a still more startling statement on celibacy. Just as marriage must be understood with reference to God's creative activity in the past, celibacy must be understood with a view to God's saving activity in the future, that is, the kingdom which is at hand.

SATURDAY

YEAR I   *First Reading: Jos 24:14–29*
          Responsorial Psalm: Ps 16:1–2a and 5, 7–8, 11
YEAR II   *First Reading: Ez 18:1–10, 13b, 30–32*
          Responsorial Psalm: Ps 51:12–13, 14–15, 18–19
YEARS I AND II *Gospel: Mt 19:13–15*

Some element of family life figures in all of today's readings. Joshua confronts the house of Israel with a decision: Whom will they serve in the land they are about to occupy? "As for me and my household," he famously declares, "we will serve the LORD" (Jos 24:15). In the Gospel, Jesus welcomes children, saying that the kingdom of God belongs to them. To choose God and to cherish children are both positive family values.

Ezekiel also has something to say about relationships within the family. Citing the proverb "Fathers have eaten green grapes, thus their children's teeth are on edge" (Ez 18:2), the prophet, in God's name, announces the reversal of conventional wisdom. No longer will the sins of their parents be visited upon children; each will be held responsible for his or her own sin. Translated into today's terms, this new teaching says that, however dysfunctional a family system may be, individual family members are always free to make for themselves a new heart and a new spirit and, by the grace of God, to return and live. For God takes "no pleasure in the death of anyone who dies, says the Lord GOD" (Ez 18:32).

Twentieth Sunday in Ordinary Time

A

First Reading: Is 56:1, 6–7
Responsorial Psalm: Ps 67:2–3, 5, 6, 8
Second Reading: Rom 11:13–15, 29–32
Gospel: Mt 15:21–28

༺≈⊙⊙≈༻

In this Sunday's readings, three men confront the privilege and the purpose of Israel in God's one will to save all humanity. Today's first reading is from Third Isaiah (56–66), the anonymous post-exilic prophet. He gives voice to God's intention to extend all the privileges of Israel, including full access to the Temple, to righteous Gentiles, "foreigners who join themselves to the LORD" (Is 56:6). That divine intention is finally realized when Jesus meets and ministers to the Canaanite woman in today's Gospel. The irrevocable privilege of Israel is made clear in Jesus' initial response to her request. "I was sent only to the lost sheep of the house of Israel," he tells her (Mt 15:24). But her great faith persuades him to reach beyond ethnic boundaries and anticipate the worldwide mission that will be revealed only after his resurrection.

In Romans, the Apostle to the Gentiles reaffirms his conviction that the privilege of Israel is irrevocable. "For the gifts and the call of God are irrevocable," he says (Rom 11:29). Therefore, for Paul, "the power of God," the plan of salvation, "of everyone who believes" is "for Jew first, and then Greek" (Rom 1:16).

B

First Reading: Prv 9:1–6
Responsorial Psalm: Ps 34:2–3, 4–5, 6–7
Second Reading: Eph 5:15–20
Gospel: Jn 6:51–58

The exhortation of Ephesians, today's second reading, consists of three contrasts, all saying essentially the same thing. Christians are to live not as foolish persons but as wise; not in ignorance but trying to understand God's will; not drunk on wine but filled with the Spirit. The same contrast is implicit in today's first reading, too. In Proverbs, Wisdom issues her invitation to those who lack understanding over and against the seductions of Folly, who also calls to those who lack understanding (see 9:13–17).

A contrast is also implied in the conclusion of the eucharistic discourse in John. With the first verse of today's reading, the discourse takes a sharp turn: the bread that in the first part of the discourse (Jn 6:35–50) referred to Jesus' teaching, in this last part of the discourse (vv. 51–59) refers with inescapable clarity to Jesus' flesh and blood. At this juncture, Jesus' claim is dramatically heightened, and the contrast between this true bread from heaven and the manna that fed the wilderness generation is razor sharp. The choice presented by this "hard saying" (v. 60) is, in the end, the only one that matters. "Whoever eats this bread will live forever" (v. 58). In faith, then, let us "Taste and see the goodness of the LORD" (Ps 34:9).

C

First Reading: Jer 38:4–6, 8–10
Responsorial Psalm: Ps 40:2, 3, 4, 18
Second Reading: Heb 12:1–4
Gospel: Lk 12:49–53

~∞∞∞~

Today's reading from Hebrews introduces an athletic image to describe the strict discipline of the Christian life. We must think of ourselves as marathoners, the author says, who must "persevere in running the race that lies before us" (Heb 12:1). To that end, we must rid ourselves of every burden so as to run unhampered toward the finish line. This we do surrounded by "a cloud of witnesses" (v. 1), not mildly curious onlookers, but martyrs, who have already competed well, finished the race, and won the crown of life (see 2 Tm 4:7). More than that, running we follow Jesus and fix our eyes on him who is "the leader and perfecter of faith" (Heb 12:2).

Just what finishing the race might entail is spelled out in the historical experience of Jeremiah in the first reading and in the dire prophecy of Jesus in Luke. For fearlessly speaking the word of God, Jeremiah is left in the muddy cistern to die. Like Elijah who called down fire from heaven to consume the holocaust on Mount Carmel, Jesus proclaims that he has come "to set the earth on fire" (Lk 12:49; see 1 Kgs 18:38). This consummation will demand of him a baptism by fire that all of us who follow him must expect to share.

Twentieth Week in Ordinary Time

MONDAY

YEAR I   *First Reading: Jdg 2:11–19*
         Responsorial Psalm: Ps 106:34–35, 36–37, 39–40, 43ab and 44
YEAR II *First Reading: Ez 24:15–23*
         Responsorial Psalm: Dt 32:18–19, 20, 21
YEARS I AND II *Gospel: Mt 19:16–22*

Matthew alone of all the Gospel writers uses the word "young" to describe the rich man who approaches Jesus. Perhaps he wants us to read Jesus' word, rendered here as "to be perfect," as "to be mature" (Mt 19:21) instead. That is one meaning of the Greek *teleios*. In this light, Jesus is inviting the rich young man not so much to give up but to grow up by dedicating himself totally to God. The two first readings offer a negative and a positive illustration of such total dedication.

The passage from Judges depicts the chronic instability of the Israelites during the period before the monarchy. "They were quick to stray from the way their fathers had taken, and did not follow their example of obedience to the commandments of the LORD" (Jdg 2:17). To paraphrase Deuteronomy, today's psalm, they forgot the one who gave them birth. The selection from Ezekiel, however, reveals the maturity of the prophet's faith. His dedication to the word of God strips him not of mere material things but of the delight of his eyes, his wife, and even of the comfort of mourning her loss. Such is the cost of true discipleship (see Mt 8:21–22).

Tuesday

YEAR I *First Reading: Jdg 6:11–24a*
       Responsorial Psalm: Ps 85:9, 11–12, 13–14
YEAR II *First Reading: Ez 28:1–10*
       Responsorial Psalm: Dt 32:26–27ab, 27cd–28, 30, 35cd–36ab
YEARS I AND II *Gospel: Mt 19:23–30*

Today's readings present a study in contrast: the call of Gideon described in the Book of Judges, and the arrogance of the king of Tyre, who is mocked in the prophecy of Ezekiel. Gideon frankly acknowledges that he is the least important in his father's house. Yet ironically, it is he who will save Israel from the power of Midian, because God will be with him and nothing is impossible with God. The king of Tyre, on the other hand, is haughty of heart. "A god am I!" he boasts (Ez 28:2). His over-weening pride will be his downfall. As the responsory from Deuteronomy foresees, "Close at hand is the day of their disaster" (32:35).

Ezekiel says that the heart of the king of Tyre has grown haughty from his riches. So can wealth corrupt even the best of us. Jesus draws this lesson from the refusal of the rich young man, much to the astonishment of his disciples. "Who then can be saved?" they ask (Mt 19:25). Jesus' answer is anticipated in the psalm taken from Deuteronomy that asks the same question: "How could one man rout a thousand ... unless ... the LORD delivered them?" (32:30).

WEDNESDAY

⟪⟫

Today's readings offer us a literary feast: a fable, an extended metaphor, and a parable. The two first readings denounce bad kings and kingship itself. The fable of Jotham is an old anti-monarchical tradition. The only tree willing to reign over the other trees is no tree at all. The buckthorn is bramble, too close to the ground to cast a shadow, so close that it causes fire to spread. Rulers in the ancient Near East described themselves as the shepherds of their people. As Psalm 23 makes clear, it was the king's responsibility as shepherd to protect and provide for his people. Ezekiel extends the metaphor as he indicts the kings of Israel who have given God's sheep over to pillage, leaving them "scattered over the whole earth, with no one to look after them" (34:6).

The owner of the vineyard in Jesus' parable might be described as a good shepherd. The generosity he extends to the workers hired late in the day is simple justice, as the Hebrew Bible defines it. It honors the claims of the relationship that exists between an employer and his workers. That may not be good business sense, but it is good shepherding, says the Lord.

Thursday

Year I   *First Reading: Jdg 11:29–39a*
         Responsorial Psalm: Ps 40:5, 7–8a, 8b–9, 10
Year II   *First Reading: Ez 36:23–28*
          Responsorial Psalm: Ps 51:12–13, 14–15, 18–19
Years I and II *Gospel: Mt 22:1–14*

T he theme of missed opportunity runs through all of today's readings. The story of Jephthah begins with the words, "The spirit of the Lord came upon Jephthah" (Jdg 11:29). Unbidden, God acts in Jephthah, assuring him of victory. But for Jephthah, God's grace is not enough; he wants a guarantee. So he makes a foolish, faithless vow and his triumph turns into tragedy. The parable of the Wedding Feast in Matthew is aimed at the Jewish leaders. Their violent refusal of the king's double invitation will have dire consequences. But it will create an opportunity for those along the byways. Yet Matthew warns that grace is not a guarantee even for them. The wedding garment symbolizes a life responsive to God's grace. Seized by grace, we must act in faith on the gift we have received.

Ezekiel addresses his words to the people of God exiled in Babylon. They are there because of a missed opportunity: they defiled their land, God's gift, "by their conduct and deeds" (Ez 36:17). But the prophet offers hope of another opportunity not because of their good behavior but because of God's good name.

FRIDAY

The rabbis counted 613 commandments in the Torah. Teachers, however, often summarized the commandments to make them easier to learn and to live, as Jesus does in today's Gospel. He says that the whole law can be summed up in two commandments: love of God, as prescribed in Deuteronomy 6:5, and love of neighbor, as in Leviticus 19:18. While Jewish rabbis routinely emphasized love of God or love of neighbor as basic, Jesus may have been the first to combine the two commandments. Clearly he means to say that true love of God—that is, covenant fidelity—is expressed concretely in love of neighbor.

The story of Ruth illustrates the teaching of Jesus. She proves her loyalty to the God of Israel in the practical love she extends to Naomi, her mother-in-law. The vision of the dry bones in Ezekiel, on the other hand, demonstrates that it is God's own creative fidelity that makes possible the covenant fidelity required of us. It is God who opens our graves, God who gives us the spirit that we may extend covenant love and loyalty to one another. Jesus says that "the whole law and the prophets depend" on this (Mt 22:40).

Saturday

At first glance, today's selection from Matthew seems to contradict itself. On the one hand, Jesus acknowledges the authority of Moses' successors and urges his hearers to "do and observe all things whatsoever they tell you" (Mt 23:3). On the other hand, he accuses these very same teachers of hypocrisy and warns against doing what they do. This seeming contradiction reflects Matthew's dual aim: to depict Jesus as he was, an observant Jew, and at the same time to discredit the Jewish rivals of his church, as well as those Christian leaders who are already imitating them. The two first readings uncover the deep truth hidden in today's Gospel. Both point to God's choice of Israel, a choice signified in Ezekiel by the restoration of the Temple. The same divine choice is evident in the person of Jesus. Jesus "did not just happen to be a Jew," writes Eugene Fisher. "We Christians believe that, in the economy of salvation, he could *only* have been born a Jew."[24] This means that we Christians are all like Ruth, foreigners who have found refuge in the house of Israel.

Twenty-first Sunday in Ordinary Time

A

First Reading: Is 22:19–23
Responsorial Psalm: Ps 138:1–2, 2–3, 6, 8
Second Reading: Rom 11:33–36
Gospel: Mt 16:13–20

❧⊶◉◉⊷❧

The historical memory of the investiture of Eliakim preserved in the oracle of Isaiah, today's first reading, sheds light on the commissioning of Peter in today's Gospel. By divine decree, Eliakim son of Hilkiah replaces Shebna as master of the palace, a promotion that makes him prominent in the royal house. His great authority is symbolized by the key of the house of David; this means that Eliakim will determine who gains admission to the palace and who does not. Similarly, the authority conferred on Simon son of Jonah means he will function as master of the palace in the kingdom established by Jesus. Jesus' words to Peter make it clear that this appointment, too, is by divine decree. "Flesh and blood has not revealed this to you, but my heavenly Father" (Mt 16:17).

It is not Peter's résumé but his response in faith to divine revelation that signals God's choice of him. Jesus announces God's initiative with a beatitude: "Blessed are you" (Mt 16:17), while Paul in Romans seems to respond to God's mysterious election of Israel with a doxology: "How inscrutable are [God's] judgments and how unsearchable his ways!" (11:33).

B

First Reading: Jos 24:1–2a, 15–17, 18b
Responsorial Psalm: Ps 34:2–3, 16–17, 18–19, 20–21
Second Reading: Eph 5:21–32 or 5:2a, 25–32
Gospel: Jn 6:60–69

Today's first reading from the Book of Joshua describes the covenant renewal that took place at Shechem before Joshua "dismissed the people, each to his own heritage" (see 24:28). What is particularly striking about the passage is that it shows how every generation must in its own way freely choose to live in covenant with God. In today's Gospel, Jesus puts a similar choice before his disciples. Jesus has spoken plainly: "Unless you eat the flesh of the Son of Man and drink his blood, you do not have life within you" (Jn 6:53). His words are a hard saying that divides the disciples. So he asks directly, "Do you also want to leave?" (v. 67). And ever since, the question has been put to each successive generation. Each of us must choose freely, fully to participate in the death and life of Jesus—or not.

Today's selection from Ephesians is also a hard saying. As we have come better to appreciate the equality of the sexes, the husband-Christ-Church-wife metaphor is no longer so compelling. However, the hard truth is that in every generation we share the death and life of Jesus most concretely in our loving service of each other.

C

First Reading: Is 66:18–21
Responsorial Psalm: Ps 117:1, 2
Second Reading: Heb 12:5–7, 11–13
Gospel: Lk 13:22–30

❦

J esus, in today's Gospel, shares the vision of Isaiah in the first reading. Both look to a day when Jews and Gentiles from all the nations, "from the east and the west and from the north and the south" (Lk 13:29) will come to share the bounty of God's kingdom. Jesus' parable makes it clear that not all will be admitted to the table in God's kingdom, however. In context, they will be shut out who have put off for too long the discipline of the narrow gate, the same discipline that Hebrews urges on us in the second reading. Such discipline, Hebrews says, seems at the time "a cause not for joy but for pain, yet later it brings the peaceful fruit of righteousness" (12:11).

Jesus' words in today's Gospel are spoken in answer to a common enough question: "Will only a few people be saved?" (Lk 13:23). Typically, refusing to speculate, Jesus turns the question into a direct command. "Strive to enter through the narrow gate," he says (v. 24). It is tempting to speculate about who will or will not be saved. But it is more important, today's readings tell us, to submit to the discipline of the narrow gate that leads to the banquet of God's kingdom. Then and only then will we be ready, as the responsorial psalm puts it, to "go out to all the world and tell the good news."

Twenty-first Week in Ordinary Time

Monday

Year I   *First Reading: 1 Thes 1:1–5, 8b–10*
          Responsorial Psalm: Ps 149:1b–2, 3–4, 5–6a and 9b
Year II   *First Reading: 2 Thes 1:1–5, 11–12*
          Responsorial Psalm: Ps 96:1–2a, 2b–3, 4–5
Years I and II *Gospel: Mt 23:13–22*

The first readings for today from 1 and 2 Thessalonians and the selection from Matthew's Gospel reflect the experience of two early Christian communities in different times and circumstances. Both 1 and 2 Thessalonians address a church founded by Paul. The passage from 1 Thessalonians makes it evident that they are Gentiles (non-Jews) who have become followers of Jesus. There Paul describes them as having "turned to God from idols" (1 Thes 1:9), and 2 Thessalonians adds that they have been constant and faithful in persecution and trial. While Paul commends the Thessalonians, Matthew's Jesus condemns the Pharisees and scribes. Matthew is writing for a Christian-Jewish group engaged in a bitter rivalry with an early rabbinic Jewish group. These are the "scribes and Pharisees" accused in today's woes of stopping their fellow Jews from embracing the Gospel of Jesus. This is what Matthew means when he says that they "lock the Kingdom of heaven before men" (Mt 23:13). These glimpses into the life of the early Church keep us mindful of the variety of religious experiences that, by the power of the Spirit, were the beginnings of the Church.

TUESDAY

Today's Gospel is taken from Matthew 23, which is an example of religious polemic. Polemic is a verbal attack on one's opponents, characterized by harsh denunciation, gross exaggeration, mockery, sarcasm, and the like. In today's selection, Matthew ridicules the values of his Jewish rivals. He says they "strain out the gnat and swallow the camel" (Mt 23:24). (The camel is an unclean animal, no less!) Note, however, that he does not say that tithes on mint and herbs and seed should not be paid; only that the weightier matters of Jewish law—justice and mercy and faith—should be given priority.

The distinction Matthew makes between the inside and the outside is also made in both first readings. They warn Christians against being moved by flattering words (1 Thes) or disquieting rumors (2 Thes). These things that come from outside may be deceptive. Rather, they must take their stand on what is inside, holding fast to the traditions they have received from those like Paul, whose hearts have been tested by God, "who judges our hearts" (1 Thes 2:4), scrutinizes our comings and goings, as Psalm 139 puts it, and finds them true.

WEDNESDAY

YEAR I   *First Reading: 1 Thes 2:9–13*
         Responsorial Psalm: Ps 139:7–8, 9–10, 11–12ab
YEAR II *First Reading: 2 Thes 3:6–10, 16–18*
         Responsorial Psalm: Ps 128:1–2, 4–5
YEARS I AND II *Gospel: Mt 23:27–32*

Religious polemic reaches a climax in today's Gospel as Jesus accuses the scribes and Pharisees of being "the children of those who murdered the prophets." Then with the words "now fill up what your ancestors measured out," he seems to point to their murder of him and of his disciples (Mt 23:31–32). Surely this is Matthew's intent: to condemn his opponents and consign them, a "brood of vipers," to the judgment of Gehenna (v. 33). However distasteful we may find such language, it is a standard feature in the Dead Sea Scrolls and other Jewish and Greco-Roman writings as well as in the Gospels. Its purpose is mainly to equip one's own constituents to resist the allure of the opponent's message.

All too often in the past, the polemic of Matthew in passages like today's was taken at face value and used to caricature and condemn Jews and Judaism. It is imperative, therefore, that when Christians read the Gospels, they take into account the historical context in which they were written and the literary conventions they employ. Only thus will we, like Paul's Thessalonians, receive their message "not as the word of men but, as it truly is, the word of God" (1 Thes 2:13).

THURSDAY

YEAR I *First Reading: 1 Thes 3:7–13*
          Responsorial Psalm: Ps 90:3–5a, 12–13, 14 and 17
YEAR II *First Reading: 1 Cor 1:1–9*
          Responsorial Psalm: Ps 145:2–3, 4–5, 6–7
YEARS I AND II *Gospel: Mt 24:42–51*

All three of today's readings resonate with the theme of Christian apocalyptic, the expectation of Christ's Second Coming. The Gospel praises the faithful, farsighted servant who is always ready to receive the Son of Man, who will come when least expected. In both letters Paul exhorts his churches to the same fidelity. He prays that they may be strong and blameless "at the coming of our Lord Jesus with all his holy ones" (1 Thes 3:13), that is, "on the day of our Lord Jesus Christ" (1 Cor 1:8).

In the Gospel parable, the delay of the Second Coming becomes the occasion for the worthless servant to abuse his fellow servants. The warning is especially urgent for us, to whom the Lord's return seems so long delayed. A delay of two thousand years naturally gives rise to doubt that may lead to dissolution. We must, therefore, resolve to stay awake and stand firm "to the end" in the knowledge that "God is faithful" (1 Cor 1:8, 9). And as we watch and wait, Paul says, we must "increase and abound in love for one another and for all" so that we may be ready for the coming of our Lord Jesus Christ (1 Thes 3:12–13).

Friday

Today's parable, found only in Matthew, again calls us to vigilance in view of the Lord's return. "You know neither the day nor the hour" (Mt 25:13). The unprepared foolish virgins are severely punished. Their cry—"Lord, Lord, open the door for us" (v. 11)—reminds us of the earlier words of Jesus: "Not everyone who says to me, 'Lord, Lord,' will enter the kingdom of heaven, but only the one who does the will of my Father in heaven" (Mt 7:21). The foolish lack the "oil" of good works; they have failed to do the Father's will. Paul's instruction is more specific still. He tells the Thessalonians that God wills that they grow in holiness and that they abstain from immorality.

Aside from its implied moral imperative, Matthew's parable also makes a massive Christological claim. In the Old Testament, God is the Bridegroom of Israel (see Hos 1–2 most notably). In this parable, however, Jesus is the Bridegroom whose return must be awaited in joyful hope. To change the metaphor, he is the wisdom of God who causes the foolish of this world to stumble.

SATURDAY

❧⸰❀⸰❧

Today's Gospel is another parable about the return of the Son of Man. This one further explains what preparedness for Christ's Second Coming entails. It requires positive, productive activity utilizing the gifts God has entrusted to us according to our abilities. That the two "good and faithful" servants both receive the same reward indicates that the quality of their activity is what counts, not the quantity of their achievement. Such committed, creative activity in response to God's grace enables "the foolish of the world to shame the wise," as Paul tells the Corinthians, and "the weak of the world to shame the strong" (1 Cor 1:27). Similarly, Paul urges the Thessalonians to work, recognizing the danger of inactivity, as does the parable.

Because this passage uses three times the Greek word for "hand over," the root of the word for tradition, some find in this parable a critique of those who "bury" religious tradition, refusing the risk of handing it on. Matthew's Christian Jews may have thought this way about the rabbinic Jews with whom they were in conflict. It is a question that we might ask ourselves.

Twenty-second Sunday in Ordinary Time

A

First Reading: Jer 20:7–9
Responsorial Psalm: Ps 63:2, 3–4, 5–6, 8–9
Second Reading: Rom 12:1–2
Gospel: Mt 16:21–27

"Do not conform yourself to this age but be transformed by the renewal of your mind, that you may discern what is the will of God" (Rom 12:2). Thus Paul exhorts the Romans in today's second reading. The challenge posed by his words is illustrated in the Gospel for today. Peter, a man still conformed to the age in which he lives, is outraged by Jesus' prediction of his passion. "No such thing shall ever happen to you," he says (Mt 16:22). Jesus' sharp rebuke cuts to the heart of the problem: "You are thinking not as God does, but as human beings do." So it is that "the rock" becomes a stumbling stone (v. 23).

To be transformed from within and enabled to think as God does is not an easy thing. The witness of Jeremiah makes that clear. Today's first reading is taken from one of the autobiographical sections of the Book of Jeremiah. His brutally honest speech is at once complaint and capitulation. He feels betrayed by God for putting in his mouth words of such unremitting outrage and violence. And yet, those words burn in his bones like the consuming fire that God is (see Ex 24:17); and he, God's man, must speak them.

B

First Reading: Dt 4:1–2, 6–8
Responsorial Psalm: Ps 15:2–3, 3–4, 4–5
Second Reading: Jas 1:17–18, 21b–22, 27
Gospel: Mk 7:1–8, 14–15, 21–23

Both Moses in Deuteronomy and James in the letter that bears his name demonstrate a lively appreciation for the word of God. In the first reading, Moses insists on the witness value of keeping God's word by observing God's law, the Torah. "For thus will you give evidence of your wisdom and intelligence to the nations," he says (Dt 4:6). Regarding the second reading, the consensus of scholars is that the James behind this letter is not one of the Twelve, but "the brother of the Lord" (see Gal 1:19) who led the early Church in Jerusalem. This James commanded the respect of Jews, as well as Christians, for his fervent observance of Torah. In today's passage he shares the concern of Moses that God's people be "doers of the word and not hearers only" (Jas 1:22).

Jesus in today's Gospel does not seem to share James's devotion to the law. But the text must be read carefully. Jesus is not, in fact, opposing Torah, the law of God, but the human "tradition of the elders" (Mk 7:3) that sought to dictate how the law must be kept. He stresses that observance of the law must proceed from within—from "the word that has been planted in you," as James puts it (1:21)—a principle the Pharisees themselves espoused.

C

First Reading: Sir 3:17–18, 20, 28–29
Responsorial Psalm: Ps 68:4–5, 6–7, 10–11
Second Reading: Heb 12:18–19, 22–24a
Gospel: Lk 14:1, 7–14

Jesus' table etiquette in today's Gospel echoes the wisdom of Sirach in the first reading. His parable about choosing the places of honor at the table illustrates Sirach's instruction "Humble yourself the more, the greater you are, / and you will find favor with God" (Sir 3:18). His teaching about inviting the poor who cannot reciprocate agrees with Sirach's dictum, "Alms atone for sins" (v. 29). At one level, today's reading depicts Jesus as a teacher in the tradition of wisdom in Israel.

On another level, the horizon of Jesus' teaching is that of the end time, the day of "the resurrection of the righteous" (Lk 14:14), when God will humble those who exalted themselves and exalt those who humbled themselves. This end-time, or eschatological, perspective is amplified in today's reading from Hebrews. With a barrage of biblical images—"a blazing fire and gloomy darkness and storm and a trumpet blast and a voice" (Heb 12:18–19)—he evokes ancient Israel's experience of God in the Exodus. Then with another profusion of images, he asks his Christian readers to push the horizon of their faith beyond the earthbound event of Sinai to the revelation of Zion, the heavenly Jerusalem, where Jesus waits in glory.

Twenty-second Week in Ordinary Time

MONDAY

YEAR I   *First Reading: 1 Thes 4:13–18*
          Responsorial Psalm: Ps 96:1 and 3, 4–5, 11–12, 13
YEAR II   *First Reading: 1 Cor 2:1–5*
          Responsorial Psalm: Ps 119:97, 98, 99, 100, 101, 102
YEARS I AND II *Gospel: Lk 4:16–30*

B oth Jesus in the selection from Luke and Paul in 1 Corinthians present themselves as coming in the power of the Spirit.
That power designates both men as prophets. The Gospel passage
is particularly significant because it stands at the very beginning
of Jesus' career and is the key to all that follows. Luke's Jesus will
be a prophetic Messiah. Anointed by the Spirit, he will announce
good news to the powerless and the poor—not socioeconomic
reform, but spiritual release from sin and death, as Paul explains
to the Thessalonians. Furthermore, as Jesus' references to the
prophets Elijah and Elisha indicate, his messianic mission will
extend beyond the boundaries of Israel to all the nations.

Today's Gospel clarifies the distinctive nature of Jesus' messiahship. As announced by Isaiah and expected by the Jews, the
Messiah was to undertake a secular mission within the national
boundaries of Israel. The spiritual messiahship of Jesus represented a transformation of the Jewish understanding. Therefore, it is
unjust to condemn the Jews for not accepting Jesus as Messiah.

Tuesday

The first full day of Jesus' ministry in Capernaum, described in today's Gospel, bears witness to his anointing by the Spirit. The close connection between the words and works of Jesus identifies him as the "prophet like Moses," a messianic figure, whose coming was announced in Deuteronomy: "I will raise up for them a prophet like you," God told Moses, "and will put my words into his mouth" (18:18). So the people are spellbound by Jesus' teaching, "because he spoke with authority" (Lk 4:32). Just as Moses had no equal in "the terrifying power that [he] exhibited in the sight of all Israel" (Dt 34:12), even so does the power of Jesus over the unclean spirits strike all who see it with astonishment.

The two first readings explore what Jesus' prophetic ministry means for all who follow him. Paul reminds the Thessalonians that having welcomed the Gospel, they are now "children of the light and children of the day … not of the night or of darkness." Therefore, they must "stay alert and sober" (1 Thes 5:5–6). And he warns the Corinthians that they have "not received the spirit of the world but the Spirit who is from God," the very "mind of Christ" (1 Cor 2:12, 16).

WEDNESDAY

YEAR I *First Reading: Col 1:1–8*
         Responsorial Psalm: Ps 52:10, 11
YEAR II *First Reading: 1 Cor 3:1–9*
         Responsorial Psalm: Ps 33:12–13, 14–15, 20–21
YEARS I AND II *Gospel: Lk 4:38–44*

Today's selection from the Gospel of Luke contains Jesus' mission statement: "To the other towns also I must proclaim the good news of the Kingdom of God, because for this purpose I have been sent" (Lk 4:43). Later Jesus will send the Twelve to continue his mission: "[He] summoned the Twelve and gave them power and authority over all demons and to cure diseases, and he sent them to proclaim the Kingdom of God ..." (Lk 9:1–2). The two first readings for today attest to the spread of the Gospel, which they describ in agricultural terms. Writing to the Corinthians, Paul compares the word of the Gospel to seed, as Jesus did. Paul planted it and Apollos watered it, but it grows by the power of God alone (1 Cor 3:6). That seed has borne fruit among the Colossians as well and it continues to grow in their midst "just as in the whole world it is bearing fruit and growing" (Col 1:6).

Like Epaphras, Apollos, and Paul, other faithful ministers of Christ and co-workers with God have proclaimed the word and planted the seed among us. We pray that by the power of God it will bear fruit in our faith and love and hope.

Thursday

Year I   *First Reading: Col 1:9–14*
          Responsorial Psalm: Ps 98:2–3ab, 3cd–4, 5–6
Year II   *First Reading: 1 Cor 3:18–23*
          Responsorial Psalm: Ps 24:1bc–2, 3–4ab, 5–6
Years I and II *Gospel: Lk 5:1–11*

U nlike Mark and Matthew, Luke delays the call of the disciples until the ministry of Jesus is well underway. When Jesus does call them in today's Gospel, the focus falls on Simon Peter. This brief encounter reveals much about Peter. First, he is a fisherman full of bluster that often causes him here as elsewhere to blurt out an objection to Jesus' word. Peter is also a sinner who recognizes his unworthiness in the presence of the Lord. He is a leader, too, whose contagious amazement seizes his shipmates, as well as James and John, Zebedee's sons. Finally, he is a follower of Jesus, and will realize in his life as a disciple the prayer of Colossians to "walk in a manner worthy of the Lord, so as to be fully pleasing, in every good work bearing fruit and growing in the knowledge of God, strengthened with every power, in accord with his glorious might, for all endurance and patience, with joy" (1:10–11).

"Put out into deep water," Jesus tells Peter, who on second thought does just that (Lk 5:4). A fool in the eyes of the world, he leaves everything only to find that everything is his, for he is Christ's and Christ is God's (1 Cor 3:22–23).

FRIDAY

Like Paul in 1 Corinthians, Jesus in today's reading from Luke comes under judgment. His opponents complain that his disciples, unlike those of John the Baptist, do not observe the traditional forms of piety, such as fasting. Jesus answers in a parable, likening his teaching to a new coat and new wine. He says that the revelation that he brings is so new that it is incompatible with the old ways. As a new cloak cannot patch an old one, and as new wine must be poured into fresh wineskins (Lk 5:36, 38), so will the new word of Jesus require new forms of piety.

Today's reading from Colossians fully expresses the newness of the revelation of Jesus. These verses are part of an early Christian hymn presenting Christ as the "image" of God. The claim that Genesis makes for all of us—that we are made in God's image—is here applied to Jesus in a unique way. As "the firstborn of all creation," he is the one through whom the world was created. As "the firstborn from the dead," he is the one through whom the world was recreated, that is, reconciled to God through the blood of his cross (Col 1:15–16, 18–20).

Saturday

Today's Gospel is the familiar story of Jesus' disciples pluck-ing heads of grain on the Sabbath. Luke has taken the story from Mark and trimmed it to fit the scheme of his Gospel. Like Mark, Luke reports Jesus' answer to his critics as an allusion to the story of David. But where in Mark's account Jesus says that David entered God's house and ate the bread, Luke adds the word "took." In Luke's version, then David took (*labon*) the bread and gave (*edoken*) it to his friends. "He went into the house of God, took the bread of offering, which only the priests could lawfully eat, ate of it, and shared it with his companions" (Lk 6:4). Thus he anticipates the action of Jesus at the Last Supper (see Lk 22:19) and gives the story a eucharistic flavor. In the Eucharist we savor and celebrate the achievement of Jesus that Paul explains to the Colossians, that is, the reconciliation that Christ has achieved for us (1:21–23).

Paul describes at what cost and under what conditions he and his fellow apostles labor, entrusted as they are with the ministry of reconciliation. He does so not to shame us but to show us the gratitude we owe to our fathers and mothers in Christ.

Twenty-third Sunday in Ordinary Time

A

First Reading: Ez 33:7–9
Responsorial Psalm: Ps 95:1–2, 6–7, 8–9
Second Reading: Rom 13:8–10
Gospel: Mt 18:15–20

The readings for this Sunday explore the parameters of individual responsibility in the context of human community. The aim of the three verses from Ezekiel is to clarify the personal responsibility of the prophet, who is Israel's watchman, for those to whom he is sent. His task is to warn the wicked, who must themselves choose to turn from their wicked ways.

According to Paul, our only responsibility is "to love one another" (Rom 13:8). But the love required may be "tough love." Today's Gospel outlines a three-step program for acting responsibly toward the brother or sister who sins. If confrontation and intervention fail, the last resort is excommunication. In the language of the Gospel, "Treat him as you would a Gentile or a tax collector" (Mt 18:17). As Raymond Brown notes, this raises the question: is the sinner "now to be shunned totally, or is he to be the subject of outreach and concern in imitation of a Jesus," who was reputed to be "a friend of tax collectors and sinners" (see Mt 11:19)?[25] "If today you hear his voice ..." (Ps 95:7).

B

First Reading: Is 35:4–7a
Responsorial Psalm: Ps 146:7, 8–9, 9–10
Second Reading: Jas 2:1–5
Gospel: Mk 7:31–37

Mark gives special attention to today's Gospel miracle, since coupled with the cure of the daughter of the Syrophoenician woman that precedes it, it anticipates and authorizes the mission to the Gentiles. Allusions to the Hebrew Bible abound in this story, particularly to the oracle of salvation from Isaiah, today's first reading. There is a verbal link to the prophecy of Ezekiel, too, in the Greek word for "be opened," which also appears in Ezekiel 24:26. And surely the acclaim of the crowd, "He has done all things well" (Mk 7:37), is meant to recall the words of Genesis, "God looked at everything he had made, and he found it very good" (1:31). All this is to say that the end-time triumph of God, who comes with divine recompense to save, has arrived in Jesus and, through him, extends even to the Gentiles.

The triumph of God that Isaiah announces and that arrives in Jesus demonstrates God's preference for the powerless and the poor—that is, the blind, the deaf, the lame, the tongue-tied. This is the point of James as well when he urges his community to "show no partiality" (2:1). He seeks to counteract, even in the community of Jesus' followers, the all too human tendency to be partial to the rich.

C

First Reading: Wis 9:13–18b
Responsorial Psalm: Ps 90:3–4, 5–6, 12–13, 14 17
Second Reading: Phlm 9–10, 12–17
Gospel: Lk 14:25–33

G od's way in the world is the way of the cross. Jesus says it
today with inescapable clarity: "Whoever does not carry his
own cross and come after me cannot be my disciple" (Lk 14:27).
Going this way with Jesus demands that we reassess all our relationships and reorder all our priorities. This is what it means for
us "to number our days aright"; this is "wisdom of heart" (Ps
90:12). Something of the sort is being asked of Philemon in
today's second reading. The slave Onesimus, who Paul implies
may not always have lived up to his name (which means "useful"),
has run away from the household of Philemon and found refuge
with Paul, who is in prison. Paul sends Onesimus back to his
master, as the law required, but only after he has baptized
Onesimus, making him, as Paul sees it, no longer Philemon's
slave but his brother "in the Lord" (Phlm 16).

The twists and turns of the way of the cross, the way of
Christ, make it a treacherous path to follow. That's why the two
parables of Jesus today urge us to consider well and calculate
costs before setting out. It is not human wisdom, but only the
wisdom of the "holy spirit from on high" (Wis 19:17) that can
guide us and make straight the difficult way we must walk.

Twenty-third Week in Ordinary Time

MONDAY

YEAR I   *First Reading: Col 1:24—2:3*
             Responsorial Psalm: Ps 62:6—7, 9
YEAR II   *First Reading: 1 Cor 5:1—8*
             Responsorial Psalm: Ps 5:5—6, 7, 12
YEARS I AND II *Gospel: Lk 6:6—11*

The Lucan reading for today again retells a story from Mark. Scholars note that Luke has softened Mark's portrayal of the Pharisees. In Mark, this story ends with the Pharisees plotting to destroy Jesus, while here they discuss what to do about Jesus. The effect of the story is to impress on the reader the high priority Jesus places on human need, not just on human life (the Pharisees would have agreed with him). In Colossians, the priority of the person becomes a theological insight. Paul makes clear that the core of his message is not a principle nor a precept but a person—the person of Jesus Christ. In light of this revelation, the priority of every person can be seen.

First Corinthians demonstrates just how difficult it is to live the mystery of God revealed in Christ. Some at Corinth have mistaken the priority of the person to mean that they can ignore social mores, in this case against incest. Paul offers a corrective. They must clean house as Jews do at Passover and rid themselves of the old yeast (a symbol of evil). They must make of themselves fresh dough, the "unleavened bread of sincerity and truth" (1 Cor 5:8).

TUESDAY

YEAR I   *First Reading: Col 2:6–15*
         Responsorial Psalm: Ps 145:1b–2, 8– 9, 10–11
YEAR II *First Reading: 1 Cor 6:1–11*
         Responsorial Psalm: Ps 149:1b–2, 3–4, 5–6a and 9b
YEARS I AND II *Gospel: Lk 6:12–19*

Today's selection from Colossians returns to the high Christology of the hymn that opened this letter. In Christ "dwells the whole fullness of the deity bodily" (Col 2:9). But before he waxes poetic, Paul warns, "See to it that no one captivate you with an empty, seductive philosophy" (v. 8). The best protection against error is to be grounded in Christ, "established in the faith as you were taught" (v. 7). In a more prosaic passage, Paul warns the Christians in Corinth against bringing lawsuits against each other in pagan courts of law. He urges them instead to bring their cases to their duly designated fellow Christians, who are destined by God to "judge the world" (1 Cor 6:2).

Both of today's first readings attest to the Church's need for authoritative teachers and guides. In today's Gospel, Jesus takes the first step toward providing for that need. He selects twelve men from among his followers to be his apostles. Later he will assign to them the dominion the Father has assigned to him. "In my Kingdom," he will tell them, "you will sit on thrones judging the twelve tribes of Israel" (Lk 22:29–30).

Wednesday

Year I   *First Reading: Col 3:1–11*
           Responsorial Psalm: Ps 145:2–3, 10–11, 12–13ab
Year II   *First Reading: 1 Cor 7:25–31*
           Responsorial Psalm: Ps 45:11–12, 14–15, 16–17
Years I and II *Gospel: Lk 6:20–26*

A ll three of today's readings reflect a distinctly apocalyptic perspective. They all have as their horizon the "what is above" to which Christians have already been raised "with Christ" (Col 3:2–3). Yet there is nothing "otherworldly" about these readings. The Beatitudes of Jesus are addressed to those who are living now in poverty, hunger, grief, and persecution. They know firsthand the emptiness of the present age and set their hearts on the promised future, the reign of God already theirs, but "hidden with Christ in God" (Col 3:3). This perspective underlies Paul's teaching, too. He tells the Colossians to "think of what is above, not of what is on earth" (3:2) and the Corinthians that "the time is running out.... For the world in its present form is passing away" (1 Cor 7:29, 31).

Luke's account does not spiritualize the Beatitudes as Matthew's does. Furthermore, in Luke, Jesus addresses his hearers directly: "Blessed are you...." He intends the materially poor and hungry, not the "poor in spirit" or those who "hunger and thirst for righteousness" (Mt 5:3, 6). In this way his Gospel comforts the afflicted while at the same time afflicting the comfortable.

THURSDAY

YEAR I   *First Reading: Col 3:12–17*
          Responsorial Psalm: Ps 150:1b–2, 3–4, 5–6
YEAR II   *First Reading: 1 Cor 8:1b–7, 11–13*
          Responsorial Psalm: Ps 139:1b–3, 13–14ab, 23–24
YEARS I AND II *Gospel: Lk 6:27–38*

A number of points from today's Gospel deserve attention as it puts forth the practical demands of the law of love. First, love here is not a noun but a verb; it is described by a series of action words: "do good … bless … pray …" (Lk 6:27–28). Also, this love must be given even if one is not loved in return. Luke's version says it twice: "Love your enemies, do good to those who hate you" (vv. 27, 35). This goes beyond the ancient norm of reciprocity. In fact, the criterion for such love is not "Do to others what you would have them do to you," but do to others what God would do, who "himself is kind to the ungrateful and the wicked" (vv. 31, 35). This principle of the imitation of God originates in Israel's covenant with God, who commanded, "Be holy, for I, the LORD, your God, am holy" (Lv 19:2).

The way the Colossians are addressed recalls the covenant context of the law of love. They must love because they are "God's chosen ones" (Col 3:12). Paul tells the Corinthians that such love surpasses knowledge, for it "builds up," like God, who builds us up into the body of Christ. Let us take the practical wisdom of today's readings to heart.

Friday

YEAR I *First Reading: 1 Tm 1:1–2, 12–14*
        Responsorial Psalm: Ps 16:1b–2a and 5, 7–8, 11
YEAR II *First Reading: 1 Cor 9:16–19, 22b–27*
        Responsorial Psalm: Ps 84:3, 4, 5–6, 12
YEARS I AND II *Gospel: Lk 6:39–42*

An athletic quality marks the commitment that today's three readings require of Christians. In 1 Timothy we learn that Paul has been strengthened for Christian service by the grace of the Lord Jesus granted to him in abundance. The selection from 1 Corinthians shows the robustness of Paul's faith. He does all that he does for the sake of the Gospel in the hope of sharing its blessings. In Luke, Jesus teaches that only strenuous self-criticism—removing the plank from one's own eye—enables one to guide others without falling into a ditch.

First Corinthians develops the metaphor as Paul compares the Christian to the athlete in the stadium. He says that a competitor must "run so as to win" (1 Cor 9:24). To that end, he submits to a rigorous discipline, never losing sight of the finish line. As was the custom among the rabbis, Paul then argues from the lighter to the weightier matter: if athletes do this "to win a perishable crown," how much more should we to win an imperishable crown (v. 25). In the words of the psalm, "Blessed are the men [and we would add the women] whose strength you are!" (see 84:6).

SATURDAY

∽୧◯ୡ∾

Today's Gospel concludes the Sermon on the Plain and gives us a succinct message: practice what Jesus preaches. "Why do you call me, 'Lord, Lord,' but not do what I command?" he asks. "I will show you what someone is like who comes to me, listens to my words, and acts on them" (Lk 6:46–47). This message is introduced by one parable about trees and illustrated by another about houses.

According to 1 Timothy, as a good tree is known by its fruit, so was the patience of Christ revealed in the exemplary life of Paul. In the excerpt from 1 Corinthians, on the other hand, Paul expresses concern that that community is being built like a house without a solid foundation. Some in Corinth profess faith in Christ by partaking of the Lord's Table, but at the same time they practice idol worship by participating in pagan temple meals. To paraphrase the words of the Gospel, they listen to the teaching of Jesus but they do not act on it (see Lk 6:49). Thus, their common union with idols threatens the communion of the one body of Christ. Paul is saying that partaking of the one loaf, that is, the body of Christ, is the one unshakable foundation of the Christian community.

Twenty-fourth Sunday in Ordinary Time

A

First Reading: Sir 27:30—28:9
Responsorial Psalm: Ps 103:1–2, 3–4, 9–10, 11–12
Second Reading: Rom 14:7–9
Gospel: Mt 18:21–35

"Whether we live or die, we are the Lord's" (Rom 14:9). With these words Paul prepares to ask in the verse immediately following today's passage, "Why then do you judge your brother?" (v. 10). This, in part, is the admonition of Sirach, too. "Think of the commandments, hate not your neighbor; / remember the Most High's covenant, and overlook faults" (Sir 28:7).

An important key to the parable of the Unmerciful Servant, the Gospel for today, lies in the enormity of the debt he owes the king. The "huge amount" (Mt 18:24), as it is rendered in our translation, was 10,000 talents, an astronomical sum that was impossible to repay. Knowing this allows us to appreciate the debtor's bravado: "Be patient with me, and I will pay you back in full" (v. 26). Because he fails to grasp the reality of his situation—that so totally beholden is he to the king that he literally belongs to him—he is unable to comprehend the king's unexpected generosity. And therefore he is incapable of showing mercy to his fellow servant "who owed him a much smaller amount" (v. 28). Which brings us back to Paul: "We are the Lord's," he says (Rom 14:9). Forgetting this truth makes us unable to forgive.

B

First Reading: Is 50:4c–9a
Responsorial Psalm: Ps 116:1–2, 3 4, 5–6, 8–9
Second Reading: Jas 2:14–18
Gospel: Mk 8:27–35

With Peter's confession at Caesarea Philippi, we arrive at the watershed of Mark's Gospel. The first seven chapters have revealed Jesus as the Messiah, who mediates the power of God by teaching and healing with authority. The climax of this first part of the Gospel is reached when Peter declares, "You are the Christ" (Mk 8:29), in answer to Jesus' question. Then immediately, the second part of the Gospel begins to reveal what kind of Messiah Jesus will be. "He began to teach them that the Son of Man must suffer greatly" (v. 31). The Son of Man, the Messiah, is a Suffering Servant. The revelation comes as a blow to Peter. He objects strenuously and is sternly rebuked by Jesus for thinking as human beings do and not as God does (v. 33).

What does it mean to think as God does? The answer is found in the poetry of Isaiah and the prophecy of Jesus. To think as God does is to set one's face like flint (Is 50:7), to take up one's cross (Mk 8:34), trusting absolutely that the Lord God is our help and, therefore, we can never be disgraced (Is 50:7). To think as God does is to dare to do what James calls the works of faith. It is, in the words of the psalmist, to "walk before the LORD / in the land of the living" (116:9).

C

First Reading: Ex 32:7–11, 13–14
Responsorial Psalm: Ps 51:3–4, 12–13, 17, 19
Second Reading: 1 Tm 1:12–17
Gospel: Lk 15:1–32 or 15:1–10

Each of today's readings tells at least one story of divine forgiveness mediated through human intercession. In the account from Exodus, Moses intercedes for sinful Israel in the wake of the debacle of the molten calf. He reminds God of God's own initiative on behalf of this people, the descendants of Abraham, Isaac, and Jacob. And remembering, God relents. As Paul sees it, it is by the intercession of Christ Jesus that he, "a blasphemer and a persecutor and [an] arrogant" man, has been mercifully treated (1 Tm 1:13). In the parables of Jesus, God's forgiveness is conveyed in three human scenarios: the stories of the Lost Sheep, the Lost Coin, and the Lost Son. These stories dramatize God's determined search for the sinful and straying, and God's delight in finding them.

Moses and Jesus in their intercession, the shepherd and the woman in their relentless searching, and the prodigal father all give value to the object of their efforts. So, the readings tell us, we are of infinite value, for we are the cherished objects of God's concern. Paul says, "This saying is trustworthy and deserves full acceptance" (1 Tm 1:15). Today's psalm is our response to the good news of the readings: "Have mercy on me, O God, in your goodness" (Ps 51:3).

Twenty-fourth Week in Ordinary Time

MONDAY

YEAR I   *First Reading: 1 Tm 2:1–8*
           Responsorial Psalm: Ps 28:2, 7, 8–9
YEAR II *First Reading: 1 Cor 11:17–26, 33*
           Responsorial Psalm: Ps 40:7–8a, 8b–9, 10, 17
YEARS I AND II *Gospel: Lk 7:1–10*

In Luke's Gospel, Jesus, the messianic prophet, began his ministry by announcing that his mission was to all nations. He did this by alluding to the work of two earlier prophets: Elijah, who was sent to a widow of Zarephath, and Elisha, who healed the Syrian Naaman (see Lk 4:25, 27). The miracle retold in today's Gospel is meant to remind us of the cure of Naaman the leper (see 2 Kgs 5). Like the centurion in today's story, Naaman was also a Gentile military officer. And just as the Jewish elders petition Jesus on behalf of the centurion, so did a Jewish girl tell Naaman about Elisha. Thus, like the cure of Naaman himself, the cure of the centurion's servant makes it known that there is indeed "a prophet in Israel" (2 Kgs 5:8), and that the God of Israel, as Paul writes to Timothy, "wills everyone to be saved and to come to knowledge of the truth" (1 Tm 2:4).

Today's excerpt from 1 Timothy ends with the wish that all might be free from dissension. Dissension characterizes the Corinthians when they assemble for the Lord's Supper. So Paul invokes the sacred tradition of the Last Supper for their instruction.

Tuesday

Year I   *First Reading: 1 Tm 3:1–13*
         Responsorial Psalm: Ps 101:1b–2ab, 2cd–3ab, 5, 6
Year II *First Reading: 1 Cor 12:12–14, 27–31a*
         Responsorial Psalm: Ps 100:1b–2, 3, 4, 5
Years I and II *Gospel: Lk 7:11–17*

Today's Gospel miracle is reminiscent of Elijah's raising of the son of the widow of Zarephath (see 1 Kgs 17). Because of this miracle, Jesus is acclaimed as a prophet and his ministry is acknowledged as a "visitation," a biblical term for God's gracious intervention in history.

The two first readings are both concerned about various roles within the Church. First Corinthians lists charismatic roles, that is, roles that derive from the gifts of the one Spirit, whom all Christians receive at Baptism. That the first three are numbered—"first, Apostles; second, prophets; third, teachers" (1 Cor 12:28)—indicates their importance in the foundation of the Church. The other roles ensure the body's continued growth and vitality. First Timothy, written some time after 1 Corinthians, attests to a development in the Church's infrastructure. Roles are no longer charismatic now, and so personal qualifications must determine who may serve as a bishop or a deacon. Yet in both letters, what finally matters is that the Church be a credible witness to the good news that "God has visited his people" (Lk 7:16).

WEDNESDAY

YEAR I   First Reading: 1 Tm 3:14–16
        Responsorial Psalm: Ps 111:1–2, 3–4, 5–6
YEAR II   First Reading: 1 Cor 12:31—13:13
        Responsorial Psalm: Ps 33:2–3, 4–5, 12 and 22
YEARS I AND II Gospel: Lk 7:31–35

In today's Gospel, Jesus uses a saying from the wisdom tradition of his people to characterize the men of his generation who lack seriousness and sincerity. They are noisy children who do not know what they want and so spend the day teasing and taunting one another. Similarly, Paul depicts the Corinthians as childish for quibbling and quarreling over spiritual gifts, when all the time they lack the one gift that surpasses all others.

The excerpt from 1 Timothy, on the other hand, is a monument to the seriousness and sincerity of the mature Paul. He urges Timothy to conduct himself in a manner that befits "the household of God, which is the Church of the living God, the pillar and foundation of truth" (1 Tm 3:15). He sums up that truth in an early creed tracing the career of Jesus, from his being "manifested in the flesh" to his resurrection "in the spirit" and his ascension among the angels (v. 16). It continues to serve as a call to Timothy and to us to commit ourselves to preaching Christ among the Gentiles so that he may be "believed in throughout the world" (v. 16).

Thursday

Year I   First Reading: 1 Tm 4:12–16
            Responsorial Psalm: Ps 111:7–8, 9, 10
Year II   First Reading: 1 Cor 15:1–11
            Responsorial Psalm: Ps 118:1b–2, 16ab–17, 28
Years I and II Gospel: Lk 7:36–50

Today's Gospel finds Jesus at the table of a Pharisee. Some scholars note that the Pharisee here and elsewhere in Luke may represent Christians in Luke's church who would prefer more rigid standards for admission to the table fellowship of the community. This Pharisee is given an object lesson on the nature of salvation. The parable of the Two Debtors provides the key to the story. The woman's great love concretely expressed by her generous actions proves that God has forgiven her many sins; her faith has saved her and set her feet on the path of peace (see Lk 1:77, 79). Conversely, the Pharisee's failure to show love for Jesus proves that his sins are not forgiven. Not only does the prophet Jesus read people's hearts, he reveals them as well (see Lk 2:35).

It is easy to read Paul's heart in the two first readings. He tells the Corinthians that in response to God's grace, hard work has characterized his own ministry as an apostle. He urges such work upon Timothy—and upon us all, young and old alike—with the promise, "for by doing so you will save both yourself and those who listen to you" (1 Tm 4:16).

FRIDAY

❧⟨❀⟩❧

Today's Gospel—all of three verses—is a film clip, a preview of the early Christian community that Luke will depict in Acts: devoted to the teaching of the apostles and sharing their property and possessions (see Acts 2:42, 45). With 1 Corinthians we fast-forward to a church in mid-50s A.D. Some in Corinth are denying the bodily resurrection of Jesus, so Paul writes to say, "If Christ has not been raised, your faith is vain" (1 Cor 15:17). This is the "religious teaching" that a church leader, writing in Paul's name, promotes in 1 Timothy, a letter that most scholars date some fifty years after the Corinthian correspondence.

Today's selection from 1 Corinthians is the earliest commentary we have on the resurrection of Jesus. We find here the key to how Paul understood the central mystery of our faith. It is in the last line of today's reading: "Christ has been raised from the dead, the firstfruits of those who have fallen asleep" (1 Cor 15:20). The resurrection of Jesus is of utmost importance because it reveals what awaits us all. This is what 1 Timothy means when it tells us to "lay hold of eternal life, to which you were called" (6:12).

Saturday

Luke's account of the parable of the Seed in today's Gospel is a comment on the stages of Christian life. Those on the footpath are almost Christians; they hear the word of God but never come to "believe and be saved" (Lk 8:12). Those on rocky ground are Christians who welcome the word of God with joy, but whose fervor fades when they are tested. Those among the briars do make some progress, but they are kept from maturing as Christians by the pressures and the pleasures of life. Thus it is possible at any stage to lose or to let go of the word of God. Only those who hold on to it "with a generous and good heart" bear fruit (v. 15). That is why Paul charges Timothy to keep God's word "without stain or reproach until the appearance of our Lord Jesus Christ" (1 Tm 6:14).

In 1 Corinthians, Paul uses the image of the seed to explain what the resurrected body is like. The physical body of the dead is sown in the earth, like seed, and raised up a spiritual body. The image of the seed allows Paul to make the point that it is the same body, though radically changed.

Twenty-fifth Sunday in Ordinary Time

A

First Reading: Is 55:6–9
Responsorial Psalm: Ps 145:2–3, 8–9, 17–18
Second Reading: Phil 1:20c–24, 27a
Gospel: Mt 20:1–16

"Fd my thoughts are not your thoughts, nor are your ways my ways, says the LORD" (Is 55:8). What Isaiah declares in the poetry of today's first reading, Jesus puts in a parable found only in Matthew. This is one of the few parables of Jesus that still has the capacity to engage and at times even to enrage the modern reader. It flies in the face of our sense of what is just and fair.

The way Jesus tells it, the parable does, indeed, take up the question of what is just and fair. The workers accept the landowner's offer of "what is just," but when that just wage is paid to them, they grumble because of the generosity of the owner to those who worked but a short time. Pheme Perkins calls our attention to the parable's setting in a time of "chronic underemployment." She notes that "the owner's behavior insures that everyone went home that day with the minimum amount needed for himself and his family"[26] in keeping with the Torah of Israel: "There should be no one of you in need" (Dt 15:4). To act justly, what Paul would consider conduct worthy of the Gospel of Christ (see Phil 1:27), may not always be popular, but for God's people it must be business as usual.

B

First Reading:Wis 2:12, 17–20
Responsorial Psalm: Ps 54:3–4, 5, 6–8
Second Reading: Jas 3:16—4:3
Gospel: Mk 9:30–37

Wisdom is first of all innocent ("pure"), James says, "then peaceable, gentle, compliant, full of mercy and good fruits" (Jas 3:17). But as the passage from Wisdom reveals, the good fruits of wisdom are obnoxious to the wicked, who determine to beset the just one. "With revilement and torture let us put the just one to the test / that we may have proof of his gentleness / and try his patience. / Let us condemn him to a shameful death" (Wis 2:12, 19–20). No wonder Jesus could predict with such grim certainty, "The Son of Man is to be handed over to men and they will kill him" (Mk 9:31).

The disciples of Jesus in today's Gospel are hardly innocent. On the contrary, they are caught up in the "jealousy and selfish ambition" that James decries (3:16). So Jesus places a child in their midst. The child was not for Jesus an icon of cuteness or disarming curiosity. Rather, the child was a symbol of the kind of innocence that in every age draws the fire of the wicked; the kind of innocence that can depend only on God to defend and deliver it from the hands of its foes. This is the posture of the psalmist who can say with total confidence, "Behold, God is my helper; / the Lord sustains my life" (Ps 54:6).

C

First Reading: Am 8:4–7
Responsorial Psalm: Ps 113:1–2, 4–6, 7–8
Second Reading: 1 Tm 2:1–8
Gospel: Lk 16:1–13 or 16:10–13

In all the readings for this Sunday, two worlds collide: the earthly realm, where business goes on as usual; and the heavenly realm, from where the one God of heaven and earth presides over all. In the first reading, Amos describes the deceitful business practices of those in Israel "who trample upon the needy / and destroy the poor of the land" (8:4). His oracle concludes with the ominous observation that God has seen and will never "forget a thing they have done" (v. 7). Instructing his community to offer prayers "for kings and for all in authority," 1 Timothy acknowledges the legitimate authority of earthly rulers. But they rule only within the sovereign, saving will of the one God and the one mediator between earth and heaven, that is, Jesus Christ (2:1–2, 5).

In today's parable, Jesus uses the deceitful business practices of the dishonest steward to make a point about the reign of God. Unlike Amos, Jesus is not concerned with passing judgment on this example of corrupt business practices. Rather, he commends to us the practical wisdom of the quick-thinking steward. We must be as realistic as he was in assessing our own situation and as resourceful in acting to secure our future.

Twenty-fifth Week in Ordinary Time

Monday

Year I   *First Reading: Ezra 1:1–6*
         Responsorial Psalm: Ps 126:1b–2ab, 2cd–3, 4–5, 6
Year II *First Reading: Prv 3:27–34*
         Responsorial Psalm: Ps 15:2–3a, 3bc–4ab, 5
Years I and II *Gospel: Lk 8:16–18*

One of today's first readings is taken from the Book of Proverbs, which is an example of "wisdom literature." Wisdom here is not esoteric knowledge but the common sense that allows individuals and communities to conduct themselves reasonably and responsibly. Such wisdom is not learned by reading books but by reflecting on one's lived experience. Often it is captured in pithy sayings that are easy to remember and to pass on. The selection for today collects five of these sayings about being a good neighbor. In today's Gospel, Jesus also resorts to proverbial wisdom—"No one who lights a lamp conceals it with a vessel or sets it under a bed ..." (Lk 8:16)—to impress on his disciples that the word of God they have heard from him must be shared with others.

Today's other first reading from the Book of Ezra records a momentous event. The edict of Cyrus the King of Persia marks the end of the Babylonian exile. This good news is greeted with a proverb in the responsorial psalm: "Those that sow in tears / shall reap rejoicing" (Ps 126:5).

TUESDAY

Today's reading from Ezra reports that the Jews, after returning from exile, have completed rebuilding the house of God,
which the Persians subsidized and the prophets Haggai and
Zechariah supported. Finally, "the children of Israel ... celebrated the dedication of this house of God with joy" (Ezra 6:16). So
the service of God resumed in Jerusalem as "prescribed in the
book of Moses" (v. 18). Echoing earlier prophets, the selection
from Proverbs says this about worship in God's house: "To do
what is right and just / is more acceptable to the LORD than sacrifice" (21:3). This is not a rejection of sacrifice, but a reminder of
the overriding importance of keeping God's commandments.

Similarly, in today's Gospel, Jesus declares that membership
in his house consists in hearing the word of God and acting on it.
In Luke's version, the passage takes on a Marian flavor, for Luke
has presented Mary from the beginning as the handmaid of the
Lord, who hears the word of God and does it (Lk 8:21; see
1:38).

Wednesday

In today's Gospel, Jesus sends the Twelve to spread the good news, as he himself has been doing by combining preaching and healing. The text emphasizes that they are to take with them only the barest necessities and to depend for the rest on God's providence. In this they are like Agur, the wise man whose words are reported in today's reading from Proverbs. He asks only for truth and the little food he needs to live (see Prv 30:7–8).

In a way, the Twelve are also like the priest-scribe Ezra, who journeyed from Babylon to bring the book of the law of God to the Jews who had returned from exile. His message was not always well received, and the conditions he found in Jerusalem greatly disturbed him. Today's selection is his prayer of lament at the sin of his people, his "testimony against them," as it were (Lk 9:5). Yet his prayer ends in gratitude to God for not abandoning Israel, but rather giving them "new life" to build the house of God and begin afresh. In a very real way, the mission of the Twelve is also a new beginning, an offer of new life, the proclamation of the kingdom of God and the restoration of the sick.

THURSDAY

Each of today's readings seems to say something about priori-ties. The prophet Haggai calls the Jews who have returned from exile in Babylon to consider their ways: "You have sown much, but have brought in little; / you have eaten, but have not been satisfied" (1:6). The reason? They did not make rebuilding the house of God their priority upon their return. So now they dwell in paneled houses, while God's house lies in ruins. Thomas à Kempis, who wrote the *Imitation of Christ*, thought that Qoheleth's totally negative portrayal of life was "the highest wis-dom," since it assessed all things as vain and futile, giving sole priority to the service of God.

In the brief selection from Luke, Herod finds himself con-fused and confounded by Jesus. Herod's past actions are called into question, such as the beheading of John the Baptist. He faces an insecure future. "Who then is this?" he wonders (Lk 9:9). The answer could reorder all his priorities and reorient his whole life. But then, it could simply satisfy his curiosity and serve his polit-ical ambition. He has a choice, and so do we.

Friday

❧⦵❧

Today's readings confirm the popular wisdom that tells us not to judge a book by its cover. The Temple built by the Jews who returned from exile lacked the glory of Solomon's Temple. In today's reading, God speaks through Haggai to reassure the people: "I [not you] will fill this house with glory" (2:7). In other words, the true glory of God's house will consist not in external trappings of silver and gold, but in the continuing presence of God. Similarly, in today's well-known excerpt from Ecclesiastes, Qoheleth suggests that a person's external achievement, the fruit of one's labor, does not determine one's true worth. Rather, "the timeless" that God has put into the human heart is what gives worth to every person (Eccl 3:11).

In today's Gospel, Peter confers on Jesus the familiar title "the Christ [the Messiah] of God" (Lk 9:20). But Jesus immediately qualifies Peter's answer by predicting the suffering and death he must endure. Thus he cautions Peter and all who would be his disciples: even messiahship does not consist in external achievements, but in hearing God's word and doing it whatever the cost.

SATURDAY

YEAR I   *First Reading: Zec 2:5–9, 14–15a*
            Responsorial Psalm: Jer 31:10, 11–12ab, 13
YEAR II   *First Reading: Eccl 11:9—12:8*
            Responsorial Psalm: Ps 90:3–4, 5–6, 12–13, 14 and 17
YEARS I AND II *Gospel: Lk 9:43b–45*

In today's Gospel, the disciples, afraid to question, cannot or will not grasp the reality of impending death. But Qoheleth, who boldly questions everything, confronts it squarely. In today's first reading, he presents old age allegorically: the idle "grinders" are the few teeth left in the mouth of an old person; the closed "doors to the street" are his deaf ears; the bloom of the almond is his white hair. The poem ends with four images: the snapped silver cord, the broken golden bowl, the shattered pitcher, and the broken pulley. Thus, he concludes, "the life breath returns to God who gave it" (Eccl 12:3–7). This is death, and the disciples fail to understand that even Jesus will not be spared.

The vision of the prophet Zechariah proclaims the future glory of Jerusalem. This city, teeming with human beings and animals, will not need walls for protection, for God "will be for her an encircling wall of fire … the glory in her midst" (Zec 2:9). This vision, meant for returning exiles, is a symbol of resurrection—of the power of God to raise what is dead—a city, a savior—to new life.

Twenty-sixth Sunday in Ordinary Time

A

First Reading: Ez 18:25–28
Responsorial Psalm: Ps 25:4–5, 6–7, 8–9
Second Reading: Phil 2:1–11 or 2:1–5
Gospel: Mt 21:28–32

Today's excerpt from Ezekiel represents a development in the religious consciousness of ancient Israel. Although the principle of individual responsibility was already in the Torah (see Dt 24:16), as long as they lived as a defined community on the land that God had given them, the Israelites tended to think of obedience to God as a collective response to God's law. In exile, however, it became important that each individual assume responsibility for living in obedient faith. This is the point of the first reading and of the Gospel. In the parable Jesus tells, each son must be judged individually on the strength of what he actually did, not what he said he would do. So it is, Ezekiel says, that the virtuous who commit iniquity will be punished and the wicked, by doing what is right, shall live (Ez 18:26–28); or, in Jesus' words, so it is that tax collectors and prostitutes are entering the kingdom of God ahead of the righteous (Mt 21:31).

In the hymn in Philippians, Jesus' whole life is summed up in his obedience. But Paul does not offer the obedience of Jesus as an example. Rather, he says that Jesus' attitude of humble obedience is already ours; we have only, individually, to act on it (Phil 2:5).

B

First Reading: Nm 11:25–29
Responsorial Psalm: Ps 19:8, 10, 12–13, 14
Second Reading: Jas 5:1–6
Gospel: Mk 9:38–43, 45, 47–48

Just how lightly the mantle of charismatic authority rested on Moses' shoulders is made clear in today's first reading. When God takes some of the spirit that was on Moses and confers it on the seventy elders, they begin to prophesy—even the two who were not with the rest. Joshua wants Moses to stop these two, to which Moses says, "Are you jealous for my sake? Would that all the people of the LORD were prophets! Would that the LORD might bestow his spirit on them all!" (Nm 11:29). In today's Gospel, John plays Joshua to Jesus' Moses. He wants to stop the exorcist who is driving out demons in Jesus' name. But Jesus tells him, "Do not prevent him. . . . Whoever is not against us is for us" (Mk 9:39–40).

The Gospel continues with a series of Jesus' sayings in which the unquenchable fire of Gehenna—"where 'their worm does not die'" (see Is 66:24)—figures prominently. The same dire imagery is used by James to condemn the rich who have amassed great wealth by depriving the workers of their wages and the righteous of their livelihood (5:2–3). We tend to recoil from such relentless rhetoric. We like our religion in small, artificially sweetened doses. But Jesus does not pander to or pamper his followers. "Everyone will be salted with fire" (Mk 9:49).

C

First Reading: Am 6:1a, 4–7
Responsorial Psalm: Ps 146:7, 8–9, 9–10
Second Reading: 1 Tm 6:11–16
Gospel: Lk 16:19–31

Amos and Luke both champion the cause of the poor, as today's readings make clear. For that matter, even 1 Timothy, in the two verses immediately following today's selection, teaches that exhorting the rich "not to rely on so uncertain a thing as wealth but rather on God" is an important duty for the "man of God" (6:17).

According to Pheme Perkins, today's parable is so arresting not so much for what it says about giving alms to the poor, a basic biblical principle, but for the pathos with which it exposes the predicament of the rich.[27] Even from the depths of the netherworld, the rich man clings to the illusion of his superior status and commands Lazarus, now safe in the bosom of Abraham, to run and fetch him water (Lk 16:24). Like the leisured and lazy classes in Jerusalem at the time of Amos who could not imagine the collapse of Joseph (Am 6:6), "the rich man is pictured as one who still does not grasp his situation."[28] He persists in thinking he can at least secure his family's future. This is the real danger of riches, Jesus says, the complacency that cannot be penetrated by Moses or the prophets or even by the one who rises from the dead.

Twenty-sixth Week in Ordinary Time

MONDAY

YEAR I   *First Reading: Zec 8:1–8*
          Responsorial Psalm: Ps 102:16–18, 19–21, 2 and 22–23
YEAR II   *First Reading: Jb 1:6–22*
          Responsorial Psalm: Ps 17:1bcd, 2–3, 6–7
YEARS I AND II *Gospel: Lk 9:46–50*

The concept of the name figures in some way in all of today's readings. The Gospel reworks the familiar saying of Jesus about the little child. In Luke, it is not so much an exhortation to be humble as an explanation of what it means to be sent. Jesus tells the disciples that being sent in his name (*epi to onomati*) makes even the least among them great, for it was understood in the Judaism of Jesus' day that the one who is sent is as the one who sent him. In Zechariah's prophecy, the presence of God in Jerusalem confers a new name on that city. It shall now "be called the faithful city and ... the holy mountain" (8:3). Finally, Job's testing is to determine if he is worthy to bear the name that God has given him, "my servant Job" (Jb 1:8). And he is. In all his trials, he does not once blaspheme, but blesses the name of the Lord.

Like Job and Jerusalem, so we who have been baptized in the name of Jesus must strive to be worthy of that name "that is above every name" (see Phil 2:9). For only thus will the prophecy of today's Psalm 102 come true: "The nations shall revere your name, O LORD" (v. 16).

Tuesday

꩜

When today's Gospel says that Jesus "resolutely determined to journey to Jerusalem" (Lk 9:51), it is rendering a Greek phrase that literally means "to harden one's face." This is the posture of Job as he mounts his verbal attack against the God who has hemmed him in on every side. Though he begins by cursing the day he was born, he will eventually come into the presence of God, who will answer him from the heart of the storm. It is the posture of Jesus, too, as he resolutely determines to go to Jerusalem, knowing full well what awaits him there. For Luke, Jesus' journey to Jerusalem, where he will be taken up from this world, is an image of the Christian life. Like the first disciples, we are all called to journey faithfully with Jesus along the road to Jerusalem, by way of the cross, into the presence of God.

The prophet Zechariah looks to the time when many peoples and nations will also firmly determine to go to Jerusalem. He says that in those days, people of every nationality and of every language will take hold of every Jew—and, we would say, of every follower of Jesus the Jew—and beg, "Let us go with you, for we have heard that God is with you" (Zec 8:23).

WEDNESDAY

In today's Gospel, Luke continues to portray Jesus as a messianic prophet. Already we have seen that, like Ezekiel, Jesus the Son of Man "hardens his face" to go to Jerusalem (see Ez 21:7–8; Lk 9:51), where he will be "taken up" to heaven like Elijah (see 2 Kgs 2:1, 9–12; Acts 1:9–11). In today's selection, the request that a would-be follower makes of Jesus echoes the request that Elisha made of Elijah first to bid farewell to his father and mother and then to follow him (1 Kgs 19:19–21; Lk 9:61). But something greater than Elijah is here. So while Elisha is allowed to kiss his parents good-bye, the would-be disciple is not. Nor is he allowed even first to bury his father. The demands of Christian discipleship supersede all other duties.

Like Jesus, Nehemiah in today's reading also sets his face to Jerusalem. He is determined to go there, "to the city of my ancestors' graves, to rebuild it" (Neh 2:5). Job, on the other hand, "hardens his face" for a confrontation with God. He wants to sue God, but has little hope of winning his case, since the defendant would also be the judge! In the end, even he will have to yield to the awesome otherness of God.

Thursday

Today's selections from Nehemiah and Luke both concern the proclamation of God's word. In the first reading, Ezra brings the book of the law of God to the whole people gathered in the liturgical assembly. He not only reads from the book, but also interprets what is read so that all can understand the word of the Lord. The people weep in repentance, but he tells them this is good news, adding, "Rejoicing in the LORD must be your strength!" (Neh 8:10).

In the Gospel, Jesus sends the seventy-two ahead of him "to every town and place he intended to visit" to announce the good news that "the Kingdom of God is at hand" (Lk 10:1, 11). They are not only to preach, but also to interpret their message by healing the sick. This is good news for those who receive it, but judgment for those who refuse.

Even Job is the bearer of good news in today's reading. "I know that my Vindicator lives" (19:25), he declares, and although commentators disagree as to who this Vindicator (*go'el*) is, there is no doubt that Job hopes against hope that he will finally be vindicated. Was it Karl Barth who said, "The good news is that the bad news is not the last word"?

FRIDAY

YEAR I   *First Reading: Bar 1:15–22*
          Responsorial Psalm: Ps 79:1b –2, 3–5, 8, 9
YEAR II   *First Reading: Jb 38:1, 12–21; 40:3–5*
          Responsorial Psalm: Ps 139:1–3, 7–8, 9–10, 13–14ab
YEARS I AND II *Gospel: Lk 10:13–16*

A ll three of today's readings announce dire consequences for
the wicked who fail to hear or to heed the word of God. The
passage from Baruch is a penitential prayer, a confession of sin
that spans "the time [when] the LORD led our ancestors out of the
land of Egypt until the present day" (1:19), that is, from the time
of the exile in Babylon. He says that evil clings to them because
"we have been disobedient to the LORD ... and only too ready to
disregard his voice" (v. 19). In the Lord's first speech, addressed
to Job out of the storm, the command of the Lord is heard and
heeded by the morning that at dawn colors the earth "as though
it were a garment," but withholds light from sinners and shatters
their pride, shaking them from the surface of the earth (Jb 38:1,
13–15). In the Gospel, Jesus says that the same fate will befall
Chorazin, Bethsaida, and Capernaum. They will "go down to the
netherworld" because they have rejected the word of life (Lk
10:15).

The readings call us in turn to heed those whom Jesus has
sent to speak his word to us. To hear them is to hear him, and the
one who sent him. To reject them is to reject him and the one
who sent him (Lk 10:16).

Saturday

Each of today's readings promises a happy ending. The passage from Baruch depicts the city of Jerusalem as a widow bereft of her children, who have been taken into exile because of their sins. Framing her lament are the prophet's words of reassurance: "Fear not," he tells the people, "for he who has brought disaster upon you will, in saving you, bring you back enduring joy" (Bar 4:27, 29). The Book of Job also ends on a happy note in the other first reading for today. Once bereft of his children like Jerusalem, Job is given back in his last days the joy of his earlier ones, and more.

The return of the seventy-two disciples after their first foray into the mission field fills Jesus with joy in today's Gospel. He rejoices in God's victory over Satan and in the part his own disciples have played in it. The joy of Jesus here is *agalliasis*, that is, joy that originates not in the self but in the Spirit. It is liturgical in character, grateful praise, delight in God's saving work. The psalms are full of *agalliasis*. As today's Psalm 69 attests, such joy is the prerogative of the poor, those lowly ones whom the Lord hears and helps and does not spurn (vv. 33–34).

Twenty-seventh Sunday in Ordinary Time

A

First Reading: Is 5:1–7
Responsorial Psalm: Ps 80:9, 12, 13–14, 15–16, 19–20
Second Reading: Phil 4:6–9
Gospel: Mt 21:33–43

⌘

T he modern reader must be alerted to two points when approaching Matthew's version of the parable of the Wicked Tenants. First, the parable as it came from Jesus has been reworked by Matthew, who received it from Mark. The most obvious change he makes is to describe the fate of the wicked tenants—"He will put those wretched men to a wretched death" (Mt 21:41)—in a way that would evoke the destruction of Jerusalem in A.D. 70. Second, historically, Christian readers have interpreted the rejection and replacement of the tenants to mean that Israel has been rejected and replaced by the Church as God's people. The parable does not support that reading. It is not the vineyard (Israel) but the tenants (the leaders of the people) who are rejected and replaced.

Given Matthew's reworking, what does this parable have to say to us? In both the parable and its biblical prototype, the song of the vineyard from Isaiah (see Is 5:1–7), the core issue is the necessity of bearing "good fruit." This is a biblical image for living in faithful obedience to God's will, the kind of life that Paul says frees us from anxiety and assures us of peace (Phil 4:6–7).

B

First Reading: Gn 2:18–24
Responsorial Psalm: Ps 128:1–2, 3, 4–5, 6
Second Reading: Heb 2:9–11
Gospel: Mk 10:2–16 or 10:2–12

In today's Gospel, Jesus and the Pharisees debate in typically rabbinic fashion the ever timely issue of divorce, where a question is often answered with a question. Jesus does not deny their interpretation of Deuteronomy 24:1–4, which does say that a man may divorce his wife if "he finds in her something indecent" (v. 1). However, he argues that the text represents not a law but a dispensation given by Moses "because of the hardness of your hearts" (Mk 10:5). Then returning to the biblical ideal of marriage—marriage as God intended it "from the beginning of creation" (v. 6; also Gn 2:24)—he prohibits divorce absolutely and reiterates the prohibition when his disciples later question him about it.

Jesus' hard line on divorce can raise difficult questions for Catholics today as it apparently did for the disciples. Wilfrid Harrington speaks to this point in his commentary on Mark: "Jesus prohibited divorce on the assumption that the marriage involved is a real marriage." And he adds, this is the same Jesus who understands our humanness and who is not ashamed to be called our brother (Heb 2:11).[29]

C

First Reading: Hb 1:2–3; 2:2–4
Responsorial Psalm: Ps 95:1–2, 6–7, 8–9
Second Reading: 2 Tm 1:6–8, 13–14
Gospel: Lk 17:5–10

The prayer of the apostles in today's Gospel is one we can all make our own. The readings for this Sunday help us to understand exactly what we are praying for when we ask the Lord to increase our faith. The first reading is from Habakkuk, who, writing in a time of turmoil not too long before the fall of Jerusalem in 586 B.C., dares to question God. Then taking his position like a guard on the rampart, he waits to see what God will say. The answer comes in the form of a vision that he is commanded to write down. It is this vision, pressing ineluctably toward fulfillment, which persuades him to wait and wait patiently, for "it will surely come" (Hb 2:3). Second Timothy offers Paul as a model of faith. His faith is a gift of the indwelling Spirit, not "a spirit of cowardice but rather of power and love and self-control" (1:7). Finally, the parable of Jesus depicts faith as humble service of a Master who is generous and loving, but Master nonetheless.

This then is faith: the gift of the Spirit that moves in Paul; the patience of Habakkuk, who waits on the rampart; and the humility of Jesus, who serves at the table, always knowing that to do so is unmerited grace.

Twenty-seventh Week in Ordinary Time

MONDAY

YEAR I   *First Reading: Jon 1:1—2:1–2, 11*
          Responsorial Psalm: Jon 2:3, 4, 5, 8
YEAR II   *First Reading: Gal 1:6–12*
          Responsorial Psalm: Ps 111:1b–2, 7–8, 9 and 10c
YEARS I AND II *Gospel: Lk 10:25–37*

The story of Jonah and the parable of the Good Samaritan both share an element of surprise. Commanded by God to preach to the Ninevites, a people the Israelites hated for their cruelty to the nations they conquered, Jonah makes for Tarshish. While he sleeps in the hold of the ship, a violent storm threatens to destroy him and everyone else aboard. The crew soon discovers that Jonah's flight from God has placed them in peril. But the unexpected humanity of these pagan sailors is meant to surprise the reader. They throw Jonah into the sea with great reluctance and only as a last resort. Similarly in the parable of Jesus, the surprise lies in the unexpected humanity of the hated Samaritan. Both stories aim to shock their hearers into new ways of seeing and acting.

Paul based his entire apostolate on this new way of seeing and acting. He proclaimed to the Gentile Galatians the Gospel he received as a revelation from Jesus Christ: that salvation is possible for all human beings who actively love God and neighbor.

Tuesday

Year I   *First Reading: Jon 3:1–10*
         Responsorial Psalm: Ps 130:1b–2, 3–4ab, 7–8
Year II   *First Reading: Gal 1:13–24*
         Responsorial Psalm: Ps 139:1b–3, 13–14ab, 14c–15
Years I and II *Gospel: Lk 10:38–42*

T he theme of repentance marks the two first readings for
today. The selection from Jonah describes the conversion of
Nineveh. Like everything else in this humorous book, this, too, is
told with deliberate exaggeration. This "enormously large" city
experiences a total repentance that extends to all, great and small,
man and beast alike. Such repentance moves God to repent, and
Nineveh is spared (Jon 3:3, 5–10). The excerpt from Galatians
relates the conversion of Paul. The text deliberately emphasizes
the totality that seems to have characterized Paul, for example, his
persecution of the Church "beyond measure" because he was
"even more a zealot" as a fervent Jew (Gal 1:13–14). But such
totality must have attracted the grace of God, for Paul is called to
spread the Gospel among the Gentiles.

    Today's Gospel is a lesson on hospitality. Jesus teaches Martha
that the one thing hospitality requires is wholly attending to the
guest, as Mary is doing. Yet this may teach us about repentance,
too. The conversion required of most of us is not dramatic, like
Nineveh's or Paul's. It may only require that we learn to give our
undivided attention to the Guest who already dwells in our
anxious and busy hearts.

Wednesday

The prayer that Jesus teaches his disciples in today's Gospel is typically Jewish. The first two petitions of the Lord's Prayer—"hallowed be your name, your kingdom come"—are paralleled in the Jewish prayer called the *Kaddish*. It begins, "Magnified and sanctified be his great Name," and goes on, "May he establish his kingdom during your life and during your days and during the life of all the house of Israel." The Jewishness of Jesus gives us an insight into the controversy Paul reports in today's passage from Galatians. The first followers of Jesus were Jews, like him. Their mission was limited to the Jews, like Jesus' mission during his earthly life. Paul's mission to the Gentiles challenged the nascent Church to make an imaginative leap of faith in a new direction. It would require an education of the heart.

The Book of Jonah describes the education of Jonah's heart. Jonah seems unable to imagine God's desire to save all people, even Ninevites. Loving and losing the gourd plant gives Jonah an inkling of God's love for all and of God's reluctance to lose any. Both of the psalms for today invite all nations to praise the Lord, who alone is God, and to glorify God's name (117:1; 86:9–10).

THURSDAY

YEAR I   *First Reading: Mal 3:13–20b*
          Responsorial Psalm: Ps 1:1–2, 3, 4 and 6
YEAR II   *First Reading: Gal 3:1–5*
          Responsorial Psalm: Lk 1:69–70, 71–72, 73–75
YEARS I AND II *Gospel: Lk 11:5–13*

Both the prophet we know as Malachi and the Apostle Paul are addressing recalcitrant members of their respective communities in today's two first readings. The prophet speaks to a post-exilic community of Jews, some of whom are struggling with the age-old question of why the wicked prosper. Disgruntled, they declare they have nothing to gain by keeping God's command. Malachi distinguishes between these scoffers and those who fear God, who alone are designated as God's "special possession" (3:17). Paul scolds the Gentile Christians of Galatia for succumbing to the influence of "Judaizers"—those who believed that Gentile converts should observe Mosaic Law. He distinguishes between the Gospel he preached and the other gospel on the basis of their experience of the Spirit. "Does, then, the one who supplies the Spirit to you … do so from works of the law or from faith in what you heard?" (Gal 3:5).

Like Paul, today's Gospel suggests that God gives us the Holy Spirit not in acknowledgement of our good works but in answer to our fervent, faithful prayer. In Matthew's version of this saying of Jesus, the Father gives "good things" to those who ask (7:11); in Luke, the Holy Spirit is the answer to every prayer (11:13).

Friday

❧⊙❧

The two first readings for today are both difficult passages. The excerpt from Joel is part of a communal lament, a special liturgy during a natural disaster when a plague of locusts devastates the land. The locusts are the vast army, "a people numerous and mighty," who overspread the mountains like dawn (Jl 2:2). But this dawn brings darkness, not light, and it portends the Day of the Lord. In the selection from Galatians, Paul marshals no less than five passages from the Hebrew Bible to support his argument: the righteousness of Abraham consisted in faith and not in the works of the law (Gal 3:8 [Gn 12:3]; 3:10 [Dt 27:26]; 3:11 [Hb 2:4]; 3:12 [Lv 18:5]; 3:13 [Dt 21:23]).

Like Paul, Jesus also makes his argument with the help of the Hebrew Bible. "If it is by the finger of God that [I] drive out demons," he says, "then the Kingdom of God has come upon you" (Lk 11:20). This is an allusion to Moses, who "by the finger of God" bested Pharaoh's magicians (see Ex 8:15–19). Here again Luke presents Jesus as a prophetic Messiah as powerful in deed as in word.

SATURDAY

Today's Gospel, all of two verses, is unique to Luke and is important for what it tells us about Mary. A woman declares the mother of Jesus blessed for the privilege of being his biological parent. Jesus replies with a second beatitude that, in spite of the English translation, does not discount the first one. As Raymond Brown and his coauthors explain in their book, *Mary in the New Testament*, the word *menoun*, rendered here as "rather," can also mean "yes, but even more." [30] Without denying Mary's unique privilege, Jesus declares her even more blessed for having heard the word of God and kept it. His mother is a model disciple. Marian devotion has often used the city of Jerusalem as an image of Mary. Today's reading from Joel explains why: it is God's presence within both Jerusalem and Mary that makes them holy—full of grace.

The selection from Galatians extends our reflection on Mary. Faith and Baptism in Christ Jesus make us children of God, but of Mary, too, that daughter of Abraham who inherited all that was promised.

Twenty-eighth Sunday in Ordinary Time

A

First Reading: Is 25:6–10a
Responsorial Psalm Ps 23:1–3a, 3b–4, 5, 6
Second Reading: Phil 4:12–14, 19–20
Gospel: Mt 22:1–14 or 22:1–10

Matthew's hand is evident in a number of places in today's parable of the Wedding Feast, which appears in Luke as the parable of the Great Supper (14:16–24). Two of the most noteworthy Matthean additions to the parable are the violence with which the king's servants are received and with which he retaliates, and the appending of the parable of the Wedding Garment. The first is an attempt to associate the rejection of the king's invitation with the destruction of Jerusalem in A.D. 70, and the second reflects Matthew's concern with the theme of judgment.

In the parable of Jesus, as in the oracle of Isaiah, today's first reading, the final triumph of God as King is imaged as "a feast of rich food and choice wines" (Is 25:6). No doubt his sure hope that this banquet awaits him allows Paul to live with feast or famine in the present. As Matthew sees it, however, the feast is ready even now. Some (his Jewish rivals) have refused the invitation, while others (his Christian community) have accepted it. But even for them, he warns, admission to the feast is not enough; they must don the wedding garment, a sign of Baptism, and live lives worthy of the Gospel.

B

First Reading:Wis 7:7–11
Responsorial Psalm: Ps 90:12–13, 14–15, 16–17
Second Reading: Heb 4:12–13
Gospel: Mk 10:17–30 or 10:17–27

In today's first reading, Solomon discovers in the spirit of Wisdom an incomparable grace that relativizes all else in his life: power and riches, health and beauty all pale in comparison to her, he says. This reading is followed by a psalm ascribed to Moses, another man who prayed for "wisdom of heart" (Ps 90:12).

In today's Gospel, a third man is offered the incomparable grace of following Jesus, of revaluing all that he has in light of this heavenly treasure. But sadly he goes away, "for he had many possessions." (Mk 10:22). Jesus' comment on the rich man's departure astounds the disciples. "How hard it is for those who have wealth to enter the kingdom of God!" he says. And when they ask him, "Who can be saved?" he tells them, "For human beings it is impossible, but not for God" (Mk 10:23, 26–27).

The words of Jesus contain a paradox. On the one hand, discipleship is a grace, impossible for human beings. On the other hand, it is a choice—a choice to accept the grace or not. So it is in Hebrews that the word of God, the call of Christ, is likened to a sharp two-edged sword. In biblical language, the sword is an instrument of judgment; it penetrates soul and spirit, joints and marrow, to see what is in our hearts (Heb 4:12).

C

First Reading: 2 Kgs 5:14–17
Responsorial Psalm: Ps 98:1, 2–3, 3–4
Second Reading: 2 Tm 2:8–13
Gospel: Lk 17:11–19

⌑⌑⌑

The liturgy today invites us to read the story of the ten lepers in today's Gospel in light of the story of Naaman the leper. The ten lepers are cured by acting on the word of Jesus, and Naaman was cured by acting on the word of Elisha, the man of God. One leper (a Samaritan) returns to thank Jesus, glorifying God in a loud voice. Similarly, Naaman the Aramaen also returned, bearing gifts to thank Elisha. The gratitude of both men is more than an act of politeness; it is a profession of true faith that acknowledges "there is no God in all the earth, except in Israel" (2 Kgs 5:15).

The story of the ten lepers in its context in Luke's Gospel also serves as an example of faith that is not true. Surely all the lepers had some faith, for the words of Jesus imply that all were healed. But the faith of those who did not return to thank and praise God was hardly more than good fortune; it was not the faith that saves. Faith that saves is not prevented by the gift from seeing the Giver. And it acknowledges, with Paul, that even if we are unfaithful or ungrateful, for that matter, "he remains faithful, for he cannot deny himself" (2 Tm 2:13). Praise him.

Twenty-eighth Week in Ordinary Time

MONDAY

YEAR I   *First Reading: Rom 1:1–7*
         Responsorial Psalm: Ps 98:1bcde, 2–3ab, 3cd–4
YEAR II   *First Reading: Gal 4:22–24, 26–27, 31—5:1*
          Responsorial Psalm: Ps 113:1b–2, 3–4, 5a and 6–7
YEARS I AND II *Gospel: Lk 11:29–32*

The sayings of Jesus in today's Gospel and the allegory of Paul in the Letter to the Galatians both make the same claim: the revelation of God in Jesus is greater than Jonah, greater than Solomon, and even greater than Moses and the covenant he mediated. On the lips of Jesus and Paul, both of them Jews, such claims did not abrogate the sign of Jonah or the wisdom of Solomon or the law of Moses. They simply affirmed that the revelation of Jesus surpassed that of Jonah and Solomon and Moses, surpassed without superseding it, that is, without making it obsolete. The Hebrew Scriptures, what we call the Old Testament, remained divine revelation, the word of God, for Jesus and Paul as they do for us.

The Gospel Paul proclaimed is summed up in the opening of Paul's Letter to the Romans. It is thoroughly Christocentric. Designating the risen Jesus as "Son of God in power," God identified him as the Messiah (Rom 1:4). The "Gospel of God" is that in Jesus and through him the messianic age of freedom and fullness of life has dawned.

Tuesday

In today's reading from Romans, Paul condemns as fools those godless people who resist the knowledge of God accessible to all who have eyes to see the world God has made. Paul says that such folly is inexcusable. Psalm 19 makes the same claim when it says, "The heavens declare the glory of God" (v. 2).

In today's Gospel, Jesus indicts as fools those among the Pharisees who care more about external observances than about internal dispositions. Along the same lines, Paul insists in Galatians that we have been set free not by external observance of the law but by the internal disposition of faith in Christ. He says this is all that matters: "only faith working through love" (Gal 5:6). This may be the sense of Jesus' concluding remark as well. "Give alms," he tells the Pharisee at whose table he is reclining, "and behold, everything will be clean for you" (Lk 11:41). In other words, not ritual washing but love—caring concretely for the needs of others—makes one clean before God. Justice requires that the view of the Jewish law and its champions in these readings must be balanced by Psalm 119, where the law is celebrated as liberating and the object of love and delight (vv. 46, 47).

WEDNESDAY

YEAR I   *First Reading: Rom 2:1–11*
         Responsorial Psalm: Ps 62:2–3, 6–7, 9
YEAR II   *First Reading: Gal 5:18–25*
          Responsorial Psalm: Ps 1:1–2, 3, 4 and 6
YEARS I AND II   *Gospel: Lk 11:42–46*

Paul's diatribe in today's selection from Romans might well be directed to the religious authorities in today's Gospel, as well as to all of us who think of ourselves as "religious." The message seems to be that those who lord their authority over others, those who lay impossible burdens on others, those who judge others will not escape the just judgment of God, who has no favorites. The responsorial psalm reinforces the lesson of the readings when it prays that the Lord may "give back to everyone according to his [or her] works" (Ps 62:13b).

Although he does not overlook the works of the flesh (unredeemed humanity), Paul concludes his letter to the Galatians on a more positive note, listing the fruits of the Spirit. He calls these "fruits" rather than "works" in order to show that they are not human achievements, but the result of belonging to Christ and living by the Spirit. For Paul, morality is not so much characterized by virtue, as by vitality; it comes from sharing the risen life of Jesus the Christ. Not surprisingly, the hallmark of life in the Spirit is love (*agape*), a term that includes both love of God and love of others as God loves them.

THURSDAY

YEAR I   *First Reading: Rom 3:21–30*
            Responsorial Psalm: Ps 130:1b–2, 3–4, 5–6ab
YEAR II   *First Reading: Eph 1:1–10*
            Responsorial Psalm: Ps 98:1, 2–3ab, 3cd–4, 5–6
YEARS I AND II   *Gospel: Lk 11:47–54*

Today's readings must be understood in light of their respective literary forms: a diatribe from Romans, a Jewish prayer form from Ephesians, and polemic in the Gospel. A diatribe is a sustained scholarly discussion with an imaginary opponent. In today's text from Romans, Paul wants to persuade a Jewish opponent that if justification is by faith and not by the works of the law, then it is open to all, and Jews no longer have grounds for boasting. Polemic is a verbal attack on one's opponents, who are routinely depicted with gross exaggeration. In today's Gospel, Jesus' prophetic criticism of certain Pharisees and lawyers has been exaggerated by the bitter rivalry that raged between the early Church and the Jewish community at the time the Gospels were written.

The Letter to the Ephesians is happily free of the hostility that tore Christianity from its Jewish roots. It opens with a prayer modeled on the Jewish blessing (*berakah*). This positive appropriation of a Jewish prayer form is evidenced in the new *Catechism* as well when it describes blessing as the human response to God's gifts. "Because God blesses, the human heart can in return bless the One who is the source of every blessing" (no. 2626).

FRIDAY

In today's selection from Romans, Paul returns to a familiar theme. He argues that Abraham is the father of all the uncircumcised (the Gentiles) who are justified by faith, since according to the Scripture Abraham was justified by believing God, long before circumcision was decreed. Thus, Paul firmly grounds his Gospel in the long history of God's people, recorded in the Hebrew Scriptures. Many scholars read the Letter to the Ephesians as a synthesis of Paul's thought. Today's passage seems to generalize from his argument in Romans. Here in Ephesians, the concept of divine election—God's choice of Israel, first revealed in the call of Abraham—is taken over from the Hebrew Scriptures. Christians now are also "chosen" by God to receive an "inheritance." The Holy Spirit that we received at Baptism is but the "first installment" of that promised inheritance (Eph 1:13–14).

Today's Gospel makes it clear that divine election is a costly grace. Jesus prepares his friends and followers for the real possibility of persecution. But he assures them—and us—that we need not be afraid; in the eyes of God we "are worth more than many sparrows," however small or insignificant we may feel (Lk 12:7).

Saturday

Year I   First Reading: Rom 4:13, 16–18
            Responsorial Psalm: Ps 105:6–7, 8–9, 42–43
Year II   First Reading: Eph 1:15–23
            Responsorial Psalm: Ps 8:2–3ab, 4–5, 6–7
Years I and II Gospel: Lk 12:8–12

In today's reading, Paul tells the Romans that all "depends on faith, so that it may be a gift" (Rom 4:16). The point is that salvation is God's gift (grace); it is not earned or owned by anyone, however religious or righteous they may be. The author of the Letter to the Ephesians, having heard of that community's faith, gives thanks for the way in which God's grace—"the surpassing greatness of his power for us who believe" (Eph 1:19)—has manifested itself in them and through them.

The vision of Ephesians is triumphant. The Gospel, however, envisions a different scenario. The promised triumph, "before the angels of God" at the judgment, will depend on the disciples' uncompromising loyalty to the Son of Man when they are brought before the judges of this world (Lk 12:8). But even here those who live by faith in the God "who gives life to the dead" (Rom 4:17) are assured of God's grace. Jesus says, "Do not worry about how or what your defense will be or about what you are to say. For the Holy Spirit will teach you at that moment what you should say" (Lk 12:11–12).

Twenty-ninth Sunday in Ordinary Time

A

First Reading: Is 45:1, 4–6
Responsorial Psalm: Ps 96:1, 3, 4–5, 7–8, 9–10
Second Reading: 1 Thes 1:1–5b
Gospel: Mt 22:15–21

⤜◦◑◦⤛

Any discussion of today's Gospel must begin with a disclaimer: this text does not address the question of the relationship between church and state. It speaks instead to what is the right relationship between the human community and the one God, who is Lord, besides whom, as Isaiah declares in no uncertain terms, "there is no other" (45:5).

As usual in Matthew, the treachery of Jesus' opponents is transparent. Their yes-or-no question aims to entrap him, but Jesus is not so easily taken. He asks for a Roman coin and puts a question of his own: "Whose image is this and whose inscription?" (Mt 22:20). This is the key to his meaning. If the image of Caesar stamped on a coin means that the coin belongs to Caesar, then the image of God stamped on each and every human being means that each and every one belongs to God. This, too, is the understanding of Isaiah when, in today's reading, he declares that Cyrus the Persian is the Lord's anointed (Messiah). Even Cyrus belongs to God, "though you know me not," God tells him (Is 45:4). This is also the conviction that sends Paul to the Thessalonians "in power and in the Holy Spirit" (1 Thes 1:5).

B

First Reading: Is 53:10–11
Responsorial Psalm: Ps 33:4–5, 18–19, 20, 22
Second Reading: Heb 4:14–16
Gospel: Mk 10:35–45 or 10:42–45

The Marcan theme of suffering servanthood dominates all the readings for today. The image originates in four "songs" in Isaiah, which describe the vocation of an anonymous servant of God. Today's first reading is excerpted from the fourth song in which the redemptive value of the servant's suffering is stated most explicitly. "Through his suffering, my servant shall justify many" (Is 53:11). Although the identity of the servant is not specified, the followers of Jesus—as they came in the light of his resurrection to understand the redemptive value of his suffering and death—applied Isaiah's songs to him.

The reader of today's Gospel, knowing how the story ends, must be struck by the irony of James and John's request. When on Calvary the time comes to take their place, one at Jesus' right, the other at his left (Mk 10:37; see 15:27), they will be conspicuous only by their absence. But Jesus, who can sympathize with our weakness (Heb 4:15), patiently tells them and us one more time: "Whoever wishes to be great among you will be your servant.... For the Son of Man did not come to be served but to serve and to give his life as a ransom for many" (Mk 10:43, 45).

C

First Reading: Ex 17:8–13
Responsorial Psalm: Ps 121:1–2, 3–4, 5–6, 7–8
Second Reading: 2 Tm 3:14—4:2
Gospel: Lk 18:1–8

The readings for this Sunday present us with two somewhat graphic examples of persistence in prayer: Moses, with arms outstretched bringing victory to Israel's army, and a relentless widow wearing down an unscrupulous judge. But these stories also contain humanness and humor that must not be missed. Moses' tiredness and his need for the support of Aaron and Hur diminish his heroic stature. And suddenly we know: Moses is no hero, but rather God's humble servant, and it is God who will give victory.

As for the widow, her victory is small and grudgingly given. The words of the judge are literally, "Otherwise she will keep coming and end up giving me a black eye!"[31] But her victory is not the point. The parable is preceded by Jesus' discourse on the end time (Lk 17:22–37) and concludes with the words, "When the Son of Man comes, will he find faith on earth?" (Lk 18:8). In this context, the judge becomes a foil for God, who will at the end time see to it that justice is done speedily for those who persist in faith and prayer—"whether it is convenient or inconvenient," as Paul tells Timothy (2 Tm 4:2).

Twenty-ninth Week in Ordinary Time

MONDAY

YEAR I   First Reading: Rom 4:20–25
           Responsorial Psalm: Lk 1:69–70, 71–72, 73–75
YEAR II First Reading: Eph 2:1–10
           Responsorial Psalm: Ps 100:1b–2, 3, 4ab, 4c–5
YEARS I AND II Gospel: Lk 12:13–21

Commenting on today's Gospel, Luke Timothy Johnson notes how astutely Luke has grasped the function of possessions in human life.[32] Luke seems to know that greed expresses fear, a massive insecurity that seeks to secure life with many possessions. The only way to dispel such fear is to recognize that life is a gift from the living God, a gift that no amount of material possessions can gain or guarantee. The man in the parable is a fool because he thinks that having insured his many possessions, he has secured his life "for many years" (Lk 12:19). Zechariah, in the response to the reading from Romans, is polar opposite of the rich fool of the Gospel. Zechariah represents the *anawim*, the poor and powerless whose dependence on God is total, like Abraham's.

For Paul in Romans, Abraham is the paradigm of the person of faith who accepts God's promise of life as a gift, never questioning or doubting it and never trying to secure it by his own power or possessions. Such faith relies rather on what Ephesians describes as "the immeasurable riches of [God's] grace" (2:7).

TUESDAY

YEAR I   *First Reading: Rom 5:12, 15b, 17–19, 20b–21*
         Responsorial Psalm: Ps 40:7- 8a, 8b–9, 10, 17
YEAR II *First Reading: Eph 2:12–22*
         Responsorial Psalm: Ps 85:9ab–10, 11–12, 13–14
YEARS I AND II *Gospel: Lk 12:35–38*

In today's Gospel, Luke gives particular force to the familiar exhortation to wait and watch for the Master's return. In Luke's version, when the Master finds his servants wide-awake, he "will gird himself, have them recline at table, and proceed to wait on them" (12:37). This striking image points in two directions. It looks ahead to the Last Supper, where Jesus will declare, "I am among you as the one who serves" (Lk 22:27). It also looks back, as does the reading from Romans, to suggest a contrast with Adam. The haughtiness of Adam, who overreached himself in his desire to be like a god, is redeemed by the humility of Jesus, who makes himself the servant of all. Or as Paul puts it, "Just as through the disobedience of one man the many were made sinners, so, through the obedience of the one the many will be made righteous" (Rom 5:19).

The Letter to the Ephesians today picks up this strain and proclaims what the obedience of Christ has achieved for us. He has not only reconciled us to God, but also to one another, making us in himself one new humanity.

Wednesday

Year I   First Reading: Rom 6:12–18
            Responsorial Psalm: Ps 124:1b–3, 4–6, 7–8
Year II   First Reading: Eph 3:2–12
            Responsorial Psalm: Is 12:2–3, 4bcd, 5–6
Years I and II   Gospel: Lk 12:39–48

Peter's question in today's Gospel alerts us that this parable of Jesus is meant not only for the Twelve, but also for all who will succeed them as leaders in the household of God. To appreciate the force of Jesus' teaching, it is important to remember that the steward who is set over the other servants remains himself subject to the authority of the Master. In other words, the leader is also a servant, a slave. His position is not a privilege. Rather, it is a test and a trust—a test of how well he knows the Master's wishes and a sacred trust that will require of him a greater degree of accountability. To him, Paul's words in Romans especially apply: "If you present yourselves to someone as obedient slaves, you are slaves of the one you obey" (6:16).

In today's selection from Ephesians, Paul shows himself to be a "faithful and prudent steward" (Lk 12:42) of God's grace. He is ever mindful of the ministry that God has entrusted to him. He claims as well to know his Master's will and purpose. This is "the mystery of Christ" that was made known to him "by revelation" (Eph 3:3, 4), that is, to make Gentiles as well as Jews sharers of the promise, and he commits himself responsibly and unreservedly to it.

THURSDAY

∽೬⟨⟩ꢒ∼

In today's selection from Luke, Jesus, the messianic prophet, is like Elijah, who called down fire on the earth (see 1 Kgs 18:38). But is it the fire of judgment as in the story of Elijah, or the fire of the Spirit? Similarly, Jesus says he has a baptism to undergo. But is he referring to his death, or to the descent of the Holy Spirit? These sayings are ambiguous. It is not ambiguous, however, that the God revealed in Jesus, the same God revealed through Elijah on Mount Carmel, demands a decision, one that may sever the closest family ties. Simeon had prophesied this when Jesus was presented in the Temple (see Lk 2:35), and Jesus himself now proclaims it.

In today's reading, Paul hints at the critical decision that the Christians at Rome have made. He reminds them of how they were once the slaves of sin; now they must be "slaves to right-eousness" (Rom 6:19). The same is implied of the Ephesians. Their decision Paul credits to their being "strengthened with power through his Spirit" (Eph 3:16). That same power is at work in us, too, enabling us, in turn, to decide to let the love of Christ be the root and foundation of our lives.

Friday

The need to discern the present time and to decide for Jesus is reiterated in today's Gospel reading—with two added features. First, Jesus insists that each one must make this decision for himself or herself. "Why do you not judge for yourselves what is right?" he asks (Lk 12:57). The short parable that concludes the reading makes the second point. In Matthew, this parable is part of a lesson in the Sermon on the Mount on how Jesus' followers should deal with one another. In Luke, however, the setting is Jesus' journey to Jerusalem. Here the opponent is not a fellow Christian but Jesus himself, who urges all he meets to decide, that is, "to settle the matter on the way" (Lk 12:58).

The two first readings for today illustrate the challenge of this decision. The law of sin that Paul describes in Romans, that centrifugal pull away from the law of God, makes impossible a decision that would re-center the whole of life, impossible except for the grace of God. Grace also makes it possible for us, as well as for the Ephesians, to live lives worthy of the calling we have received.

SATURDAY

YEAR I   *First Reading: Rom 8:1–11*
         Responsorial Psalm: Ps 24:1b–2, 3–4ab, 5–6
YEAR II *First Reading: Eph 4:7–16*
         Responsorial Psalm: Ps 122:1–2, 3–4ab, 4cd–5
YEARS I AND II *Gospel: Lk 13:1–9*

"**G**row up!" Paul tells the Ephesians in the first reading, so that they may no longer be "infants, tossed by waves and swept along by every wind of teaching arising from human trickery" (4:14). Today's Gospel is surely not for children. Found only in Luke, it begins with two reports of sudden and violent death, which Jesus turns into dire warnings for his listeners. "If you do not repent, you will all perish as they did!" (13:5). Since we cannot secure our lives, death is always near for all of us, so we must not postpone repentance. Although Luke's version of the parable of the Fig Tree suggests that a little more time has been given, without repentance the end remains the same. If the fig tree does not bear fruit, it will surely be cut down.

For Paul as for Luke, repentance is not simply turning away from sin, but turning toward Jesus in faith. He tells the Romans, "Now there is no condemnation for those who are in Christ Jesus," that is, for those in whom the Spirit of God dwells (8:1). The reading from Ephesians reminds us that the Spirit has given to each and every one of us gifts that enable us to live the truth in love and so grow, as one body, to the full maturity of Christ our head (4:15).

Thirtieth Sunday in Ordinary Time

A

First Reading: Ex 22:20–26
Responsorial Psalm: Ps 18:2–3, 3–4, 47, 51
Second Reading: 1 Thes 1:5c–10
Gospel: Mt 22:34–40

Matthew wrote his Gospel in the aftermath of the destruction of the Temple in Jerusalem in A.D. 70. The loss of the Temple as the center of Jewish life evoked a variety of responses from within Judaism. One of the most important was the effort by a coalition of priests and scribes and Pharisees to fashion a program of Jewish life that revolved around the Torah as they interpreted it. This was the beginning of rabbinic Judaism as we know it. Matthew's Christian Jewish community was another minority response to the destruction of the Temple. The program advocated by this community also revolved around Torah, but as interpreted by Jesus and those authorized to teach in his name. In today's Gospel we learn that the key to Jesus' interpretation of the "whole law and the prophets" (Mt 22:40) is the double commandment.

The two greatest commandments, though distinct, cannot be separated, for love of God finds practical expression in love of neighbor. Similarly in the code of Exodus, fidelity in covenant with God is expressed in compassion toward the neighbor in need, and in 1 Thessalonians, the Gospel never comes in word alone but in every good work.

B

First Reading: Jer 31:7–9
Responsorial Psalm: Ps 126:1–2, 2–3, 4–5, 6
Second Reading: Heb 5:1–6
Gospel: Mk 10:46–52

Throughout most of Mark's Gospel, Jesus seems deliberately to dodge messianic acclaim of any kind. But in today's reading, he accepts without protest the messianic title "Son of David" from the blind beggar Bartimaeus (Mk 10:47–48). In the mouth of the blind man the words identify Jesus as the deliverer of his people, who, as Jeremiah promises the exiles in today's first reading, "will gather them from the ends of the world, with the blind and the lame in their midst" (Jer 31:8). Or as the reading from Hebrews says, citing Psalm 2 as a proof text, as Son of David he is also Son of God, a title that every son of David was given upon his accession to the throne.

In Mark's scheme, Bartimaeus is one of those outsiders who, though blind, sees Jesus more clearly than his own disciples do. This is underscored in today's story as Jesus puts to Bartimaeus the very same question he put to the sons of Zebedee in last Sunday's Gospel: "What do you want me to do for you?" (Mk 10:51). But where James and John wanted to advance themselves, Bartimaeus asks only to see. The story of Bartimaeus is a call narrative as well as a miracle story. Three times in one verse the verb "call" is used (v. 49). So having received his sight, Bartimaeus followed Jesus on the way (v. 52).

C

First Reading: Sir 35:12–14, 16–18
Responsorial Psalm: Ps 34:2–3, 17–18, 19, 23
Second reading: 2 Tm 4:6–8, 16–18
Gospel: Lk 18:9–14

In today's Gospel, a Pharisee is offered as an example for "those who were convinced of their own righteousness and despised everyone else" (Lk 18:9). It must be noted, however, that Jesus is not passing judgment on the Pharisaic movement. Pharisees were no more prone to self-righteousness than were other religious groups, including Jesus' followers. Nor should the prayer of the Pharisee be judged too harshly. Such prayers were not unusual, and generally they acknowledged that it was only by God's grace that a person could live righteously. In fact, the words Timothy puts on Paul's lips in the second reading—"I have competed well; I have finished the race; I have kept the faith. From now on the crown of righteousness awaits me" (2 Tm 4:7–8)—are not unlike the Pharisee's prayer.

By choosing a tax collector instead of a Pharisee to serve as an example of one who was justified because he humbled himself in prayer, Jesus makes two important points. Both points are found in Sirach as well: first, that "the prayer of the lowly pierces the clouds" (35:17); and second, that "he is a God of justice, / who knows no favorites" (v. 12). The familiar refrain, "The Lord hears the cry of the poor" is the point here, be they Pharisees or tax collectors.

Thirtieth Week in Ordinary Time

MONDAY

YEAR I   *First Reading: Rom 8:12–17*
         Responsorial Psalm: Ps 68:2 and 4, 6–7ab, 20–21
YEAR II   *First Reading: Eph 4:32—5:8*
         Responsorial Psalm: Ps 1:1–2, 3, 4 and 6
YEARS I AND II *Gospel: Lk 13:10–17*

A t first glance today's Gospel seems like just another controversy over Sabbath regulations. But a closer look takes us to
the heart of Jesus' ministry. The messianic prophet, who came "to
proclaim liberty to captives" (Lk 4:18), releases a woman from
bondage and restores her dignity as a daughter of Abraham. "She
at once stood up straight and glorified God" (13:13). Furthermore, as Jesus himself argues, his action is not in conflict but in
continuity with the meaning of Sabbath. It was to be a day of rest
and release from the bondage of hard labor for beasts of burden
as well as for human beings, for women as well as for men.

For Paul, as we have seen, to be a daughter or a son of
Abraham is to be by faith an adopted child of God. In today's
reading, Paul tells the Romans that no less than God's Spirit
testifies to our adoption, and that adoption secures our inheritance with Christ. To this, the passage from Ephesians adds an
ethical note: as children of God, we must also "be imitators of
God" (5:1), loving others as Christ has loved us.

TUESDAY

YEAR I   *First Reading: Rom 8:18–25*
         Responsorial Psalm: Ps 126:1b–2ab, 2cd–3, 4–5, 6
YEAR II *First Reading: Eph 5:21–33*
         Responsorial Psalm: Ps 128:1–2, 3, 4–5
YEARS I AND II *Gospel: Lk 13:18–21*

Today's selection from Ephesians is an example of a household code. Household codes sought to order the roles and relationships in Roman households between husbands and wives, parents and children, masters and slaves. Christian writers sometimes adapted these codes, as in today's reading. Here it emphasizes the husband's obligation to love his wife. Although the implied lack of equality between the two may offend our modern sensibilities, the requirement that Christian husbands love their wives "even as Christ loved the church" (Eph 5:25) would, in fact, ensure that women be treated with respect. Luke often attests to Jesus' equal treatment of men and women. In today's Gospel, for example, a parable about a man is paired with a matching parable about a woman.

In the twin parables of Jesus, the mustard seed and the yeast are metaphors for the action of the Spirit that Paul describes in the excerpt from Romans. Together with all creation, we who have the Spirit "groan within ourselves" (Rom 8:23) as we await the quiet revolution that the power of God is working within us.

WEDNESDAY

As often happens in the Gospels, Jesus turns the question of an interested bystander into a dire warning as he goes about his work en route to Jerusalem. Grammatically, the question does not read, "Will only a few people be saved?" in the future, but, "Are only a few people being saved?" here and now (Lk 13:23). In answer, Jesus warns that occasionally sharing his table or listening to his teaching does not satisfy the demands of true discipleship, rather a rigorous rite of passage through a notoriously "narrow gate" is required (v. 24).

Jesus' answer evokes an image from the Hebrew prophets who often described the messianic age as a banquet where scattered Israel would be assembled from east and west, from north and south. Here Jesus, the messianic prophet, warns those who rely on cheap grace that they may not be admitted. The household code from Ephesians issues the same warning to Christian masters who are called with their slaves to the same heavenly table of the one Master, for "with him there is no partiality" (6:9). And Paul reminds the Romans that the Spirit groans within them like hunger pains for the promised banquet of eternal life.

THURSDAY

YEAR I   *First Reading: Rom 8:31b—39*
              Responsorial Psalm: Ps 109:21—22, 26—27, 30—31
YEAR II   *First Reading: Eph 6:10—20*
              Responsorial Psalm: Ps 144:1b, 2, 9—10
YEARS I AND II *Gospel: Lk 13:31—35*

Taken together, today's three readings constitute something of a call to arms. In the Gospel, Jesus, the messianic prophet, ignores the warning of the Pharisees and renews his resolve to go to Jerusalem, "for it is impossible that a prophet should die outside of Jerusalem" (Lk 13:33). In the selection from Romans, Christians who, like Jesus, "are being slain all the day," declare that "in all these things we conquer overwhelmingly" because of the love of Christ (8:36-37). The conclusion of the Letter to the Ephesians calls all Christians to "put on the armor of God"—the belt of truth, the breastplate of justice, the footgear of zeal for peace, the shield of faith, the helmet of salvation and the sword of the word of God (6:11, 13—17).

The conviction of all holy warriors that God is with them and for them underlies all the readings. So Ephesians counsels constant prayer "for all the holy ones" (6:18), while Paul tells the Romans that nothing can separate us from the love of God. In the Gospel, Jesus offers that same love to Jerusalem in the biblical image of the mother bird who, gathering her young under her wings, keeps them safe.

FRIDAY

YEAR I   *First Reading: Rom 9:1–5*
          Responsorial Psalm: Ps 147:12–13, 14–15, 19–20
YEAR II   *First Reading: Phil 1:1–11*
          Responsorial Psalm: Ps 111:1–2, 3–4, 5–6
YEARS I AND II *Gospel: Lk 14:1–6*

T he two first readings for today uncover two sides of Paul's concern as a Christian missionary. In Romans 9–11, Paul takes up the difficult question of God's plan for the Jews, while in Philippians he writes to his first foundation among the Greeks. As apostle to the Gentiles, Paul had a vested interest in the faith development of his non-Jewish converts. That interest met with a generous response among the Philippian church, who made themselves sharers in Paul's work by giving him material support. The Letter to the Philippians was written in part as a thank-you note to these Christians whom Paul held so dear. As a Jew, however, Paul also had a vested interest in the destiny of his brothers, his kinsmen the Israelites. Paul never doubted God's choice of them. He fully agreed with the psalmist, "He has not done thus for any other nation" (Ps 147:20). Therefore, their refusal of the Gospel of Jesus caused him heartfelt grief.

This concern of Paul runs through much of the New Testament. Today's Gospel dramatizes the controversy that Jesus' ministry created among the Jews. In this story the hostile scrutiny of Jesus by his opponents and their ominous silence (Lk 14:4) prepare us for their eventual rejection of him.

Saturday

T he ancient world was just as preoccupied with social status as ours is. Conventional wisdom advised guests to seek the last places, "for it is better that you be told, 'Come up closer!' than that you be humbled before the prince" (Prv 25:7). In today's Gospel, Jesus seems to say the same thing until he gets to the punch line: "For everyone who exalts himself will be humbled, but the one who humbles himself will be exalted" (Lk 14:11). The use of the passive voice here is a biblical way of indicating God's action, that is, everyone who exalts himself shall be humbled *by God*, and he who humbles himself shall be exalted *by God*, who does not defer to our social arrangements.

In the Letter to the Romans, Paul warns Christians not to make the mistake of exalting themselves over and against the Jews. For the Jews are God's beloved, he says, the chosen people of God, whose gifts and whose call are irrevocable (Rom 11:29). In the Letter to the Philippians, Paul, imprisoned for preaching the Gospel, trusts that he will never be put to shame for his hope, but that Christ will be exalted through him, and he with Christ.

Thirty-first Sunday in Ordinary Time

A

First Reading: Mal 1:14b—2:2b, 8–10
Responsorial Psalm: Ps 131:1, 2, 3
Second Reading: 1 Thes 2:7b–9, 13
Gospel: Mt 23:1–12

❦

Both Malachi and Jesus in today's readings concern themselves with abuses of power and privilege among the leaders of their respective communities. In Malachi, the priests are condemned for failing to live up to the priestly ideal, the "covenant of Levi" (2:8), causing the people to falter by their teaching. The last verse invokes the Sinai covenant, which constituted Israel as one family with one Father, as the basis for both priests and people to act with integrity toward one another. In the Gospel, Jesus cautions his followers against the honorific titles and trappings used by religious leaders, mainly priests in his day but "scribes and Pharisees" by Matthew's time. It is not religious authority that Jesus condemns but its abuse as a means of self-promotion.

Paul suggests an interesting alternative to Jesus' "Call no one on earth your father; you have but one Father in heaven" of today's Gospel (Mt 23:9). Paul calls himself "a nursing mother" as regards his beloved Thessalonians (1 Thes 2:7). In this way, he evokes the power of the parental image but avoids the privilege that fatherhood claimed in a patriarchal world. So does the psalmist when he describes the quiet, trusting soul as a "weaned child on its mother's lap" (Ps 131:2).

B

First Reading: Dt 6:2–6
Responsorial Psalm: Ps 18:2–3, 3–4, 47, 51
Second Reading: Heb 7:23–28
Gospel: Mk 12:28b–34

For his own pastoral reasons, the author of Hebrews tends to stress the discontinuity between Judaism and Christianity— as in today's reading. It is easy to misconstrue his words, especially when they are taken out of context, to mean that there are two covenants, theirs and ours. Jesus' affirmation of the scribe in today's Gospel—"You are not far from the kingdom of God" (Mk 12:34)—is an important reminder of our common heritage with the Jewish people. From them we first learned that God loves us and wants our love in return. Today's psalm is part of a shared tradition of prayer (see Ps 18:2).

One of the distinctive features of Mark's version of the double commandment is that the commandment to love God wholeheartedly begins with the words that Jews know as the *Shema Yisrael* ("Hear, O Israel!"), the first two words of Deuteronomy 6:4. What then follows is the most basic statement of Israel's faith in one and only one God. Mark's adding this verse reminds us that the one God, whom we are called to love with all our heart and soul and strength, was revealed first to Israel and only by extension to us who, in Christ and through him, have come to know the one God, the God of Israel, who is the God of Jesus the Jew.

C

First Reading: Wis 11:22—12:2
Responsorial Psalm: Ps 145:1–2, 8–9, 10–11, 13, 14
Second Reading: 2 Thes 1:11—2:2
Gospel: Lk 19:1–10

In today's readings, the Thessalonians' anxiety over the future "coming of our Lord Jesus Christ" (2 Thes 2:1) is juxtaposed to the surprise of his coming "today" to the house of Zacchaeus. The joy that Jesus' visit brings to the unsuspecting tax collector marks it as a divine visitation. "Today salvation has come to this house" (Lk 19:9). This is the work of the same God extolled by Wisdom for having mercy on all and overlooking "people's sins that they may repent" (11:23).

Luke almost surely intends the story of Zacchaeus as a contrast to the earlier story of the rich official (see Lk 18:18–23). Both are rich, and each in his own way looks for Jesus. But the official is a righteous man, having observed the commandments from his youth, and Zacchaeus is a tax collector, only marginally a son of Abraham. While the official is saddened by Jesus' call to sell all and give it to the poor, Zacchaeus responds with joy. And although he is already a generous man, he pledges even more. So the question raised by the refusal of the rich official—"Then who can be saved?" (Lk 18:26)—is answered by the open-handed hospitality of Zacchaeus, the tax collector.

Thirty-first Week in Ordinary Time

Monday

Year I   *First Reading: Rom 11:29–36*
          Responsorial Psalm: Ps 69:30–31, 33–34, 36
Year II *First Reading: Phil 2:1–4*
          Responsorial Psalm: Ps 131:1bcde, 2, 3
Years I and II *Gospel: Lk 14:12–14*

In the social world of Luke's Jesus—as in our own—generosity to others was governed by the law of reciprocity, that is, by others' ability to repay the gift or return the favor. In today's Gospel, Jesus challenges this conventional code of behavior. He says instead that we should invite precisely those who cannot reciprocate, those whom God would invite and is inviting to the banquet of the kingdom through the ministry of Jesus—the poor, the lame, the blind (see Lk 7:22). Here again Jesus makes imitation of God the norm for Christian behavior. Paul does too in the Letter to the Philippians when he instructs them always to place the interests of others above their own self-interest.

The selection from Romans not only declares that "the gifts and the call of God are irrevocable" (11:29), but also that they are nonrepayable (v. 35)—except in the reciprocity of call and gifts that exist between Christians and Jews. It then goes on to describe how the gifts and the call of God have created a dynamic of reciprocity between Jews and Christians, so "that [God] might have mercy upon all" (v. 32) to the glory of his name.

TUESDAY

YEAR I   *First Reading: Rom 12:5–16ab*
         Responsorial Psalm: Ps 131:1bcde, 2, 3
YEAR II   *First Reading: Phil 2:5–11*
         Responsorial Psalm: Ps 22:26b–27, 28–30ab, 30e, 31–32
YEARS I AND II *Gospel: Lk 14:15–24*

In today's Gospel, a casual comment by an invited guest becomes the occasion for a parable of reversal. Jesus speaks not to second or to support the guest's exclamation—"Blessed is the one who will dine in the Kingdom of God" (Lk 14:15)—but to challenge his assumption. Who will eat bread in God's kingdom? Not the invited guests, as it turns out. They are too busy with their own affairs, with their investments and their intimate relationships. Their excuses betray their self-interests. How different the attitude of Christ, portrayed in the hymn in Philippians. "He emptied himself, / taking the form of a slave, / coming in human likeness" (Phil 2:7).

In the same vein, Paul tells the Romans that self-emptying, not self-interest, must characterize the attitude of Christians as well. They must be disinterested in their service of others and place whatever gifts they may have at the disposal of others, showing "the same regard for one another" (Rom 12:16a). This is what it means to be "one Body in Christ," to be "individually parts of one another" (v. 5). And the God who in Christ goes out to the highways and byways to find us, calls us to his table.

WEDNESDAY

YEAR I   *First Reading: Rom 13:8–10*
         Responsorial Psalm: Ps 112:1b–2, 4–5, 9
YEAR II *First Reading: Phil 2:12–18*
         Responsorial Psalm: Ps 27:1, 4, 13–14
YEARS I AND II *Gospel: Lk 14:25–33*

I n today's Gospel, Jesus reiterates the conditions for discipleship. Luke's version is particularly harsh. He uses the Greek
verb *misein*, meaning "to hate." However, the saying does not dictate what one should feel as a family member, but what one must
do as a follower of Jesus. Discipleship demands a total commitment. Therefore, it is a decision that must be carefully considered, like building a tower or going to war. For in the end it may
require renouncing all possessions, relinquishing family ties, and
taking up one's cross.

Paul's total commitment as a disciple of Christ is evident in the
excerpt from his letter to the Philippians. There is no doubt that by
the grace of God he will finish the race and complete the work he
has begun. He says he is ready to be "poured out as a libation" (Phil
2:17). This outpouring, in imitation of the one who emptied himself (v. 7), is the essence of Christian discipleship and expresses
itself concretely in love of others, as Paul tells the Romans: "Owe
nothing to anyone, except to love one another" (Rom 13:8). Such
love not only fulfills the law, it also brings to its fullest expression
the life project, which is the following of Christ.

THURSDAY

YEAR I   *First Reading: Rom 14:7–12*
         Responsorial Psalm: Ps 27:1bcde, 4, 13–14
YEAR II *First Reading: Phil 3:3–8a*
         Responsorial Psalm: Ps 105:2–3, 4–5, 6–7
YEARS I AND II *Gospel: Lk 15:1–10*

Today's reading from Romans seems to comment on the setting of the Gospel for today. "Why then do you judge your brother or sister?" Paul asks. "Why do you look down on your brother or sister?" (Rom 14:10). Jesus addresses two parables to those who are doing just that by criticizing him for welcoming sinners. The parables are a matched set: a male example is paired with a female example to depict God's desire to save. In both stories something small and insignificant is lost; a single sheep and a paltry sum seem altogether unworthy of the seeking—until he or she finds it (Lk 15:4, 8)—and the celebrating that follows when the lost is found. Yet Jesus says, "there will be rejoicing among the angels of God over one sinner who repents" (v. 10). So it seems, to return to Paul, that the Master to whom we belong in life and death is determined and diligent in seeking the lost, even if they are the least.

And that is good news, as Paul declares to the Philippians. His own life is a case in point. All those things he once considered gain, he reassessed as loss when he was found by the Lord Jesus Christ. For Paul, as for us, everything pales in comparison with "the supreme good of knowing Christ Jesus my Lord" (Phil 3:8).

Friday

YEAR I   *First Reading: Rom 15:14–21*
            Responsorial Psalm: Ps 98:1, 2–3ab, 3cd–4
YEAR II *First Reading: Phil 3:17——4:1*
            Responsorial Psalm: Ps 122:1–2, 3–4ab, 4cd–5
YEARS I AND II *Gospel: Lk 16:1–8*

Today's Gospel may seem to affront our moral sensibilities. Is Jesus really presenting the devious manager of the parable as an example? Yes, but for *what* he does, not *how* he does it. Because the accounting methods of Jesus' day are not well known to us, it is impossible for us to understand exactly what the manager did to extricate himself from his predicament. Did he reduce the actual amount owed? Or did he hide the interest in the principal? Or did he forego his commission? Yet the point is not his action, but his reaction. His employer's demand for an audit precipitates a crisis for the manager. He shows initiative as he realistically assesses his situation and resourcefully acts to save himself. He is commended for responding boldly and decisively in crisis. Jesus urges this mode of action on his hearers, for whom his ministry precipitates a crisis of a different kind—one that is not "of this world" (Lk 16:8).

The two first readings, both from Paul, give us "snapshots" of a man who responded boldly and decisively in crisis throughout his whole life. He is worthy of imitation.

SATURDAY

Luke has appended many sayings to the parable of the Devious Manager, which indicates that the early Church found it as difficult to understand as we do. The parable's main point was to call for a decisive response to the crisis precipitated by Jesus' ministry. Although the parable itself was not directly concerned with the ethics of the manager, Luke knew that ethical obligations do devolve upon those who recognize the arrival of God's kingdom in the ministry of Jesus. Taken as a whole, all these sayings about managing money tell us that how we handle money says much about what is in our hearts. It should be noted that the generalization about Pharisees being avaricious is Luke's bias. Almsgiving was a cornerstone of the ethics of the rabbis.

The reading from Philippians shows us Paul's attitude toward money. Thanking his beloved Philippians for their financial support, he tells them that he has learned to live in poverty and in plenty by finding his strength in Christ alone. He most appreciates not their gift but what it signifies, a share in his ministry. In the same way in Romans, he gratefully acknowledges all his fellow workers in the service of Christ.

Thirty-second Sunday in Ordinary Time

A

First Reading:Wis 6:12–16
Responsorial Psalm: Ps 63:2, 3–4, 5–6, 7–8
Second Reading: 1 Thes 4:13–18 or 4:13–14
Gospel: Mt 25:1–13

The two New Testament readings for this Sunday, Paul's pastoral letter to the Thessalonians and Jesus' parable of the Ten Virgins, take up the theme of the Second Coming of Christ. The parable, found only in Matthew, reflects his tendency to identify Jesus with divine wisdom, which is personified as a woman in today's first reading. Jesus' followers are urged to keep vigil, watching at dawn for Wisdom, "resplendent and unfading" (Wis 6:12), the glorified and risen Lord, graciously to appear.

What it means to live in the hope of Jesus' coming again in glory is Paul's concern in 1 Thessalonians. For these early Christians expecting Jesus' imminent return, the death of one of their members raises a troubling question: Will the dead also share in the glory of the risen Lord? Paul's answer is a firm yes. Therefore, he says, they should not grieve "like the rest, who have no hope" (1 Thes 4:13). This is not to say that Christians do not grieve, but that their grief is, in some sense, contained by the sure hope that God, who raised Jesus from the dead, will raise the dead with Jesus.

B

First Reading: 1 Kgs 17:10–16
Responsorial Psalm: Ps 146:7, 8–9, 9–10
Second Reading: Heb 9:24–28
Gospel: Mk 12:38–44 or 12:41–44

At first glance, an obvious theme links today's first reading and the Gospel. At the center of each is a generous widow who acts in simple faith on the word of God. In this light, Jesus justly condemns the scribes for exploiting these defenseless women who, according to the law and the prophets, were the object of God's providence and protection.

On closer reading, a connection may also exist between this Gospel and the passage from Hebrews. It revolves around the Temple. As usual, the author of Hebrews wants to draw a contrast between the one sacrifice of Jesus and the sacrifice offered yearly on the Day of Atonement, Yom Kippur. His point is that the sacrifice of Jesus, who entered into heaven itself, has rendered all other sacrifices offered in the "sanctuary made by hands" (Heb 9:24) obsolete. This was Mark's view as well (see Mk 14:58). Today's Gospel story takes place in the Temple and immediately precedes Jesus' prediction that it will be destroyed. For Jesus, the widow's coins may be one more sign of a Temple cult so out of touch that it deprived even widows of what little livelihood they had.

C

First Reading: 2 Macc 7:1–2, 9,14
Responsorial Psalm: Ps 17:1, 5–6, 8, 15
Second Reading: 2 Thes 2:16–3:5
Gospel: Lk 20:27–38 or 20:27, 34–38

Explicit belief in resurrection appears in Judaism only during the persecution under the Greek king Antiochus IV (he ruled from 167 to 164 B.C.). This is the background for today's first reading. In this abridged version of the martyrdom of seven brothers in the presence of their mother, we hear in the brave words of these young Jewish martyrs the hope that God will restore the just to life. This hope is expressed most fully by the second brother, who says, "You are depriving us of this present life, but the King of the world will raise us up to live again forever" (2 Macc 7:9).

Even in Jesus' day, not all Jews believed in resurrection. The Sadducees were among those who did not. The elaborate question they put to Jesus in today's Gospel is an attempt to reduce the idea of resurrection to absurdity. In answer, Jesus draws a sharp distinction between this age and the age to come. He indicates that resurrection is not the continuation of this life, but its complete transformation by the living God to whom "all are alive" (Lk 20:38). This is also the hope and the encouragement Paul leaves with the Thessalonians. "May the Lord direct your hearts to the love of God and to the endurance of Christ" (2 Thes 3:5).

Thirty-second Week in Ordinary Time

MONDAY

YEAR I   *First Reading:Wis 1:1–7*
          Responsorial Psalm: Ps 139:1b–3, 4–6, 7–8, 9–10
YEAR II   *First Reading:Ti 1:1–9*
          Responsorial Psalm: Ps 24:1b–2, 3–4ab, 5–6
YEARS I AND II *Gospel: Lk 17:1–6*

All the readings for today speak to the need for discipline. The selection from the Book of Wisdom exhorts those in authority to "love justice" (1:1). The vital principle that will enable them to act justly is none other than "the holy Spirit of discipline," which "flees deceit ... withdraws from senseless counsels" (v. 5) and roundly rebukes injustice. The excerpt from the Letter to Titus also concerns those who wield authority. It says that presbyters must know how to discipline their children, and bishops must be self-disciplined.

In today's Gospel, Jesus continues to teach the daily demands of Christian life. Here again disciplined vigilance—"Be on your guard!" (Lk 17:3)—will enable his disciples not to give scandal and to forgive as unstintingly as God does. As though in response to Jesus' teaching, the disciples pray, "Increase our faith" (v. 5). Perhaps that should be our prayer, too, as we, in turn, undertake the daily discipline of following Jesus. With faith barely the size of a mustard seed, let us rely, as Wisdom teaches us, on the Spirit that not only fills the whole world, but also the huge gaps in our faith and knowledge of God.

TUESDAY

YEAR I   *First Reading:Wis 2:23—3:9*
            Responsorial Psalm: Ps 34:2–3, 16–17, 18–19
YEAR II   *First Reading:Ti 2:1–8, 11–14*
            Responsorial Psalm: Ps 37:3–4, 8 and 23, 27 and 29
YEARS I AND II *Gospel: Lk 17:7–10*

In today's Gospel, Jesus concludes his instruction on disciple-ship with a homey example. He points out that nothing is particularly heroic in going the hard way with him. He tells the disciples, "When you have done all you have been commanded," —relativizing family ties and renouncing all possessions (Lk 14:26, 33), avoiding scandal and forgiving whenever asked (Lk 17:2–4)—"say, 'We are unprofitable servants. We have done what we were obliged to do'" (v. 10).

Those words may seem somewhat deflating to us who so often falter as we follow in Jesus' steps. The reason may be, as the Book of Wisdom explains, that although we were made in the image of God's own nature, sin has distorted that image of God in us. Discipleship restores to us the dignity God willed for us in the beginning. As the Letter to Titus puts it, the grace of God revealed in Christ is "training us to reject godless ways and worldly desires and to live temperately, justly, and devoutly" as we await the appearance of God's glory (2:12–13). And as Wisdom promises, "In the time of their visitation, they [and we] shall shine" (3:7).

WEDNESDAY

YEAR I   *First Reading: Wis 6:1–11*
          Responsorial Psalm: Ps 82:3–4, 6–7
YEAR II   *First Reading: Ti 3:1–7*
          Responsorial Psalm: Ps 23:1b–3a, 3bc–4, 5, 6
YEARS I AND II *Gospel: Lk 17:11–19*

Found only in Luke, the story of the healing of the ten lepers illustrates the teaching of the Book of Wisdom: "The Lord of all shows no partiality" (6:7). The same point is made in the Letter to Titus when the author notes that God has saved us "not because of any righteous deeds we have done but because of his mercy" (3:5). In Jesus' day lepers were outcasts, the least of all people, but God's mercy extended to them, too. All ten were made whole. Their faith—even if it was small as mustard seed—was their salvation.

The surprise element in the story lies in the response of the one leper who happened to be a Samaritan. The least of all the lepers, he was not just an outcast but an outsider. Jesus underlined the irony: "Has none but this foreigner returned to give thanks to God?" (Lk 17:18). The Letter to Titus brings home the lesson here. We were all foreigners once, it says, and we were saved "through the bath of rebirth and renewal by the Holy Spirit" not because of our merits but solely because of God's mercy (3:5). Like the Samaritan, let us realize what has been done for us and give thanks without ceasing.

Thursday

Scholars often describe the reign of God as "already but not yet," and Jesus' words in today's Gospel may be construed in just this way. He tells the Pharisees that the reign of God is already among them; it is being inaugurated by his prophetic activity, his healing and teaching, though they cannot see it. He promises his disciples the day of the Son of Man, which they will long to see. But that day is not yet. "First . . . he must suffer greatly and be rejected by this generation" (Lk 17:25). Thus Jesus distinguishes between the arrival of God's kingdom in his ministry and its full realization on that day when the Son of Man lights up the sky.

Some manuscripts substitute "Spirit" for "kingdom" in the Lucan version of the Our Father (see Lk 11:2–4). Both the Spirit and the kingdom are ways of talking about the pure, pervasive power of God that "renews everything," as the author of Wisdom says. The effect of this power to produce "friends of God" (Wis 7:27) is evidenced in Paul's note to Philemon when he declares that the power of God has transformed Onesimus from a slave to a beloved brother (see Phlm 16).

FRIDAY

L uke puts a peculiar twist on the story of Lot's wife in today's Gospel. As the story goes, Lot and his family were fleeing from Sodom and Gomorrah, and "Lot's wife looked back" (Gn 19:26). In Luke's view, she is an example of those who, having set out with Jesus on the way of salvation, look back at what they have left behind. They are not fit for the kingdom of God (see Lk 9:62). So he warns: "Remember the wife of Lot" (17:32). Luke appreciates the danger that material possessions pose to salvation. Genesis attests that Lot was a wealthy man when it says that he and Abram could not live together because they had too many possessions (see Gn 13:6).

Yet Luke does not despise the material world and neither can we. As the author of Wisdom reminds us today, "From the greatness and beauty of created things their original author, by analogy, is seen" (13:5). To which Psalm 19 responds, "The heavens declare the glory of God" (v. 2). As 2 John warns, to deny the sacramentality of the material world is to be deceived by those who would deny the humanity of Jesus, "who do not acknowledge Jesus Christ as coming in the flesh" (v. 7).

Saturday

Year I   First Reading: Wis 18:14–16; 19:6–9
             Responsorial Psalm: Ps 105:2–3, 36–37, 42–43
Year II   First Reading: 3 Jn 5–8
             Responsorial Psalm: Ps 112:1–2, 3–4, 5–6
Years I and II Gospel: Lk 18:1–8

The parable of the Widow and the Unjust Judge provides comic relief in a discourse full of foreboding about the end time. Who cannot laugh at an unscrupulous judge who is finally defeated by the nagging of a persistent widow? From this lighter moment Jesus moves to the weightier one: If a corrupt judge can be converted by the cry of a widow, will not the Judge of all the earth "secure the rights of his chosen ones who call out to him day and night?" (Lk 18:7).

The foreboding mood reasserts itself with the question that concludes the parable: "When the Son of Man comes, will he find faith on earth?" (Lk 18:8). The Book of Wisdom says he will come like "a fierce warrior, into the doomed land, bearing the sharp sword of [God's] inexorable decree" (18:15–16). In what does such faith consist? The readings tell us: in Luke, it is the persistence of the widow's prayer; in 3 John, it is the ready welcome one church extends to another; and in Wisdom, it is the boundless praise of those who behold the stupendous wonders of God's saving power.

Thirty-third Sunday in Ordinary Time

A

First Reading: Prv 31:10–13, 19–20, 30–31
Responsorial Psalm: Ps 128:1–2, 3, 4–5
Second Reading: 1 Thes 5:1–6
Gospel: Mt 25:14–30 or 25:14–15, 19–21

Today's readings prepare us for the anticipated return of Jesus on the last day. Although they are a generation apart, Paul and Matthew, like Jesus before them, refuse to speculate as to when that day will be. Paul draws the familiar analogy: "The day of the Lord will come like a thief at night" (1 Thes 5:2). Without a timetable, we must always be prepared. To be prepared is not to be passive, however. This is one of the lessons of today's parable. Good and faithful servants entrusted with their master's possessions must be responsible and resourceful—like the worthy wife in the first reading.

But today's parable, one of a series that looks to the Second Coming, is more than an object lesson on using our talents well. What possession has the Master entrusted to us with the clear expectation that we will make it grow? Matthew's answer is that we each and everyone have a measure of responsibility for the spread of the Gospel of Christ in the world in which we find ourselves. To act on this responsibility may be risky business, but if today's parable is any indication, playing it safe may be riskier still.

B

First Reading: Dn 12:1–3
Responsorial Psalm: Ps 16:5, 8, 9–10, 11
Second Reading: Heb 10:11–14, 18
Gospel: Mk 13:24–32

Today's first reading from the apocalyptic Book of Daniel is significant, among other things, because it contains the earliest explicit statement of belief in resurrection of the dead. "Many of those who sleep in the dust of the earth shall awake; some shall live forever, others shall be an everlasting horror and disgrace" (Dn 12:2). Christian apocalypses, like Mark 13 from which today's Gospel is taken, set themselves apart from similar Jewish writings by the central role they gave to Christ in the unfolding end-time drama.

The Gospel for today takes us to the heart of Jesus' discourse on the end time. The description of the coming of the Son of Man, who according to Hebrews waits now "until his enemies are made his footstool" (10:13), is a patchwork of images from the Hebrew Bible. But the main concern of the passage is to answer the question posed by Jesus' disciples at the start of the chapter: "When will this happen and what sign will there be when all these things are about to come to an end?" (Mk 13:4). Jesus' answer does not satisfy our curiosity: "Of that day or hour, no one knows, neither the angels in heaven, nor the Son, but only the Father" (v. 32). We must take a lesson from the fig tree and learn to read the signs of the times.

C

First Reading: Mal 3:19–20a
Responsorial Psalm: Ps 98:5–6, 7–8, 9
Second Reading: 2 Thes 3:7–12
Gospel: Lk 21:5–19

Luke's version of Jesus' discourse on the end time is more narrowly focused than Mark's on the destruction of the Temple and the city of Jerusalem. Unlike Mark, who wants his readers to understand their present distress as the "beginnings of the labor pains" (Mk 13:8)—the beginning of the end—Luke wants instead to build his readers' confidence in the prophet Jesus. To that end, he invites us to hear in Jesus' discourse an echo of the Temple sermon of Jeremiah, who also prophesied the impending fall of Jerusalem. But for those who stand firm there are words of comfort, too: "Not a hair on your head will be destroyed," says Jesus. "By your perseverance you will secure your lives" (Lk 21:18–19). The end-time imagery of Malachi in the first reading is similarly two-sided: fiery wrath for the proud and all evildoers, but the healing rays of the sun of justice "for you who fear my name" (3:20). This two-pronged promise is taken up in Psalm 98:9 when it urges us to await the Lord's coming with joy as he comes to rule with justice.

The selection from 2 Thessalonians describes one response to the expectation of an imminent end time. Some in the Church are unwilling to work and are becoming a burden on others. Offering himself as a model, Paul counsels the hard work of tough love.

Thirty-third Week in Ordinary Time

MONDAY

YEAR I   *First Reading: 1 Macc 1:10–15, 41–43, 54–57, 62–63*
         Responsorial Psalm: Ps 119:53, 61, 134, 150, 155, 158
YEAR II *First Reading: Rev 1:1–4; 2:1–5*
         Responsorial Psalm: Ps 1:1–2, 3, 4 and 6
YEARS I AND II *Gospel: Lk 18:35–43*

T he two first readings are very much alike. Maccabees records the time when the Jewish community was divided by the introduction of Greek ways among them. Some were willing enough to adapt to and even adopt certain Greek customs, while others resisted. Maccabees takes the uncompromising view of those "who preferred to die rather than ... to profane the holy covenant" (1 Macc 1:63). Revelation was written at a time when the question of civic duty under the Romans divided the Christian community. Some were willing to conform within reasonable limits and show themselves good citizens, while others resisted. The author of Revelation took the uncompromising view, placing him on a collision course with Rome. In today's reading he commends the church in Ephesus for its patient endurance, but cautions it, too. The stress of their stance toward Rome has cooled their love for one another.

The challenges we face are not so different. Like the blind beggar in the Gospel, we sit on the side of the road and are often confused by the din of the world around us. At those times let us pray as he did, "Lord, please let me see" (Lk 18:41).

TUESDAY

YEAR I   *First Reading: 2 Macc 6:18–31*
            Responsorial Psalm: Ps 3:2–3, 4–5, 6–7
YEAR II   *First Reading: Rev 3:1–6, 14–22*
            Responsorial Psalm: Ps 15:2–3a, 3bc–4ab
YEARS I AND II *Gospel: Lk 19:1–10*

Today's readings commend two men: Eleazar and Zacchaeus; and condemn two churches: Sardis and Laodicea. At first glance Eleazar and Zacchaeus seem to be polar opposites: one, a highly respected scribe, the other, a rich and disreputable tax agent. But as their stories show, they are both sons of Abraham. The joy with which they greet the visitation of the Lord in their lives makes them both worthy of this title. The venerable Eleazar submits to the blows of the torturer and says that he suffers "with joy" (2 Macc 6:30) because of his devotion to the Lord and to his holy laws. Zacchaeus welcomes Jesus with joy and declares himself ready to make full restitution as the law of God requires.

The harsh words addressed to the churches of Sardis and Laodicea in the Book of Revelation are also a visitation of the Lord, not a verdict. "I stand at the door and knock," says the One who searches out the lost (Rev 3:20). They have only to open wide the door and welcome the salvation that comes to their house. "I will enter his house and dine with him, and he with me" (v. 20). Only thus will salvation ever come to our houses. "Whoever has ears ought to hear what the Spirit says to the churches" (v. 22).

Wednesday

A ll three of today's readings are shaped in a context of imminent persecution and offer a particular perspective on what
is about to befall. The two first readings do this by shifting the
point of view from earth to heaven. The brave mother of seven
sons in 2 Maccabees encourages her sons to consider the power
of God the Creator, the Giver of life. Surely, she reasons, the God
who mysteriously "shapes each man's beginning" can and will
give back both life and breath to those who defy death in order
to keep the law (2 Macc 7:23). In the scene from Revelation,
John, a Christian prophet exiled on the island of Patmos for proclaiming God's word (see Rev 1:9), is taken in vision to the
throne of God and shown "what must happen afterwards," that is,
the tribulation and the eventual triumph of God (4:1).

The perspective of the Gospel is encoded in a parable.
Nearing Jerusalem, Jesus interprets what is about to happen
there by telling a story about kingship. In the events about to
unfold in Jerusalem, he will claim his kingdom and confer it on
the Twelve. And "after he had said this, he proceeded on his journey up to Jerusalem" (Lk 19:28).

THURSDAY

YEAR I   *First Reading: 1 Macc 2:15–29*
         Responsorial Psalm: Ps 50:1b–2, 5–6, 14–15
YEAR II   *First Reading: Rev 5:1–10*
         Responsorial Psalm: Ps 149:1b–2, 3–4, 5–6a and 9b
YEARS I AND II *Gospel: Lk 19:41–44*

The prospect of war looms in each of today's three readings. The episode recounted in 1 Maccabees marks the start of the Maccabean revolt against the Greeks. Sparked by the just fury of Mattathias, the revolt will rally those righteous people who are zealous for the law and who stand by the covenant. These are the people, the psalmist tells us, who can confidently call upon God in time of distress (see Ps 50:15). The scene from Revelation sets the stage for holy war. The divinely appointed leader of this final campaign against the enemies of God and of God's people will be the Lion of the tribe of Judah, the Lamb who was slain, the already victorious risen Lord. It is he who will adorn the lowly with victory (see Ps 149:4).

In today's Gospel, Luke's Jesus, the messianic prophet, foresees the fate of the city of Jerusalem at the hands of the Roman army and weeps over it. Having failed to recognize the arrival of the peaceable kingdom in his ministry, which was indeed the time of their visitation (Lk 19:44), the people remain oblivious to their impending doom. "If this day you only knew what makes for peace—but now it is hidden from your eyes" (v. 42).

FRIDAY

The readings from 1 Maccabees and Luke are both concerned with the dedication of the Temple. The Greek king Antiochus IV Epiphanes desecrated the sanctuary by erecting a pagan idol on the altar of holocausts. Therefore, having retaken the Temple, Judas and his men restored and rededicated it. This is the origin of the Jewish feast known to us as Hanukkah. In the Gospel, Luke's Jesus is again cast as a prophet. Like the messenger announced by Malachi (see 3:1), he comes to the Temple. With words from Isaiah (see 56:7) and Jeremiah (see 7:3–20), he reclaims and, as it were, reconsecrates it for his own teaching. This prophetic gesture divides the people: on one side are the leaders who want to destroy him, and on the other are the people who hang on his every word.

Jesus reclaims the Temple not just for his own teaching but for that of the apostles and prophets who will follow him. In the Book of Revelation, John is one of these. Although God's word is not always easy to digest, Jesus is sent to speak his word not in the Temple in Jerusalem but from the throne of God in heaven.

SATURDAY

YEAR I   *First Reading: 1 Macc 6:1–13*
          Responsorial Psalm: Ps 9:2–3, 4 and 6, 16 and 19
YEAR II *First Reading: Rev 11:4–12*
          Responsorial Psalm: Ps 144:1, 2, 9–10
YEARS I AND II *Gospel: Lk 20:27–40*

First Maccabees reports the death of the Greek king Antiochus "in bitter grief, in a foreign land" (6:13), which marks the end of one period of persecution, while John's vision in the Book of Revelation marks the start of another. In the imagery of Revelation, the two witnesses representing all Christian martyrs are likened to messianic figures: Joshua and Zerubbabel, "the two olive trees and the two lampstands" (Rev 11:4; see Zec 4:1, 11–14); the prophet Elijah, who had the "power to close up the sky" (Rev 11:6; see 1 Kgs 17:1); and Moses, who had the "power to turn water into blood" (Rev 11:6; see Ex 7:14–23). Having given their testimony, they are martyred. But three and a half days later, they are raised to new life and taken up to heaven in a cloud.

Jesus' answer to the Sadducees, who did not believe in resurrection, provides a basis for the Christian view. God "is not God of the dead, but of the living" (Lk 20:38). Baptism makes us children of the resurrection and so children of God. Therefore, like the two witnesses of Revelation, we must seek to conform to Christ's death, confident that someday even our lowly bodies will conform to his glorified one (see Phil 3:10, 21).

Christ the King
Last Sunday in Ordinary Time

A

First Reading: Ez 34:11–12, 15–17
Responsorial Psalm: Ps 23:1–2, 2–3, 5, 6
Second Reading: 1 Cor 15:20–26, 28
Gospel: Mt 25:31–46

Celebrating the kingship of Christ heightens our expectation of his coming again in glory. Today's readings share that end-time view. The prophecy of Ezekiel is addressed to Jewish exiles in Babylon. They are the sheep scattered in every place whom God will seek out and bring back. They "shall dwell in the house of the LORD / for years to come" (Ps 23:6). Disappointment with the return from exile caused the people to postpone their hopes of a more glorious restoration to the indefinite future; so the redemptive activity of the Good Shepherd became an image of the end time, as it is in today's Gospel. Paul's metaphor of Christ as the firstfruits is also an end-time image. The firstfruits promise the complete harvest, which is still another image of the end.

Compared with these lofty images, today's parable is a comic deflation. "Imagine," says Pheme Perkins, "this glorious scene of judgment reduced to the problem of a shepherd separating sheep from goats."[33] But describing final judgment as such a mundane task may be Jesus' way of warning us that the coming judgment happens closer to home than we think.

B

First Reading: Dn 7:13–14
Responsorial Psalm: Ps 93:1, 1–2, 5
Second Reading: Rev 1:5–8
Gospel: Jn 18:33b–37

D ramatic irony characterizes the two New Testament readings for today. The Gospel is one scene from John's carefully choreographed production of the trial of Jesus before Pilate.
For John, the crucifixion is Jesus' "lifting up" (see Jn 3:14; 8:28;
12:32); this is evident in the authority with which Jesus speaks to
Pilate. He asks as many questions as he answers and with quiet
dignity explains, "My kingdom does not belong to this world" (Jn
18:36). It is difficult to remember that Jesus is the one on trial,
when Pilate seems so powerless. Borrowing the imagery of
Daniel in today's first reading, the passage from Revelation proclaims the coming of the Son of Man "amid the clouds" (1:7; see
Dn 7:13). He comes as sovereign Lord, "ruler of the kings of the
earth" (Rev 1:5). Yet, he is introduced to us as the faithful witness, that is, the martyr, the firstborn of the dead (v. 5), who was
pierced as every eye shall see (v. 7; see Zec 12:10).

For us, to honor Christ as King means to hold together in
one thought the Son of Man amid the clouds and the sovereign
Lord upon the cross. To him—whose throne "stands firm from
of old; / from everlasting" (Ps 93:2)—be glory and power forever. Amen.

C

First Reading: 2 Sm 5:1–3
Responsorial Psalm: Ps 122:1–2, 3–4, 4–5
Second Reading: Col 1:12–20
Gospel: Lk 23:35–43

In today's Gospel, Jesus' kingship is mockingly proclaimed by those who have rejected him while the people stand by and watch—the same people who will later return home beating their breasts (Lk 23:48). The Jewish rulers mock Jesus as "the Christ of God" (v. 35), a title meaning "God's anointed," associating him with David, who in the first reading is "anointed . . . king of Israel" (2 Sm 5:3). The Roman soldiers, on the other hand, mock Jesus as "King of the Jews" (Lk 23:36), as does the inscription over his head. Even one of the criminals hanging on a cross beside him joins in mocking him as Messiah. In this way Luke dramatizes the division that the divine visitation has created among the people.

But Luke's artistry in today's Gospel does more. It shows us Jesus exercising his power as King even from the cross. In answer to the prayer of the other criminal, Jesus solemnly decrees, "Amen, I say to you, today you will be with me in Paradise" (Lk 23:43). Thus we see for ourselves what Colossians means when it tells us that God "transferred us to the kingdom of his beloved Son, in whom we have redemption, the forgiveness of sins" (1:13–14).

Thirty-fourth or Last Week in Ordinary Time

MONDAY

YEAR I   *First Reading: Dn 1:1–6, 8–20*
         Responsorial Psalm: Dn 3:52, 53, 54, 55, 56
YEAR II   *First Reading: Rev 14:1–3, 4b–5*
          Responsorial Psalm: Ps 24:1bc–2, 3–4ab, 5–6
YEARS I AND II *Gospel: Lk 21:1–4*

~∽∽◎∽∾~

Today's readings are all about people who know who they are because they know whose they are. Daniel and his friends are Israelites in the court of the king of Babylon. Still, they resolve not to compromise their identity as God's people: they refuse to risk violating the traditional dietary laws, a distinctive mark of Jewish identity, by eating from the royal table. And their loyalty is rewarded: they surpass all their rivals in wisdom. In Revelation, the Lamb stands victorious surrounded by the 144,000 faithful. These are the witnesses "who follow the Lamb wherever he goes" (Rev 14:4), even to death. The name of God and of the Lamb is inscribed on their foreheads, an indelible identifying mark.

The action of the widow in today's Gospel also speaks of self-possession. She stands for those who having received the promise of the kingdom renounce all their possessions. They define themselves not by what they have but by whose they are—Christ's, the Lamb of God.

Tuesday

YEAR I   *First Reading: Dn 2:31–45*
          Responsorial Psalm: Dn 3:57, 58, 59, 60, 61
YEAR II   *First Reading: Rev 14:14–19*
          Responsorial Psalm: Ps 96:10, 11–12, 13
YEARS I AND II *Gospel: Lk 21:5–11*

The three readings for today all predict the future. King Nebuchadnezzar's dream becomes a test of Daniel's wisdom. He interprets the four metals that make up the composite statue—gold, silver, bronze, and iron mixed with clay—to correspond to the four kingdoms that ruled Israel from the exile in the sixth century B.C. to Hellenization in the second century B.C.: the Babylonians, the Medes, the Persians, and the two Greek dynasties (Ptolemies and Seleucids). During the time of the Greeks (when the Book of Daniel was written), Daniel says that God will establish a kingdom—Israel—that will supplant all these others and stand forever.

The Gospel is the beginning of Luke's version of Jesus' discourse about the future. He foresees the destruction of the Jerusalem Temple by the Romans during the First Jewish Revolt (A.D. 66–70).

The biblical imagery in Revelation makes that prediction of the future a more general prophecy of divine judgment. The first pair of angels harvest the grain (the just), and a second pair harvest the grapes (the unjust) to be thrown into the winepress of God's wrath. The message is clear: All time is in God's hand. "See that you not be deceived" (Lk 21:8).

WEDNESDAY

"The writing is on the wall," as the saying goes, not just in the Book of Daniel but in all of today's readings. In Daniel, the desecration of the sacred vessels from the Jerusalem Temple is answered by an ominous sign. The fingers of a human hand write on the plaster wall three words that announce the end of the Babylonian empire. For as Daniel explains, "the God in whose hand is your life breath and the whole course of your life, you did not glorify" (Dn 5:23). In the same way, in Revelation the prophet John sees in a vision the seven angels who stand ready to bring the wrath of God to a climax by inflicting the seven final plagues.

In the Gospel, the followers of Jesus, not the enemies of God, are warned of persecution. All three readings are sure of God's final victory, but Revelation is most explicit. Its biblical imagery takes us back to the crossing of the Red Sea. Here, however, the victory song of Moses is also the song of the Lamb, taken up by the Christian martyrs. Thus are we reassured: "By your perseverance you will secure your lives" (Lk 21:19).

Thursday

Year I   First Reading: Dn 6:12–28
         Responsorial Psalm: Dn 3:68, 69, 70, 71, 72, 73, 74
Year II First Reading: Rev 18:1–2, 21–23; 19:1–3, 9a
         Responsorial Psalm: Ps 100:1b–2, 3, 4, 5
Years I and II Gospel: Lk 21:20–28

All three readings today attest to the vindication of God's faithful people. When Daniel's enemies persuade King Darius to outlaw prayer, Daniel continues to pray three times a day as Jewish piety required. His accusers demand that he be thrown into the lion's den, and even the deeply grieved king cannot save him. But the God whom Daniel serves constantly and courageously can and does save him. "For he is the living God, enduring forever" (Dn 6:27). In Revelation, the assembly of heaven rejoices over the fall of Babylon, a code name for the Roman Empire. "Salvation, glory and might belong to our God," they sing. "He has avenged the blood of his servants" (Rev 19:1–2).

Luke's Jesus unfolds the escalating drama of the "time of punishment" when Jerusalem "will be trampled underfoot by the Gentiles" (21:22, 24). To this he appends a list of the signs of the last days, when earth and heaven will be shaken at the advent of the Son of Man. On that judgment day, fear will yield to joy for God's people, whose salvation is near at hand.

FRIDAY

YEAR I   *First Reading: Dn 7:2–14*
          Responsorial Psalm: Dn 3:75, 76, 77, 78, 79, 80, 81
YEAR II *First Reading: Rev 20:1–4, 11—21:?*
          Responsorial Psalm: Ps 84:3, 4, 5–6a and 8a
YEARS I AND II *Gospel: Lk 21:29–33*

The passing of time features in all three of today's readings. The vision of Daniel reviews the rise and fall of the four major kingdoms that ruled over God's people from the exile to the time when Daniel was written (second century B.C.). In God's good time, the eventual triumph of Israel is announced when "One like a son of man," a symbol of God's holy ones, receives "dominion, glory, and kingship" from the Ancient One (Dn 7:13–14). Revelation introduces the notion of millennium, the "thousand years" when Satan will be chained in the abyss (20:2). This passage has evoked much speculation, especially among those who interpret the Bible literally. But Jesus himself warns against such speculation, refusing to give his disciples a timetable for the last days. In today's Gospel he only says that the signs of the arrival of God's kingdom will be as obvious as the change of seasons.

The readings tell us always to know what time it is, not clock and calendar time but the time of our visitation, when the reign of God draws near—in the events of history, in the mystery of word and sacrament, and in the majesty of the Second Coming.

SATURDAY

YEAR I   *First Reading: Dn 7:15—27*
         Responsorial Psalm: Dn 3:82, 83, 84, 85, 86, 87
YEAR II *First Reading: Rev 22:1—7*
         Responsorial Psalm: Ps 95:1—2, 3—5, 6—7ab
YEARS I AND II *Gospel: Lk 21:34—36*

Today's two first readings sound a triumphant note. The passage from Daniel is an interpretation of his previous vision of the four beasts. The author is primarily concerned about the fourth beast, the kingdom of the Greek king Antiochus IV, who is oppressing "the holy ones of the Most High, thinking to change the feast days and the law." But his domination will end "by final and absolute destruction," and his dominion will be given "to the holy people of the Most High" (Dn 7:25—27). The conclusion of Revelation is a vision of Eden regained. There the trees of life produce fruit and provide healing, the curses of Genesis are reversed, and God's faithful servants "shall reign forever and ever" (Rev 22:5).

Coming after these poetic flights, the Gospel is frankly prosaic. It is a program for Christians like us who have reckoned with the long delay of the triumphant Son of Man. It calls for careful vigilance, constant prayer, and the consistent discipline that keeps us free of dissipation and the distraction of worldly cares. It means being continually on edge but with complete heart's ease, ever ready to stand before the coming Son of Man.

Feasts and Solemnities

Presentation of the Lord

February 2

First Reading: Mal 3:1–4
Responsorial Psalm: Ps 24:7, 8, 9, 10
Second Reading: Heb 2:14–18
Gospel: Lk 2:22–40 or 2:22–32

The presentation of Jesus in the Temple marks his first appearance there. Hence the entrance liturgy of Psalm 24 is apt. It greets the "king of glory" as none other than "the LORD of hosts" (Ps 24:10). The selection of readings for today also invites us to see him, in the words of Malachi, as the Lord whom we seek, suddenly come to the Temple. Surely this is the way Simeon greets him. "For my eyes have seen your salvation," he declares, "a light for revelation to the Gentiles, / and glory for your people Israel" (Lk 2:30, 32). This Lord who comes to the Temple is also our "merciful and faithful high priest," Hebrews reminds us. He will "expiate the sins of the people," but he will be tested (Heb 2:17–18). And Simeon foresees this, too, when he says that the child will be "a sign that will be contradicted" (Lk 2:34).

With the Presentation, Luke's account of the infancy of Jesus comes full circle. The story that began in the Temple with the sacrifice of Zechariah now ends in the Temple with another sacrifice. And just as that first sacrifice was the occasion for prophecy, so is this one. "This child is destined for the fall and rise of many" (Lk 2:34); "Who will endure the day of his coming?" (Mal 3:2).

Joseph, Husband of Mary

March 19

First Reading: *2 Sm 7:4–5a, 12–14a, 16*
Responsorial Psalm: *Ps 89:2–3, 4–5, 27, 29*
Second Reading: *Rom 4:13, 16–18, 22*
Gospel: *Mt 1:16, 18–21, 24a or Lk 2:41–51a*

So little is known about Joseph, the husband of Mary and the legal father of Jesus, that even today's two Gospel selections combined do not give us much to go on. What Matthew says explicitly in his Gospel—"He was a righteous man" (1:19)—is implied in the text from Luke, who describes Joseph with his family keeping Passover in Jerusalem as the law of the Lord required. The first reading from 2 Samuel 7—which is recapitulated in today's psalm—adds another piece by recounting the story of the foundation of David's house. It reminds us that it was through Joseph—whose role it was to name the child—that Jesus came to be a son of David, as both Matthew and Luke attest (Mt 1:20; Lk 1:27).

For Matthew, a believer in Jesus who remains nonetheless a Jew, Joseph is the ideal—a Torah-observant Jew who accepts Jesus as the Messiah, the one "who will save his people from their sins" (Mt 1:21). If today's second reading is any indication, that would make Joseph Paul's ideal as well, a true son of Abraham whose faith in God's promise "'was credited to him as righteousness'" (Rom 4:22; see Gn 15:6).

Annunciation

March 25

First Reading: Is 7:10–14; 8:10
Responsorial Psalm: Ps 40:7–8a, 8b–9, 10, 11
Second Reading: Heb 10:4–10
Gospel: Lk 1:26–38

The Indian poet Rabindranath Tagore once observed that the birth of every child is a sign that God has not given up on the world. In a sense, that is the meaning of the oracle with which the prophet Isaiah confronts King Ahaz in today's first reading. The birth of a child, perhaps even a royal son, will be a sign that God remains with the people of Judah in their present crisis that is exacerbated by the faithlessness of their king. Therefore, the child will be named "Immanuel," meaning "God with us" (Mt 1:23; see Is 7:14).

The angel Gabriel announces the same news to Mary in today's Gospel. The message contains two parts. The first renews God's firm promise to David's house by announcing the birth of a royal son: "The Lord God will give him the throne of David his father ... and of his Kingdom there will be no end" (Lk 1:32–33). But there is more. "The Holy Spirit will come upon you," the angel tells Mary. "Therefore the child to be born will be called holy, the Son of God" (v. 35). For this there is no precedent in the house of David or the history of Israel. This is not old news, but Good News (Gospel), to which Mary says, "May it be done to me according to your word" (v. 38).

Birth of John the Baptist

June 24
Vigil Mass

First Reading: Jer 1:4–10
Responsorial Psalm: Ps 71:1–2, 3–4a, 5–6ab, 15ab, 17
Second Reading: 1 Pet 1:8–12
Gospel: Lk 1:5–17

The readings for today underscore the unity and continuity of God's unfolding plan. In today's first reading, God dedicates Jeremiah from the womb to be a prophet to the nations. John is also dedicated from the womb to be the prophet of the Most High (see Lk 1:76). Like Samuel, he is a Nazirite, drinking "neither wine nor strong drink" (Lk 1:15; see 1 Sm 1:11). Like Elijah, he is sent "to prepare a people fit for the Lord" (v. 17). Within his account of the annunciation to Zechariah as well, Luke makes a number of similar connections. For example, Zechariah and Elizabeth are like Abraham and Sarah, too advanced in years to be capable of having a child. They also resemble Elkanah and Hannah, the parents of Samuel, whose birth was announced to them in the sanctuary where they were making their annual visit to offer sacrifice.

All these interconnections are Luke's way of "reassuring" us (see 1 Pet 1:4), as Peter reassures his churches in the second reading that the new thing God has done in Christ, though essentially unpredictable, is of a piece with all prior acts of God in Israel's history.

Mass During the Day

First Reading: Is 49:1–6
Responsorial Psalm: Ps 139:1b–3, 13–14ab, 14c–15
Second Reading: Acts 13:22–26
Gospel: Lk 1:57–66, 80

That the second Servant Song of Isaiah has been chosen as the first reading for today demonstrates the versatility of the image. In four poems (Is 42:1–4; 49:1–6; 50:4–9; 52:13— 53:12), the prophet presents a servant of God whose identity is not specified. As a result, the poems are easily appropriated. Christians have tended to apply them to Jesus, but today's selection suggests a connection with John the Baptist. This poem describes the servant's commissioning as God's prophet. Having been called from his mother's womb—a grace echoed by today's responsorial psalm: "You knit me in my mother's womb" (Ps 139:13)—he has been honed as a "sharp-edged sword" (Is 49:2) to be an effective instrument of God's word. But he is also concealed for a time, like John in the desert, waiting for the day of his manifestation to Israel.

In today's Gospel, the birth of John, whom Luke describes as herald of the coming of Jesus (see Acts 13:24–25), is briefly told. The story revolves around the naming of the child. Zechariah's announcement, "John is his name" (Lk 1:63), becomes the sign that he who doubted the angel's words has come to believe at last.

Peter and Paul, Apostles

June 29
Vigil Mass

First Reading: Acts 3:1–10
Responsorial Psalm: Ps 19:2–3, 4–5
Second Reading: Gal 1:11–20
Gospel: Jn 21:15–19

In the plan of Luke's two-volume work (Luke and Acts), the followers of Jesus, having received his Spirit, are empowered to continue his saving ministry. In today's first reading, Peter and John are doing just that. Lest we miss the point, Luke describes the crippled beggar, now healed, in words that echo Isaiah's prophecy of the arrival of the end time: "Then will the lame leap like a stag" (Is 35:6). So the beggar was "walking and jumping and praising God" (Acts 3:8). It is important to realize that the same prophecy of Isaiah stands behind Jesus' description of his own ministry that he sends to John the Baptist (see Lk 7:22). Later, this good deed done to a cripple will make Peter a target for persecution, and soon enough he will learn "by what kind of death he would glorify God" (Jn 21:19).

To the Galatians, Paul declares that he received the Gospel from the risen Lord himself. This is the basis of his claim that he is indeed an apostle, specifically the Apostle to the Gentiles. He describes his commissioning in language that recalls Isaiah's servant, who was called from his mother's womb to be a light to the nations (Gal 1:15; see Is 49:1, 6).

Mass During the Day

First Reading: Acts 12:1–10
Responsorial Psalm: Ps 34:2–3, 4–5, 6–7, 8–9
Second Reading: 2 Tm 4:6–8, 17–18
Gospel: Mt 16:13–19

I n today's readings, figuratively speaking, both Peter and Paul are "rescued from the lion's mouth" (2 Tm 4:17). This is Paul's way of attesting to the grace of God that he is sure has and will rescue him from every evil threat and bring him safe to the kingdom of heaven.

God's rescue of Peter is dramatically recounted in Acts. The dramatic effect is heightened by the author's note that Peter is being guarded by no less than four squads of four soldiers each. But the church is praying fervently for him, and nothing is impossible for God. The angel of the Lord who is sent to Peter's rescue has his work cut out for him, for wakened from sleep, Peter is uncomprehending. His movements are trancelike, and the angel must attend even to the details of his dress. All this to say that his escape is wholly by God's grace. For Peter, as for Paul, this is by no means the first time that he has received the unmerited grace of God. In fact, in Matthew's account of Peter's commissioning, the Gospel for today, Jesus himself tells Peter that God's grace alone has revealed to him that Jesus is indeed "the Christ [Messiah], the Son of the living God" (Mt 16:17, 16).

Transfiguration of the Lord

August 6

First Reading: Dn 7:9–10, 13–14
Responsorial Psalm: Ps 97:1–2, 5–6, 9
Second Reading: 2 Pet 1:16–19
A Gospel: Mt 17:1–9
B Gospel: Mk 9:2–10
C Gospel: Lk 9:28b–36

In all three of the synoptic Gospels—Matthew, Mark, and Luke—the transfiguration affords a glimpse of Jesus' future glory. Mark's is the earliest version, on which Luke and Matthew depend. In it, we discern the influence of the apocalyptic vision of Daniel in today's first reading. "His clothes became dazzling white" (Mk 9:3; see Dn 7:9). The influence of Daniel is even more pronounced in Matthew's account in the reaction of the disciples, who "fell prostrate and were very much afraid" until Jesus touched them and made them stand up (Mt 17:6–7). This was Daniel's response as well to the vision of the end time (Dn 8:17–18). Luke, who presents Jesus as the "prophet like Moses" (see Dt 18:15), is the only one who tells us that Moses and Elijah were speaking with Jesus "of his exodus that he was going to accomplish in Jerusalem" (Lk 9:31). Typically, Luke situates the transfiguration in the context of prayer. This perhaps is most helpful, for it is in prayer that we now gaze into the face of Christ, as 2 Peter puts it, "as to a lamp shining in a dark place, until day dawns and the morning star rises in your hearts" (1:19).

Assumption of Mary

August 15
Vigil Mass

First Reading: 1 Chr 15:3–4, 15–16; 16:1–2
Responsorial Psalm: Ps 132:6–7, 9–10, 13–14
Second Reading: 1 Cor 15:54b–57
Gospel: Lk 11:27–28

The feast of the Assumption celebrates the completion of God's triumph in Mary. As the ark of the Lord is borne into the city of Jerusalem, so Mary is brought into the presence of God in heaven. Paul explains to the Corinthians that when the body, "which is corruptible clothes itself with incorruptibility and this which is mortal clothes itself with immortality, then the word that is written shall come about: 'Death is swallowed up in victory'" (1 Cor 15:54). This victory is Mary's now through the grace of Christ.

In today's Gospel, Mary is declared doubly blessed. A woman in the crowd indirectly compliments Jesus by using an idiomatic expression that declares his mother blessed for giving birth to one like him. Jesus answers by redirecting the compliment to his mother, who is blessed, he says, because she hears the word of God and keeps it (Lk 11:28). In this brief exchange, which is found only in Luke's Gospel, the two foci of devotion to Mary are named. We honor Mary, on the one hand, for her unique privilege of having given birth to Jesus, and we hope, on the other hand, to imitate her faithful, faith-filled following of him.

Mass During the Day

First Reading: Rev 11:19a; 12:1–6a, 10ab
Responsorial Psalm: Ps 45:10, 11, 12, 16
Second Reading: 1 Cor 15:20–27
Gospel: Lk 1:39–56

∽◦◦◦∾

E ach of today's readings celebrates the triumph of God in its own striking imagery. Without a doubt, the most dramatic is the sign of "a woman clothed with the sun" in the vision from Revelation (12:1). This woman is described in a way that evokes the woman of Genesis 3. She is threatened by the dragon/Satan (Rev 12:4; see Gn 3:1), she gives birth in pain (Rev 12:2; see Gn 3:16), and the dragon wages war on her offspring (Rev 12:17; Gn 3:15). Since it is she who gives birth to the Messiah, "destined to rule all the nations with an iron rod" (Rev 12:5), she must be Israel, and her victory, though delayed, is assured by the power of God and his Anointed. In 1 Corinthians, God's final triumph is guaranteed in the metaphor of the firstfruits. Here, too, the imagery depends on Genesis 3: "For just as in Adam all die, so too in Christ shall all be brought to life" (1 Cor 15:22; see Gn 3:17–19).

By comparison, the imagery of Mary's canticle seems quite conventional, drawn as it is from the Hebrew Scriptures. But it also proclaims nothing less than the final victory of God, which has already begun among us. God in Christ "has shown the strength of his arm ... and has lifted up the lowly" (Lk 1:51–52). Mary, whom we honor today, is living proof.

Triumph of the Cross

September 14

First Reading: Nm 21:4b–9
Responsorial Psalm: Ps 78:1nc–2, 34–35, 36–37, 38
Second Reading: Phil 2:6–11
Gospel: Jn 3:13–17

Writing to the Philippians, Paul uses an early baptismal hymn to exhort the members of that church to put on the mind of Christ. The hymn itself is an example of how some of the first Christians articulated their understanding of the death and resurrection of Jesus. The structure of the hymn depicts two movements in the lived experience of Jesus. In the first, a gloss on the sin of Adam, he emptied himself by coming in human likeness (Phil 2:6–8); in the second, an echo of Isaiah 45:23, God exalted him by giving him the divine name at which every knee should bend (Phil 2:9–11). The hinge that holds the two movements together is the phrase "because of this" (v. 9). So the hymn teaches us, as Paul teaches the Philippians, that Jesus was exalted not because he died, but because his death on the cross was the summation of his whole life given to God in humble obedience.

In today's Gospel, Jesus alludes to the action of Moses in the first reading, announcing that "the Son of Man [must] be lifted up" (Jn 3:14). This is at once a prediction of his crucifixion and a promise of his exaltation by the Father. And precisely because it is both, we who believe in him have eternal life.

All Saints' Day

November 1

First Reading: Rev 7:2–4, 9–14
Responsorial Psalm: Ps 24:1bc–2, 3–4ab, 5–6
Second Reading: 1 Jn 3:1–3
Gospel: Mt 5:1–12a

The feast of All Saints gathers all God's holy ones in heaven and on earth to celebrate the triumph of God which is already and not-yet. Today's readings reflect this eschatological perspective. The scene depicted in Revelation takes place in the presence of God and the Lamb. There the vast multitude of the saints gather, their robes made white by the blood of the Lamb and with the palm of victory in their hands, to give glory and praise to God. Their hymn is a song of thanksgiving that joyfully acknowledges that "salvation comes from our God, who is seated on the throne, / and from the Lamb" (Rev 7:10).

With today's Gospel, the Matthean version of the Beatitudes, the perspective shifts from heaven to earth. Psalm 24 asks, "Who can ascend the mountain of the Lord?" (v. 3). And Matthew answers: the poor in spirit, those who mourn, those who hunger and thirst for righteousness. Although for them the triumph of God seems as yet unrealized, the promise of future glory is assured because, as John says, even now we are God's children, though what we shall be has not yet been revealed. But this we do know: "When it is revealed, we shall be like him, for we shall see him as he is" (1 Jn 3:2).

All Souls' Day

November 2

1

First Reading: Wis 3:1–9
Responsorial Psalm: Ps 23:1–3a, 3b–4, 5, 6
Second Reading: Rom 6:3–9
Gospel: Mt 25:31–46

Since very few Old Testament books talk about immortality, today's first reading is a rare exception. Of the souls of the just, the writer affirms, "Their hope is full of immortality" (Wis 3:4). Commenting on this text, Roland Murphy observes, "Immortality is not rooted in the human makeup, but in one's relationship to God." Something like this is suggested in today's Gospel. The last line of the parable declares that those on his left [the goats, in the code of the parable] "will go off to eternal punishment, but the righteous [the sheep] to eternal life" (Mt 25:46). "Righteousness," as Murphy also notes, "is a relationship, not a human achievement."[34] And in the parable, righteousness is described as a relationship to God, who is identified with the last and the "the least" of our brothers and sisters (Mt 25:40, 45).

In the reading from Romans, Paul elaborates on this relationship to God in which we now stand by virtue of our Baptism into Christ's death. This righteousness, that is, this "newness of life" (Rom 6:4) is now ours only because of the death and resurrection of Jesus. Thus Paul grounds our hope of immortality in Christ.

2

First Reading:Wis 4:7–14
Responsorial Psalm: Ps 25:6 and 7b, 17–18, 20–21
Second Reading: 1 Cor 15:51–57
Gospel: Jn 11:17–27

The three readings for today offer consolation to the bereaved. Each one presents us with a different scenario. The first, from the Book of Wisdom, addresses the tragedy of one who dies too young. "Having become perfect in a short while," the writer argues, "he reached the fullness of a long career" (Wis 4:13). Though this may seem small comfort to the bereaved, it is a standard argument among the rabbis. In the reading from 1 Corinthians, Paul confronts the reality of death with prophetic proclamation instead of carefully reasoned arguments. His theme is the victory over death that is ours now because of Christ. "Where, O death, is your victory?" he asks, paraphrasing Hosea. "Where, O death, is your sting?" (1 Cor 15:55; see Hos 13:14). This is the Christian perspective with which Jesus challenges Martha in today's Gospel.

The raising of Lazarus draws us into Jesus' inner circle. This family is beloved of Jesus (see Jn 11:5). It is impossible to miss the thinly veiled reproach in Martha's greeting: "Lord, if only you had been here ..." (v. 21). But this is not a bereavement call. Jesus, the Resurrection and the Life, comes to make present the glory of God. And so in the face of death, he asks Martha as he asks us, "Do you believe this?" (v. 26).

3

First Reading: Is 25:6–9
Responsorial Psalm: Ps 27:1, 4, 7 and 8b and 9a, 13–14
Second Reading: 1 Thes 4:13–18
Gospel: Jn 14:1–6

Today's first reading from Isaiah, like the selection from John, can sometimes distract us with their references to place—"this mountain" (Is 25:6) and the "many dwelling places" in the Father's house (Jn 14:2). Certainly the mountain of Isaiah recalls both Sinai and Zion, and the dwelling places in John sound the theme of divine indwelling that dominates Jesus' last discourse. But more to the point on this All Souls' Day is the good news of salvation announced by Isaiah that finally arrives in Jesus. "He will destroy death forever," Isaiah declares (25:8). What Jesus' disciples resist in today's reading, however, is that the destruction of death forever will require the death of Jesus, that is, his going away from them for a time. Hence Thomas's question—"We do not know where you are going; how can we know the way?" (Jn 14:5). We also ask this question as we come to terms with the death of those we love. And the same answer is given to us: "I am the way" (v. 6).

So it is that when we remember our faithful departed, it is not with the grief of those who have no hope (1 Thes 4:13). Rather, our remembering is the joyful hope that the victory that is theirs now will someday be ours through Christ, who is for us "the way and the truth and the life" (Jn 14:6).

Dedication of St. John Lateran

November 9

First Reading: Ez 47:1–2, 8–9, 12
Responsorial Psalm: Ps 46:2–3, 5–6, 8–9
Second Reading: 1 Cor 3:9c–11, 16–17
Gospel: Jn 2:13–22

❦◆❦

Although today's feast was created to honor a significant church building, this day's readings remind us, as the *Catechism* does, that "the worship 'in Spirit and in truth' of the New Covenant is not tied exclusively to any one place" (no. 1179*). The Gospel for today, John's account of the cleansing of the Temple, is the setting for Jesus' announcement that he would soon raise up the ideal temple promised by Israel's prophets. "On that day," Zechariah had declared, there would "no longer be any merchant in the house of the Lord" (Zec 14:21). But John hears more in Jesus' words: "He was speaking about the temple of his Body," (Jn 2:21).

In Corinthians, Paul reverses John's image and speaks of the body of Christ, the Church, as a building, a temple wherein dwells the Spirit of God. The gift of that indwelling, life-giving Spirit is symbolized in Ezekiel's vision of the stream that flows from the ideal temple. In the words of the psalm, this is "the stream whose runlets gladden the city of God" (Ps 46:5). The abundance of the end time is portrayed in the fish and fruit of every kind and the promise of healing that constitutes every new covenant.

* Jn 4:24; 1 Pet 2:4–5.

IMMACULATE CONCEPTION   *561*

Immaculate Conception of Mary

December 8

First Reading: Gn 3:9–15, 20
Responsorial Psalm: Ps 98:1, 2–3ab, 3cd–4
Second Reading: Eph 1:3–6, 11–12
Gospel: Lk 1:26–38

The feast of the Immaculate Conception honors Mary as the first truly liberated woman. Her liberation, however, was achieved not by consciousness raising or by social activism but by God, who blessed her "in Christ with every spiritual blessing in the heavens." It was God who chose her in Christ, "before the foundation of the world, to be holy and without blemish before him" (Eph 1:3–4). Therefore, the angel greets her as having found "favor" by God's grace (Lk 1:28), and the poet Wordsworth calls her "our tainted nature's solitary boast."

The grace that was Mary's from the moment of her conception became ours at the time of our Baptism. Now we, like her, must exist "for the praise of [God's] glory" (Eph 1:6). And this is possible because the old enmity that entered the world when sin did has been overcome by this woman's offspring, who is none other than the Son of God. So with her and through her, who first hoped in Christ, we are now a new creation, and we join her on this day in singing "a new song / for he has done wondrous deeds" (Ps 98:1).

Acknowledgments

We wish to express a special word of thanks for the use of certain materials cited in this book:

Reprinted by permission of the publishers and the Trustees of Amherst College from THE POEMS OF EMILY DICKINSON, Thomas H. Johnson, ed., Cambridge, Mass.: The Belknap Press of Harvard University Press, Copyright © 1951, 1955, 1979, 1983 by the President and Fellows of Harvard College.

"Basic Jewish and Christian Beliefs in Dialogue: Covenant, Part 2: A Christian Perspective," by Leon Klenicki and Eugene J. Fisher. PACE, vol. 13, January 1983. Copyright © 1982–1983 by Saint Mary's Press, www.smp.org

DODD. PARABLES OF THE KINGDOM, 1st Edition, © 1977, p. 5. Reprinted by permission of Pearson Education, Inc., Upper Saddle River, NJ.

Excerpts from Hearing the Parables of Jesus, by Pheme Perkins, Copyright © 1981 by Pheme Perkins. Paulist Press, Inc., New York/ Mahwah, NJ. Reprinted by permission of Paulist Press, Inc. www.paulistpress.com.

Excerpts from The Churches the Apostles Left Behind, by Raymond E. Brown, S.S., Copyright © 1984 by Raymond E. Brown, S.S. Paulist Press, Inc., New York/Mahwah, NJ. Reprinted by permission of Paulist Press, Inc. www.paulistpress.com.

Excerpts from Jesus and Passover, by Anthony J. Saldarini, Copyright © 1984 by Anthony J. Saldarini. Paulist Press, Inc. New York/Mahwah, NJ. Reprinted by permission of Paulist Press, Inc. www.paulistpress. com.

Excerpts from Mary in the New Testament, edited by Raymond E. Brown, Karl P. Donfried, Joseph A. Fitzmeyer and John Reumann Copyright © 1978 by Fortress Press. Paulist Press, Inc., New York/ Mahwah, NJ. Reprinted by permission of Paulist Press, Inc. www.paulistpress.com.

Excerpts from The Prophets, by Abraham Heschel. Copyright © 1962 by Abraham Heschel. Reprinted by permission of HarperCollins Publishers.

Excerpt from *Revelation: The Torah and the Bible*, by Bruce D. Chilton and Jacob Neusner, © 1995. Reprinted by permission of the publisher, The Continuum International Publishing Group.

Excerpt from *The Rock That Is Higher*, by Madeleine L'Engle, copyright © 1993, 2002, Crosswicks, Ltd. Reprinted with permission of McInstosh & Otis, Inc.

Notes

1. Daniel Harrington, *The Gospel of Matthew, Sacra Pagina 1* (Collegeville: Liturgical Press, 1991), 160.

2. James Sanders, *Canon and Community* (Philadelphia: Fortress Press, 1984), 59.

3. Thomas Johnson, ed., *The Complete Poems of Emily Dickinson*, 13th ed. (Boston: Little, Brown and Company, 1960), 428.

4. Neal Flanagan, "John," *The Collegeville Bible Commentary, New Testament* (Collegeville: Liturgical Press, 1992), 982.

5. Anthony Saldarini, *Jesus and Passover* (New York: Paulist Press, 1984), 108, 111.

6. Raymond Brown, *A Risen Christ in Eastertime* (Collegeville: Liturgical Press, 1991), 50.

7. Jerome Neyrey, *The Resurrection Stories* (Wilmington: Michael Glazier, 1998), 79.

8. Cf. Lionel Swain, *Reading the Easter Gospels, Good News Studies 35* (Collegeville: The Liturgical Press, 1993), 100.

9. Madeleine L'Engle, *The Rock That Is Higher* (Wheaton: Harold Shaw, 1993), 248.

10. Lionel Swain, *Reading the Easter Gospels Good News Studies 35* (Collegeville: The Liturgical Press, 1993), 65.

11. Luke Timothy Johnson, *The Acts of the Apostles, Sacra Pagina 5* (Collegeville: Liturgical Press, 1992), 141.

12. Walter Brueggemann, *In Man We Trust* (Eugene: Wipf & Stock, 2006), 33–34.

13. C. H. Dodd, *Parables of the Kingdom* (New York: Scribner's, 1961), 5.

14. Walter Brueggemann, *Power, Providence and Personality* (Louisville: Westminster/John Knox Press, 1990), 103.

15. Jacob Neusner and Bruce D. Chilton, *Revelation: The Torah and the Bible* (Valley Forge: Trinity Press International, 1995), 77.

16. Pheme Perkins, *Hearing the Parables of Jesus* (New York: Paulist Press, 1981), 191–92.

17. Daniel Harrington, *The Gospel of Matthew, Sacra Pagina 1* (Collegeville: Liturgical Press, 1991), 83.

18. Joachim Jeremias, *The Sermon on the Mount*, trans. Norman Perrin, Facet Books—Biblical Series 2 (Philadelphia: Fortress Press, 1963), 23.

19. Pheme Perkins, *Hearing the Parables of Jesus* (New York: Paulist Press, 1981), 88.

20. Abraham Heschel, *The Prophets*, Vol. 1, (New York: Harper & Row, 1962), 59–78.

21. Megan McKenna, *Not Counting Women and Children* (Maryknoll: Orbis Books, 1994), 185.

22. Sean McEvenue, "The Elohist at Work," *Interpretation and Bible* (Collegeville: Liturgical Press, 1994), 131.

23. Daniel Harrington, *The Gospel of Matthew, Sacra Pagina 1* (Collegeville: Liturgical Press, 1991), 236.

24. Dr. Eugene J. Fisher and Rabbi Leon Klenicki, eds., "Basic Jewish and Christian Beliefs in Dialogue: Covenant," *Understanding the Jewish Experience* (Education Department, USCC, ADL), 3.

25. Raymond Brown, *The Churches the Apostles Left Behind* (New York: Paulist Press, 1984), 144.

26. Pheme Perkins, *Hearing the Parables of Jesus* (New York: Paulist Press, 1981), 137–146.

27. Pheme Perkins, *Hearing the Parables of Jesus* (New York: Paulist Press, 1981), 71.

28. Ibid.

29. Wilfrid Harrington, *New Testament Message 4* (Wilmington: Michael Glazier, 1979), 153.

30. Raymond E. Brown, Karl P. Donfried, et al. eds., "Mary in the Gospel of Luke and the Acts of the Apostles," *Mary in the New Testament* (New York: Paulist Press, 1978), 171.

31. Luke Timothy Johnson, *The Gospel of Luke, Sacra Pagina 3* (Collegeville: The Liturgical Press, 1991), 268–273.

32. Ibid., 201.

33. Pheme Perkins, *Hearing the Parables of Jesus* (New York: Paulist Press, 1981), 159.

34. Roland Murphy, *The Tree of Life* ABRL. (New York: Doubleday, 1990), 86.

About the Author

CELIA SIROIS holds an M.A. in biblical studies from Providence College. Currently an adjunct professor of Sacred Scripture in the Master of Arts in Ministry Program at St. John's Seminary, Brighton, Massachusetts, she also teaches in the Permanent Diaconate Formation Program and is a coordinator and instructor for CHRISM, a Bible study program serving the parishes of the South Region of the Boston Archdiocese. For fifteen years she has co-directed New Directions in Catholic-Jewish Dialogue, an interfaith educational initiative jointly sponsored by the Archdiocese of Boston and the Anti-Defamation League. She is the author of *My Jewish Friend: A Young Catholic Learns About Judiasm* and the translator of *Paul: Least of the Apostles*, both published by Pauline Books & Media.

Pauline
BOOKS & MEDIA

The Daughters of St. Paul operate book and media centers at the following addresses. Visit, call or write the one nearest you today, or find us on the World Wide Web, www.pauline.org

CALIFORNIA

3908 Sepulveda Blvd, Culver City, CA 90230 — 310-397-8676
2650 Broadway Street, Redwood City, CA 94063 — 650-369-4230
5945 Balboa Avenue, San Diego, CA 92111 — 858-565-9181

FLORIDA

145 S.W. 107th Avenue, Miami, FL 33174 — 305-559-6715

HAWAII

1143 Bishop Street, Honolulu, HI 96813 — 808-521-2731
Neighbor Islands call: — 866-521-2731

ILLINOIS

172 North Michigan Avenue, Chicago, IL 60601 — 312-346-4228

LOUISIANA

4403 Veterans Memorial Blvd, Metairie, LA 70006 — 504-887-7631

MASSACHUSETTS

885 Providence Hwy, Dedham, MA 02026 — 781-326-5385

MISSOURI

9804 Watson Road, St. Louis, MO 63126 — 314-965-3512

NEW JERSEY

561 U.S. Route 1, Wick Plaza, Edison, NJ 08817 — 732-572-1200

NEW YORK

150 East 52nd Street, New York, NY 10022 — 212-754-1110

PENNSYLVANIA

9171-A Roosevelt Blvd, Philadelphia, PA 19114 — 215-676-9494

SOUTH CAROLINA

243 King Street, Charleston, SC 29401 — 843-577-0175

TENNESSEE

4811 Poplar Avenue, Memphis, TN 38117 — 901-761-2987

TEXAS

114 Main Plaza, San Antonio, TX 78205 — 210-224-8101

VIRGINIA

1025 King Street, Alexandria, VA 22314 — 703-549-3806

CANADA

3022 Dufferin Street, Toronto, ON M6B 3T5 — 416-781-9131

¡También somos su fuente para libros, videos
y música en español!